Lecture Notes in Computer Science   15547

Founding Editors

Gerhard Goos
Juris Hartmanis

Editorial Board Members

Elisa Bertino, *Purdue University, West Lafayette, IN, USA*
Wen Gao, *Peking University, Beijing, China*
Bernhard Steffen, *TU Dortmund University, Dortmund, Germany*
Moti Yung, *Columbia University, New York, NY, USA*

The series Lecture Notes in Computer Science (LNCS), including its subseries Lecture Notes in Artificial Intelligence (LNAI) and Lecture Notes in Bioinformatics (LNBI), has established itself as a medium for the publication of new developments in computer science and information technology research, teaching, and education.

LNCS enjoys close cooperation with the computer science R & D community, the series counts many renowned academics among its volume editors and paper authors, and collaborates with prestigious societies. Its mission is to serve this international community by providing an invaluable service, mainly focused on the publication of conference and workshop proceedings and postproceedings. LNCS commenced publication in 1973.

Claus Pahl · Andrea Janes · Tomas Cerny ·
Valentina Lenarduzzi · Matteo Esposito
Editors

Service-Oriented and Cloud Computing

11th IFIP WG 6.12 European Conference, ESOCC 2025
Bolzano, Italy, February 20–21, 2025
Proceedings

Editors
Claus Pahl
Free University of Bozen-Bolzano
Bolzano, Bolzano, Italy

Andrea Janes
Free University of Bozen-Bolzano
Bolzano, Italy

Tomas Cerny
The University of Arizona
Tucson, AZ, USA

Valentina Lenarduzzi
University of Oulu
Oulu, Finland

Matteo Esposito
University of Oulu
Oulu, Finland

ISSN 0302-9743   ISSN 1611-3349 (electronic)
Lecture Notes in Computer Science
ISBN 978-3-031-84616-8   ISBN 978-3-031-84617-5 (eBook)
https://doi.org/10.1007/978-3-031-84617-5

© IFIP International Federation for Information Processing 2025

This work is subject to copyright. All rights are solely and exclusively licensed by the Publisher, whether the whole or part of the material is concerned, specifically the rights of translation, reprinting, reuse of illustrations, recitation, broadcasting, reproduction on microfilms or in any other physical way, and transmission or information storage and retrieval, electronic adaptation, computer software, or by similar or dissimilar methodology now known or hereafter developed.
The use of general descriptive names, registered names, trademarks, service marks, etc. in this publication does not imply, even in the absence of a specific statement, that such names are exempt from the relevant protective laws and regulations and therefore free for general use.
The publisher, the authors and the editors are safe to assume that the advice and information in this book are believed to be true and accurate at the date of publication. Neither the publisher nor the authors or the editors give a warranty, expressed or implied, with respect to the material contained herein or for any errors or omissions that may have been made. The publisher remains neutral with regard to jurisdictional claims in published maps and institutional affiliations.

This Springer imprint is published by the registered company Springer Nature Switzerland AG
The registered company address is: Gewerbestrasse 11, 6330 Cham, Switzerland

If disposing of this product, please recycle the paper.

Preface

Service-oriented computing and cloud computing continue to impact the software industry and the research community profoundly. Today, these technologies are fundamental in building large-scale software ecosystems and delivering individual software services to end-users. Services are now independently developed, deployed, and composed using diverse technologies—a key factor driving business agility and innovation. On the other hand, cloud computing enables flexible, centralized resource sharing. It has become the dominant paradigm for provisioning scalable, on-demand computational resources to meet the growing need for agile IT systems.

However, significant challenges remain. Developers, providers, and integrators must continuously advance methods, tools, and techniques to ensure cost-effective, secure, and reliable development and deployment of service-oriented applications, platforms, and services in cloud environments.

The European Conference on Service-Oriented and Cloud Computing (ESOCC) remains Europe's premier venue for presenting the latest advances in these domains. ESOCC aims to foster exchange and collaboration between researchers and practitioners, explore emerging trends, and strengthen cooperation within Europe and beyond.

The 11th edition of ESOCC (ESOCC 2025) was hosted at the Free University of Bozen-Bolzano in Bolzano, Italy. Based on previous editions' success, ESOCC 2025 featured a comprehensive program tailored to academic and industrial audiences, presenting cutting-edge service-oriented and cloud computing contributions.

The conference offered two inspiring keynote talks from Elisabetta Di Nitto (Politecnico di Milano) and Fabio Massacci (Vrije Universiteit Amsterdam and University of Trento), addressing critical challenges and opportunities in service-oriented and cloud computing and related areas such as security, automation, and resource management.

ESOCC 2025 was a multi-event conference that attracted both an academic and industrial audience, with its leading research track focusing on the presentation of cutting-edge research in both the service-oriented and cloud computing areas. Overall, we aimed to bring together academia and industry by showcasing the application of service-oriented and cloud-computing research, especially case studies. Overall, 28 submissions were received, of which 12 outstanding full and six short papers were accepted. Thus, the overall acceptance rate for full papers was 42.8%.

Each submission was peer-reviewed by three main reviewers from the Program Committee (PC).

The PC Chairs would like to thank all the reviewers who participated in the reviewing process. Their comments were essential for improving the quality of the received manuscripts and especially for giving constructive comments to the authors of papers that, in their current forms, were rejected from ESOCC 2025.

ESOCC 2025 continued to encourage a vibrant and engaged community. We thank all contributors, including authors, reviewers, presenters, and participants, for their role in advancing research and practice. Their active engagement drives ESOCC's success as a platform for impactful discussions, new collaborations, and shared learning.

December 2024

Tomas Cerny
Valentina Lenarduzzi

Organization

General Chairs

Andrea Janes Free University of Bozen-Bolzano, Italy
Claus Pahl Free University of Bozen-Bolzano, Italy

Program Committee Chairs

Tomas Cerny University of Arizona, USA
Valentina Lenarduzzi University of Oulu, Finland

Steering Committee

Antonio Brogi University of Pisa, Italy
Schahram Dustdar TU Wien, Austria
Paul Grefen Eindhoven University of Technology, Netherlands
Einar Broch Johnson University of Oslo, Norway
Kyriakos Kritikos ICS-FORTH, Greece
Winfried Lamersdorf University of Hamburg, Germany
Flavio de Paoli University of Milano-Bicocca, Italy
Ernesto Pimentel University of Málaga, Spain
Pierluigi Plebani Politecnico di Milano, Italy
Ulf Schreier Hochschule Furtwangen University, Germany
Stefan Schulte TU Wien, Austria
Massimo Villari University of Messina, Italy
Olaf Zimmermann Eastern Switzerland University of Applied Sciences, Switzerland
Wolf Zimmermann Martin Luther University Halle-Wittenberg, Germany

Program Committee

Adam Przybylek Gdańsk University of Technology, Poland
Amr Elsayed University of Arizona, USA
Antonio Brogi Università di Pisa, Italy

Daniel Morandini	KIM Keep In Mind, GmbH, Italy
Darek Gajewski	Cloud Engineering Technologies Inc., Canada
Davide Taibi	University of Oulu, Finland
Ebaa Alnazer	University of Stuttgart, Germany
Erik Johannes Husom	SINTEF, Norway
Ernesto Pimentel	University of Málaga, Spain
Fabian Stricker	Hochschule Karlsruhe (HKA), Germany
Fabrizio Montesi	University of Southern Denmark, Denmark
Francisco Ponce	University of Pisa, Italy
Gianluigi Zavattaro	University of Bologna, Italy
Hernán Astudillo	Universidad Andrés Bello, Chile
Ilche Georgievski	University of Stuttgart, Germany
Indika Weerasingha Dewage	JADS, Tilburg University, Netherlands
Jacopo Massa	Università di Pisa, Italy
Jacopo Mauro	University of Southern Denmark, Denmark
Jacopo Soldani	University of Pisa, Italy
Jonas Fritzsch	University of Stuttgart, Germany
José Antonio Peregrina Pérez	Universidad de Cádiz, Spain
José Merseguer	Universidad de Zaragoza, Spain
Larisa Safina	Inria - Lille Nord Europe, France
Luciano Baresi	Politecnico di Milano, Italy
Marco Comuzzi	Ulsan National Institute of Science and Technology, South Korea
Matteo Esposito	University of Oulu, Finland
Md Arfan Uddin	University of Arizona, USA
Md Showkat Hossain Chy	University of Arizona, USA
Minh-Tri Nguyen	Aalto University, Finland
Mirko Stocker	Eastern Switzerland University of Applied Sciences, Switzerland
Muhammad Ashfakur Arju	Montana State University, USA
Nour Ali	Brunel University of London, UK
Raadesh Gupta Balanarasimmagupta	Oracle, USA
Rustem Dautov	SINTEF, Norway
Stefan Kapferer	Eastern Switzerland University of Applied Sciences, Switzerland
Stefan Schulte	TU Hamburg, Germany
Stefano Forti	University of Pisa, Italy
Ulf Schreier	Furtwangen University, Germany
Uwe Breitenbücher	Reutlingen University, Germany
Vasilios Andrikopoulos	University of Groningen, Netherlands

Wolf Zimmermann	Martin Luther University Halle-Wittenberg, Germany
Xiaozhou Li	University of Oulu, Finland

Contents

AI and Data-Driven Systems

Adaption via Selection: On Client Selection to Counter Concept Drift
in Federated Learning 3
   *Julius Thomas, Finn Saile, Mathias Fischer, Dominik Kaaser,
and Stefan Schulte*

Applying a Prompt Pattern Sequence for Decision-Making in Microservices
Architectures 18
   João José Maranhão Junior, Jorge Melegati, and Eduardo Guerra

SemT: A Framework for Enhancing Tabular Data Through
Enrichment-as-a-Service 33
   Abubakari Alidu, Michele Ciavotta, and Flavio De Paoli

Towards WebAssembly-Based Federated Learning 40
   *Felix Gottschalk, Stefan Schulte, Nisal Hemadasa, Elmira Ebrahimi,
Janick Edinger, and Dominik Kaaser*

Edge and Resource Management

A Bio-inspired Leader-Based Energy Management System for Drone Fleets ... 57
   Rosario Napoli, Antonio Celesti, Massimo Villari, and Maria Fazio

Carbon-Aware Software Services 65
   Stefano Forti, Jacopo Soldani, and Antonio Brogi

Comparative Analysis of Lightweight Kubernetes Distributions for Edge
Computing: Performance and Resource Efficiency 81
   Diyaz Yakubov and David Hästbacka

Comparative Analysis of Lightweight Kubernetes Distributions for Edge
Computing: Security, Resilience and Maintainability 96
   Diyaz Yakubov and David Hästbacka

Enhancing Failure Resilience of Cloud-Edge Microservices: The FREEDA
Approach 105
   Francisco Ponce, Stefano Forti, Jacopo Soldani, and Antonio Brogi

ML-Based Performance Modeling in Edge FaaS Systems 112
   *Federica Filippini, Luca Cavenaghi, Nicolas Calmi, Marco Savi,
and Michele Ciavotta*

Privacy and Trust Management

A Quantitative Privacy Evaluation Method Based on Tsallis Entropy
for Trustworthy Data Sharing 131
   Shudan Yang and Pierluigi Plebani

SafeAR: Privacy-Maintenance in Augmented Reality Applications 146
   *Rogério Luís de C. Costa, Anabela Marto, Leonel Santos,
Alexandrino Gonçalves, and Carlos Rabadão*

Serverless and Cloud Systems

Deep Surrogate Models of Serverless Batch Processing Services 155
   Yicheng Gao, Roberto Sala, Danilo Ardagna, and Giuliano Casale

pyStorageLess: Leveraging Von Neumann's Architecture to Abstract
Storage Heterogeneity in Serverless Applications 171
   *Sashko Ristov, Mika Hautz, Philipp Gritsch, Isabella Schmut,
Peter Koll, and Michael Felderer*

Software Architecture

A Conceptual Framework for API Refactoring in Service-Oriented
Architectures 181
   *Fabrizio Montesi, Marco Peressotti, Valentino Picotti,
and Olaf Zimmermann*

A Survey Study About the Impacts of Introducing a Microservices
Cataloging Tool in a Large Software Development Unit 197
   Matheus C. Leite, André A. S. Ivo, João F. L. Daniel, and Eduardo Guerra

TOSCARISMA: Modeling CARISMA-Based Service Communication
Using TOSCA 219
   Kevin Klein, Pascal Hirmer, Alexander Walz, and Steffen Becker

Workflow Net Compositions for the Analysis of Service-Oriented Systems 235
   Mandy Weißbach, Wolf Zimmermann, and Thomas Kühn

Author Index 251

AI and Data-Driven Systems

Adaption via Selection: On Client Selection to Counter Concept Drift in Federated Learning

Julius Thomas[1], Finn Saile[1], Mathias Fischer[2], Dominik Kaaser[1(✉)], and Stefan Schulte[1]

[1] Christian Doppler Laboratory for Blockchain Technologies for the Internet of Things, TU Hamburg, Hamburg, Germany
{julius.thomas,finn.saile,dominik.kaaser,stefan.schulte}@tuhh.de
[2] University of Hamburg, Hamburg, Germany
mathias.fischer@uni-hamburg.de

Abstract. Federated Learning is a Machine Learning paradigm in which multiple devices jointly train a shared model without the need to share their local data. Most Federated Learning approaches assume that the data remains static. However, this assumption is unrealistic in real-world scenarios where data may change over time. In this paper we study the impact of concept drift on Federated Learning models with heterogeneous data distribution.

Client selection directly impacts the model's performance, and we observe that the local loss of clients under concept drift deviates. Nevertheless, most applications select clients randomly for each training round. Our main contribution therefore is a probabilistic client selection algorithm that introduces a bias towards clients with higher local loss in order to counter concept drift. Extensive evaluations show that our algorithm recovers a drop in accuracy incurred by concept drift up to five times faster than random sampling while retaining competitive performance.

Keywords: Federated Learning · Concept Drift · Client Selection · Machine Learning

1 Introduction

Federated Learning (FL) is a Machine Learning (ML) paradigm in which multiple distributed clients collaborate to train a model. The data remain on the clients, which has significant advantages for the privacy, security, and scalability of the system. These characteristics of FL make it applicable, for instance, when developing models for keyboard input suggestions [36] or electronic health records [2]. Since its introduction in 2016 [24], research in the domain of FL has gained significant momentum [38].

In many FL applications it is possible to achieve highly accurate models while using only a subset of clients, reducing the computational load, preserving bandwidth, and providing high availability. Prominent frameworks such as TensorFlow Federated or PySyft sample clients randomly in each training round. An adaptive selection method, however, can lead to a significant benefit w.r.t. performance and load [8]. Client selection becomes particularly attractive when working with real-world data: it helps to overcome two challenges faced by real-world applications of FL, namely *data heterogeneity* and *concept drift*. Data heterogeneity describes a situation where the statistical distributions of the underlying data differ between clients. Common examples are regional differences in client behavior or differences in the hardware or connectivity of devices. Data heterogeneity tends to have a significant impact on the accuracy of a model [12,22]. Concept drift is another challenge in FL (and, in general, in ML). Most FL approaches assume that the underlying data is stationary. However, in many real-world datasets, the data may change over time. As a consequence, the model loses accuracy unless the FL system is retrained to adapt to the new concepts. The phenomenon of concept drift has been extensively studied in ML [9]. Interestingly, when it comes to FL the research on concept drift is still in its infancy.

Results in a Nutshell. We investigate active sampling for FL systems under concept drift. Our experiments on multiple datasets confirm a significant negative impact of concept drift on model performance. To improve the performance of FL during and after concept drift, we present a novel FL algorithm that employs probabilistic client selection based on the clients' loss. Our loss-based selection favors clients for which the drift occurs over clients where the data has remained mostly unchanged. The main idea is that clients which exhibit a larger loss must have a bigger impact on the improvement of the global model. Indeed, our experiments confirm that loss-based selection leads to a significantly faster convergence.

Outline. This paper is structured as follows. In the following section we give an overview of related work on concept drift and client selection in FL. In Sect. 3 we present our probabilistic client selection algorithm, and in Sect. 4 we evaluate our approach. Finally, in Sect. 5 we draw our conclusions and present some open problems for future work.

2 Background and Related Work

Our work is based on *Federated Averaging* (FedAvg) [24]. FedAvg is a seminal FL algorithm that was originally implemented with Stochastic Gradient Descent (SGD) [28], random client selection, and a weighted average aggregation function. Nowadays, FedAvg is often combined with a variety of optimizers, selection schemes and aggregation functions [21]. Many modifications of FedAvg have been proposed to improve its performance or address specific issues, and it continues to serve as a foundational framework for various implementations, advancements, and applications [18,22,27]. Numerous studies have investigated data heterogeneity [12,19,32], communication efficiency [15], and privacy preservation properties [25,31] of FedAvg.

Concept Drift. Concept drift describes a phenomenon where the statistical properties of the underlying data change over time. Without compensation, this leads to a decrease in model accuracy, potentially rendering the model obsolete. Concept drift can arise when a model does not capture hidden trends that arise in the real world such as seasonal changes or changes in user behavior [23]. For example, a model trained during December for text suggestions on mobile device keyboards might return "Christmas" when prompted "Merry". However, this behavior is probably no longer desirable during the summer. Many other factors could also affect the model over time, such as the introduction of new vocabulary or a long-term change in the way a language is spoken [9].

Concept drift in ML was first described by Schlimmer and Granger [30] and later expanded on by Widmer and Kubat [33]. They identify that the statistical properties of target labels might change over time, either due to a change in behavior or hidden information that the model has not encountered in the training phase. The challenges posed by concept drift are grouped into three categories: drift detection, drift understanding, and drift adaptation [23]. Drift detection refers to noticing whether drift occurs and drift understanding is the investigation of real-world causes for concept drift. Drift adaptation deals with counteracting concept drift. Gama et al. [9] suggest different types of drift that either occur instantaneously or incrementally over a longer period of time. While concept drift is widely explored in ML and identified as one of the most important challenges in FL [20], results on concept drift in FL are surprisingly scarce.

Chen et al. [5] employ a two-step process with active drift detection and, should drift be detected, a local drift adaptation algorithm. Concept drift is detected by storing an accuracy value in a bounded queue for each client and using a statistical normality test on the newest entry over the queue to measure its deviation. When an outlier is detected, local drift adaptation is triggered. The drift adaptation mechanism is based on *FedProx* [21]. A regularization component based on the client's loss is added to the local objective function and a solver is used to find those model parameters that minimize this error.

Canonaco et al. [4] tackle the problem of concept drift in FL by adapting the learning rate to improve the reactivity during the drift phase. An adaptive optimizer based on exponential moving averages is used to control the learning rate on the server side. This strategy is often employed on the client side in non-distributed environments, e.g., by the *RMSprop* [37] and *ADAM* [14] optimizers.

Jothimurugesan et al. [13] treat concept drift as a two-dimensional time-varying clustering problem. They explore the setting in which drift occurs for different clients at different times. Groups of clients are divided into clusters where each cluster learns an individual model. Clients that observe a new concept are split off into a new cluster, and client clusters that observe the same concept are re-merged.

In our own work [29] we present an FL algorithm that is deployed on the client side. We use a dynamic learning rate at each client which adapts automatically in presence of concept drift. To calculate the dynamic learning rate we use exponentially moving averages based on the individual training loss. In contrast to the work at hand, the algorithm in [29] explicitly requires a uniform distribution of data among clients, leaving heterogeneous data an open problem.

Client Selection. The authors of *FedCS* [26] discuss client selection based on a greedy algorithm that prioritizes clients with more powerful computational resources. However, they only consider system (device) heterogeneity and do not take data heterogeneity into account.

Loss-based selection was introduced by Goetz et al. [10], who proposed the *Active Federated Learning* algorithm. Clients with a higher loss function are preferred in the selection process. The authors argue that loss-based selection has multiple advantages: For one, the model loss is already calculated on the client side and thus cheap to access. If there is a weak separation of the classes or strong heterogeneous tendencies, the algorithm will prefer the minority classes and yield a stronger correction to the overall model. Lastly, should all data points be equally valuable, users with more trained data will be preferred.

Lai et al. [17] view loss-based selection as an approximation of importance sampling [39] where for each client the statistical utility is computed, i.e., the benefit of the client to the overall model.

Cho et al. [6] employ a biased, loss-based selection strategy in their algorithm *Power-of-Choice*. The loss is calculated for clients in a randomly chosen candidate set and those clients with the largest loss are selected for training.

Further strategies of client selections are explored by Amiri et al. [1]. The authors measure the channel conditions and significance of the local model update via the l_2 norm. The authors of *FedPNS* [34] avoid adverse model updates by comparing the local and global gradients to encourage faster model convergence.

To the best of our knowledge, there is no prior research that investigates the intersection of concept drift and client selection. This is precisely the setting of this paper: we will show that our algorithm achieves faster convergence of the model under concept drift by exploiting that some clients experience a stronger drift than others and thus yield a greater utility to the global model.

3 Our Contribution

We model, design, and simulate an FL system that allows us to enact and evaluate our probabilistic client selection algorithm. We simulate the FL system with one centralized server and 100 distributed clients. The clients train a Convolutional Neural Network (CNN) on three different datasets that are commonly used as benchmarking datasets in ML. Our FL system is based on the architecture developed for the FedAvg [24] algorithm. The source code for our system and all necessary tools to reproduce our figures are publicly available at https://github.com/dcmx/concept-drift-selection/.

Before we go into details about our algorithm, we first present hardware and software configurations of the underlying frameworks. Then we explain the CNN architecture and motivate the chosen hyperparameters. Next we describe the datasets that we use. Finally, we outline how we model concept drift.

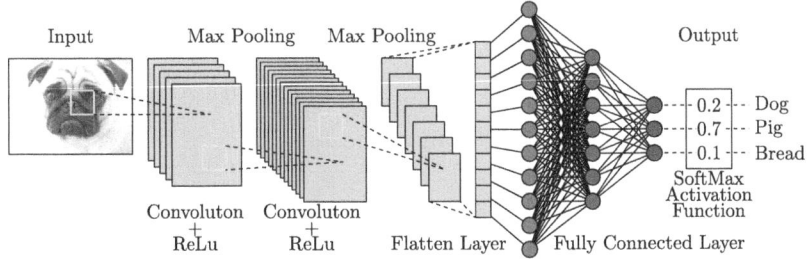

Fig. 1. Illustration of the CNN used in our evaluation

3.1 Implementation Details

System Setup. All of our experiments are carried out in a Windows Subsystem for Linux environment running Ubuntu 20.04. The system uses an AMD Ryzen 5 1600X processor with 6 cores and 12 threads backed by 32 GiB of DDR4 memory and equipped with an NVIDIA GeForce GTX 1080 Ti graphics card with 11 GB of graphics memory.

Our system is implemented in a Python 3.10.10 virtual environment based on the *Federated Learning in PyTorch* [11] research repository. Our implementation depends on *PyTorch*, *NumPy*, *scikit-learn*, and *TensorBoard*.

Model Architecture Our model architecture is based on [24]. We use a CNN which consists of two convolutional layers with a ReLU activation function, each followed by a max-pooling layer. The output is flattened into a one-dimensional vector and fed into a fully connected layer consisting of two hidden layers and an output layer. A schematic is shown in Fig. 1.

Parameters and Hyperparameters. Table 1 shows the parameters used in our evaluation. To facilitate the comparison of our results with related work our parameters are taken from [24] such that they align well with related works in FL that build upon [24]. Table 2 shows the hyperparameters of our model chosen for specific datasets. Network topology, fraction of selected clients C, batch size B, learning rate η, decay rate, decay step and the testing holdout sets are adopted from [24]. Again, these are the parameters of choice in related works [4,29].

Datasets. We evaluate our approach using the MNIST [7] and FMNIST [35] datasets, two popular research and benchmarking datasets that are commonly used in FL. The datasets provide inputs and labels for image classification. They feature 10 classes, simplifying the comparison of the performance between datasets. Following the approach described by Zhao et al. [40], our heterogeneous data distribution follows a pathological split where each client is limited in the number of labels it trains on. This approach was also utilized in the evaluation of FedAvg [24] and FedProx [21]. The MNIST and FMNIST datasets each consist of 70,000 28×28-pixel grayscale images, divided into 10 different classes. MNIST features the handwritten digits 0 to 9 while FMNIST features items of clothing.

Table 1. Parameters used in our evaluation

Parameter	Value
Number of clients	$K = 100$
Number of local epochs	$E = 3$
Optimizer	SGD
Loss function	Cross-entropy loss
Fraction of clients trained per round	$C = 0.1$

Table 2. CNN hyperparameters used for MNIST and FMNIST

Parameter	Value
Image Size	28×28
Number of hidden neurons per layer	200
Fraction of clients selected C	0.1
Mini-Batch Size B	10
Learning Rate η	0.1
Learning Rate decay rate	0.99
Learning Rate decay step	10
Train/Test split	$6:1$

Simulating Concept Drift. We simulate concept drift via label flipping, also known as *sudden drift* [9]. It occurs when the data distribution F_t changes between two consecutive rounds r_0 and $r_0 + 1$ from the initial distribution $F_0 = F_{r_0}$ to a target distribution $F_{r_0+1} = F_\infty$. This means, in round r_0 the drift occurs instantly, and it persists thereafter. To model the drift we select two pairs of classes and switch the associated labels in the datasets in a pairwise manner. We remark that selecting two pairs of classes to flip their labels models a strong drift that has, if not countered properly, a substantial impact on model performance.

When discussing concept drift, the *recovery time* refers to the time in rounds it takes for the model to regain the original accuracy before the drift. Similarly, the term *recovery phase* refers to those rounds during which the algorithm attempts to compensate for the loss in accuracy due to the concept drift.

3.2 Concept Drift in Federated Learning

Understanding concept drift is vital for designing effective counter measures. To this end we assess the impact of concept drift in a series of preliminary simulations. In these simulations we run FedAvg for 100 rounds on the MNIST and FMNIST datasets. After every round we gather the server's accuracy. Concept drift is simulated after half of the rounds have elapsed in round $r_0 = 50$. The number of rounds was chosen to allow sufficient time for the model to converge.

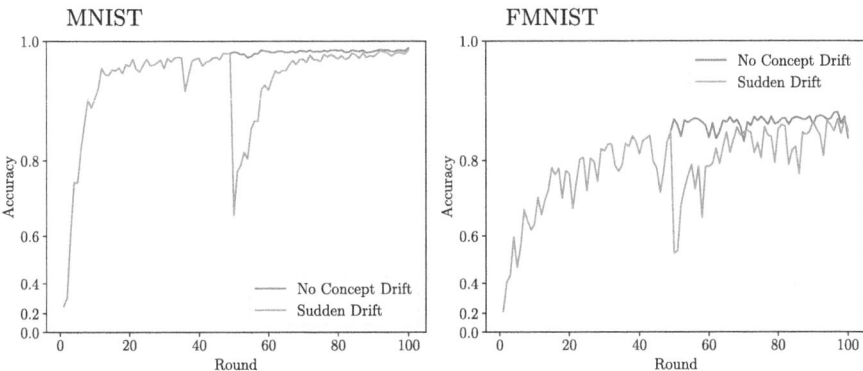

Fig. 2. Accuracy of FedAvg under concept drift

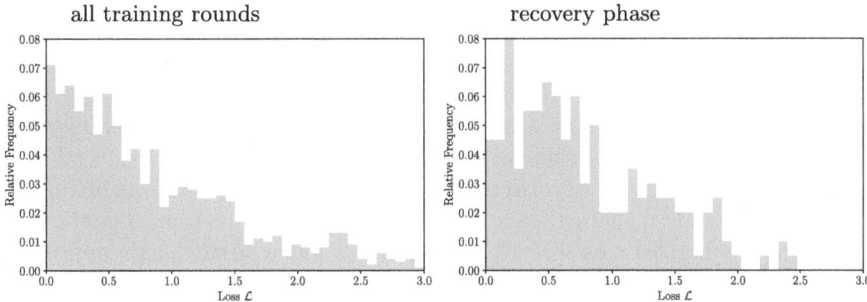

Fig. 3. Loss distribution in the FMNIST dataset

Figure 2 shows the server accuracy for each round for the MNIST and FMNIST datasets. In round 50 we flip the labels '3' with '7' and '8' with '9'. For both datasets, the server accuracy plummets after the initial label switch, losing up to 33% model accuracy. The recovery times are roughly 20 rounds.

For independent and identically distributed (IID) data we would expect all clients to show a consistent, homogeneous, increase in loss during the drift recovery phase. In Fig. 3 this would be represented by a right-shift of the frequency distribution. This, however, is not the case: some clients retain a small loss during drift, while other clients having a larger proportion of flipped labels in their training data are affected more drastically, exhibiting a larger loss. This leads to the following assumption that forms the basis of our probabilistic client selection algorithm: when we prefer high-loss clients, the model accommodates the flipped labels more quickly. Likewise, clients with a small proportion of the flipped labels provide less value to the global model. Therefore, training on clients with larger loss results in faster recovery of the model after concept drift.

Algorithm 1: Probabilistic Client Selection
---
1 **Function** sampleClients(m, d, τ):
2      $A \leftarrow$ Random sample of $d \leq K$ clients
3   Request from each client $i \in A$ its loss $\mathcal{L}_i$
4   Compute $p_i = \dfrac{e^{\mathcal{L}_i/\tau}}{\sum_{j=1}^{N} e^{\mathcal{L}_j/\tau}}$ for all clients $i \in A$
5   Draw m elements without replacement from A with probabilities p_i
---

3.3 Probabilistic Client Selection Algorithm

We now present our probabilistic client selection algorithm that accommodates for concept drift. Our algorithm builds upon work by Cho et al. [6] who propose to use a candidate set and, instead of sending the model to all clients, only request the loss from a small fraction of clients.

We remark that one has to be cautious about an implicit risk with maximum-loss selection. Namely, some clients may possess such unfavorable training data that they continuously exhibit a high loss without a chance of convergence. In that case they would not provide any benefit to the global model but nevertheless be selected for training all the time. Our goal is to refashion the algorithm to provide more stability against such erratic behavior. Rather than selecting the clients with the highest loss directly, we therefore follow a stochastic approach. The main difference of our approach to maximum-loss selection is that we use a probabilistic approach to sample the clients on the server side.

Server Side. At the server side our algorithm samples clients according to the Boltzmann distribution. To this end we use the *Boltzmann Softmax Function* [3]

$$p_i = \frac{e^{\mathcal{L}_i/\tau}}{\sum_{j=1}^{N} e^{\mathcal{L}_j/\tau}}, \quad (1)$$

where $\mathcal{L}_i$ is the local loss of client i and τ is a so-called *temperature* parameter. Depending on τ, our algorithm mimics the behavior of other known client selection schemes. For $\tau = 1$, the Boltzmann Softmax Function behaves like the regular softmax function. If $\tau \to \infty$, the client selection probabilities p_i follow a uniform distribution. In this case our algorithm behaves identically to FedAvg with random sampling. For small values of τ, differences between inputs have a larger effect in the produced distribution. Thus if $\tau \to 0$, clients with larger loss are favored and the algorithm behaves like Power-of-Choice [6]. For large values of τ, the produced distribution approaches a uniform distribution.

Our algorithm is formalized in Algorithm 1. In this algorithm we first sample a random candidate set A of $d \leq K$ clients. Then we request the loss from all clients in A. In order to draw the clients from a Boltzmann distribution over their loss values we compute in Algorithm 4 of Algorithm 1 the sampling probabilities using the Boltzmann Softmax function from Eq. (1). The clients are then drawn according to their Boltzmann probabilities p_i without replacement.

Client Side. On the client side it is possible to evaluate the exact loss over the client's entire dataset. However, to reduce the computational load, we employ a computationally more efficient variant where we estimate the loss over only one mini-batch of training as suggested in [6].

4 Evaluation

4.1 Evaluation on MNIST and FMNIST

We now present an evaluation of our probabilistic client selection algorithm on the MNIST and FMNIST datasets. We focus on the standalone performance of our algorithm under concept drift and analyze the server-side test accuracy and model loss. The training is orchestrated by the server which is initialized with an empty model with random parameters. In each round a C-fraction the K clients are selected for training. The server then broadcasts the model and incorporates model updates from the selected clients using weighted averaging. For our evaluation we use a train/test split of 6:1.

To assess the effects of the temperature parameter τ, we evaluate our algorithm for two temperature parameters, $\tau = 0.5$ and $\tau = 1$. Recall that a value of $\tau = 1$ implements the softmax function while $\tau = 0.5$ resembles a maximum loss strategy. As a reference, we use an implementation of the FedAvg algorithm.

Figures 4 and 5 show the accuracy and the loss, respectively, for the MNIST and FMNIST datasets under concept drift. For both datasets we simulate concept drift in round $r_0 = 50$. The training is conducted on $K = 100$ clients. For the client selection algorithms, the loss is requested from $d = 40$ clients, and $m = 10$ clients are sampled for training. These parameters are consistent with the configuration used by Cho et al. [6]. In terms of accuracy and loss, both client selection models perform almost identically.

We observe a similar behavior of all three models up to round r_0. Once the drift occurs in round r_0, the accuracies drop. On the MNIST dataset, the accuracy drops from 98% to 66%, and on the FMNIST dataset, the accuracy drops from 85% below 60%. Following the drift, our client selection algorithm is faster in regaining accuracy (Fig. 4) and reducing the loss (Fig. 5). On the MNIST dataset, both client selection models pass 95% accuracy in round 56, while the FedAvg algorithm passes the same threshold only after round 62. On the FMNIST dataset, both client selection models pass 85% accuracy in round 53, while the FedAvg algorithm passes the same threshold only after round 65.

Figure 6 compares the client selection frequencies during overall training and during the drift adaptation phase in rounds 50 to 70. The change in client selection frequencies indicates that the server prefers different clients during drift recovery than during general training. We highlight that the faster recovery time achieved by the client selection algorithm can be attributed to the fact that clients with a larger proportion of flipped labels are preferred after the drift.

Under a purely random selection strategy and $K = 100$ clients, each individual client would be selected with a probability of 1%. For the MNIST dataset,

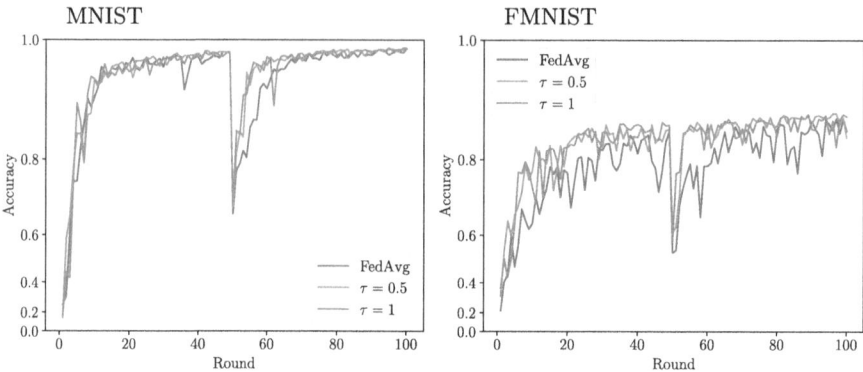

Fig. 4. Accuracy per round under concept drift

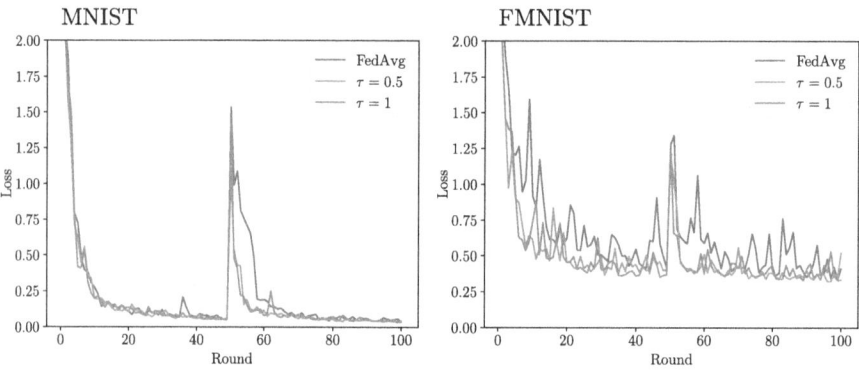

Fig. 5. Loss per round under concept drift

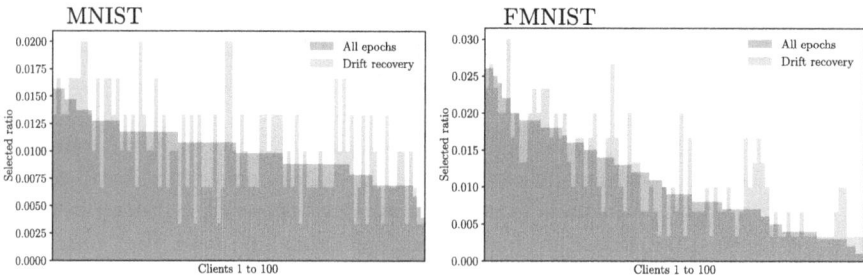

Fig. 6. Client selection profiles, $\tau = 0.5$

our data in Fig. 6 show that most clients are drawn with a frequency in the range of 0.75% to 1.25%. For the FMNIST dataset, however, we observe much stronger fluctuations: clients are drawn with a frequency in the range of almost 0% to 2%. Interestingly, this implies a significantly larger variance in client loss in the

FMNIST dataset compared to the MNIST dataset and ultimately explains the noise in the accuracy and loss in Figs. 4 and 5 for the FMNIST dataset.

4.2 Evaluation on CIFAR-10

Besides the evaluations on the MNIST and FMNIST datasets, we also evaluated our approach on the CIFAR-10 [16] dataset. The CIFAR-10 dataset consists of 60,000 32×32-pixel color images with three color channels featuring animals and vehicles. Under the given condition of heterogeneous data distributions, this turned out to be particularly challenging: our results either fell short of comparable experiments from related research or required excessive amounts of training. In particular, we were not able to replicate the convergence speed of the max-loss client selection employed by Cho et al. [6]. In addition, our experiments suffer from a large amount of noise which makes it impossible to assess the performance of client selection strategies.

Figure 7 shows the accuracy under concept drift for the CIFAR-10 dataset. The learning rate η was chosen according to [24] and the remaining parameters were adapted from the evaluation on the MNIST and FMNIST datasets.

Our data show an exceptionally large amount of noise throughout all three selection algorithms. This not only makes a clear distinction between the performance of the selection strategies impossible but also confirms research by Zhao et al. [40] who investigate the effects of highly skewed non-IID data and observe similar results with the CIFAR-10 dataset. As a consequence, we exclude the CIFAR-10 dataset from further evaluation.

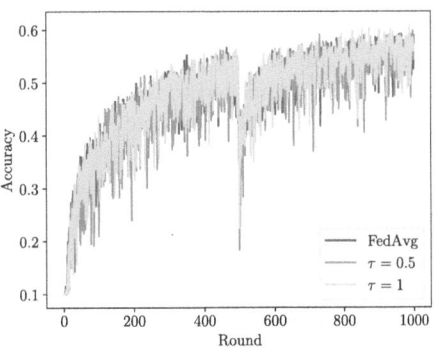

Fig. 7. Evaluation on CIFAR-10.

4.3 Comparison to Related Work

We now compare our probabilistic client selection algorithm with *Power-of-Choice* [6] and the *Adaptive-FedAvg* (Ada-FedAvg) algorithm for FL under concept drift [4]. For our algorithm we use the parameter $\tau = 1$, and as before we keep FedAvg as a reference. The Ada-FedAvg algorithm builds upon FedAvg. It uses Exponential Moving Averages (EMAs) to calculate the current effective learning rate in order to continuously adapt the model to potential concept drift. This guarantees sufficient decaying properties required for convergence while providing a more reactive behavior in presence of concept drifts. We implement Ada-FedAvg with the settings suggested by Canonaco et al. [4]. All other hyperparameters are identical to the previous evaluation.

Figure 8 shows the performance of the algorithms under concept drift. On the MNIST dataset, both the probabilistic client selection algorithm as well as

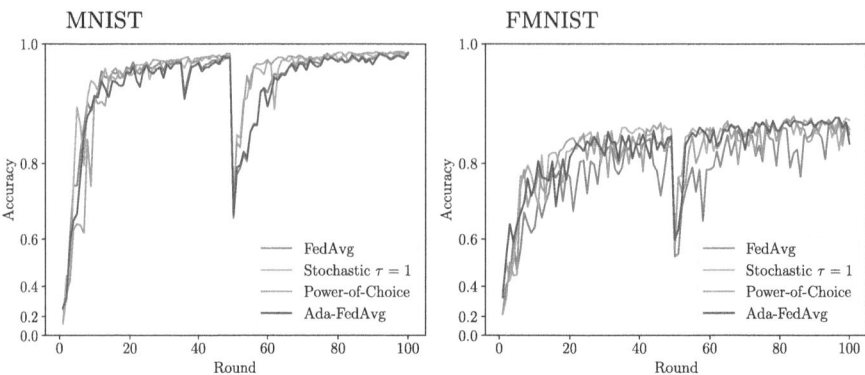

Fig. 8. Comparison with Ada-FedAgv and Power-of-Choice

the maximum loss selection utilized by the Power-of-Choice algorithm achieve a much faster convergence after the label flip. Both selection schemes have slightly higher fluctuations in accuracy during the initial training phase but reach convergence with 98% accuracy by round 50. During the drift adaptation phase, both selection algorithms perform very well, converging to above 95% accuracy by round 56 as opposed to round 63 for the FedAvg algorithm. The selection algorithms achieve a 98% accuracy by round 60, which is reached by FedAvg only in round 76. Ada-FedAvg performs almost identically to the FedAvg baseline.

On the FMNIST dataset, the server accuracy drops after the drift from approximately 85% below 60% for every model. Our algorithm recovers to 85% accuracy by round 53, Ada-FedAvg by round 54 and Power-of-Choice by round 55, while it takes FedAvg until round 68. This confirms that our algorithm improves upon FedAvg in terms of convergence speed and accuracy when concept drift in the data occurs. The maximum loss selection strategy of Power-of-Choice achieves similar results to our algorithm on both datasets, while Ada-FedAvg performs poorly on the MNIST dataset.

5 Conclusions

We study the performance of loss-based client selection in FL. Observing the effect of concept drift on the seminal FedAvg algorithm, we introduce a probabilistic loss-based client selection algorithm that favors more relevant clients to speed up the convergence during drift recovery. Extensive simulations demonstrate that under concept drift our algorithm consistently achieves faster drift adaptation and thus reduces the recovery time. Our algorithm achieves particularly promising results in non-IID data distributions where the drift affects different clients in a heterogeneous way: in these settings, our algorithm reduces the recovery time by up to 60%.

Loss-based selection performs particularly well in situations where some clients experience a stronger drift than others. We simulate this scenario under non-IID data with label flipping, where some clients carried more of the affected labels than others. Here the algorithm shows a distinct change in the client selection frequencies. Consequently, the our algorithm recovers up to three times faster on the MNIST dataset and five times faster on the FMNIST dataset than the classical FedAvg algorithm.

The temperature parameter τ allows to control the extent of bias that the model shows when choosing clients, allowing a seamless transition between random selection and maximum loss selection schemes. Proper choice of this temperature parameter yields a more stable algorithm and limits excessive fluctuations displayed, e.g., by the maximum loss selection approach of Power-of-Choice. Ultimately, our probabilistic client selection algorithm captures the benefits of loss-based selection without incurring the drawbacks of maximum-loss selection in unfavorable environments.

Open Problems. We highlight that we simulate two major prerequisites for the algorithm to be effective on real-world data, namely concept drift and data heterogeneity. Nevertheless, all client selection schemes come at the cost of increased communication as well as server- and client-side computation and it is an open problem to assess whether the benefits of the selection strategy still outweigh the added costs in a real-world application.

It remains an open question if more conservative choices for the temperature parameter τ yield a similar performance, while further reducing the risk of large fluctuations in the model. On the other hand, more aggressive configurations of τ may be beneficial in environments under heavy drift. It is an open problem to design and evaluate an adaptive algorithm that automatically adjusts the temperature parameter in a *simulated annealing* fashion to first allow for a rapid response to concept drift but ultimately retain a stable model. It would be interesting to see if such an algorithm could also handle highly-skewed non-IID data and counter concept drift on, e.g., the CIFAR-10 dataset.

Arguably, label flipping captures the complexity of real-world data only to some extent. However, we are not aware of standardized implementations of concept drift on non-IID data distributions. Future research would therefore greatly benefit from a robust definition of concept drift that replicates concept drift as experienced in real-world data.

Acknowledgments. The financial support by the Austrian Federal Ministry for Digital and Economic Affairs, the National Foundation for Research, Technology and Development, as well as the Christian Doppler Research Association is gratefully acknowledged.

References

1. Amiri, M.M., Gündüz, D., Kulkarni, S.R., Poor, H.V.: Convergence of update aware device scheduling for federated learning at the wireless edge. IEEE Trans. Wirel. Commun. **20**(6), 3643–3658 (2021)

2. Antunes, R.S., André da Costa, C., Küderle, A., Yari, I.A., Eskofier, B.: Federated learning for healthcare: systematic review and architecture proposal. ACM Trans. Intell. Syst. Technol. **13**(4) (2022)
3. Asadi, K., Littman, M.L.: An alternative softmax operator for reinforcement learning. In: 34th International Conference on Machine Learning, ICML, pp. 243–252 (2017)
4. Canonaco, G., Bergamasco, A., Mongelluzzo, A., Roveri, M.: Adaptive federated learning in presence of concept drift. In: International Joint Conference on Neural Networks, IJCNN, pp. 1–7 (2021)
5. Chen, Y., Chai, Z., Cheng, Y., Rangwala, H.: Asynchronous federated learning for sensor data with concept drift. In: 2021 IEEE International Conference on Big Data, pp. 4822–4831 (2021)
6. Cho, Y.J., Wang, J., Joshi, G.: Towards understanding biased client selection in federated learning. In: International Conference on Artificial Intelligence and Statistics, AISTATS, pp. 10351–10375 (2022)
7. Deng, L.: The MNIST database of handwritten digit images for machine learning research [best of the web]. IEEE Signal Process. Mag. **29**(6), 141–142 (2012)
8. Fu, L., Zhang, H., Gao, G., Zhang, M., Liu, X.: Client selection in federated learning: principles, challenges, and opportunities. IEEE Internet Things J. **10**(24), 21811–21819 (2023)
9. Gama, J., Zliobaite, I., Bifet, A., Pechenizkiy, M., Bouchachia, A.: A survey on concept drift adaptation. ACM Comput. Surv. **46**(4), 44:1–44:37 (2014)
10. Goetz, J., Malik, K., Bui, D., Moon, S., Liu, H., Kumar, A.: Active Federated Learning (2019). arXiv:1909.12641 [cs.LG]
11. Hahn, S.-J.: Federated Learning in PyTorch, GitHub repository (2023). https://github.com/vaseline555/Federated-Learning-in-PyTorch
12. Hsu, T.-M., Qi, H., Brown, M.: Measuring the effects of non-identical data distribution for federated visual classification (2019). arXiv:1909.06335 [cs.LG]
13. Jothimurugesan, E., Hsieh, K., Wang, J., Joshi, G., Gibbons, P.B.: Federated learning under distributed concept drift. In: International Conference on Artificial Intelligence and Statistics, AISTATS, pp. 5834–5853 (2023)
14. Kingma, D., Ba, J.: Adam: a method for stochastic optimization (2014). arXiv:1412.6980 [cs.LG]
15. Konečný, J., McMahan, H.B., Yu, F.X., Richtárik, P., Suresh, A.T., Bacon, D.: Federated Learning: Strategies for Improving Communication Efficiency (2016). arXiv:1610.05492 [cs.LG]
16. Krizhevsky, A.: Learning multiple layers of features from tiny images. Technical report (2009). https://www.cs.toronto.edu/~kriz/learning-features-2009-TR.pdf. University of Toronto
17. Lai, F., Zhu, X., Madhyastha, H.V., Chowdhury, M.: Oort: efficient federated learning via guided participant selection. In: 15th USENIX Symposium on Operating Systems Design and Implementation, OSDI, pp. 19–35 (2021)
18. Leroy, D., Coucke, A., Lavril, T., Gisselbrecht, T., Dureau, J.: Federated learning for keyword spotting. In: IEEE International Conference on Acoustics, Speech and Signal Processing, ICASSP, pp. 6341–6345 (2019)
19. Li, Q., He, B., Song, D.: Model-contrastive federated learning. In: IEEE Conference on Computer Vision and Pattern Recognition, CVPR, pp. 10713–10722 (2021)
20. Li, T., Sahu, A.K., Talwalkar, A., Smith, V.: Federated learning: challenges, methods, and future directions. IEEE Signal Process. Mag. **37**(3), 50–60 (2020)

21. Li, T., Sahu, A.K., Zaheer, M., Sanjabi, M., Talwalkar, A., Smith, V.: Federated optimization in heterogeneous networks. In: Third Conference on Machine Learning and Systems, MLSys (2020)
22. Li, X., Huang, K., Yang, W., Wang, S., Zhang, Z.: On the Convergence of FedAvg on Non-IID Data (2019). arXiv:1907.02189 [stat.ML]
23. Lu, J., Liu, A., Dong, F., Gu, F., Gama, J., Zhang, G.: Learning under concept drift: a review. IEEE Trans. Knowl. Data Eng. **31**(12), 2346–2363 (2019)
24. McMahan, B., Moore, E., Ramage, D., Hampson, S., Arcas, B.A.: Communication-efficient learning of deep networks from decentralized data. In: 20th International Conference on Artificial Intelligence and Statistics, AISTATS, pp. 1273–1282 (2017)
25. Mothukuri, V., Parizi, R.M., Pouriyeh, S., Huang, Y., Dehghantanha, A., Srivastava, G.: A survey on security and privacy of federated learning. Future Gener. Comput. Syst. **115**, 619–640 (2021)
26. Nishio, T., Yonetani, R.: Client selection for federated learning with heterogeneous resources in mobile edge. In: 2019 IEEE International Conference on Communications, ICC, pp. 1–7 (2019)
27. Reddi, S.J., et al.: Adaptive federated optimization. In: 9th International Conference on Learning Representations, ICLR (2021)
28. Ruder, S.: An overview of gradient descent optimization algorithms (2016). arXiv:1609.04747 [cs.LG]
29. Saile, F., Thomas, J., Kaaser, D., Schulte, S.: Client-side adaptation to concept drift in federated learning. In: 2nd IEEE International Conference on Federated Learning Technologies and Applications, FLTA (2024)
30. Schlimmer, J.C., Granger, R.H.: Incremental learning from noisy data. Mach. Learn. **1**(3), 317–354 (1986)
31. Truex, S., et al.: A hybrid approach to privacy-preserving federated learning. In: 12th ACM Workshop on Artificial Intelligence and Security, AISec@CCS, pp. 1–11 (2019)
32. Wang, J., Liu, Q., Liang, H., Joshi, G., Poor, H.V.: Tackling the objective inconsistency problem in heterogeneous federated optimization. In: Annual Conference on Neural Information Processing Systems, NeurIPS (2020)
33. Widmer, G., Kubat, M.: Learning in the presence of concept drift and hidden contexts. Mach. Learn. **23**(1), 69–101 (1996)
34. Wu, H., Wang, P.: Node selection toward faster convergence for federated learning on non-IID data. IEEE Trans. Netw. Sci. Eng. **9**(5), 3099–3111 (2022)
35. Xiao, H., Rasul, K., Vollgraf, R.: Fashion-MNIST: a Novel Image Dataset for Benchmarking Machine Learning Algorithms (2017). arXiv:1912.01703 [cs.LG]
36. Yang, T., et al.: Applied Federated Learning: Improving Google Keyboard Query Suggestions, arXiv:1812.02903 [cs.LG]
37. Zaheer, M., Reddi, S.J., Sachan, D.S., Kale, S., Kumar, S.: Adaptive methods for nonconvex optimization. In: Annual Conference on Neural Information Processing Systems 2018, NeurIPS, pp. 9815–9825 (2018)
38. Zhang, C., Xie, Y., Bai, H., Yu, B., Li, W., Gao, Y.: A survey on federated learning. Knowl. Based Syst. **216**, 106775 (2021)
39. Zhao, P., Zhang, T.: Stochastic optimization with importance sampling for regularized loss minimization. In: 32nd International Conference on Machine Learning, ICML. JMLR Workshop and Conference Proceedings, pp. 1–9 (2015)
40. Zhao, Y., Li, M., Lai, L., Suda, N., Civin, D., Chandra, V.: Federated Learning with Non-IID Data (2018). arXiv:1806.00582 [cs.LG]

Applying a Prompt Pattern Sequence for Decision-Making in Microservices Architectures

João José Maranhão Junior[1], Jorge Melegati[2], and Eduardo Guerra[2](✉)

[1] Institute for Technological Research, São Paulo, Brazil
[2] Free University of Bozen-Bolzano, Bolzano, Italy
{jorge.melegati,eduardo.guerra}@unibz.it

Abstract. Software architecture decisions are critical in a software project to ensure that systems meet functional and non-functional requirements. Microservice architectures have become popular in the industry, having a high amount of material available that was used in the training of large language models (LLMs). This paper explores the use of generative AI tools, such as ChatGPT, guided by a prompt pattern sequence to support architectural decision-making in microservices architectures. The proposed approach aims to provide structured guidance to software architects, helping them navigate in complex design challenges. To evaluate the prompt sequence, we conducted studies that revisited important architectural decisions made by large companies in the context of microservices architectures. Two industry case studies are presented: one involving the management of a large set of components in a financial institution, and the other focused on the front-end approach for a large-scale e-commerce platform in a pharmaceutical chain. The results demonstrate how five distinct prompt patterns deliver actionable insights tailored to each project's unique technical and business constraints, enabling more informed decision-making. Retrospective feedback from architects highlights the effectiveness of the proposed prompt pattern sequence, which proposed solutions aligned to what was actually implemented. The findings suggest that generative AI, guided by well-structured prompt patterns, can support the decision-making process in microservice architectures.

Keywords: Prompt Patterns · Software Architecture · Generative AI · Microservices

1 Introduction

In recent years, rapid advancements in software engineering practices have led to the widespread adoption of microservices architectures, particularly in large-scale, complex systems. Microservices is an architectural approach in which an application is composed of loosely coupled and independently deployable services [13,16]. Each service focuses on a specific business capability and can be developed, deployed, and scaled independently [15]. While this architectural style offers benefits such as modularity, scalability, and fault isolation, it also presents significant challenges in both design and implementation [6].

A microservices architecture is a distributed software system architecture that comprises highly cohesive but loosely coupled services [4]. A key challenge in this architecture is defining the boundaries of each microservice, which is essential to ensuring that the system remains with a good performance, fault-tolerant, and scalable [2]. Poorly designed microservices can lead to a high number of dependencies between services, lack of fault tolerance, and overlapping responsibilities, ultimately degrading system performance [17]. Defining microservice boundaries requires a deep understanding of the system and domain knowledge, a process that is often iterative and error-prone. This task is typically performed by software architects and domain experts, whose skills and understanding of customer needs strongly influence the quality of the resulting architecture [5].

The complexity of microservice design has led to the exploration of new technologies to aid the process. One such technology is generative AI, with GPT models having recently emerged as a valuable resource in software development. Generative AI has demonstrated capabilities in various software engineering tasks, including code generation [9], testing, refactoring, and software design [8]. Studies have shown that generative AI can aid in requirements analysis [22], domain concept identification, and the generation of design artifacts such as class and sequence diagrams. In the context of microservices, the potential of generative AI and similar large language models lies in their ability to identify microservices [20], analyze requirements, and provide design recommendations that align with system needs and architectural best practices [12]. The large amount of material related to microservices architecture available that was consumed in the training of large language models (LLMs) creates a huge potential for its usage to support decision-making.

Due to the difficulties in obtaining the information using the conversational interface from tools based on LLMs, such as ChatGPT, a discipline named prompt engineering emerged [14]. Prompt engineering can be defined as the process of structuring an instruction that can be interpreted and understood by a generative AI model. In this context, the prompt patterns [21] propose recurrent solutions that can be used in this interaction. For instance, some specific prompt patterns were proposed in the context of code quality improvement, refactoring, requirements elicitation, and software design [22].

This paper proposes a prompt pattern sequence to support software architects in making critical architectural decisions based on the project's technical premises, quality attributes, uncertainties, and project context. Through this sequence, composed of five prompt patterns that guide interactions with ChatGPT, we aim to provide insights into how architects perceive this new interaction in decision-making in microservice architectures [1,23]. This work evaluated the prompt pattern sequence in two industry use cases, revisiting past architectural decisions: one regarding a solution for managing a large number of software components and the other regarding a change in the front-end approach. The software architects involved in these decisions participated in an interview evaluating the prompt results and the approach itself. As a result, both architects evaluated that the obtained answers would be useful in the decision-making, reporting that they were aligned with what was implemented in practice. On the other hand, they also pointed out the lack of detail in some cases and suggested a more iterative approach to be able to go deeper into them.

2 Prompt Patterns Sequence

This work proposes new prompt patterns and a prompt sequence to be applied using generative AI conversational interfaces for architectural decision-making. They were described in more detail in a pattern paper targeted to practitioners [10], which did not present any evaluation of them. These five prompt patterns emerged from practice by adapting concepts of other documented prompt patterns [21] and introducing steps related to some architecture design approaches, such as ArchHypo [19]. The next paragraphs describe each proposed pattern.

`Software Architect Persona` describes in the prompt a specialized persona for software architects, defining what is their decision scope to prevent answers that suggest actions outside of what can be done. It guides AI-generated responses to reflect the specific roles, objectives, and constraints architects face in complex projects. The goal is to tailor responses to be technically precise and contextually relevant, helping architects make informed decisions based on their current responsibilities.

`Technical Premises` is a pattern that introduces prompts to validate the technical premises used in architectural decision-making. Given the potential for AI-generated "hallucinations" (misleading or incorrect responses) [12], this pattern ensures that the AI justifies its suggestions with a list of specific technical premises. It allows architects to critically evaluate the accuracy and reliability of the AI's outputs.

`Uncertain Requirement Statement` suggests creating prompts that explicitly state in the prompt what the uncertainties related to the software architecture [19]. It helps architects plan for potential risks and impacts associated with these uncertainties, ensuring that the architecture is flexible enough to accommodate future changes. By proactively managing uncertain requirements, architects can better align the system with long-term business needs and technological trends.

Finally, the pattern `Quality Attribute Question` creates prompts to assist architects in evaluating the trade-offs and balancing quality attributes, such as scalability, security, and performance. Through an interactive questioning process, the AI tool gathers information about the system's functional and non-functional requirements, helping architects make balanced decisions that optimize the integration of these quality attributes in architectural design.

Finally, `Architectural Project Context` integrates key project constraints into the decision-making process, such as development time, team size, and budget. It ensures that architectural solutions are theoretically sound and practically feasible within the project's limitations. The pattern helps architects design architectures that align with the business and technical requirements while navigating these constraints.

These patterns can be applied independently or in combination. After interactively evaluating various sequences and combinations, we propose a prompt sequence based on these prompt patterns, as illustrated in Fig. 1. The process begins by defining the role and objectives of the architect. Then, it moves on to assess technical premises and ask for solutions to handle uncertainties and balance quality attributes. The process concludes by prompting about the restrictions of the project context.

3 Research Design

The objective of this study is to evaluate whether the prompt pattern sequence proposed by this work can support the architectural decision-making processes, especially in scenarios involving microservices architectures. This study was guided by the following research question: *What are the perceived benefits and challenges of using the proposed prompt sequence with generative AI tools in the decision-making in microservice architectures from the perspective of software architects?*

To achieve that goal, we identified important architectural decisions made in real software projects to be used as the basis for this evaluation. Based on the project information collected, we recreated the existing scenario when the decision was made in the prompts and used the prompt pattern sequence to retrieve information from ChatGPT that could support the decision-making. After that, we interviewed a software architect who participated in the decision and followed the implementation of the solution, having information regarding its consequences and the challenges faced by the team. Based on that, we assessed the applicability of the proposed approach in supporting architectural decision-making.

The research method used in this study is inspired by characteristics of case studies [18] and retrospective studies [3]. From case studies, we considered observation of real scenarios to address relevant and realistic factors. Since architectural decisions usually involve complex specific attributes and relationships, using real cases allows the representation of the complexity of this process. Considering similarities with retrospective studies, we reviewed decisions and their consequences from completed projects, as performed by other studies [7]. However, in our case, we not only analyzed past decisions but simulated their context to evaluate the proposed technique.

3.1 Research Steps

The research methodology for this study was executed in the following five steps: (1) recruit companies to participate in the study, (2) select and document target design decision, (3) execute the prompt pattern sequence, (4) present the results and interview a software architect involved in the decision, and (5) perform

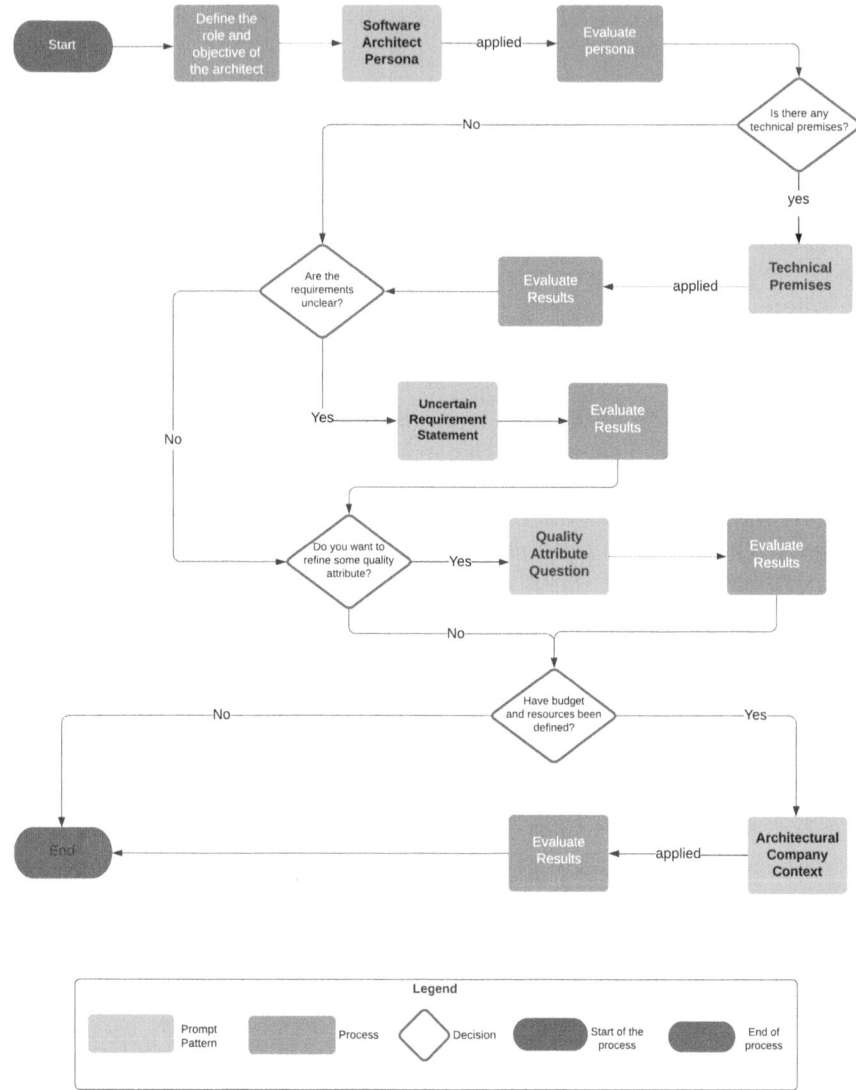

Fig. 1. Decision Flow To Prompt Patterns Sequence

a qualitative analysis of the prompts and interview answers. The study was conducted between October 2023 and March 2024, and GPT-4o was used to execute the prompts.

For the recruitment phase, we considered that projects had to meet three inclusion criteria: (a) be a recently completed project to ensure up-to-date and relevant architectural practices; (b) it must involve significant architectural decisions related to microservices; (c) participating company should be willing to provide detailed project data, including technical specifications, decision-making processes, and results.

Recruiting such companies posed a challenge due to confidentiality concerns [18]. To address this, convenience sampling was used, focusing on companies with professionals inside the contact network of the researchers [11]. After the prerequisites and methods were presented, two Brazilian companies operating in the Brazilian market agreed to participate in the study. Company A (leader in car financing) and Company B (leader in pharmaceutical retail with more than 3000 stores) were selected. Both of them have systems with microservices architectures that face interesting technical challenges.

As the second step, a relevant design decision was selected for each project and analyzed through meetings with their architects. The goal was to select a specific architectural decision to focus and retrieve information to be used to create the prompts of the prompt pattern sequence. In the third step, the prompt patterns were used to create the prompts according to each company's specific architectural scenario. The prompts were executed for each scenario and prepared to be presented to the software architects.

As the fourth step, the results of the prompt sequence were presented to the architects, and interviews were conducted following the protocol presented in the next subsection. The questions were focused on asking the architects to evaluate AI-generated responses based on the prompt pattern sequence and their usefulness in the retrospective scenarios. Questions about the architects' expertise were also collected to understand their professional background, making sure they have the appropriate experience to judge the results. In the fifth step, we conducted a qualitative analysis focused on the architects' perceptions regarding the AI-generated responses, considering the challenges in the project and the developments that happened later. We also evaluated how they evaluated the prompt patterns and the respective prompt pattern sequence to extract relevant information from the AI tool.

3.2 Interview Protocol

The interview started with a comprehensive introduction in which the participants are reminded of the consent terms to ensure their complete understanding and agreement. Following this, a clear explanation of the research objectives was provided to help participants understand the study's aims. The research protocol was also outlined, giving participants a clear understanding of the procedures and expectations during the study. Finally, participants were asked permission to record the sessions for further analysis.

As the first interview section, participants are asked detailed questions to gather background information and assess their expertise in software architecture. They are first asked about their experience working with software architecture, followed by a request to describe their professional trajectory and main experiences in software architecture. Participants are also asked about the duration of their employment at their current or previous companies (Company A or B) and the roles they have performed there, which provides context on their responsibilities and influence on decision-making processes within the company.

Further, the interview moves to the prompt patterns section, where we seek to gain insight into the perspective of architects regarding the architectural recommendations generated by AI using prompt patterns created in this work. The questions presented in Table 1 were used to guide the interview, which followed a semi-structured format. For each prompt pattern, the pattern was explained and the prompt and the respective answer presented. The architect then answer the questions regarding that pattern. In the end, the questions regarding the pattern sequence were asked.

Table 1. Questions about the prompt patterns and prompt patterns sequence.

Prompt Pattern Questions
Would the information generated by the prompt have been useful at the time of the project?
Which of the responses generated coincides with what was implemented?
Is there any information in the generated responses that you disagree with?
Is there information you agree with in the generated responses that you would implement?
Prompt Patterns Sequence Questions
What do you think of the proposed sequence?
Does this sequence fulfill the objective of supporting architectural decision-making?
Were any steps unnecessary and could be removed?
Are there any steps that need to be added?
Would you make any changes to the sequence of prompts applied?

For each pattern, we started asking the participants a fundamental question: whether AI-generated information would have been helpful during the project to evaluate the practical applicability of prompt patterns. Further, the participants were requested to elaborate if the responses were aligned with what was implemented and discuss any discrepancies or agreements with the AI suggestions.

Following that, the sequence of prompt patterns was assessed. Participants were asked for their thoughts on the proposed sequence and whether it meets the objective of supporting architectural decision-making. They were encouraged not just to criticize but also to suggest if any steps are unnecessary or if any additional steps could be added to enhance the process.

4 Industrial Case Studies Description

This section reports the results of applying the prompt pattern sequence in the context of projects from two companies, a financial institution, and a pharmaceutical company, that will be referred respectively to as COMPANY A and

COMPANY B. The focus is on evaluating the perceived benefits and difficulties of applying prompt pattern sequences through generative AI to assist in the architectural decision-making process from the perspective of software architects. In the description of each case, a link to the execution of the prompts is provided, and all names used in the prompts are fictitious for confidentiality reasons.

In both cases, the software architect who participated in the interview had experience in microservices architectures and had appropriate knowledge to judge the answers. They also participated in the decision process targeted by the study, following the implementation of the solution and the developments that followed it. Based on that, we judged their experience appropriate to evaluate the result of the prompt sequences.

4.1 Financial Institution - COMPANY A

COMPANY A[1] has a system that adopts a microservices architecture and manages over 18,000 software components using various technologies and frameworks. The scenario chosen to be analyzed concerns COMPANY A's change management process, which is critical in this type of architecture. The software versions could not be released if code coverage fell below a threshold or had critical security issues, and the fact that analysts manually gathered quality and security metrics caused delays and increased risks. The focus of this study was on the architectural decision regarding how to implement an automated solution to centralize and streamline the change management process by integrating several key technologies.

For the first prompt pattern, `Software Architect Persona`, Architect A emphasized the significance of defining a specific persona to enable the AI to tailor its responses more effectively to their needs. This approach made the interaction more relevant and practical. Architect A also confirmed that this pattern helped to narrow the scope of the AI's responses, ensuring that the information generated aligned with the project's architectural requirements.

Architect A appreciated the detailed technical context in the second prompt pattern, `Technical Premises`, noting its reflection on practical project considerations. He emphasized the importance of technical assumptions in checking the validity of AI-generated solutions to specific technologies. Architect A highlighted the effectiveness of the prompts in the guidance present in the answers. He believed that it could help the team to implement solutions, such as a dashboard using Angularand TypeScript, ensuring alignment with the project's architecture and security practices.

He also noted that the prompts could have addressed resilience-related issues by suggesting appropriate delays for report availability. Architect A shared an example: *"When we integrated with a tool like Veracode, a report with security information was generated, but we didn't realize it wasn't available instantly. This*

---

[1] Full prompt: https://chat.openai.com/share/5604c457-13b2-4213-90da-8b598386 73fc.

led to a problem when we checked the report prematurely". He explained that a delayed query job could have resolved the issue and that using this approach earlier would have saved time. The prompts could have proactively guided the team in implementing such resilience measures.

The answer to the third pattern Unclear Requirement Statement suggested developing API contract integrations for consuming microservice APIs using contract-first and testing them in the CI/CD pipeline. Architect A noted that while adopting an API management tool can help, it is not always feasible, especially with off-the-shelf products like Veracode and Sonar that offer limited customization. However, due to tight deadlines, this strategy was not implemented, although Architect A believed it could have mitigated the issues at the time, even if it did not completely solve them.

Architect A found that the prompt stimulated the generative AI to ask insightful questions when using the fourth Quality Attribute Questions pattern to ask about scalability and resilience. According to him, the considerations about quality attributes generated by the prompt pattern demonstrated its ability to highlight critical aspects of system design that may not be immediately obvious, helping architects build more robust systems. All necessary points were addressed, and as more information was provided, the AI developed a more detailed solution, proposing improvements for performance, quality, and scalability. Architect A found it particularly valuable that the AI suggested additional solutions, such as implementing caching mechanisms, increasing horizontal and vertical scalability, and delegating certain functionality to other system components. These efforts went beyond what was initially requested. The extra attention to detail and proactive suggestions were greatly appreciated and exceeded the architect's expectations.

When prompting about the Architectural Project Context, ChatGPT underestimated the implementation timeline compared to what was actually needed. Even though Architect A appreciated aligning the AI's suggestions with effective software architecture practices. The suggestions provided a vision consistent with the project's architectural goals, even if the timeline required adaptation.

Architect A confirmed that the Prompt Patterns Sequence would be helpful for architectural decision-making in the described scenario. The detailed guidance provided by the AI aligned well with the project's needs, and its recommendations closely matched what was implemented in practice. While no steps were considered unnecessary, Architect A suggested making some parts more concise and adding an interactive element for exploring specific topics further.

Architect A emphasized that the sequence effectively supported architectural decision-making, particularly in areas like resilience and quality. It would have been extremely useful during the project's development, potentially facilitating faster delivery of high-quality solutions. The prompts' structured and detailed approach provided valuable and relevant guidance that aligned well with the project's practical needs. While no steps were unnecessary, Architect A reiterated the benefit of adding an interactive feature for deeper exploration of specific topics if needed. The following quote represents Architect A assessment: *"I wouldn't change the chat prompts significantly. The sequence was engaging and made sense. Some minor modifications might be needed to adapt to specific needs, but the accuracy of the chat's recommendations, which closely resembled what we applied in practice, was impressive".*

4.2 Pharmacy Chain - COMPANY B

COMPANY B[2], one of the Brazilian largest pharmacy retail chains, is overhauling its customer service interface across 3,000 stores to improve efficiency and modernize interactions. Each store's system handles tasks like price checks, order processing, and compliance with Brazil's LGPD, emphasizing the need for a robust solution. The problem that was chosen to be targeted was the inefficiency of the front-end approach, which was leading to potential customer dissatisfaction and maintenance issues. The pharmacy chain needed a scalable, user-friendly, and highly available front-end system to handle operations, including 24/7 locations, with minimal disruptions. The project team had to decide on a new architectural approach for the front-end system.

Architect B emphasized the importance of defining the `Software Architect Persona` to guide project decisions and confirmed that it should be the first prompt in the sequence. Regarding `Technical Premises`, Architect B agreed that the prompt's suggestion for the adoption of micro front-ends [15] aligned with the project's technical requirements and praised the detailed comparison of architectural approaches. He confirmed that the architectural decision generated by the prompt patterns was the same decision made in the project, as stated in the following: *"We reached the same conclusion: that micro front-ends, given the scalability and multidisciplinary team, would fit the product."* He also appreciated the presentation of the advantages and benefits of each architectural approach, which provided a solid basis for comparison. Even though the suggestion was agreed upon, the architect missed a question about the current backend configuration before recommending the usage of micro front-ends.

The pattern `Uncertain Requirement Statement` addressed technical variations, network reliability, system integration, and user adoption uncertainties. Architect B acknowledged the importance of having more intuitive interfaces and noted that 90% of the system screens were redesigned in that direction, as suggested by the prompt. He also appreciated the recommendation to consider technologies such as GraphQL or BFF, which aligned with the project's modernization efforts. As a critic of the answers received, the architect expected more specific and technical recommendations, such as including Kubernetes for management and scaling.

The `Quality Attribute Question` addressed quality attributes such as usability, scalability, and testability. The participant expressed satisfaction with

---

[2] Full prompt: https://chat.openai.com/share/775a0eae-b826-4ab3-95ac-eca4f60bf649.

how the prompt clarified doubts and decision-making based on the specified quality attributes. He found the suggestions helpful for generating features to collect user feedback. Architect B remarked: *"It's nice to have continuous evolution and faster feedback... I thought it was cool; it's something we don't have today"*. As in the other questions, Architect B missed more details in the answers, this time in the testing recommendations. He mentioned that the discussion could include more details on the types of tests that would be most effective, such as integration or unit tests.

The prompt for the `Architectural Project Context` focused mainly on the team organization and the delivery strategy. Architect B valued the insights related to the team structure and sprint cycles. He also appreciated the recommendation for using the micro front-ends to improve component scalability. On the negative side, Architect B expressed concern about potential bias in the cloud vendor recommendations, specifically the exclusion of Google Cloud Platform (GCP) in favor of AWS and Azure. He suggested that the prompt should take a more neutral stance toward specific vendors.

Evaluating the prompt sequence, Architect B confirmed that the `Prompt Pattern Sequence` effectively would support architectural decision-making in the evaluated context, particularly regarding resilience and quality. The sequence offered valuable guidance, leading to suitable solutions quickly, highlighting that the AI's recommendations were closely aligned with the solutions implemented in practice. Architect B suggested reorganizing the sequence, bringing the Quality Attribute Question pattern closer to Technical Premises, as he felt that non-functional requirements are closely related to technical assumptions. He also recommended adding an interactive element, allowing for additional specific questions to explore topics more deeply.

5 Discussion

Integrating generative AI tools into the architectural decision-making process by using the proposed prompt pattern sequence has demonstrated substantial benefits and has surfaced areas for improvement, as noted by software architects. This discussion delves into these aspects, emphasizing the value of prompt patterns and their sequence in enhancing architectural decision-making.

From their professional perspective, software architects identified numerous advantages in using sequence prompt patterns with generative AI tools. A key benefit is the structured guidance that prompt patterns offer, allowing architects to address various architectural questions systematically. The AI's ability to generate relevant, context-specific information boosts the efficiency of the decision-making process. Furthermore, the prompts' focus on critical factors such as resilience, scalability, and technical premises ensures that essential architectural considerations are not overlooked.

However, using generative AI also poses challenges. Architects observed that the AI sometimes generates generic or overly broad recommendations that need more specificity for complex technical environments. Additionally, there is a need for more iterative and detailed follow-up questions to explore issues further, which the current prompt patterns may need to address fully. This lack of interaction can also be due to the sequence adopted in the study, in which the prompts were generated before the interview. In a real setting, the software architects do not need to be restricted only to these patterns and strictly follow the proposed sequence. By using it as a guide, it is possible to explore some of the answers in more detail with some additional prompts.

According to the participants, the information generated by the prompt patterns would have been beneficial during past projects. For example, prompts for patterns like `Technical Premises`, `Quality Attribute Question`, and `Uncertain Requirement Statement` could have provided more precise direction for architectural decisions, potentially preventing integration and performance issues. The structured approach to identifying and addressing uncertainties would have been valuable in mitigating potential risks.

AI-generated responses also aligned with actual implementations in the two industry case studies. For instance, the micro front-end solution recommended as answers to the `Technical Premises` and `Uncertain Requirement Statement` prompts in the pharmacy chain project was adopted. This enabled independent development and scaling of features across multiple stores. Similarly, strategies implemented in the project mirrored the AI's emphasis on cloud-based solutions for scalability and resilience to microservices.

In both studies, architects also noted divergences between AI-generated responses and their specific needs, particularly regarding the generality of particular recommendations. In the case of the financial institution, suggestions for API management and integration approaches sometimes needed to be more abstract or fully aligned with the project context, as reflected in prompts like `Uncertain Requirement Statement` and `Architectural Project Context`. In the pharmacy case, some recommendations to address uncertainties were general and, according to Architect B, needed to be more specific.

Controversial points in the AI's output also emerged. In the financial institution case, disagreements arose concerning project delivery deadlines, highlighting a potential limitation in the AI's understanding of complex project timelines regarding using the `Architectural Project Context` pattern. Similarly, in the pharmacy scenario, the AI's recommendation of a specific cloud vendor, while omitting others, raised concerns about its ability to provide comprehensive, unbiased information.

Despite these challenges, architects agreed on several AI-generated suggestions they would implement. In the case of financial institutions, AI recommended more robust contract testing to ensure API consistency and a message broker approach to maintain loose coupling and guarantee message delivery. These recommendations were noted in the `Technical Premises` and `Uncertain Requirement Statement` prompts patterns. In the pharmacy case, the AI's suggestion to include a "suggestions and improvements" feature in the front end to enhance quality attributes was appreciated, as reflected in the `Quality Attribute Question` prompt pattern.

Architects responded positively to the sequence of prompt patterns, praising its logical flow and comprehensive coverage of critical architectural considerations. The sequence effectively guides architects through a structured decision-making process, ensuring that all critical aspects are addressed thoroughly. Overall, they judged that the sequence supports architectural decision-making by providing a clear structure for evaluating and resolving architectural challenges, ensuring decisions are well-informed and aligned with project requirements.

While architects did not identify any unnecessary steps in the sequence, they suggested that some prompts could be more concise and focused on avoiding redundancy, streamlining the decision-making process, and increasing their effectiveness. Additionally, they recommended adding more interactions, allowing the architect to ask follow-up questions to explore specific topics in greater depth. While this lack of interaction was also due to the structure of the study, as stated previously, we agree that the sequence could have this aspect more explicitly represented. One architect proposed reorganizing the sequence, suggesting that quality attribute-related issues be addressed earlier, closer to the `Technical Premises` prompt. This change was argued to improve accuracy, as non-functional requirements are closely tied to technical assumptions.

Limitations. One of the main limitations of this study is related to the number of participants interviewed and the number of case studies analyzed. While the results are promising, evaluating the prompt pattern sequence in more projects and retrieving the assessment from more professionals would allow a stronger evaluation of it. In these studies, one researcher generated the prompts, so the approach was not evaluated in cases in which the professionals were responsible for writing the prompts.

Another limitation of this study is that the decisions targeted in this study were in the context of microservice architecture, which is a popular architectural style in the industry with plenty of material available. That has an influence on the material used for training the generative AI, which also contributes to the correctness and precision of the answers. Because of that, the results of this study should be considered in the context of this specific architectural style.

6 Conclusion

The adoption of generative AI tools, guided by the proposed prompt pattern sequence, has demonstrated potential in supporting architectural decision-making for microservices architectures. This study applied the sequence in two real-world scenarios, in a financial institution and in a pharmaceutical company, highlighting how AI-generated insights, structured through prompt patterns, can enhance decision-making by providing architects with relevant, context-specific guidance. According to the participants, the five proposed prompt patterns provided a systematic approach in the usage of generative AI tools to address critical architectural challenges while ensuring that technical and business constraints were considered. The prompt pattern sequence, including the pattern themselves, and its assessment study are the main contributions of this paper.

Architects who participated in the study provided valuable feedback on the sequence, underscoring its practical relevance. They particularly highlighted its effectiveness in ensuring that critical considerations like scalability, resilience, and quality attributes were not overlooked. The study also identified areas for improvement, such as the need for more interactive and detailed follow-up questions and suggestions to streamline some prompts to avoid redundancy. Moreover, the architects recommended reordering certain patterns to better align with their practical decision-making processes.

Despite the challenges identified, the architects overwhelmingly recognized the potential of using generative AI tools to generate structured, actionable insights that closely aligned with the solutions they implemented. This approach, when leveraged effectively, allows software architects to explore different options and brainstorm about the candidate solutions and alternatives for their more detailed implementation. In conclusion, the prompt pattern sequence can provide a valuable structure for integrating AI tools into the architectural decision-making process.

Future work should refine the sequence by incorporating more interactive elements and exploring how the approach can be adapted to more specific project contexts. Further studies with projects involving other architectural styles could be used to evaluate the applicability of the prompt pattern sequence in other contexts.

References

1. Ayas, H.M., Leitner, P., Hebig, R.: Facing the giant: a grounded theory study of decision-making in microservices migrations. In: Proceedings of the 15th ACM / IEEE International Symposium on Empirical Software Engineering and Measurement (ESEM), ESEM 2021. Association for Computing Machinery, New York (2021). https://doi.org/10.1145/3475716.3475792
2. Balalaie, A., Heydarnoori, A., Jamshidi, P.: Microservices architecture enables devops: migration to a cloud-native architecture. IEEE Softw. **33**(3), 42–52 (2016)
3. Desouza, K.C., Dingsøyr, T., Awazu, Y.: Experiences with conducting project postmortems: reports versus stories. Softw. Process: Improv. Pract. **10**(2), 203–215 (2005). https://doi.org/10.1002/spip.224
4. Dragoni, N., et al.: Microservices: yesterday, today, and tomorrow. Present Ulterior Softw. Eng. **100**, 195–216 (2017)
5. Evans, E.: Domain-Driven Design: Tackling Complexity in the Heart of Software. Addison-Wesley Professional (2003)
6. Fowler, M., Lewis, J.: Microservices: a definition of this new architectural term (2014). https://martinfowler.com/articles/microservices.html. Accessed 07 Oct 2024
7. Hayes, D., Grossman, F., Knapp, C., Rising, L.: The impact of project retrospectives on process improvement initiatives: a case study. In: 2011 IEEE Long Island Systems, Applications and Technology Conference (2011). https://doi.org/10.1109/lisat.2011.5784234
8. Jiang, S., Zhang, H., Wang, T., Liu, J.: A survey on deep learning for software engineering. IEEE Trans. Softw. Eng. (2021)

9. Liu, C., et al.: Improving chatgpt prompt for code generation. arXiv preprint arXiv:2305.08360 (2023)
10. Maranhão, J.J.J., Guerra, E.M.: A prompt pattern sequence approach to apply generative AI in assisting software architecture decision-making. In: 2024 Proceedings of the 29th European Conference on Pattern Languages of Programs, People, and Practices, Europlop. ACM (2024). https://doi.org/10.1145/3698322.3698324
11. Marshall, M.N.: Sampling for qualitative research. Fam. Pract. **13**(6), 522–526 (1996)
12. Meyer, J.G., et al.: Chatgpt and large language models in academia: opportunities and challenges. BioData Min. **16**(1), 20 (2023). https://doi.org/10.1186/s13040-023-00339-9
13. Newman, S.: Building Microservices: Designing Fine-Grained Systems. O'Reilly Media (2015)
14. Phoenix, J., Taylor, M.: Prompt Engineering for Generative AI. O'Reilly Media Inc. (2024)
15. Richard, C.: Microservice architecture essentials: deployability (2022). https://microservices.io/post/architecture/2022/05/04/microservice-architecture-essentials-deployability.html. Accessed 07 Oct 2024
16. Richard, C.: Microservice architecture essentials: loose coupling (2023). https://microservices.io/post/architecture/2023/03/28/microservice-architecture-essentials-loose-coupling.html. Accessed 07 Oct 2024
17. Richardson, C.: Microservices Patterns: With Examples in Java. Manning Publications (2018)
18. Runeson, P., Host, M., Rainer, A., Regnell, B.: Case Study Research in Software Engineering: Guidelines and Examples. Wiley (2012). https://books.google.com.br/books?id=T7rXoaxqPIAC
19. Silva, K., Melegati, J., Wang, X., Ferreira, M., Guerra, E.: Using hypotheses to manage technical uncertainty and architecture evolution in a software start-up. IEEE Softw. **41**(4), 7–13 (2024)
20. Stojanovic, T., Lazarević, S.D.: The application of chatgpt for identification of microservices. In: E-Business Technologies Conference Proceedings, vol. 3, pp. 99–105 (2023)
21. White, J., et al.: A prompt pattern catalog to enhance prompt engineering with chatgpt (2023)
22. White, J., Hays, S., Fu, Q., Spencer-Smith, J., Schmidt, D.C.: Chatgpt prompt patterns for improving code quality, refactoring, requirements elicitation, and software design. In: Generative AI for Effective Software Development, pp. 71–108. Springer, Cham (2024)
23. Zdun, U., Stocker, M., Zimmermann, O., Pautasso, C., Lübke, D.: Guiding architectural decision making on quality aspects in microservice APIs. In: Pahl, C., Vukovic, M., Yin, J., Yu, Q. (eds.) ICSOC 2018. LNCS, vol. 11236, pp. 73–89. Springer, Cham (2018). https://doi.org/10.1007/978-3-030-03596-9_5

SemT: A Framework for Enhancing Tabular Data Through Enrichment-as-a-Service

Abubakari Alidu(✉), Michele Ciavotta, and Flavio De Paoli

Department of Informatics, Systems and Communication, University of
Milano-Bicocca, Milan, Italy
`a.alidu@campus.unimib.it, {michele.ciavotta,flavio.paoli}@unimib.it`

Abstract. Tabular data enrichment involves leveraging external data sources to enhance the content of a source table through automated pipelines. This paper proposes a service model that standardizes API definitions for accessing specialized, single-task services, transforming them into modular components for seamless integration into various workflows. This approach facilitates dynamic composition and execution of services, providing flexibility to meet diverse enrichment needs while lowering the expertise barrier for users. The model supports the *extend by linking* paradigm, reconciling and linking relevant columns in a source table to external datasets, typically knowledge graphs, to enrich the table with new content. Grounded in REST and microservices principles, the service model supports a lightweight, modular architecture and complies with the W3C reconciliation API for data matching, ensuring interoperability.

Keywords: Data Enrichment · Data linking · Semantic annotation · Service model · Data pipeline

1 Introduction

The adoption of AI solutions is becoming widespread across various human activities, relying heavily on massive amounts of data. A significant portion of this data is in tabular format and often requires extensive preparation before it can be used. Raw data typically lacks standardized formats, contains errors, and may require enrichment. Therefore, early-stage data preparation operations, including structural, syntactical, and semantic transformations, are essential.

According to a recent survey [7], data preparation operations can be classified into several categories: discovery, validation, structuring, enrichment, filtering, and cleaning. Data preparation involves multiple steps organized into a pipeline to gradually transform a dataset into the desired output. Effective data preparation benefits from a comprehensive, extensible set of operators, allowing for more intelligent and self-service techniques. Once established, pipelines can be optimized and customized to meet specific business needs.

This paper discusses the enrichment of tabular data to prepare it for analytics and other downstream activities. We discuss a reference scenario focusing on a company's need for periodic data enrichment, highlighting the importance of repeatability addressed by the definition of enrichment data pipelines.

The research contribution of this paper is the definition of a service model aiming to support the development and provisioning of EaaS (enrichment-as-a-service) services, which can be exploited to support data exploration and composed to create data enrichment pipelines. The approach is based on the *extend by linking* paradigm, which involves reconciling and linking the content of column cells in a source table to shared datasets that define systems of identifiers, typically knowledge graphs, thereby extending the table with new content [4,5,8,9].

The service model implements REST and microservices principles to support the design of a modular software architecture. The data model is compliant with the W3C protocol for semantic data matching [10]. It aims to overcome some limitations of current solutions: unify API definitions for single-task services, create composable components for different pipelines, and simplify the development of user-friendly interactive tools. The adoption of a shared API enhances service management and interoperability across both new and legacy services.

The proposed SemT Service model has been used to implement a framework that supports the *Explore-Design-Operate* workflow to support the development and operation of enrichment applications. A key advantage of this workflow is its logical separation of tasks based on the roles, skills, and expertise required: exploration relies on domain expertise to focus on the meaning of the managed content, design demands technical skills to program the necessary components, while operation requires engineering expertise to efficiently package and run the applications within workflow execution platforms.

The core component of the framework is the extendable backend, named SemT-backend, which provides a flexible set of EaaS services. These services are accessible through multiple channels, including a Graphical User Interface (GUI), named SemT-UI [3,6], for seamless interaction by end-users, and a Python library, named SemT-Py, which enables programmatic access.

In Sect. 2, we present a detailed case study to motivate our work and describe the approach that supports the proposed service model. Section 3 introduces the service model, the framework, and its components. Finally, Sect. 4 concludes the paper and outlines future developments.

2 Motivation

A digital marketing use case illustrates the application of the SemT service model to enhance marketing data analytics. The initial dataset, containing campaign metrics such as dates, keywords, impressions, clicks, and location information, faces challenges due to imprecise geolocations and a lack of contextual data. To overcome these limitations, the data is enriched with accurate geographical coordinates, local weather data, and standardized location identifiers. The goal is to support analytics and gain insights into how weather affects campaign performance, identify geographical trends, and develop targeted strategies.

The SemT service model supports the definition of a flexible set of operations for data enrichment, enabling domain experts to explore data, data scientists to design replicable pipelines, and data engineers to deploy them efficiently. The process includes data loading, geographic reconciliation, meteorological augmentation, and column formatting, to prepare data for analytics.

Figure 1 shows a portion of the enriched dataset. Location data is first reconciled to obtain city latitude and longitude, which, together with dates, is used to retrieve weather information. This information is then used to add new columns to the original table, enriching the dataset with contextual details.

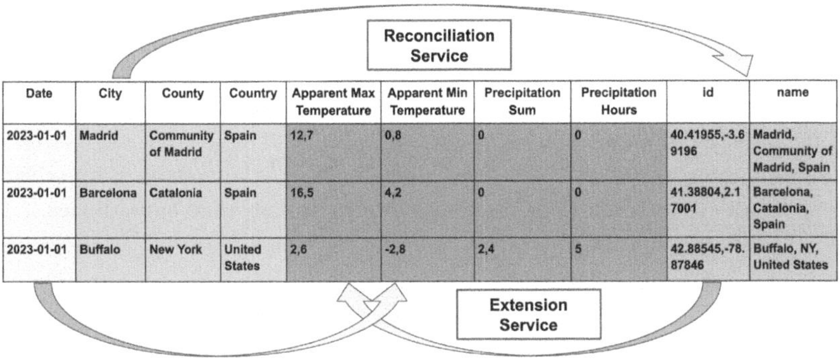

Date	City	County	Country	Apparent Max Temperature	Apparent Min Temperature	Precipitation Sum	Precipitation Hours	id	name
2023-01-01	Madrid	Community of Madrid	Spain	12,7	0,8	0	0	40.41955,-3.69196	Madrid, Community of Madrid, Spain
2023-01-01	Barcelona	Catalonia	Spain	16,5	4,2	0	0	41.38804,2.17001	Barcelona, Catalonia, Spain
2023-01-01	Buffalo	New York	United States	2,6	-2,8	2,4	5	42.88545,-78.87846	Buffalo, NY, United States

Fig. 1. Example of Enriched Data with Geographical and Weather Information

This simple setup shows the effectiveness of the SemT service model in addressing data enrichment challenges, enabling the creation of a robust framework for broader applications beyond this initial use case.

3 The SemT Service Model and Framework

The aim of the proposed SemT Service Model and Framework is to address the complexities of data enrichment through a structured approach that encompasses exploration, design, and operation phases.

The service model defines a REST API, based on the annotation formats of the W3C Reconciliation Service API v0.2 specification [10], and specialized for enriching tabular data. Table representations are exchanged in JSON-LD format, incorporating semantic annotations for headers (schema annotations) and cells (entity annotations), as shown in Listing 1.1. The only required fields are the labels in the tables; an optional metadata field can store the semantic annotations.

Listing 1.1. Column and Cell interfaces in TypeScript

```typescript
interface Column {
  label: string;
  context?: Record<ID, {prefix: string; uri: string}>;
  metadata?: ColumnMetadata[];
  kind?: 'entity' | 'literal';
  role?: 'sbj' | 'obj';
  cells: Record<string, Cell>;
}

interface Cell {
  label: string;
  metadata?: EntityMetadata[];
}
```

The SemT Framework is built on the *Explore-Design-Operate* paradigm, which guides stakeholders through the enrichment process. Domain experts can explore data sources and select relevant services, data scientists can create and test replicable pipelines, and data engineers can deploy these pipelines on execution platforms to enhance efficiency and scalability. The architecture (Fig. 2) is modular and microservices-based, featuring a backend that serves as an advanced gateway to an ecosystem of enrichment services and storage capabilities.

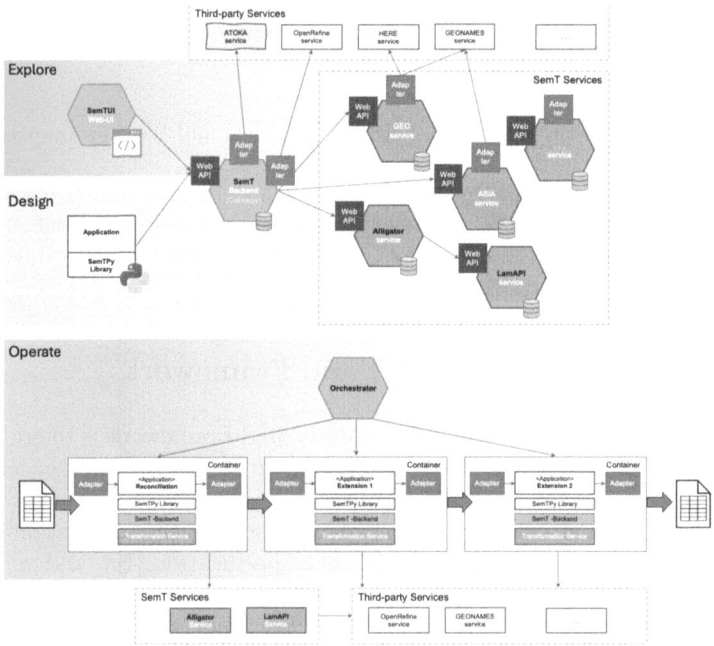

Fig. 2. The architecture of the SemT framework

The SemT backend enables seamless integration of enrichment services, allowing users to transform and enrich source tables through automatic annotation, reconciliation, and content extension. Services are wrapped by adapters that standardize requests and responses, ensuring a consistent data format throughout the process. The SemT backend gives access to three types of services: i) **Built-in services** are on-premise and integrated into the SemT ecosystem, ensuring stable and fast performance. For example, Alligator service uses machine learning and heuristics with knowledge graphs (e.g., Wikidata) to annotate tables with column types, properties, and entity links, accompanied by confidence scores [3]. ii) **Third-party services** operate remotely and include tools like the OpenRefine API for Wikidata and OpenMeteo to retrieve weather data [2,5]. iii) **Hybrid services** combine on-premise control with external data sources. For instance, the GEO service relies on GeoNames and HERE APIs, implementing caching logic for location data for efficiency.

On top of the backend, the SemT-UI graphical user interface has been developed to support the exploration phase, helping domain-expert users identify suitable services for enriching a source table. Complementing this, the SemT-Py library enables the programmatic definition of enrichment processes, allowing data scientists to design pipelines that transform source data into the desired enriched table.

Referring to the example in Fig. 1, the process begins with exploration in SemT-UI, where users identify services such as the GEO service for *reconciliation* and OpenMeteo for *extension*. During this phase, users may also identify the need to *adjust* the source table (e.g., converting the date format to ISO8601). In the next stage, pipeline design in SemT-Py translates these insights into a set of tasks that can be executed as a linear pipeline, leading to results like the one illustrated in Fig. 3. Each component in the pipeline is a Docker container that encapsulates the required transformation logic, an instance of the backend, and the necessary service to ensure high cohesion and independent deployability. Pipelines can thus be organized as distinct Directed Acyclic Graphs (DAGs) to address specific business needs, including data size and infrastructural constraints.

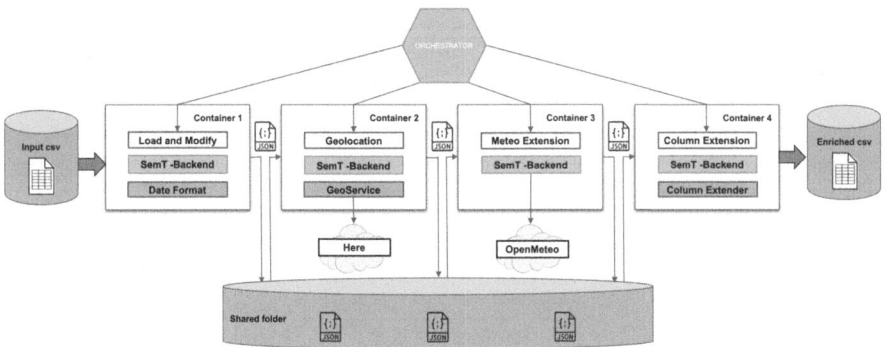

Fig. 3. Enrichment pipeline for the DM use case

4 Conclusions and Future Works

This work introduces a service model for data enrichment, aimed at addressing the increasing demands of data preparation for AI and machine learning applications. The model adopts an *extend by linking* approach to develop a *Explore-Design-Operate* framework, simplifying tool development, unifying API definitions, and enabling composable components for diverse pipelines. The model reduces user expertise requirements while maintaining modularity, scalability, and interoperability, allowing for the creation of context-aware, enriched datasets.

The proposed model was validated through real business use cases addresses in European innovation projects, demonstrating its capability and flexibility to transform raw data into enriched datasets by adding contextual information to enhances data quality, analytical potential, and usability across domains.

The system's modular design, based on containerized components and shared folders, ensures ease of maintenance, scalability, and seamless integration with external services through REST and W3C-compliant protocols. Additionally, user-friendly interfaces promote accessibility for individuals with domain expertise and varying technical expertise.

Future work focuses on efficiently creating and sustainably executing pipelines. Current experiments explore using Large Language Models (LLMs) to organize complex pipelines by generating DAGs from natural language descriptions [1].

Acknowledgments. Work funded by the EU innovation action *enRichMyData* (101070284) and the Italian PRIN Next Generation EU *Discount Quality for Responsible Data Science: Human-in-the-Loop for Quality Data* (202248FWFS).

References

1. Alidu, A., Ciavotta, M., De Paoli, F.: LLM-based DAG creation for data enrichment pipelines in semt framework. In: Proceedings of the 20th International Workshop on Engineering Service-Oriented Applications and Cloud Services (2024)
2. Avogadro, R., Cremaschi, M., D'Adda, F., De Paoli, F., Palmonari, M., et al.: LamAPI: a comprehensive tool for string-based entity retrieval with type-base filters. In: 17th ISWC Workshop on Ontology Matching (OM) (2022)
3. Avogadro, R., Ciavotta, M., De Paoli, F., Palmonari, M., Roman, D.: Estimating link confidence for human-in-the-loop table annotation. In: IEEE/WIC International Joint Conference on Web Intelligence and Intelligent Agent Technology (WI-IAT), Venice, Italy (2023)
4. Ciavotta, M., Cutrona, V., De Paoli, F., Nikolov, N., Palmonari, M., Roman, D.: Supporting semantic data enrichment at scale. In: Technologies and Applications for Big Data Value, pp. 19–39. Springer, Cham (2022)
5. Cutrona, V., Ciavotta, M., De Paoli, F., Palmonari, M., et al.: ASIA: a tool for assisted semantic interpretation and annotation of tabular data. In: International Workshop on the Semantic Web, vol. 2456, pp. 209–212. CEUR-WS (2019)

6. De Paoli, F., et al.: An interactive approach to semantic enrichment with geospatial data. Data Knowl. Eng. 102341 (2024)
7. Hameed, M., Naumann, F.: Data preparation: a survey of commercial tools. SIGMOD Rec. **49**(3), 18–29 (2020)
8. Liu, J., Chabot, Y., Troncy, R., Huynh, V.P., Labbé, T., Monnin, P.: From tabular data to knowledge graphs: a survey of semantic table interpretation tasks and methods. J. Web Semant. **76**, 100761 (2023)
9. Ripamonti, M., De Paoli, F., Palmonari, M.: SemTUI: a framework for the interactive semantic enrichment of tabular data. arXiv:2203.09521 (2022)
10. w3c.org: Reconciliation service API v0.2 (2023). https://www.w3.org/community/reports/reconciliation/CG-FINAL-specs-0.2-20230410/. Accessed 24 July 2024

Towards WebAssembly-Based Federated Learning

Felix Gottschalk[1], Stefan Schulte[1(✉)], Nisal Hemadasa[1], Elmira Ebrahimi[1], Janick Edinger[2], and Dominik Kaaser[1]

[1] Christian Doppler Laboratory for Blockchain Technologies for the Internet of Things, Institute for Data Engineering, TU Hamburg, Hamburg, Germany
{felix.gottschalk,stefan.schulte,nisal.hemadasa,elmira.ebrahimi,
dominik.kaaser}@tuhh.de
[2] University of Hamburg, Hamburg, Germany
janick.edinger@uni-hamburg.de

Abstract. WebAssembly is a portable binary instruction format designed to serve as a compilation target for high-level languages. While originally developed to run performance-intensive applications directly in Web browsers, WebAssembly supports these days a number of different hardware platforms across the compute continuum. This makes it a promising option to run services for training and inference in Federated Learning.

To the best of our knowledge, there have been only a few practical approaches to realize Federated Learning using WebAssembly. Therefore, in this paper, we present a framework to achieve this. Our prototypical implementation shows that WebAssembly-based Federated Learning applications are highly portable while providing acceptable runtime overhead during model training.

Keywords: Federated Learning · WebAssembly · Machine Learning

1 Introduction

In traditional Machine Learning (ML), a centralized cloud server collects data from multiple sources to train a model that can then be used for inference. This centralized approach raises concerns related to the privacy of the data since organizations and people are not always willing to share sensitive data with a cloud provider. An alternative would be to train an ML model only on local data. However, there are settings where the amount of locally available data will not be sufficient to train highly accurate models, e.g., in industrial scenarios where each operator only has a small number of machines of a certain type and therefore possesses only a very limited amount of training data [9].

A prominent approach to tackle this challenge is Federated Learning (FL), which is a privacy-preserving way of sharing knowledge between collaborating nodes without revealing raw data [6]. In its basic form, FL allows clients to train a model based on locally available data, then forward the local models to an aggregator which generates a global model and shares it with the clients for inference and further training rounds [16]. Very often, the concept of FL is combined with the utilization of (lightweight) edge devices as nodes for training of the local models and inference of the global model [42], since client nodes can be hosted anywhere in the cloud-edge compute continuum [14]. Especially in large-scale FL topologies, the heterogeneity of devices may become an issue, since an FL client software needs to support many different hardware architectures. Also, devices may be very heterogeneous w.r.t. CPU power and available memory, with some devices being very powerful, while others have only limited resources available. This makes it necessary to apply a well-performing virtualization approach.

WebAssembly was originally proposed to provide client-side near-native execution speed of applications running in a Web browser [13]. In recent years it has evolved to non-Web environments [39] and can be seen as a lightweight alternative to other virtualization techniques like Virtual Machines or Docker containers [25,33]. In this work, we exploit this lightweight virtualization provided by WebAssembly and present a framework that enables FL. Our framework can be used efficiently on resource-constrained devices, as often encountered in the Internet of Things (IoT) and enables portability of FL client software. To evaluate our framework, we compare the model training runtime with state-of-the-art technologies. To the best of our knowledge, our framework is the first implementation of FL based on WebAssembly which takes into account both model training and inference.

The remainder of this paper is organized as follows. In Sect. 2 we provide some technical background information about WebAssembly and in Sect. 3 we discuss the related work. Afterwards, in Sect. 4 we discuss the design of our framework. Finally, Sect. 5 provides the results of our benchmark, and Sect. 6 concludes this paper.

2 Background: WebAssembly

WebAssembly was originally developed as a low-level binary code format designed to run applications in Web browsers and is today supported by major Web browsers like Safari, Edge, Firefox, and Chrome. Major applications running in WebAssembly are, e.g., Google Photos and Adobe Photoshop Web. In addition, it is also possible to run WebAssembly code in a standalone, non-browser fashion. In 2019, WebAssembly became a W3C recommendation [43] and is therefore now an open standard.

WebAssembly provides a layered architecture based on available hardware and the host operating system. It runs on all major operating systems including Windows, macOS, Linux, iOS, and Android and supports multiple processor architectures including x64, x86, ARM, and RISC-V. The *WebAssembly System Interface (WASI)*[1] provides standard API specifications for applications that are compiled to the WebAssembly standard. Through the WASI, system resources

---
[1] https://github.com/WebAssembly/WASI.

like file system access become available [8]. This relieves the software developer from adapting their applications to the specific needs of a particular operating system and hardware architecture. On top of the WASI, a *WebAssembly runtime* like Wasmtime, WAMR or Wasm3 provides a sandbox to compile and execute WebAssembly modules (see below). This makes it possible to run WebAssembly bytecode on arbitrary platforms for which a WebAssembly runtime exists.

WebAssembly bytecode is generated by compiling it once from high-level languages like C, C++, Golang, or Rust. Importantly, these languages are directly supported by WebAssembly due to their ability to generate low-level machine code. Dynamically-typed languages like Python need additional runtimes or interpreters, which comes with several drawbacks such as slower execution, larger binary sizes, and limited language feature support. *WebAssembly modules* provide the actual functionalities of applications without the boilerplate code necessary to run it on the WebAssembly stack.

If compared to technologies like Docker containers, WebAssembly modules do not contain a rich set of libraries, binaries, and dependencies. This makes it harder to develop complex applications, but leads to modules that are very lightweight: WebAssembly modules often have a size of a few Kilobytes [10] to a few Megabytes [7], and startup times are often in the order of a few milliseconds [18]. WebAssembly is therefore suitable to provide applications in a Function-as-a-Service style [37], including FL.

In Web browser settings, the WebAssembly runtime is part of the Web browser engine, while the WASI is not needed. Instead, system calls are provided via JavaScript APIs available in Web browsers. This allows running a complete application with all of its features, running just the main components, or bringing some libraries to the Web. The most significant advantage of WebAssembly in Web browser environments is its performance. Studies have shown [4,39] that WebAssembly is faster and provides better energy efficiency in comparison to standard technologies like JavaScript and asm.js.

In this work, we focus on WebAssembly in non-browser environments. Here, both WASI APIs and WebAssembly runtime, as described above, are necessary. Given that it is a very recent technology, WASI is still in preview mode at the time of writing this paper and there has not been a stable release yet. In addition, current implementations do not yet match the speed of Web browsers [11].

3 Related Work

To the best of our knowledge, our work constitutes the first WebAssembly-based framework for FL. In the following, we start with a general overview of FL. Then we give a brief overview of FL frameworks. Afterwards, we discuss the utilization of WebAssembly in related areas including the IoT and ML.

Ever since it was introduced by McMahan et al. [29], the research field of FL has experienced rapid growth. While the original Federated Averaging (FedAvg) algorithm continues to serve as a foundation for various subsequent implementations, advancements, and applications [21,23,34], numerous studies have extended the original approaches to FL by investigated data heterogeneity [12,22,41], communication efficiency [19], privacy preservation [31], and the effects of concept drift on FL [3,15,36,40]. For a more detailed overview of FL, we refer to the survey by Zhang et al. [44].

In a recent survey, Riedel et al. [35] compare 15 open-source FL frameworks. They take various qualitative and quantitative evaluation criteria into account. Given that FL is very often carried out in IoT settings on edge devices, one interesting result is that only five out of the 15 frameworks can be run on a Raspberry Pi. The authors also highlight that 13 out of 15 frameworks provide Docker images such that the frameworks can be run readily using a Docker engine. WebAssembly is not mentioned in the analysis by Riedel et al.

Different researchers have investigated the use of WebAssembly in IoT settings. For instance, Mäkitalo et al. [28] propose the idea of liquid IoT applications which are able to migrate seamlessly between different devices. Similarly to our work, the authors use WebAssembly modules as a kind of lightweight container. They, however, do not take the special case of FL or ML into account. Ménétrey et al. [30] compared WebAssembly and native execution on x86 and ARM architectures. They come to the conclusion that WebAssembly is a viable alternative with acceptable overhead compared to native execution. They also highlight the increased level of security provided by WebAssembly thanks to the sandboxed environment it uses.

Most existing works regarding the use of WebAssembly for ML focus on inference. For instance, Smilkov et al. [38] introduce a WebAssembly backend for TensorFlow.js which is built for inference; for training they recommend making use of an existing WebGL backend. Brown and Sun [1] propose *wasi-nn*, a WASI API for ML inference focusing on neural networks. Khelifa et al. [17] provide a case study where pre-trained models are used with different WebAssembly runtimes to analyze their performance w.r.t. execution time and memory consumption. Kotilainen et al. [20] present a prototypical implementation of ML inference in WebAssembly, aiming at data from IoT devices and allowing distribution of the applications anywhere along the cloud-edge compute continuum.

In all of these approaches, training does not play a role. This is not surprising, since training is a complex task when large amounts of data are involved. In the case of FL, however, the local amount of data is not excessive, giving us the opportunity to evaluate the feasibility of WebAssembly for FL training. To the best of our knowledge, this is the first study to provide a working framework for WebAssembly-based FL.

4 Framework Design and Implementation

4.1 Basic Considerations and General Architecture

Before giving the details for the design of the ML/FL and WebAssembly parts of our framework, we discuss basic considerations that we have taken into account.

First, WebAssembly has only native support for statically typed programming languages and primarily targets languages that can be compiled directly to

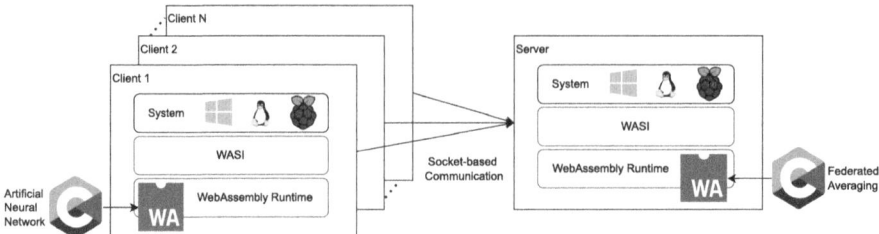

Fig. 1. Architecture Overview

native machine code. We therefore investigate the use of either C or C++ as the underlying programming language for our framework. This decreases the number of applicable FL frameworks. For instance, common frameworks like TensorFlow Federated and PySyft have neither C nor C++ bindings which prevents their use in WebAssembly. This is also the case for most other production-ready FL frameworks, making it necessary to investigate the use and adaptation of classical ML frameworks in our work. Second, while frameworks like TensorFlow are very powerful, they also require computational resources that are not always available on edge devices. Third, the compatibility of ML frameworks with WebAssembly might be further decreased due to a lack of features in WebAssembly. For instance, exception handling has been proposed only rather recently, and some WebAssembly runtimes do not yet support it.

A high-level overview of our framework design is shown in Fig. 1. As it can be seen, both client and server software are implemented using WebAssembly and make use of the software stack discussed in Sect. 2. In the following sections, we discuss in more detail the implementation of the Artificial Neural Network (ANN) on client-side (see Sect. 4.2), the socket-based communication (see Sect. 4.3), and the implementation of FedAvg on the server (see Sect. 4.4). The source code could be provided in C as well as other languages not shown in the figure, which is then compiled into WebAssembly modules running on the WebAssembly runtime. The WebAssembly runtime interacts with the local operating system via the WASI. Our prototypical framework presented in this section is available at GitHub[2]. We use Wasmtime[3] as WebAssembly runtime for all our experiments.

4.2 Federated Learning

Since we cannot identify FL frameworks that allow the training of models in a federated way and provide either C or C++ bindings, we focus on generic ML frameworks for the implementation of our framework. We remark that both the

---

[2] https://github.com/VerFlix/WASM-FL.
[3] https://wasmtime.dev/.

FATE[4] [24] and IBM FL[5] [26] frameworks provide C++ bindings, but they rely on TensorFlow or PyTorch for model training [35]. They are thus not applicable in our case, where training and inference should take place using WebAssembly.

Due to the lack of readily available frameworks we develop our own implementation of a basic FL algorithm based on FedAvg [29]. Our implementation is based on an already existing solution to train an ANN and hence our main goal is to find a lightweight implementation for the latter. To this end we analyze the generic ML frameworks *LiteRT*[6] (formerly known as *TensorFlow Lite*), *mlpack*[7], *Maxent*[8], *LibTorch*[9], and *Fast Artificial Neural Network (FANN)*[10] [32].

In our framework we opt to use the FANN library for ML. The library is simple, dependency-free, versatile, and open-source, making it an ideal choice for WebAssembly, where minimizing dependencies to ensure compatibility is crucial. The library implements an ANN in C, supporting fully and sparsely connected networks. Unlike LiteRT, it is designed for the training of ANNs. It does not rely on Python, which would present a prohibitive challenge for our WebAssembly implementation. The simplicity of FANN facilitates the adaption of the library to our needs, and it supports the addition of new features and more complex ML models like Convolutional Neural Networks to the framework.

While this decision limits our framework to ANNs for now, the advantages of simplicity, compatibility, and lightweight implementation make it an ideal choice for our FL framework with WebAssembly. Furthermore, we remark that ANNs have been commonly used with FedAvg since the advent of the technology [29], even though other types of ML algorithms could have been applied as well. Therefore, the features of FANN are well suited for the purposes of our research.

4.3 Client-Server Communication

For the communication between FL clients and server (i.e., the aggregator), we apply sockets as defined in the WASI Sockets Proposal[11]. An alternative would have been to use the WASI HTTP Proposal[12], which however introduces additional overhead such as headers and status codes which we want to avoid in a scenario where communication might also be necessary between resource-constrained edge devices.

The WASI Sockets Proposal provides low-level access to TCP/UDP sockets. This enables developers to design custom protocols and have low-level control over the communication, allowing them to optimize and adapt to specific use cases. Sockets enable persistent connections, which allow the implementation of

---

[4] https://github.com/FederatedAI/FATE.
[5] https://github.com/IBM/federated-learning-lib.
[6] https://ai.google.dev/edge/litert.
[7] https://www.mlpack.org/.
[8] https://github.com/minhpqn/maxent.
[9] https://pytorch.org/cppdocs/.
[10] https://github.com/libfann/fann.
[11] https://github.com/WebAssembly/wasi-sockets.
[12] https://github.com/WebAssembly/wasi-http.

unusual communication patterns if necessary. On the downside, this low-level control makes communication management more complex and makes communication with existing, standardized systems more challenging.

For the communication design, our framework uses a one-way active communication architecture. In this architecture, the clients can communicate with the server to request the current global model or post the locally trained model. After receiving a certain number of trained models, the server aggregates the new global model. A flag in the model's metadata indicates whether the model needs further training. Also, the version ID of the model can be found in the metadata, allowing the clients to ensure that they do not participate in the same training round more than once.

Restricting the communication to one direction simplifies the communication protocol, as the server does not need to initiate communication with clients. The server only needs to handle incoming connections and does not have to manage connections with all the clients. In addition, this allows the clients to request the model or participate in training based on their circumstances. This allows the clients to use their resources most efficiently, e.g., by only training the model when computational resources are available and the device is connected to a power supply. When a client loses the connection or runs out of power, it does not impact the FL process because the server does not depend on the clients to be available. In this case, other clients can still continue to train the model.

4.4 Federated Averaging

As discussed above, we implement our own version of FedAvg for the aggregation of the global model. The variant of FedAvg that we use is given in simplified form in Algorithm 1. The algorithm shows a single aggregation round that is invoked whenever an update of the global model is necessary. It takes as an input the total number of clients and the clients selected for the current aggregation. The output is an aggregated global model.

Algorithm 1: Federated Averaging (simplified)

Input: number of clients n, selected clients C
Result: global model $\mathcal{G}$

1 $\mathcal{N} \leftarrow \texttt{init}()$ ▷ initialize an empty neural network $\mathcal{N}$
2 **for each** *selected client* $c \in C$ **do**
3 $\quad$ $\mathcal{N}_c \leftarrow \texttt{load}(c)$ ▷ retrieve the neural network from client c
4 $\quad$ **for each** edge $(u,v) \in \mathcal{N}_c$ **with** weight w **do**
5 $\quad\quad$ add weight $\dfrac{1}{n} \cdot w$ to edge (u,v) in $\mathcal{N}$ ▷ aggregate the average weight

6 $\mathcal{G} \leftarrow \mathcal{N}$ ▷ update the global model $\mathcal{G}$ with aggregated weights in $\mathcal{N}$

We start by initializing an empty neural network $\mathcal{N}$ for the current round of training, see Line 1. In the main loop in Lines 2 to 5 we iterate over all selected clients and retrieve for each selected client the weights for its ANN (see Line 3). In the inner loop in Lines 4 to 5, we aggregate the average weight of all clients' ANNs in the neural network $\mathcal{N}$. At this step, we perform in our implementation additional checks to verify that the network structure (connections between neurons) matches between clients. Finally, the averaged weights are used to update the network model, creating the new global model in Line 6. This global model can now be sent to the clients.

Our implementation of FedAvg is slightly simplified: we do not take the weighting of clients into account. This however perfectly serves the purposes of our prototypical implementation, since our goal is to show that training of ANNs is possible using WebAssembly on lightweight devices. The server-side aggregation therefore is only a helper functionality to confirm that we can generate a global model and use WebAssembly for both model training and inference.

5 Evaluation

5.1 Goals and Setup

The goal of the evaluation of the implemented prototypical framework is to assess its runtime performance during model training and compare it to an existing framework. For comparison we have chosen to use TensorFlow Federated, one of today's most applied FL frameworks. Note that TensorFlow Federated only provides Python bindings and therefore cannot be used in WebAssembly without considerable overhead. Furthermore, TensorFlow Federated cannot be used in all envisioned settings, and we therefore also make use of regular TensorFlow and TensorFlow.js (see below). Regarding our implemented FL client software, we compile it to WebAssembly and also as a native binary. The latter is expected to show a smaller overhead than the version using WebAssembly, but it cannot be ported to other platforms so easily.

Since one of the main motivations for using WebAssembly is the portability of applications across heterogeneous devices, we make use of different hardware: we perform evaluation runs on a desktop computer with a Ryzen 9 7950X processor running Ubuntu Linux and Windows 11 as operating systems and on a Raspberry Pi 3 Model B+ running Raspberry Pi OS (64bit).

We adopt the configuration proposed by Ma et al. [27] and operate with 1, 2, 3, 4, or 8 hidden layers and 64, 128, or 256 neurons in each of the layers. All models are fully connected ANNs. When using TensorFlow (Federated) for comparison purposes, we make use of the same settings for the trained ANNs. Regardless of the use of our solution or TensorFlow (Federated), we apply the hyperbolic tangent activation function for the hidden layers and the sigmoid activation function for the output layer.

The goal of FL in this context is the correct *classification* in terms of assigning labels to instances. Nevertheless, this is not the focus of our work: We explicitly not present the accuracy of the models, since we make use of the same ANN configurations in all settings. The evaluation runs were carried out with two rounds of FL training; further preliminary experiments were carried out with four and eight rounds of training, respectively. As expected, the runtime increases linearly with the number of rounds.

For our evaluation, we use the Federated Extended MNIST (FEMNIST) digit recognition dataset [2] for training and inference. The dataset consists of 805,263 28x28-pixel grayscale images of handwritten letters and digits, divided into 3,550 users. It shares the same image structure and parameters as the original MNIST dataset [5], which is a prominent benchmark for ML systems and which we also apply for parts of our evaluations. MNIST contains 60,000 images for training and 10,000 for testing.

5.2 Results

Figure 2 shows the results for WebAssembly, the native binary, and TensorFlow Federated in the Linux environment on the desktop PC with an increasing number of clients, using FEMNIST as training and testing data. In the figure, we report the average of ten independent evaluation runs for different combinations of hidden layers (first number of each pair on the x-axis) and neurons (second number); both training and aggregation are covered here.

As it can be seen, the native binary of our FL client software is the fastest and thus performs best. This is not surprising: the WebAssembly modules in the client software add some overhead, while the native binary does not need a specific runtime and is therefore more lightweight. However, the native binary needs to be compiled individually for each hardware and operating system and thus lacks portability. It is interesting to see that the native binary is even faster than TensorFlow Federated. This is particularly surprising, given that TensorFlow Federated is a highly professional and production-ready software.

For all three implementations, we can see that the time increases with the complexity of the ANNs and the number of clients. However, the extent varies: For WebAssembly and the native binaries, the increase in complexity and the increase in number of clients roughly lead to the same increase in time. For TensorFlow Federated, the impact of the increase in client numbers is larger. This is most likely due to its highly optimized handling of complex models.

Figure 3 shows the average runtime over all combinations of numbers of clients and complexities tested. The time consumed by TensorFlow Federated when restricted to a single thread is also added for better comparison. Compared to the TensorFlow Federated library in a single thread, our framework based on WebAssembly is 83% faster. It even performs better than the multi-threaded version, requiring 35% less time. However, it is 3.9 times slower than the native version. This again shows the performance overhead of WebAssembly.

Figure 4 shows the evaluation results for our client solution (both native and WebAssembly) on the Windows PC and on the Raspberry Pi. We also evaluate our client solution on the Linux PC. However, the results on the Linux PC are virtually identical to the results on the Windows PC. We therefore only present our data for the Windows PC and the Raspberry Pi in Fig. 4 and omit the data

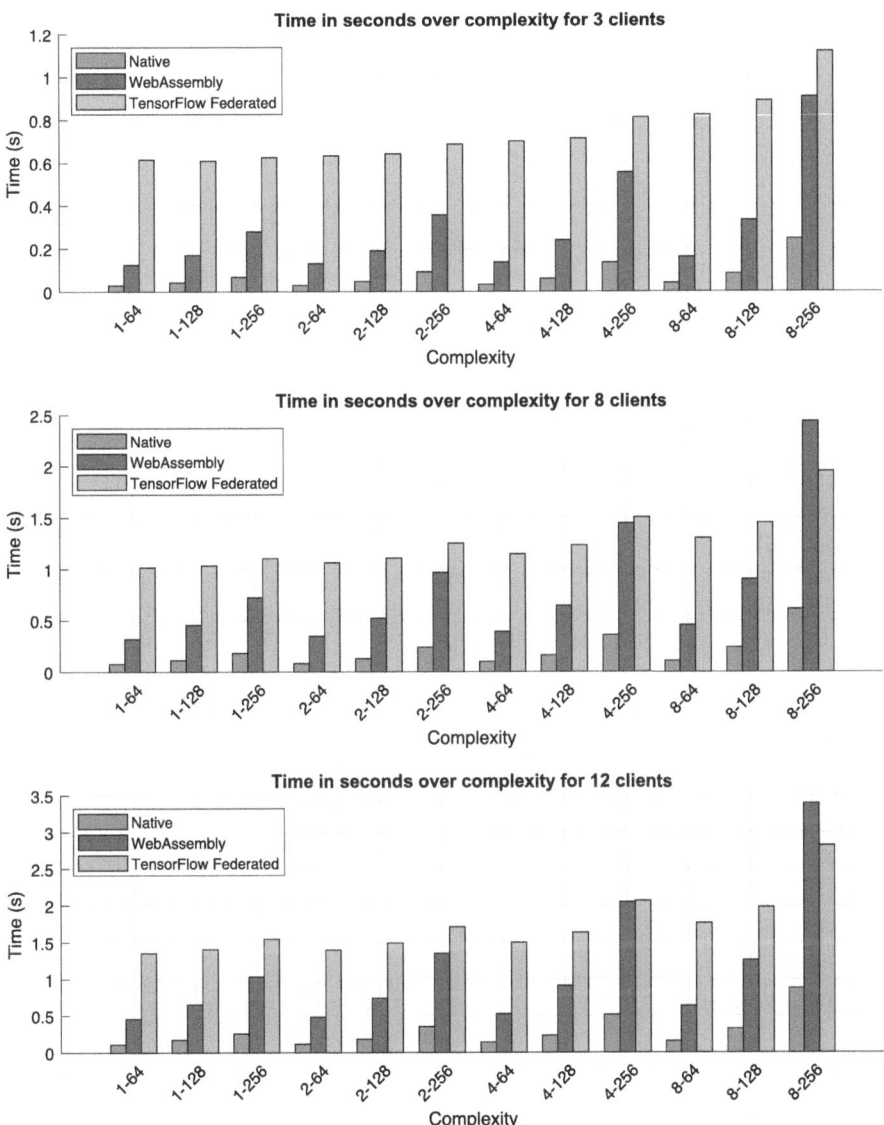

Fig. 2. Time measurements for different ANN complexities and numbers of clients

for the Linux PC. For comparison purposes we also evaluate the TensorFlow and the JavaScript-based TensorFlow.js libraries, even though they do not provide built-in FL capabilities. Nevertheless, we reimplement the ANNs also for these libraries. The reason for not using TensorFlow Federated in these experiments is that it is neither available for Windows nor ARM-based Raspberry Pis. Unfortunately, it is also not possible to run Tensorflow.js on a Raspberry Pi: after

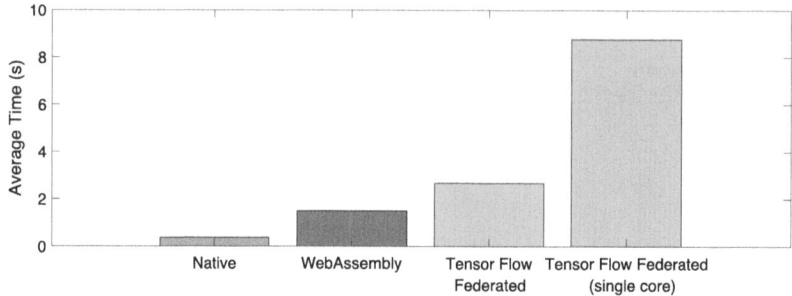

Fig. 3. Average time of all runs for different frameworks

adjusting the maximum swap size and the allowed heap size for the JavaScript runtime, training still takes hours even for simple models due to the lack of computational resources on this device. Note that for the comparison in Fig. 4 we use the smaller MNIST [5] dataset.

From our data, we observe that the Windows PC shows the best performance over all configurations. Among the evaluated libraries, TensorFlow performs best, while TensorFlow.js performs worst. As expected, the WebAssembly version of our own implementation comes with some overhead. It is nevertheless interesting to see that our WebAssembly version outperforms TensorFlow.js on the Windows PC. This can be traced back to the significant overhead introduced by TensorFlow.js compared to our framework based on WebAssembly. Not surprisingly, the Raspberry Pi cannot provide a similar level of performance. As before, we observe that TensorFlow performs best. Interestingly, the lack of computational resources leads to remarkably similar results (within the same small constant factors) for all three available frameworks, TensorFlow, our WebAssembly-based client software, and the native client software.

5.3 Discussion

The presented evaluation results provide some interesting insights. Most notably, WebAssembly delivers exactly what it promises, since the client software provided as WebAssembly modules can be easily ported to different hardware setups at negligible overhead. The native code is faster but leads to compatibility issues when porting it from one setup to another one.

The WebAssembly trade-off between portability and performance enables efficient computation in resource-constrained environments. Together with the security provided by the sandboxing, this makes WebAssembly a promising solution for FL tasks. Altogether, our framework is well-suited for heterogeneous hardware settings where portability is essential, like in an IoT setting. This cannot be achieved with any of the existing FL and ML frameworks discussed in Sect. 4.2. Also, none of the three variants of TensorFlow used for comparison in the evaluation can be applied in such settings.

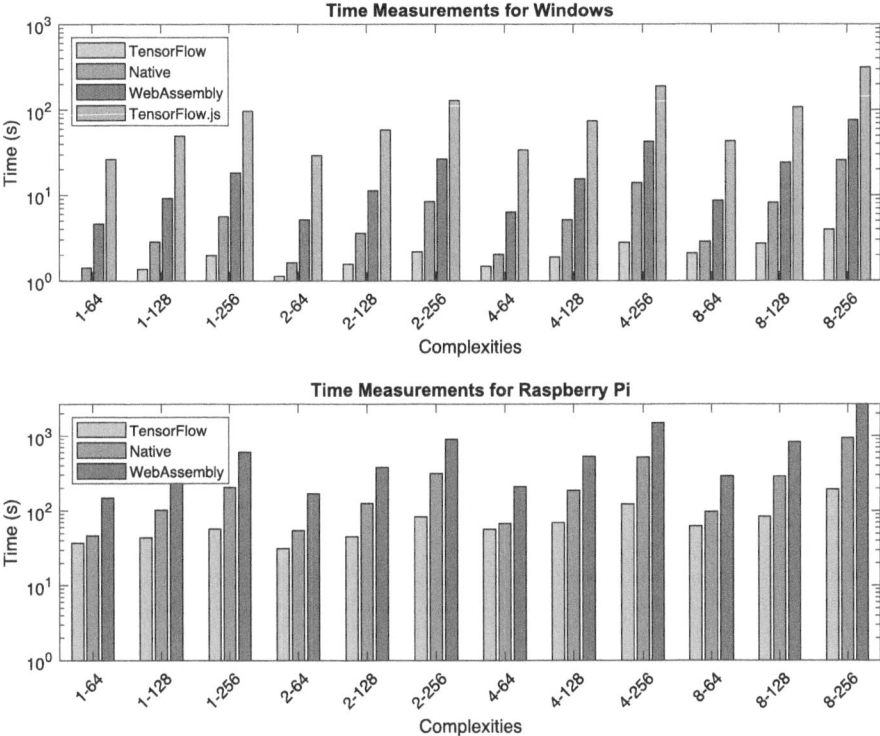

Fig. 4. Time measurements for different ANN complexities and various frameworks

As mentioned in Sect. 2, current non-browser WebAssembly implementations do not yet match the speed of in-browser usage of WebAssembly. Hence, we assume that the results would even become better with more mature implementations in the future.

6 Conclusions

WebAssembly is a recent technology to enable portability between computational platforms with different hardware and operating systems with comparably little overhead. Despite these advantages, to the best of our knowledge, WebAssembly has not yet been used for FL in heterogeneous settings. We therefore provide a framework to conduct FL based on WebAssembly. Our evaluation shows that the solution is indeed able to provide portability with comparable little overhead.

We consider the work presented in this paper as the first step towards WebAssembly-based FL. Nevertheless, the presented solution does not yet constitute a full-fledged FL framework. From an engineering perspective, turning our framework into a production-ready system remains a challenging task. From a research perspective, it would be interesting to assess the impact of integrating security and privacy mechanisms. An open question is whether the overhead of differential privacy or encryption would still be acceptable w.r.t. the introduced overhead. Furthermore, it might be interesting to investigate a setting in which the server software is provided as a native application, while the client software is provided via WebAssembly. This could lead to further improvements in performance.

Acknowledgement. The financial support by the Austrian Federal Ministry for Digital and Economic Affairs, the National Foundation for Research, Technology and Development as well as the Christian Doppler Research Association for the Christian Doppler Laboratory for Blockchain Technologies for the Internet of Things is gratefully acknowledged.

References

1. Brown, A., Sun, M.: WASI-NN Proposal (2020). https://github.com/WebAssembly/wasi-nn
2. Caldas, S., et al.: LEAF: A Benchmark for Federated Settings (2018). arXiv:1812.01097 [cs.LG]
3. Chen, Y., Chai, Z., Cheng, Y., Rangwala, H.: Asynchronous federated learning for sensor data with concept drift. In: 2021 IEEE International Conference on Big Data, pp. 4822–4831 (2021)
4. De Macedo, J., Abreu, R., Pereira, R., Saraiva, J.: WebAssembly versus JavaScript: energy and runtime performance. In: 2022 International Conference on ICT for Sustainability, pp. 24–34 (2022)
5. Deng, L.: The MNIST database of handwritten digit images for machine learning research [best of the web]. IEEE Signal Process. Mag. **29**(6), 141–142 (2012)
6. Ding, A.Y., et al.: Roadmap for edge AI: a Dagstuhl perspective. ACM SIGCOMM Comput. Commun. Rev. **52**, 28–33 (2022)
7. Gackstatter, P., Frangoudis, P.A., Dustdar, S.: Pushing serverless to the edge with webassembly runtimes. In: 2022 22nd IEEE International Symposium on Cluster, Cloud and Internet Computing, pp. 140–149 (2022)
8. Gohman, D., et al.: WebAssembly/WASI: v0.2.1 (2024)
9. Hiessl, T., Lakani, S.R., Kemnitz, J., Schall, D., Schulte, S.: Cohort-based federated learning services for industrial collaboration on the edge. J. Parallel Distrib. Comput. **167**, 64–76 (2022)
10. Hilbig, A., Lehmann, D., Pradel, M.: An empirical study of real-world web-assembly binaries: security, languages, use cases. In: Web Conference 2021, pp. 2696–2708 (2021)
11. Hoque, M.N., Harras, K.A.: WebAssembly for edge computing: potential and challenges. IEEE Commun. Stand. Mag. **6**(4), 68–73 (2022)
12. Hsu, T.-M., Qi, H., Brown, M.: Measuring the effects of non-identical data distribution for federated visual classification (2019). arXiv:1909.06335 [cs.LG]
13. Jangda, A., Powers, B., Berger, E.D., Guha, A.: Not so fast: analyzing the performance of webassembly vs. native code. In: 2019 USENIX Annual Technical Conference, pp. 107–120 (2019)
14. Jansen, M., Al-Dulaimy, A., Papadopoulos, A.V., Trivedi, A., Iosup, A.: The SPEC-RG reference architecture for the compute continuum. In: IEEE 23rd International Symposium on Cluster, Cloud and Internet Computing, pp. 469–484 (2023)

15. Jothimurugesan, E., Hsieh, K., Wang, J., Joshi, G., Gibbons, P.B.: Federated learning under distributed concept drift. In: International Conference on Artificial Intelligence and Statistics, pp. 5834–5853 (2023)
16. Khan, L.U., et al.: Federated learning for edge networks: resource optimization and incentive mechanism. IEEE Commun. Mag. **58**(10), 88–93 (2020)
17. Khelifa, S.E., Bagaa, M., Messaoud, A.O., Ksentini, A.: Case study of webassembly runtimes for AI applications on the edge. In: 2024 Global Information Infrastructure and Networking Symposium, pp. 1–6 (2024)
18. Kluften, M.N.: Nebula: performance and energy efficiency in serverless computing. Master's thesis, University of Oslo (2024)
19. Konečný, J., McMahan, H.B., Yu, F.X., Richtárik, P., Suresh, A.T., and Bacon, D.: Federated learning: strategies for improving communication efficiency (2016). arXiv:1610.05492 [cs.LG]
20. Kotilainen, P., Heikkilä, V., Systä, K., and Mikkonen, T.: Towards liquid AI in IoT with webassembly: a prototype implementation. In: 19th International Conference on Mobile Web and Intelligent Information Systems, pp. 129–141 (2023)
21. Leroy, D., Coucke, A., Lavril, T., Gisselbrecht, T., Dureau, J.: Federated learning for keyword spotting. In: IEEE International Conference on Acoustics, Speech and Signal Processing, pp. 6341–6345 (2019)
22. Li, Q., He, B., Song, D.: Model-contrastive federated learning. In: IEEE Conference on Computer Vision and Pattern Recognition, pp. 10713–10722 (2021)
23. Li, X., Huang, K., Yang, W., Wang, S., Zhang, Z.: On the Convergence of FedAvg on Non-IID Data (2019). arXiv:1907.02189 [stat.ML]
24. Liu, Y., Fan, T., Chen, T., Xu, Q., Yang, Q.: FATE: an industrial grade platform for collaborative learning with data protection. J. Mach. Learn. Res. **22**(226), 1–6 (2021)
25. Long, J., Tai, H.-Y., Hsieh, S.-T., Yuan, M.J.: A lightweight design for serverless function as a service. IEEE Softw. **38**(1), 75–80 (2020)
26. Ludwig, H., et al.: IBM Federated Learning: an Enterprise Framework White Paper V0.1 (2020). arXiv:2007.10987 [cs.LG]
27. Ma, Y., Xiang, D., Zheng, S., Tian, D., Liu, X.: Moving deep learning into web browser: how far can we go? In: The World Wide Web Conference, pp. 1234–1244 (2019)
28. Mäkitalo, N., et al.: WebAssembly modules as lightweight containers for liquid IoT applications. In: 21st International Conference on Web Engineering, pp. 328–336 (2021)
29. McMahan, B., Moore, E., Ramage, D., Hampson, S., Arcas, B.A.: Communication-efficient learning of deep networks from decentralized data. In: 20th International Conference on Artificial Intelligence and Statistics. Machine Learning Research, pp. 1273–1282 (2017)
30. Ménétrey, J., Pasin, M., Felber, P., Schiavoni, V.: WebAssembly as a common layer for the cloud-edge continuum. In: 2nd Workshop on Flexible Resource and Application Management on the Edge, pp. 3–8 (2022)
31. Mothukuri, V., Parizi, R.M., Pouriyeh, S., Huang, Y., Dehghantanha, A., Srivastava, G.: A survey on security and privacy of federated learning. Future Gener. Comput. Syst. **115**, 619–640 (2021)
32. Nissen, S.: Implementation of a Fast Artificial Neural Network Library (FANN). Graduate project, Department of Computer Science, University of Copenhagen (2003)

33. Pham, S., Oliveira, K., Lung, C.-H.: WebAssembly modules as alternative to docker containers in IoT application development. In: 2023 IEEE 3rd International Conference on Electronic Communications, Internet of Things and Big Data, pp. 519–524 (2023)
34. Reddi, S.J., et al.: Adaptive federated optimization. In: 9th International Conference on Learning Representations (2021)
35. Riedel, P., Schick, L., von Schwerin, R., Reichert, M., Schaudt, D., Hafner, A.: Comparative analysis of open-source federated learning frameworks – a literature based survey and review. Int. J. Mach. Learn. Cybern. (2024)
36. Saile, F., Thomas, J., Kaaser, D., Schulte, S.: Client-side adaptation to concept drift in federated learning. In: 2nd IEEE International Conference on Federated Learning Technologies and Applications (2024)
37. Semjonov, A., Bornholdt, H., Edinger, J., Russo, G.R.: Wasimoff: distributed computation offloading using webassembly in the browser. In: 2024 IEEE International Conference on Pervasive Computing and Communications Workshops and other Affiliated Events, pp. 203–208 (2024)
38. Smilkov, D., Thorat, N., Yuan, A.: Introducing the WebAssembly backend for TensorFlow.js (2020). https://blog.tensorflow.org/2020/03/introducingwebassembly-backend-for-tensorflow-js.html
39. Spies, B., Mock, M.: An evaluation of webassembly in non-web environments. In: 2021 XLVII Latin American Computing Conference, pp. 1–10 (2021)
40. Thomas, J., Saile, F., Fischer, M., Kaaser, D., Schulte, S.: Adaption via selection: on client selection to counter concept drift in federated learning. In: 11th European Conference on Service-Oriented and Cloud Computing (2025)
41. Wang, J., Liu, Q., Liang, H., Joshi, G., Poor, H.V.: Tackling the objective inconsistency problem in heterogeneous federated optimization. In: Advances in Neural Information Processing Systems 33: Annual Conference on Neural Information Processing Systems (2020)
42. Wang, S., et al.: Adaptive federated learning in resource constrained edge computing systems. IEEE J. Sel. Areas Commun. **37**(6), 1205–1221 (2019)
43. WebAssembly Working Group, WebAssembly Core Specification (2019). W3C Recommendation. https://www.w3.org/TR/2019/REC-wasm-core-1-20191205/
44. Zhang, C., Xie, Y., Bai, H., Yu, B., Li, W., Gao, Y.: A survey on federated learning. Knowl. Based Syst. **216**, 106775 (2021)

Edge and Resource Management

A Bio-inspired Leader-Based Energy Management System for Drone Fleets

Rosario Napoli^(✉), Antonio Celesti, Massimo Villari, and Maria Fazio

University of Messina, 98122 Messina, ME, Italy
rosario.napoli2@studenti.unime.it

Abstract. Drones are embedded systems used across a wide range of fields, however, their limited battery life and high energy consumption are very important challenges, especially in networked systems, where multiple drones must communicate with a Ground Base Station (GBS). This study addresses these limitations by proposing a bio-inspired leader-based energy management system for drone fleets that dynamically chooses a cluster's leader to handle long-range communication with the GBS, allowing other drones to preserve their energy. The results demonstrate that our approach significantly increases network efficiency and service time by removing useless communications.

Keywords: Drones · Leader Election · Battery management · Energy optimization · Bio-inspired algorithm · Network lifespan

1 Introduction

Embedded Systems are electronic devices designed to execute a specific task. They interact with the environment through sensors and actuators, satisfying strict requirements in terms of power consumption, size and cost. Drones are small-medium size Embedded Systems which enhance geolocalized data collection and computation. They are generally equipped with high-definition cameras and thermal sensors to capture data, even from areas difficult to access by humans [1], and are used in many different fields, such as agriculture [2] and emergency services [3].

In large-scale applications, drones typically work in groups, setting up a distributed computing environment to cooperate for a common goal, such as wildlife monitoring, search and rescue, firefighting and so on. To this aim, they communicate with each other to synchronize their activities and with the Ground Base Station (GBS) for remote control and transfer of collected data. The GBS acts as a computing node at the Edge of the area where the drones are deployed and can interact with remote Cloud computing services for advanced processing [4].

Despite advances in drone technologies, energy management is still a critical aspect that influences their efficiency, overall performance and service time. Energy Management Strategies (EMSs) identify methods to extend the life of a drone network by optimizing the average power consumption of the whole system. EMSs monitor the consuming tasks and communication activities, implementing different policies for minimizing energy consumption [5].

In this paper, we present an EMS solution that aims to optimize the energy consumption of drone networks during communication with the GBS. Generally, the long distance between drones and the GBS, due to the altitude during flight, becomes an issue for energy depletion, since transmission power in wireless interactions increases with the square of the distance. However, the idea of implementing a Leader-based communication of a cluster of close drones with the GBS can drastically reduce the average battery drain due to messaging transmissions.

The solution we propose is based on a Bio-inspired algorithm for Leader election that uses the principles of natural selection and evolution, allowing us to find optimal or near-optimal solutions to complex problems. By studying natural phenomena, researchers have developed algorithms that mimic these behaviors to solve complex problems in more efficient ways, especially important in Internet of Things (IoT) applications and ES, where conditions can change rapidly and systems must adapt without human intervention [6]. This paper explores the effectiveness of such bio-inspired EMS through simulations under different conditions, focusing on its ability to increase network's lifespan.

2 State of the Art

Some works in the literature deal with leader election in drone fleets to manage specific issues, particularly on how to improve the network's performance. [7] presents a solution to connect drones to multiple GBSs, maximizing communication throughput and minimizing energy consumption. To this aim, the optimal connection between drones and the nearest GBS is continuously calculated, may causing interferences and congestion problems. The implementation of a proxy signature-based authentication mechanism in a drone fleet for device-to-device communication in 5G architectures is presented in [8]. The leader is responsible for managing communications between the fleet and a 5G core network, handling: authentication, authorisation and access functions. Although it is an interesting work, implemented polices do not consider energy constraints. Trusted Dynamic Leader Selection (TDLS) [9] is another algorithm based on a trusted drone in charge to manage secure communications. The system uses a trust-based mechanism to identify trusted drones and isolate potentially malicious ones. However, from an EMS perspective, the exclusion of malicious drones introduces a significant limitation to the system lifespan for energy constraints.

Bio-inspired approaches are not yet widely used in literature but have already shown significant results. In [10], the way ants organise work within their colony was used to develop a distributed control approach, where control actions focus on the interactions between system components. The algorithm works around the Response Threshold Model (RTM), which is based on the way that ants react to external stimuli, showing better performance compared to classical control approaches. [11] presents a bio-inspired algorithm based on the Elephant Search

Algorithm (ESA) to solve the NP-hard travelling salesman problem (TS). The proposed algorithm is based on observing the group's dynamics and positions of elephants, in particular how they form clans and follow a matriarch, which is the leader. [12] proposes a bio-inspired approaches for the coordination of drone fleets, achieving significant results in terms of energy savings (15% more than classical approaches). Here, the leader not only has to manage communications with the GBS but also to coordinate and assign tasks to the other members of the fleet, resulting in a high communication overhead. is only activated when the leader's battery level falls below 40%.

3 Bio-inspired Approach for Energy Management

Our work aims to improve the performance and duration of a fully connected drone network, assuming that drones maintain a certain altitude for their tasks while keeping communication with the GBS. However, as altitude increases, communication with their GBS becomes more energy-intensive as the wireless signal for communication must be amplified. Normally, every drone in the network has to maintain direct communication with the GBS, causing significant energy consumption challenges. To address this, in our architecture the network is divided into n clusters made of m drones. A leader for each cluster is elected, carrying out all the non-leader drones communications to the GBS. Since it is positioned between them, the altitude required for communication is reduced, allowing energy preservation. All the messages from the non-leader drones are stored into a messages buffer with a fixed size. When the buffer is full or the leader must be changed, all the pieces of information are communicated to the GBS and then sent to a remote processing unit in the Cloud.

In this paper, we have implemented a Bio-Inspired Leader-Based EMS for drone fleet management based on Particle Swarm Optimization (PSO). PSO is an algorithm that simulates the social behavior of birds searching for food, where individual agents (particles) adjust their position based on personal and general experiences to preserve energy. This bio-inspired methodology not only enhances the search for optimal solutions but also increases adaptability in dynamic environments. In PSO, each particle adjusts its position based on its own experience (the best solution it has identified, known as *pBest*) and the one of the entire swarm (the best solution found, known as *gBest*). Then, the particle with *gBest* is chosen as the leader, taking on the responsibility of searching for food. This cooperation allows particles to share information and complete their task, avoiding useless waste of energy [13]. The core of our proposed solution is to choose a drone to act as the PSO *gBest* to communicate with the GBS, relieving other drones from energy-intensive long-range communications, and improving the network's lifespan.

Our model enhances efficiency by rotating the role of the leader drone. When the current leader's battery level drops below a predefined battery threshold, a new leader (*gBest*) is elected. Each drone has a routine that dynamically changes according to the role it plays (see Fig. 1).

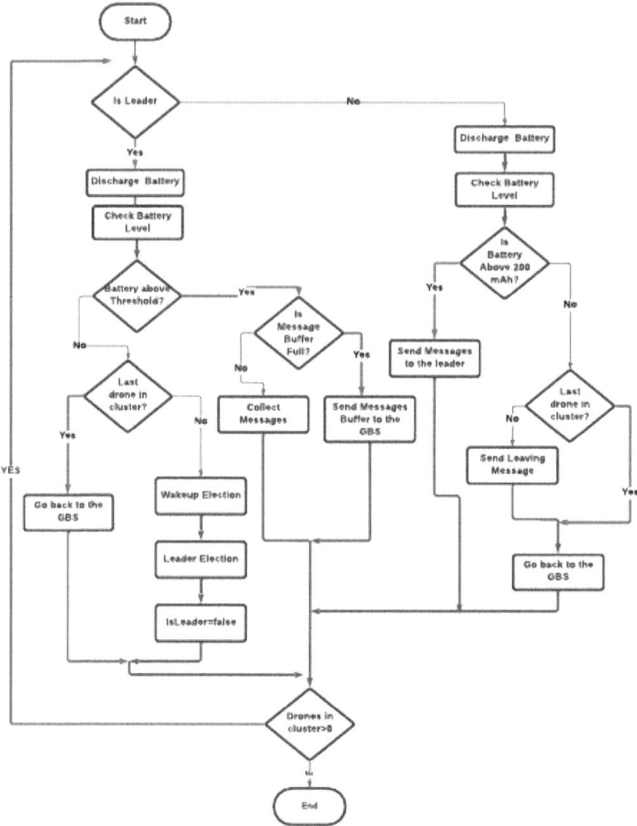

Fig. 1. Drone's Routine.

At the beginning of the fleet activity, all the drones have the same energy. So, the leader can be selected according to a default policy, such as the one with the lowest identifiers (IDs), which is a common practice in this kind of algorithms. Formally, we introduce the threshold parameter as a percentage of the battery energy of the current Leader that enables a new Leader election. Let be B_0 the battery capacity of a drone when it is elected as leader of the fleet, the new election will start when its battery level drops below the threshold value B_T, which is given by the following equation:

$$B_T = B_0 \times \left(1 - \frac{T}{100}\right) \quad (1)$$

where: 1) B_0 is the drone's battery capacity when it becomes leader, expressed in milliampere-hours (mAh); 2) T is the threshold value, expressed as a percentage (e.g., $T = 60\%$). When a new Leader is elected, the previous one can leave the fleet and go back to the GBS to recharge its battery. The condition under which a drone leaves its fleet and returns safely to GBS is defined when B_T (see Eq. 1) falls below a critical value of 200 mAh.

The EMS algorithm proposed in this paper is composed of the following 5 phases:

1) **Initialization Phase** Leaders broadcast an initialization message to the other drones within their respective clusters. This message prompts the drones to begin their routines.
2) **Update Phase** Non-leader drones continuously send data in form of messages with a fixed rate to their leader, which communicates with the GBS. The leader drone has a fixed-size buffer to collect data from other. When the buffer is full, it sends the data to the GBS. The remaining battery levels of the leaders are monitored to determine when a new election is needed, by analyzing the threshold value with respect to their remaining energy.
3) **Election Initialization Phase** When a leader's remaining battery level reaches the threshold (see Eq. 1), it sends its buffer to the GBS an then begins the Election Initialization Phase. A "wakeupElection" message is sent and each drone within the cluster replays with its: ID, clusterID and remaining battery level. The leader evaluates these responses to determine who is the $gBest$, then it starts the election phase.
4) **Election Phase** The current leader broadcasts an election message to all the nodes in the cluster, announcing the new $gBest$. After receiving this message, each drone updates its global knowledge. A new update phase starts and when the Eq. 1 is satisfied by the new leader, it eventually triggers a new Election Initialization Phase by broadcasting a "wakeUpElection" message.
5) **Termination Phase** The algorithm includes a termination phase that is triggered when a drone's battery reaches a critically low level, indicating that it must return to its base station for recharging. When a non-leader drone needs to leave the cluster, it sends a "leaveMessage" to the current leader. After receiving this message, the leader updates its local knowledge, reducing the cluster size by one. Instead, if the leader has to leave and the cluster size is greater than one, a new election starts, otherwise the algorithm ends.

4 Results

We have evaluated the proposed solution using the OMNeT++ simulator together with the INET framework [14] was used to make simulations, as it offers a wide set of models for managing nodes and edges. The network was modelled by defining a simple Omnet++ module called *Drone* that represents each drone within the simulation. It includes parameters for managing: 1) position; 2) local battery, initially set to 2500 mAh; 3) leader battery; 4) leader-id. Each drone has also attributes to monitor and to handle communication, in particular: 1) the message rate, which is set to 10; 2) cluster size; 3) buffer size, which is $clusterSize \times 3$; 4) election battery threshold.

The first experiment focuses on the average cluster lifetime (Omnet++ time steps) as the number of drones in the network and the threshold increases. The idea is to compare the results obtained with no EMS, against the proposed algorithm. The results in Fig. 2 show how the algorithm actually contributes significantly to increase the average network lifetime. This suggests that the EMS works as expected, as communication with the GBS is distributed among the different leaders during the activity, making it a promising approach for applications requiring continuous service.

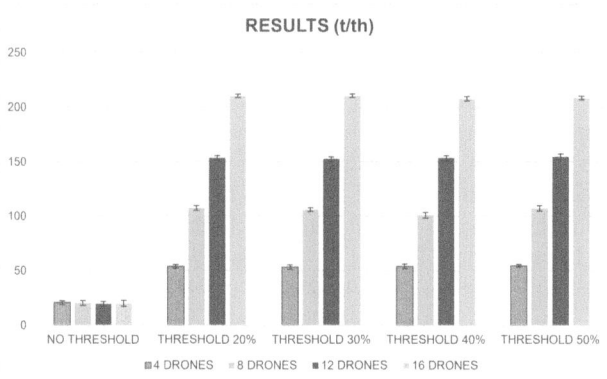

Fig. 2. Time/Threshold Results.

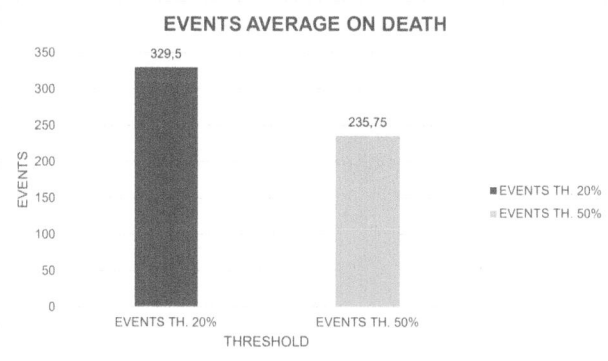

Fig. 3. Events on death.

The threshold values analysis made on events on death (see Fig. 3) revealed that lower threshold led to a higher number of messages exchanged, due to more frequent elections in the end of network's lifespan. This means that a balance between the number of election messages and the operational ones is needed in order to avoid messages overhead. In further applications, this overhead can be used to piggyback other useful messages, depending on the context.

A final analysis was also conducted to evaluate the increase in the number of election messages as the threshold changes (see Fig. 4). For lower thresholds, the number of elections increases because of the leader switch condition that, in the final stages of the cluster's life, is reached faster. These results suggest that low level of thresholds cause frequent elections that enhance responsiveness at the cost of communication overhead. The balance has to be found with respect to the final task. For example, in crisis management more network responsiveness is required in face off message complexity overhead.

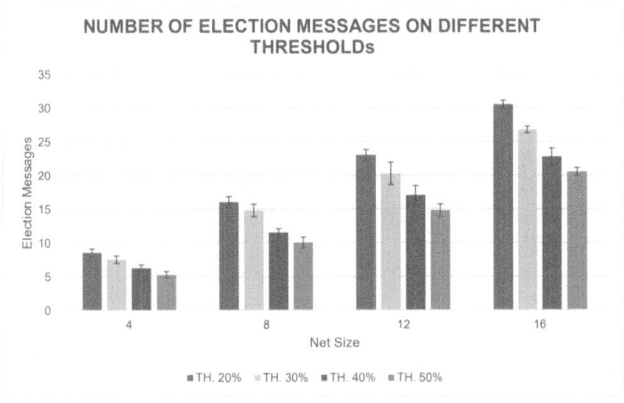

Fig. 4. Number of election messages on different thresholds

5 Conclusions

The research presented in this paper demonstrates the effectiveness of our leader-based energy management system in enhancing the overall lifespan of drone networks. Through a series of simulations, it has been established that the implementation of our algorithm significantly increases the efficiency and duration of the network, thereby addressing one of the primary limitations associated with drone battery life. In addition, as the number of drones increases, the average duration of the cluster also increases, suggesting that the distributed battery system allows better management of communications and, therefore, of each individual drone's battery. By reducing the threshold value, the number of messages exchanged is higher because of the increasing messages complexity. This means that we have to pay attention to the main goal of our service, in order to have a good balance between the number of elections and messages exchanged. This can be advantageous in some specific applications, such as image capture, where the cluster must be active for as long as possible.

Acknowledgment. Rosario Napoli is a PhD student enrolled in the National PhD in Artificial Intelligence, XL cycle, course on Health and life sciences. This work has been partially funded by the Italian Ministry of Health, Piano Operativo Salute (POS) trajectory 2 "eHealth, diagnostica avanzata, medical device e mini invasività" through the project "Rete eHealth: AI e strumenti ICT Innovativi orientati alla Diagnostica Digitale (RAIDD)" (CUP J43C22000380001) and "SEcurity and RIghts in the CyberSpace (SERICS)" project (PE00000014), under the MUR National Recovery and Resilience Plan funded by the European Union - NextGenerationEU (CUP: D43C22003050001) and the Italian Ministry of University and Research (MUR) "Research projects of National Interest (PRIN-PNRR)" through the project "Cloud Continuum aimed at On-Demand Services in Smart Sustainable Environments" (CUP: J53D23015080001-IC: P2022YNBHP).

References

1. Kyrkou, C., Timotheou, S., Kolios, P., Theocharides, T., Panayiotou, C.: Drones: augmenting our quality of life. IEEE Potentials **38**(1), 30–36 (2019)
2. Van der Merwe, D., Burchfield, D., Witt, T., Price, K., Sharda, A.: Drones in agriculture. Adv. Agron. (2020)
3. Wankmüller, C., Kunovjanek, M., Mayrgündter, S.: Drones in emergency response - evidence from cross-border, multi-disciplinary usability tests. Int. J. Disaster Risk Reduction **65**, 102567 (2021)
4. Wu, H., Hu, J., Sun, J., Sun, D.: Edge computing in an IoT base station system: reprogramming and real-time tasks. Complexity **2019**, 4027638 (2019)
5. Tlili, F., Fourati, L.C., Ayed, S., Ouni, B.: Investigation on vulnerabilities, threats and attacks prohibiting UAVs charging and depleting UAVs batteries: assessments and countermeasures. Ad Hoc Netw. **129**, 102805 (2022)
6. Devika, G., Karegowda, A.G.: Bio-inspired optimization: algorithm, analysis and scope of application. IntechOpen, Rijeka (2023)
7. Yu, X., Xiao, L., Yang, D., Cuthbert, L., Wang, Y.: Energy-efficient UAV communication with multiple GTS based on trajectory optimization. Mob. Inf. Syst. **2018**, 5629573 (2018)
8. Abdel-Malek, M.A., Akkaya, K., Bhuyan, A., Ibrahim, A.S.: A proxy signature-based swarm drone authentication with leader selection in 5G networks. IEEE Access **10**, 57485–57498 (2022)
9. Kundu, J., Alam, S., Koner, C., Piran, M.J.: Trust-based dynamic leader selection mechanism for enhanced performance in flying ad-hoc networks (FANETs). IEEE Trans. Intell. Transp. Syst. (2024)
10. García, M., Aguilar, J.: A bio-inspired emergent control approach for distributed processes. Appl. Soft Comput. **141** (2023)
11. Hossam, A., Bouzidi, A., Riffi, M.E.: Elephants herding optimization for solving the travelling salesman problem. In: Ezziyyani, M. (ed.) AI2SD 2018. AISC, vol. 912, pp. 122–130. Springer, Cham (2019). https://doi.org/10.1007/978-3-030-12065-8_12
12. Ganesan, R., Raajini, X.M., Nayyar, A., Sanjeevikumar, P., Hossain, E., Ertas, A.H.: Bold: bio-inspired optimized leader election for multiple drones. Sensors **20**, 3134 (2020)
13. Sengupta, S., Basak, S., Peters, R.A.: Particle swarm optimization: a survey of historical and recent developments with hybridization perspectives (2019)
14. Holzinger, B., Bachmeier, K., Jaeger, S.: Network simulation with OMNeT++ (2020)

Carbon-Aware Software Services

Stefano Forti[✉][iD], Jacopo Soldani[iD], and Antonio Brogi[iD]

Department of Computer Science, University of Pisa, Pisa, Italy
{stefano.forti,jacopo.soldani,antonio.brogi}@unipi.it

Abstract. The significant carbon footprint of the ICT sector calls for methodologies to contain carbon emissions of running software. This article proposes a novel framework for implementing, configuring and assessing carbon-aware interactive software services based on forecasts for carbon intensity and service request rates. An open-source prototype of such framework is used to configure a software service implemented as per our methodology and assessed against traditional non-adaptive implementations of the same service. Experiments show the capability of our framework to control the average quality of output results of carbon-aware services and to reduce carbon emissions from 8% to 50%.

Keywords: carbon-aware services · green design patterns · carbon footprint reduction · mathematical optimisation

1 Introduction

The Information and Communication Technologies (ICT) sector is producing around 2% of the worldwide carbon emissions, i.e. as much as airplane traffic, with an energy consumption estimated at between 6% and 9% of the global demand and expected to grow up to 20% by 2030 [2,25]. Such exponential growth is due to the increase in the amounts of data produced, transmitted, and consumed worldwide through software services (e.g., video streaming services, social networks, and Internet-of-Things-based applications). This, along with the urge to reduce carbon emissions to ensure a future for our Planet by meeting the Paris Agreement objectives, poses non-trivial challenges.

As Dennard's scaling and Moore's law slow down [17], further improvements towards a more sustainable future for ICT will require combining enhancements in hardware efficiency with suitable energy-aware and carbon-aware software engineering tools and methodologies that are currently lacking. Said otherwise, we need to start treating *"energy and carbon as a first-class resource"* [1] in our code. Apropos, Verdecchia et al. [23] call for methodologies to write sustainable software by blending decision-making with the software execution context. To this end, much research has lately targeted the optimisation of renewable energy usage through suitable service orchestration [7].

However, few efforts have been devoted to designing software which is natively carbon-aware [13]. Indeed, existing approaches to implement sustainable applications (e.g., [3,4,19]): (*a*) mostly focus on only reducing the energy consumption

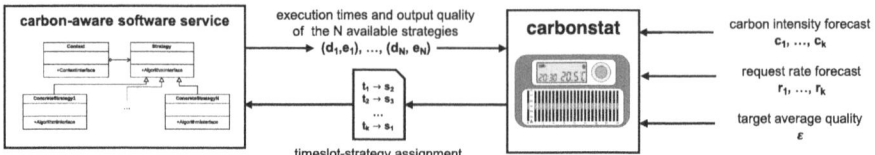

Fig. 1. Bird's-eye view of the proposed framework.

of running software, without explicitly considering the carbon intensity of the energy mix that powers up application servers nor target result quality, (*b*) rely on additional software modules to manage adaptation features, thus increasing overall energy consumption, and (*c*) do not feature open-source releases.

In this article, we propose a framework (Fig. 1) to implement, configure and assess carbon-aware request-response software services, made from

(i) a *methodology*, illustrated via a case study, to design and implement carbon-aware software services by relying on the *Strategy* pattern [8], which features alternative implementations of the same functionality, each associated with their own output *quality scores* (e.g., error, QoE) and *execution times*,
(ii) an *optimisation schema* and its Python *prototype*[1], CARBONSTAT, to suitably *configure* such adaptive software services by selecting which functionality implementation to use so as to minimise carbon emissions and ensure target average output quality, and
(iii) an *experimental assessment* of different service configurations obtained via CARBONSTAT for a software service implemented as per the proposed methodology, and relying on real carbon intensity data and lifelike requests' patterns as contextual data for the experiments.

This work enables developers to implement different versions of the same request-response service, retaking the key idea of approximate computing [16], i.e., that shorter execution times usually result in lower energy consumption at the price of lower output quality scores. By considering this, the forecast service requests and the carbon intensity of the energy mix powering up deployment servers, CARBONSTAT suitably selects the version to run at different times of the day to minimise the carbon emissions of a running service and to keep the average results' quality above a set-point. Notably, our methodology can also be used to reconfigure existing application services so as to accommodate carbon-awareness, aiming at reducing their environmental footprint.

By analogy, consider thermostats that measure the temperature of a building and trigger its heating system to maintain such temperature near a desired set-point throughout the day. Thermostats allow users to move sliders to specify different set-points for different times of the day, depending on their thermal comfort preferences, presence in the building, and weather forecasts. Similarly, based on the forecasts of the carbon intensity of the employed energy mix and

---

[1] Open-sourced at: https://github.com/di-unipi-socc/carbonstat.

the number of incoming service requests, via mixed integer linear programming (MILP), CARBONSTAT decides which version (viz. strategy) to use of a service at different times of the day so to minimise carbon emissions due to service computation and keep the average result quality close to a set threshold.

CARBONSTAT considers the average error on the returned output as the quality metric to optimise. It is assessed against four different baseline configurations by relying on forecast and real data traces from the carbon intensity of the United Kingdom[2] from 2023. Results show how CARBONSTAT– fed with reliable forecasts – can ensure consistent reduction on carbon emissions and average error rates within set thresholds under different request load conditions, whereas static naïve policies might incur in unpredictable behaviour. Note that the employed experimental setup and code can also be used to assess and fine-tune services designed as per our methodology, by varying contextual data. Overall, in contrast with the state of the art, our proposal explicitly considers the forecast of energy carbon intensity and service request rates to minimise carbon emissions while guaranteeing the quality of output results. Besides, it allows making informed decisions from within the application code, without relying on additional modules. Last, but not least, it is available open-source.

The rest of this article is organised as follows. We illustrate, through a case study, our methodology to implement carbon-aware software services (Sect. 2). Then, we describe the MILP formulation of CARBONSTAT to configure the behaviour of such services, based on forecast contextual data and target quality of output results (Sect. 3). Subsequently, we assess the use case service, configured via CARBONSTAT, by relying on forecast and real data for carbon intensity and on a set of lifelike request patterns (Sect. 4). We conclude by discussing some related efforts (Sect. 5) and possible future work (Sect. 6).

2   Carbon-Aware Service Design

The *Strategy* pattern is a behavioural pattern exploiting a family of algorithms that offer a same functionality, enabling the dynamic selection of those algorithms at runtime, independently from clients and based on contextual information, e.g., current system states [8]. Strategies are each implemented in a separate class and offer the Strategy interface. A Context class then acts as an interface between the application's client and the different available strategies, by selecting the most appropriate one to serve incoming requests.

We employ the *Strategy* pattern to implement carbon-aware software services. We assume service functionalities – accessible through a REST API – can be provided in a set of different flavours, each associated to a different result quality (e.g., average error), execution time, and, therefore, energy consumption. In general, the lower the execution time, the lower the result quality and energy consumption. Figure 2 and 3 show an example of the Strategy pattern within CARBONSTAT. Consider a RESTful service featuring a single operation

---

[2] Data available at: https://carbonintensity.org.uk.

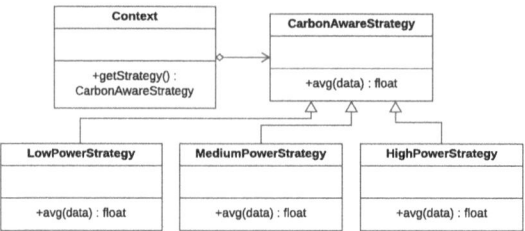

Fig. 2. UML diagram of CARBONSTAT case study.

/avg that returns the average value of a given list of integers. The service is associated with a Context object that is in charge of selecting a suitable strategy to compute the average, by relying on the three concrete implementations available for the abstract interface CarbonAwareStrategy, viz. LowPowerStrategy, MediumPowerStrategy, HighPowerStrategy.

Figure 3 lists the Python code for the abstract class CarbonAwareStrategy. Such interface only offers the avg(data) method, which supposedly inputs a list of data and returns its average, and can be implemented into different classes, i.e., concrete strategies. By running controlled experiments, the application developers can associate each concrete strategy with its average execution time and average error on output results over the deployment servers[3]. The strategies we consider are defined in terms of the function avg(2) listed in Fig. 3. Such function inputs a list data of integers and a step value, which allows skipping some integers when accumulating values to compute the average of data.

Overall, our service implements:

- a *low-power* strategy that computes a statistical average over one fourth of the values in the list, by picking one every four items in the list (i.e., step = 4), with associated average execution time of 35.3 ms and an average error on the results of 13.4%,
- a *medium-power* strategy that also computes a statistical average over half of the values in the list, by picking one every two items in the list (i.e., step = 2), with associated average execution time of 66.3 ms and an average error on the results of 4.5%, and
- a *high-power* strategy which computes the exact average over all values in the list (i.e., step = 1), with associated average execution time of 100.2 ms and no error on output results.

The above strategies are offered to end-users as a service to compute the average of a list of integers. Figure 4 shows the Context class, fed with a strategy assignment array (line 4) by the __init__() constructor, which loads a pre-computed assignment of strategies to time slots within a certain period of time (lines 5–7). The Context then exposes a getStrategy() method (lines 9–13) that

---

[3] This can be achieved, for instance, by using the code provided at https://github.com/di-unipi-socc/carbonstat/tree/main/data/time_error.

```
class CarbonAwareStrategy(ABC):
    @abstractmethod
    def avg(data) -> float:
        pass

    def avg(data, step=1):
        sum = 0
        count = 0
        size = len(data)
        for i in range(0,size,step):
            count += 1
            sum += data[i]
        return round(sum/count)
```

Fig. 3. Abstract carbon-aware strategy.

```
1   class Context:
2
3       def __init__(self):
4           self.assignment = {}
5           assignment = open(environ["ASSIGNMENT"])
6           self.assignment = load(assignment)
7           assignment.close()
8
9       def getStrategy(self,force_strategy) -> CarbonAwareStrategy:
10          if force_strategy is not None:
11              return CarbonAwareStrategies[force_strategy].value
12          now = datetime.now()
13          return self.assignment[now.hour + 0.5*floor(now.minute/30)]
```

Fig. 4. Context implementation.

either returns the strategy set for the current time (line 12–13), or a specific strategy, `force_strategy`, forced by the caller (i.e. lines 10–11), e.g., for those applications that do not tolerate errors on the computed results (e.g., life-critical applications). Our application is wrapped as a Flask service to expose a REST endpoint /avg featuring the average function implemented by the three strategies, invoked through the `Context` object. Every incoming request is handled by retrieving the strategy to be used from the `Context` instance.

3 Setting Strategies, with CARBONSTAT

In this section, we show how, based on forecast carbon intensity and forecast request rates for our service, CARBONSTAT can map strategies to different time slots across the day to keep the average quality of output results above a set thresholds and, subsequently, to minimise carbon emissions. In detail, we first present the formulation of our problem as a bilevel optimisation (Sect. 3.1), then illustrate it through a running example (Sect. 3.2). We assume that predictions on both service demand and carbon intensity are available within a time horizon (e.g. 24–48 h). Many accurate techniques exist to predict such values, like [18,20] for service demand and [14,15] for carbon intensity.

Table 1. Notation recap.

Symbol	Meaning
ε	tolerated average error
x	assignment matrix
x_{ij}	assignment of strategy j to time slot i
t	total number of time slots
c_i	estimated carbon emissions for time slot i
r_i	user requests received at time slot i
s	total number of available strategies
d_j	average execution time for strategy j
e_j	average error for strategy j

3.1 Problem Formulation

Consider a time interval represented by a sequence of t discrete time slots, for which a forecast of carbon emissions c_i and user requests r_i is available (with $i = 1, \ldots, t$). Suppose that the target service is available with s implemented strategies, each with its own average error e_j and execution time d_j (with $j = 1, \ldots, s$). We aim at assigning a strategy to each time slot to minimise the overall carbon emissions and keep the average error of the results returned by the target service within a tolerated error threshold ε. Among the assignments that minimise carbon emissions, we then aim at minimising the average error of returned results.

By exploiting the notation of Table 1, the above is formalised by the following bilevel optimisation [22] problem, defined over the binary decision variable x_{ij} that is set to 1 to indicate that strategy j is assigned to time slot i, to 0 otherwise:

$$\min_{x \in X} \sum_{i=1}^{t} \sum_{j=1}^{s} x_{ij} r_i e_j \quad (1)$$

subject to

$$X = \arg\min_{x \in Y} \left\{ \sum_{i=1}^{t} \sum_{j=1}^{s} x_{ij} c_i r_i d_j \right\} \quad (2)$$

where

$$Y = \left\{ x \in V \mid \sum_{i=1}^{t} \sum_{j=1}^{s} x_{ij} r_i e_j \leq \varepsilon \sum_{i=1}^{t} \sum_{j=1}^{s} x_{ij} r_i \right\} \quad (3)$$

$$V = \left\{ x \in \{0,1\}^{t \times s} \mid \sum_{j=1}^{s} x_{ij} = 1, \ i = 1, \ldots, t \right\} \quad (4)$$

Solutions to the above problem are within the domain of binary $t \times s$ matrices denoting assignments of strategies to time slots, with each time slot obviously assigned with a single strategy (Eq. 4). We further restrict assignments to those maintaining the average error within ε (Eq. 3). Then, the lower-level optimisation task minimises the overall carbon emission (Eq. 2), and the upper-level optimisation task minimises the average error of the results returned by the target service (Eq. 1).

The above formulation makes it clear that the upper-level optimisation task strictly depends on determining the optimal Pareto front for the lower-level optimisation task. This naturally induces a priority between tasks, which requires to first solve the lower-level and, then, the upper-level one. It is worth noting that this type of problems are inherently NP-hard [6].

3.2 CARBONSTAT at Work

The considered problem was encoded in an open-source Python prototype[4], CARBONSTAT, by relying on Google's optimisation suite OR-tools[5].

Our prototype first determines all possible solution x optimising the inner objective set by Eq. 2 and meeting Eq. 3 and Eq. 4. Among these, it then determines one solution that also optimises the outer objective of Eq. 1. We now show the solutions it finds over a small motivating example considering six time slots only. The prediction values for those time slots are as follows:

$$r = \begin{pmatrix} 350 \\ 500 \\ 1000 \\ 750 \\ 400 \\ 100 \end{pmatrix} \quad c = \begin{pmatrix} 260 \\ 350 \\ 220 \\ 530 \\ 610 \\ 1100 \end{pmatrix}$$

where, for instance, at time slot $i = 1$ there is a forecast of 350 incoming requests and of a carbon intensity of 260 gCO$_2$-eq/kWh, while at $i = 6$ there is a forecast of 100 incoming requests and of a carbon intensity of 1100 gCO$_2$-eq/kWh.

We assume the strategies that can be selected are those of the case study of Sect. 2, that is they are denoted by the following average execution times and error on output results:

$$d = \begin{pmatrix} 35.3 \\ 66.3 \\ 100.2 \end{pmatrix} \quad e = \begin{pmatrix} 13.4 \\ 4.5 \\ 0 \end{pmatrix}$$

By using CARBONSTAT over the above input data, we can solve the bilevel optimisation problem of Sect. 3.1 for different values of the maximum tolerated error ε. Running our prototype after setting the maximum tolerated error $\varepsilon =$

---
[4] Available at: https://github.com/di-unipi-socc/carbonstat/blob/main/carbonstat/carbonstat.py.
[5] *Google OR-tools*, https://developers.google.com/optimization.

0%, naturally returns the optimal assignment that always exploits the "ero-error" strategy, i.e., the *high-power* strategy. Considering running our service on a 50 W server, this configuration emits 1.72 gCO$_2$-eq over the considered time slots. This first solution incurs no error but, on the other hand, gives no control over the produced carbon emissions. Similarly, setting $\varepsilon = 15\%$ we obtain the assignment which always runs the *low-power* strategy – as 15% is above the 13.4% average error of the *low-power* strategy. Considering again running our service on a 50 W server, this latter configuration emits 0.6 gCO$_2$-eq over the considered time slots, i.e., 65.1% less than the *high-power* configuration. It incurs, however, the highest average error on output results of 13.4%. In contrast with the previous case, this configuration minimises emissions but gives no control over the error on output results.

Last, setting $\varepsilon = 5\%$, we get the following optimal assignment, with an average error on output results of 4.98% and minimising overall carbon emissions:

$$x = \begin{pmatrix} 0 & 0 & 1 \\ 0 & 1 & 0 \\ 0 & 0 & 1 \\ 1 & 0 & 0 \\ 0 & 1 & 0 \\ 1 & 0 & 0 \end{pmatrix}$$

Such assignment exploits the *high-power* strategy at time slots 1 and 3, the *medium-power* strategy at time slots 2 and 5, and the *low-power* strategy at time slot 4 and 6. Notably, CARBONSTAT selects the best strategy to handle situations in which a lower carbon intensity allows to handle large amounts of requests at *high-power* (e.g. time slot $i = 3$) or, vice versa, a higher carbon intensity in spite of few requests is better handled at *low-power* (e.g. time slot $i = 6$). With a 50W server, this configuration emits 1.07 gCO$_2$-eq, i.e. 37.8% less than the *high-power* configuration and 43.9% more than the *low-power*. To conclude this example, note that CARBONSTAT allows to control the average quality of output results while minimising carbon emissions as much as possible.

4 Evaluation

In this section, we illustrate and discuss the results of a controlled experiment[6] executed by relying on the service described in Sect. 2, configured by running CARBONSTAT over realistic carbon intensity data and request load patterns.

Setup. Our experiments aimed at comparing the amount of carbon emissions and the average error of running the carbon-aware average software service

---

[6] All experimental code and data are publicly available on GitHub at https://github.com/di-unipi-socc/carbostat/tree/main/data/experiment. Experimental results (included average execution times and error for the considered strategies) were obtained over a Ubuntu 20.04 LTS server, equipped with 4 CPUs and 32 GB of RAM. Experiments were repeated two times to mitigate experimental errors.

(Sect. 2), with each time slot's strategy selected according to seven different configurations, against a standard version featuring only the *high-power* strategy. Namely, we considered the following configurations:

- always low and always medium, which always run the *low power* and *medium power* strategy of the service, respectively, independently of the carbon intensity or user requests of each time slot,
- naïve, which runs the *high power* strategy of the service in a time slot if the carbon intensity is low and user requests are below 1/3 of the maximum expected number of user requests, the *medium power* strategy if the carbon intensity is at most moderate and user requests are below 2/3 of the maximum expected number of user requests, and the *low power* strategy in any other case,[7]
- CARBONSTAT ($\varepsilon = x$), with $x \in \{1\%, 2\%, 4\%, 8\%\}$, which assigns strategies to time slots by running CARBONSTAT with the tolerated error threshold x.

We first measured the *average error* of the output results and *service time* for each strategy of the approximated average service, with the service time being the time between the service receiving a request and sending its corresponding reply. We then considered 12 different days of the year 2023, each taken from a different month so to account for a meaningful variety of possible carbon intensities. The values of forecast and actual carbon intensity for each 30-minutes time slot of each considered day were obtained via the Carbon Intensity API. For instance, Fig. 5(d) plots forecast and actual carbon intensity values for a day in January 2023. Instead, the values of forecast and actual user requests per each day's time slot were randomly generated by means of three different probability distributions following three lifelike requests' profiles. Namely:

- a profile with peaks around 1000 requests occurring at early in the morning and late in the afternoon, see e.g., Fig. 5(a),
- a profile with stable load around 300 requests, see e.g., Fig. 5(b), and
- a profile with stable load around 500 requests, see e.g., Fig. 5(c).

Actual profiles were obtained by perturbing the amounts of requests specified above by a random variance of ±10%. For each considered day, we passed the forecast values of carbon intensity and user requests, and the strategies' average service time and error, as input to CARBONSTAT to obtain the assignments of CARBONSTAT ($\varepsilon = x$), $x \in \{1\%, 2\%, 4\%, 8\%\}$. We used the actual values of carbon intensity from the Carbon Intensity API and user requests obtained by varying forecast requests by a random amount between 0 and ±5% to simulate the execution of the approximated average service on each time slot of each considered day as if strategies were assigned by each of the seven considered policies. A time slot was simulated by invoking the deployed instance of the approximated average service for a number of times equal to the time slot's

---

[7] The thresholds for "low" or "moderate" carbon intensity were aligned to those of the Carbon Intensity API, published at https://carbonintensity.org.uk.

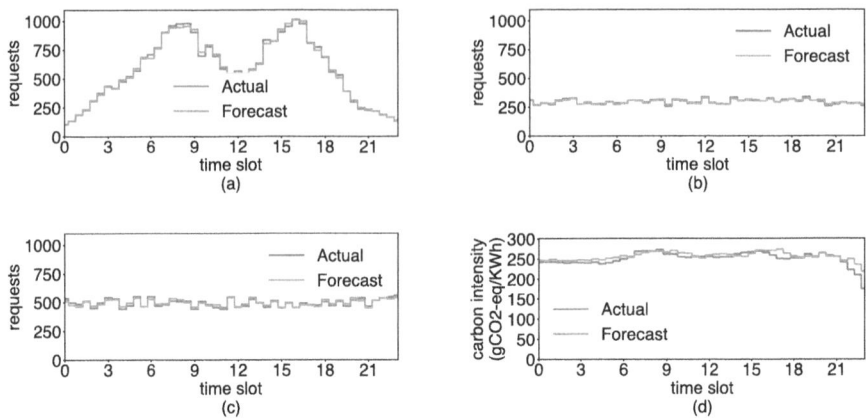

Fig. 5. Example of evolution of the values of (a-c) user requests and (d) carbon intensity in one of the considered days.

actual user requests, and by assuming that they were served by consuming energy produced with the time slot's actual carbon intensity.

We then measured the average error and overall carbon emissions as the average and sum of those measured on each time slot, respectively. The error was computed as a percentage denoting the distance from the returned average and the actual one, with the latter obtained by initially forcing a request to be served with the *high power* strategy. The carbon emissions for serving each request, instead, were estimated based on the service time for such request. More precisely, the carbon emissions for each request were obtained by multiplying the corresponding service time by the time slot's carbon intensity and by the server's power consumption (i.e., 50 W).

Results. Figure 6 illustrates the average results obtained in our experiments for each given configuration, in terms of average error and carbon emissions reduction in comparison to the service only featuring the *high-power* functionality. Particularly, Fig. 6(a), (b), and (c) concerns the experiments corresponding to the request profiles sketched in Fig. 5(a), (b) and (c), respectively. In all experiments, as expected, the always low and the always medium strategies show an average error on output results equal to that of the corresponding strategies, viz., 13.4% and 4.5%, respectively. Similarly, across all experiments, the configurations obtained via CARBONSTAT guarantee that the average error on output results settles exactly around the set maximum error threshold $\varepsilon \in \{1\%, 2\%, 4\%, 8\%\}$.

It is worth analysing how the average desired average error threshold is not exceeded by the CARBONSTAT instances across the three experiments, i.e. guaranteeing the desired quality for output results. With $\varepsilon = 1\%$ as the maximum average tolerated error on output results, CARBONSTAT ($\varepsilon = 1$) is the sole configuration that can guarantee such average error, also reducing carbon emissions with respect to the *high-power* baseline. Indeed, independently of the considered request profile, CARBONSTAT ($\varepsilon = 1$) guarantees an average error of 1% and

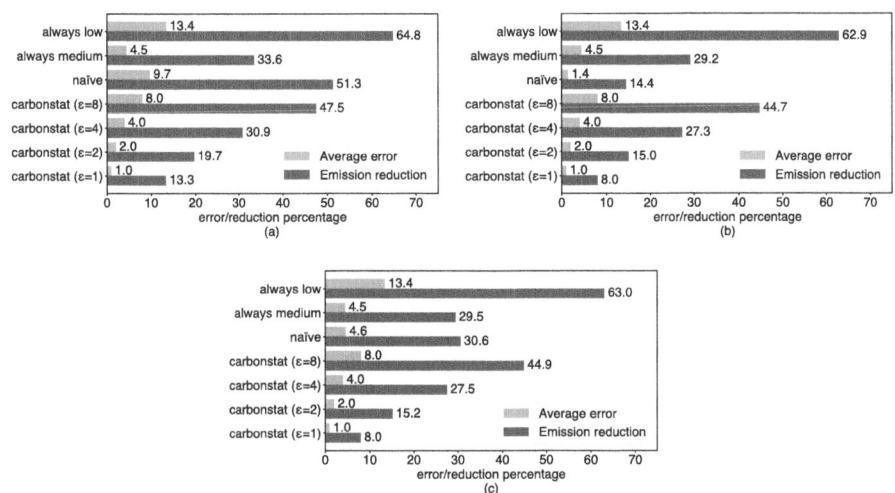

Fig. 6. Experimental results.

reduces emissions by 13.3% in for the peaky request profile (a) and by 8% for the stable request profiles (b) and (c).

With $\varepsilon = 2\%$ as the maximum average tolerated error on output results, CARBONSTAT ($\varepsilon = 2$) is the only configuration capable of satisfying such requirement both in the case of peaky load (a) and stable load of 500 requests (c), also achieving a carbon reduction of 19.7% and 15.2%, respectively. In the case of stable load profile of 300 requests (b), both the naïve and the CARBONSTAT ($\varepsilon = 2$) configuration manage to meet the error threshold. However, CARBONSTAT ($\varepsilon = 2$) achieves a slightly higher reduction of carbon emissions (15%) in comparison with the naïve approach (14.4%). Naturally, also CARBONSTAT ($\varepsilon = 1$) meets the requirement on the average error of 2% for all request profiles, at the price, however, of a lower reduction of carbon emissions in all considered scenario.

If $\varepsilon = 4\%$, CARBONSTAT ($\varepsilon = 4$) still is the only approach to meet the maximum error threshold for peaked requests (a) and stable requests (c), reducing carbon emissions by 30.9% and 27.5%, respectively. In the case of stable requests (b), the naïve policy also does not exceed the maximum tolerated error but has a reduction in carbon emissions which is around half the one achieved by CARBONSTAT ($\varepsilon = 4$) (14.4% vs 27.3%). As before, CARBONSTAT ($\varepsilon = 1$) also meets the requirement on the average error of 4%, producing higher carbon emissions than CARBONSTAT ($\varepsilon = 4$), in (a), (b), and (c), and naïve in (b). Similarly, CARBONSTAT ($\varepsilon = 2$) satisfies the requirement set on the average error in all cases, with higher emissions than CARBONSTAT ($\varepsilon = 4$) for request profiles (a), (b) and (c), and with higher error than naïve for request profile (b) at a similar reduction in the carbon emissions.

Last, when considering $\varepsilon = 8\%$ as the maximum average tolerated error on output results, the CARBONSTAT configuration still works fine with all requests profiles with a reduction of emissions of 47.5% for peaky requests (a), and of 44.7% for stable request loads (b) and (c). The always medium configuration works for the peaky load (a) but causes a more modest reduction in carbon emissions, settling around 33.6%. The always medium and naïve configurations also meet the 8% set-point for request profiles (b) and (c), however they reduce carbon emissions less, when compared with CARBONSTAT configuration. Particularly, naïve achieves a reduction of 14.4% in case (b) and of 30.6% in case (c), while always medium reaches a reduction of 29.2% in case (b) and 29.5% in case (c). Again, the configuration obtained with CARBONSTAT ($\varepsilon = 1$), ($\varepsilon = 2$), and ($\varepsilon = 4$) would support the requirement on the average error of at most 8% incurring in lower reduction in carbon emissions w.r.t. CARBONSTAT ($\varepsilon = 8$), i.e. without fully exploiting the potential reduction in carbon emissions.

Discussion. Our experimental assessment against varying carbon intensity of the available energy mix and of the incoming requests shows that our framework: (*i*) can guarantee average error rates within the set thresholds, both in case of constant and peaked requests' load profiles, (*ii*) can dynamically adapt the behaviour of the configured service to minimise carbon emissions, while naïve static configuration might fail on this objective (as, e.g., in Fig. 6(b)), and (*iii*) can consistently balance the performance of the service and its carbon footprint, achieving a reduction of carbon emissions between 8% and 50% in the considered scenarios. Speaking of static policies, like always low, they can further minimise carbon emission in comparison to CARBONSTAT, at the price of higher error rates. Analogously, naïve thresholds do not dynamically adapt to different service contexts, viz. energy mix and request rates.

5 Related Work

To enable intrinsic application sustainability, some authors designed energy-aware programming languages. For instance, Canino & Liu [5] devise a proactive and adaptive framework based on mixed type checking to embed energy information in written program. Similarly, Sampson et al. [21] and Han et al. [9] propose approximate type systems that support different data precision levels at different energy consumptions. These works, however, requires rethinking CPU design to support both precise and approximate data types.

More closely related to our effort, Bunse & Höpfner [3,4] were among the first to focus on energy-awareness of communication within component-based software. They propose the development and usage of an *energy management component* (EMC) to handle communication via resource substitution strategies (e.g., caching, replication or hoarding) to balance the trade-offs between energy, performance and hardware usage (e.g., compute results vs use cached values vs invoke a remote service). Despite relying on the *Strategy* pattern, they require, differently from us, the deployment of the EMC, the dynamic (un)deployment

Table 2. Comparison of our work with the state of the art.

Ref.	Carbon intensity	Energy consumption	Request rate	QoS	No external modules
Bunse & Höpfner [3,4]		✓		✓	
Kavanagh et al. [12]		✓		✓	
Hasan et al. [10,11]	✓	✓		✓	
de Oliveira & Ledoux [19]		✓		✓	
Xu et al. [24]	✓	✓	✓	✓	
Our work	✓	✓	✓	✓	✓

of components and do not consider carbon emissions nor incoming requests to optimise software configuration.

Still only considering energy usage optimisation and Software-as-a-Service architectures, de Oliveira & Ledoux [19] propose a framework targeting BPEL-based service compositions, based on an orchestration component to trigger reconfiguration events and make application deployment more sustainable in terms of energy footprint. Hasan et al. [10,11] propose an autonomic self-adaptive auto-scaler for Software-as-a-Service architectures, which accounts for response times, application availability and energy quality (green vs brown). Also Xu et al. [24] study how to adapt Cloud application deployments based on information about the current energy mix and (interactive/batch) workload. Differently from our work, their focus is how to manage applications by reacting to monitored events through external controllers, instead of configuring them based on context predictions. Based on energy consumption and QoS, Kavanagh et al. [12] focus on runtime migration of high-performance computing tasks across heterogeneous accelerated infrastructure resources.

Table 2 graphically compares our work to the closely related work analysed above. To the best of our knowledge, our proposal is the first to propose *both* a software engineering methodology and an optimisation scheme to code and tune carbon-aware software services. Particularly, it enables writing applications that are natively carbon-aware, i.e., do not rely on external components for achieving adaptation at runtime, and considers holistically carbon intensity of the available energy mix, energy consumption, request rate and QoS.

6 Conclusions

In this article, we proposed a framework to implement and configure adaptive carbon-aware software services. It comprises a methodology to implement adaptive services based on established software engineering principles (i.e. the *Strategy* pattern) *and* a MILP approach to optimally configure those services. The MILP approach has been released an open-source tool named CARBONSTAT and the overall framework has been assessed by controlled experiments over a case study. Interestingly, our framework can also be used to enhance existing applications with carbon-aware features so as to reduce their environmental footprint.

Our experimental assessment of a software service implemented and tuned with CARBONSTAT shows the feasibility of our framework and its capability to adapt the service behaviour in response to lifelike carbon emissions and request patterns, with reduction on carbon emissions between 8% and 50%, corresponding to guaranteed average error rates between 1% and 8%. We have also shown that static configurations do not provide the same flexibility and might end up with different behaviours depending on the service execution context.

As future work, we plan to: (i) add continuous service re-configuration to adapt the service behaviour in case of sudden changes in the forecast of carbon emissions or incoming requests, as well as in response to unexpected events, (ii) evaluate our approach over more complex software services and in Cloud-Edge settings, relying on real applications (e.g., from the field of generative artificial intelligence or high-performance computing) and involving end-users to include an assessment of their Quality of Experience, and (iii) extend our methodology to accommodate other classes of services that can tolerate delays (e.g. batch processing) also considering the possibility of shifting service execution in time to further save on carbon emissions and considering the environmental footprint of involved Internet-of-Things devices.

Acknowledgments. Work partly funded by projects: *Energy-aware management of software applications in Cloud-IoT ecosystems* (RIC2021_PON_A18) funded over ESF REACT-EU resources by the *Italian MUR* through *PON Ricerca e Innovazione 2014–20*; *FREEDA* (CUP: I53D23003550006), funded by the frameworks PRIN (MUR, Italy) and Next Generation EU; *OSMWARE* (UNIPI_PRA 2022 64), funded by the University of Pisa, Italy. The Authors wish to thank Giandomenico Mastroeni for his feedback on the mathematical model presented in this work.

References

1. Anderson, T.E., et al.: Treehouse: a case for carbon-aware datacenter software. ACM SIGENERGY Energy Inform. Rev. **3**(3), 64–70 (2023). https://doi.org/10.1145/3630614.3630626
2. Belkhir, L., Elmeligi, A.: Assessing ICT global emissions footprint: trends to 2040 & recommendations. J. Clean. Prod. **177**, 448–463 (2018). https://doi.org/10.1016/j.jclepro.2017.12.239
3. Bunse, C., Höpfner, H.: Resource substitution with components - optimizing energy consumption. In: Proceedings of the 3rd International Conference on Software and Data Technologies (ICSOFT 2008), pp. 28–35. INSTICC Press (2008)
4. Bunse, C., et al.: Choosing the "best" sorting algorithm for optimal energy consumption. In: Proceedings of the 4th International Conference on Software and Data Technologies, ICSOFT 2009, vol. 2, pp. 199–206. INSTICC Press (2009)
5. Canino, A., Liu, Y.D.: Proactive and adaptive energy-aware programming with mixed typechecking. In: Proceedings of the 38th ACM SIGPLAN Conference on Programming Language Design and Implementation, PLDI 2017, pp. 217–232. ACM (2017). https://doi.org/10.1145/3062341.3062356

6. Dempe, S., Zemkoho, A.: Bilevel optimization. In: Springer Optimization and Its Applications, vol. 161. Springer, Cham (2020)
7. Gaglianese, M., et al.: Green orchestration of cloud-edge applications: state of the art and open challenges. In: IEEE International Conference on Service-Oriented System Engineering, SOSE 2023, pp. 250–261. IEEE (2023). https://doi.org/10.1109/SOSE58276.2023.00036
8. Gamma, E., et al.: Design Patterns: Elements of Reusable Object-Oriented Software. Addison Wesley (1994)
9. Han, J., Orshansky, M.: Approximate computing: an emerging paradigm for energy-efficient design. In: 18th IEEE European Test Symposium, ETS 2013, pp. 1–6. IEEE Computer Society (2013). https://doi.org/10.1109/ETS.2013.6569370
10. Hasan, M.S., et al.: Enabling green energy awareness in interactive cloud application. In: 2016 IEEE International Conference on Cloud Computing Technology and Science, CloudCom 2016, pp. 414–422. IEEE Computer Society (2016). https://doi.org/10.1109/CLOUDCOM.2016.0071
11. Hasan, M.S., et al.: Investigating energy consumption and performance trade-off for interactive cloud application. IEEE Trans. Sustain. Comput. **2**(2), 113–126 (2017). https://doi.org/10.1109/TSUSC.2017.2714959
12. Kavanagh, R.E., Djemame, K., Ejarque, J., Badia, R.M., García-Pérez, D.: Energy-aware self-adaptation for application execution on heterogeneous parallel architectures. IEEE Trans. Sustain. Comput. **5**(1), 81–94 (2020). https://doi.org/10.1109/TSUSC.2019.2912000
13. Lee, S.U., Fernando, N., Lee, K., Schneider, J.: A survey of energy concerns for software engineering. J. Syst. Softw. **210**, 111944 (2024). https://doi.org/10.1016/J.JSS.2023.111944
14. Leerbeck, K., et al.: Short-term forecasting of CO2 emission intensity in power grids by machine learning. Appl. Energy **277**, 115527 (2020)
15. Maji, D., et al.: Multi-day forecasting of electric grid carbon intensity using machine learning. ACM SIGENERGY Energy Inform. Rev. **3**(2), 19–33 (2023)
16. Mittal, S.: A survey of techniques for approximate computing. ACM Comput. Surv. **48**(4), 62:1–62:33 (2016). https://doi.org/10.1145/2893356
17. Muralidhar, R., et al.: Energy efficient computing systems: architectures, abstractions and modeling to techniques and standards. ACM Comput. Surv. **54**(11s), 236:1–236:37 (2022). https://doi.org/10.1145/3511094
18. Nishimatsu, K., et al.: Service-demand-forecasting method using multiple data sources. In: Networks 2006. 12th International Telecommunications Network Strategy and Planning Symposium, pp. 1–6. IEEE (2006)
19. Alvares de Oliveira, F.G., Ledoux, T.: Self-optimisation of the energy footprint in service-oriented architectures, pp. 4–9 (2010). https://doi.org/10.1145/1925013.1925014
20. Qiu, C., Shen, H.: Dynamic demand prediction and allocation in cloud service brokerage. IEEE Trans. Cloud Comput. **9**(4), 1439–1452 (2019)
21. Sampson, A., et al.: EnerJ: approximate data types for safe and general low-power computation. In: Proceedings of the 32nd ACM SIGPLAN Conference on Programming Language Design and Implementation, PLDI 2011, pp. 164–174. ACM (2011). https://doi.org/10.1145/1993498.1993518
22. Sinha, A., et al.: A review on bilevel optimization: from classical to evolutionary approaches and applications. IEEE Trans. Evol. Comput. **22**(2), 276–295 (2018). https://doi.org/10.1109/TEVC.2017.2712906
23. Verdecchia, R., et al.: Green IT and green software. IEEE Softw. **38**(6), 7–15 (2021). https://doi.org/10.1109/MS.2021.3102254

24. Xu, M., et al.: A self-adaptive approach for managing applications and harnessing renewable energy for sustainable cloud computing. IEEE Trans. Sustain. Comput. **6**(4), 544–558 (2021). https://doi.org/10.1109/TSUSC.2020.3014943
25. Zulfiqar, M., et al.: Digitalized world and carbon footprints: does digitalization really matter for sustainable environment? Environ. Sci. Pollut. Res. **30**, 88789–88802 (2023). https://doi.org/10.1007/s11356-023-28332-z

Comparative Analysis of Lightweight Kubernetes Distributions for Edge Computing: Performance and Resource Efficiency

Diyaz Yakubov[✉] [iD] and David Hästbacka [iD]

Tampere University, 33014 Tampere, Finland
{diyaz.yakubov,david.hastbacka}@tuni.fi

Abstract. Edge computing environments increasingly rely on lightweight container orchestration platforms to manage resource-constrained devices. This paper provides an empirical analysis of five lightweight kubernetes distributions (KD)—k0s, k3s, KubeEdge, OpenYurt, and Kubernetes (k8s)—focusing on their performance and resource efficiency in edge computing scenarios. We evaluated key metrics such as CPU, memory, disk usage, throughput, and latency under varying workloads, utilizing a testbed of Intel NUCs and Raspberry Pi devices. Our results demonstrate significant differences in performance: k3s exhibited the lowest resource consumption, while k0s and k8s excelled in data plane throughput and latency. Under heavy stress scenarios, k3s and k0s accomplished the same workloads faster than the other distributions. OpenYurt offered balanced performance, suitable for hybrid cloud-edge use cases, but was less efficient in terms of resource usage and scalability compared to k0s, k3s and k8s. KubeEdge, although feature-rich for edge environments, exhibited higher resource consumption and lower scalability. These findings offer valuable insights for developers and operators selecting appropriate KD based on specific performance and resource efficiency requirements for edge computing environments.

Keywords: Kubernetes · Lightweight Kubernetes · Benchmark · Container orchestration · Performance Testing · Load testing · Edge Computing · Resource-constrained Devices

1 Introduction

In recent years, the edge computing demand has grown significantly resulting in more research [7,10,11] and springing up new software solutions to cope with new issues. The enablers of such growth are improvements in communication (5G, such as 5G IoT [2]) and ways of managing/maintaining the software on the edge devices (containerization). While many data systems successfully pioneered the orchestration techniques for containerization, the Internet of Things (IoT) was lagging in that area, though many of the kubernetes distributions (KD) can be used for it. However, IoT has slightly different requirements that are not widely considered in common-purpose orchestration tools, such as Kubernetes (k8s). To benefit from battle-tested orchestration of k8s technology and to address IoT-specific requirements on resource-constrained devices, many lightweight KDs have been devised recently.

Lightweight KDs like k0s, k3s, KubeEdge, and OpenYurt are evolving rapidly, each with unique features and components. This diversity complicates the choice for developers, especially for resource-constrained edge devices in factories, autonomous vehicles, or smart cities, where container orchestration overhead can be critical. Application performance on these distributions is influenced by factors like container runtime, control plane, data plane storage, and networking. These factors are crucial for assessing resource efficiency, analyzing cluster behavior under stress, and optimizing resource usage.

Performance and capacity planning for microservice architectures are key challenges in the performance engineering community. Previous studies [3,8,9] have compared full and managed KDs, but research on lightweight distributions like k0s and k3s is limited and often inconsistent. Newer distributions like k0s and OpenYurt remain understudied.

This paper presents an empirical study of popular lightweight KDs. We evaluated resource utilization, throughput and response times under stress scenarios. Our benchmarking setup involved two Intel NUCs (Next Unit of Computing, small form factor computer) and three Raspberry Pi 4 Model B single-board computers, netdata for data collection, MongoDB for storage, Python for analysis and visualization, and Ansible with bash scripts for automation and provisioning which can be replicated by other researchers. The following research questions (RQ) were formulated to explain the test results and provide a comprehensive analysis:

– RQ1 Resource Utilization Comparison: Assess and compare the resource efficiency of various lightweight KDs when deployed on resource-constrained devices, such as Raspberry Pis. Focus on metrics like CPU, memory, and storage utilization to determine which distributions are most suitable for such environments.
– RQ2 Cluster Behavior Characterization: Analyze the behavior of kubernetes clusters under various stress conditions, including: 1) Light and heavy CPU loads to gauge processing efficiency. 2) Network-intensive activities to understand bandwidth and latency implications.
– RQ3 Resource Optimization: Identify which KD is most suitable for specific environments, focusing on efficient workload scheduling, auto-scaling, and resource management to optimize performance on constrained devices.

The results will provide valuable guidance for both practitioners and researchers selecting KDs in edge computing environments.

The paper is structured as follows: Sect. 2 describes KDs and reviews previous performance analyses. Section 3 details the experimental setup. Section 4 presents the benchmarking results answering research questions, followed by Sect. 5 which discusses the results. Section 6 concludes the paper and highlights future work.

2 Background and Related Work

2.1 Kubernetes Distributions Under Test

Kubernetes has become the de facto standard for container orchestration, automating deployment, scaling, and management of containerized applications. Various distributions have been developed for different use cases, particularly resource-constrained environments like edge devices and IoT gateways. This section overviews notable distributions: k0s, k3s, k8s, OpenYurt, and KubeEdge, each offering varying levels of complexity, resource consumption, and features tailored to specific deployment needs, from robust cloud infrastructures to resource-limited edge devices.

Kubernetes[1] is an open-source orchestration platform originally developed by Google and now maintained by the Cloud Native Computing Foundation (CNCF). It is designed to automate deploying, scaling, and operating application containers supporting a broad ecosystem of tools for monitoring, logging, networking, security, etc. Still, its resource intensity makes it less suitable for limited-resource environments.

k3s[2], developed by Rancher Labs (now part of SUSE), is a lightweight KD designed for edge computing, IoT, and CI/CD pipelines. Packaged as a single binary (around 100 MB), it simplifies the installation process and requires less memory and CPU. Likewise, it supports ARM processors making it suitable for devices like Raspberry Pi.

k0s[3], created by Mirantis, is another lightweight distribution focused on minimal resource consumption and ease of installation. It supports various storage options like etcd and SQLite, and it is designed for bare metal, edge, and cloud environments, emphasizing security and versatility across ARM and x86 platforms into a single binary file.

OpenYurt[4], developed by Alibaba Cloud, extends Kubernetes to edge computing, enhancing it for cloud-edge hybrid environments. It supports edge autonomy and edge-cloud synergy with features like YurtHub for traffic routing and YurtTunnel for secure communication between cloud and edge nodes, making it ideal for smart cities, industrial IoT, and remote monitoring.

KubeEdge[5], a CNCF project, extends Kubernetes to edge computing environments, offering infrastructure and APIs to manage applications on edge nodes. It supports offline autonomy, allowing edge nodes to function independently of the cloud, and simplifies IoT and Industrial Internet communications with components like EdgeHub for device communication and EdgeController for managing edge nodes from the cloud.

---

[1] https://kubernetes.io/.
[2] https://k3s.io/.
[3] https://k0sproject.io/.
[4] https://openyurt.io/.
[5] https://kubeedge.io/.

2.2 Related Work

Over the last years, performance studies have been conducted on lightweight KDs. Each cover specific KDs and metrics thoroughly, though there are still areas that require further investigation. Following, we describe previous works and discuss the differences with our work.

Koziolek et al. [6] compared lightweight KDs, specifically Microk8s, k3s, k0s, and MicroShift, focusing on resource usage as well as control plane and data plane performance under stress scenarios. They found that k3s and k0s had slightly higher control plane throughput, while MicroShift excelled in data plane throughput, providing useful insights for selecting distributions.

Cilic et al. [12] evaluated Kubernetes, k3s, KubeEdge, and ioFog in edge computing, assessing deployment complexity, memory footprint, and performance. Kubernetes stood out with its low memory footprint and strong performance, but the study also noted specific challenges for each tool in edge environments.

Kjorveziroski and Filiposka et al. [5] examined KDs for serverless edge computing using OpenFaaS, finding k3s and Microk8s performed best in most benchmarks, while full Kubernetes excelled under sustained loads.

Fogli et al. [4] assessed KDs in tactical networks with limited bandwidth and high latency, concluding that KubeEdge outperformed k8s and k3s in maintaining cluster stability under degraded conditions, making it ideal for tactical applications.

Bahy et al. [1] compared KubeEdge, k3s, and Nomad, focusing on resource utilization in edge computing. They found Nomad was the most efficient in CPU and memory usage, while k3s excelled in storage efficiency, offering insights into choosing the best container orchestrator for resource-constrained environments.

While the provided works offer valuable insights into the performance of various lightweight KDs, our research differentiates itself by conducting detailed stress tests covering light and heavy CPU loads, and network-intensive activities on real devices with some KDs that are not well covered, such as k0s, KubeEdge and OpenYurt. By addressing these aspects, our work aims to provide a more holistic understanding of the performance and efficiency of lightweight KDs in edge computing environments.

3 Methodology

3.1 Test Setup and Equipment

In this section, we detail the equipment and configurations utilized to empirically evaluate several lightweight KDs, including Kubernetes itself: k0s, k3s, k8s, OpenYurt, and KubeEdge, listed in Table 1.

Our primary objective is to gauge and compare resource utilization, specifically focusing on CPU, network bandwidth, disk I/O, and RAM. To provide a holistic view, we incorporate test cases that load kubernetes clusters differently in order to overview the consumption of resources and the cluster behavior in different use cases. Figure 1 depicts the setup deployment view.

Table 1. Setup attributes of kubernetes distributions

Feature	k0s	k3s	Kubernetes (k8s)	KubeEdge	OpenYurt
Version	v1.28.4+k0s.0	v1.27.4+k3s1	v1.29	1.14.4	v1.4.0
Container Network Interface (CNI)	kube-router (default, v1.1.1)	flannel (default, v0.22.0)	flannel (v0.24.3)	flannel^a (v0.24.3) + edgemesh^b (v1.14.0)	flannel^a(v0.24.3) + raven^c (0.4.1)
Container Runtime Interface (CRI)	containerd (v1.7.11)	containerd (v1.7.11)	containerd (v1.7.11)	containerd (v1.7.11)	containerd (v1.7.11)
Control Plane Storage	etcd(v3.5.10)	SQLite(3.39.2)	etcd(v3.5.10)	etcd^a(v3.5.10)	etcd^a(v3.5.10)
Type of distribution	lightweight	lightweight	full-fledged	edge extension for k8s	edge extension for k8s

^{a} KubeEdge and OpenYurt extend the k8s to the edge, consequently, the cloud part is still requiring CNI to operate and dictate what control plane storage is.
^{b} https://github.com/kubeedge/edgemesh.
^{c} https://openyurt.io/docs/core-concepts/raven/.

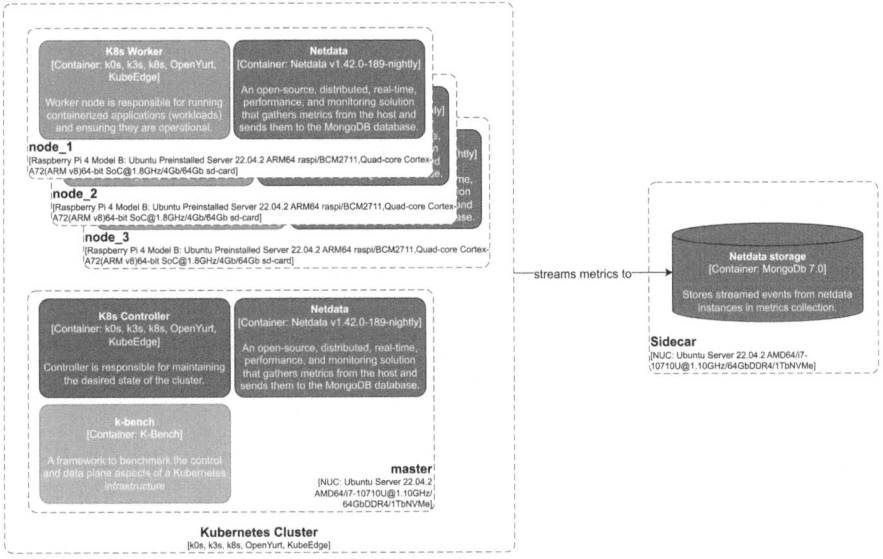

Fig. 1. Deployment diagram

In the diagram, there are several NUC and Raspberry Pi 4 Model B (RPi) machines. One NUC (master) and three RPi (workers) machines form the kubernetes cluster, while the second NUC machine acts as a side container machine monitoring and storing data. Apart from KDs, all machines in this cluster have netdata installed to gather metrics and stream them to the sidecar machine to the MongoDB database. Likewise, the master machine has additional software installed for performing performance tests (k-bench[6]).

---

[6] https://github.com/vmware-tanzu/k-bench with the last commit's sha hash: 53a82d316effaaf562d81a7cd306bf5f0d40cfc6.

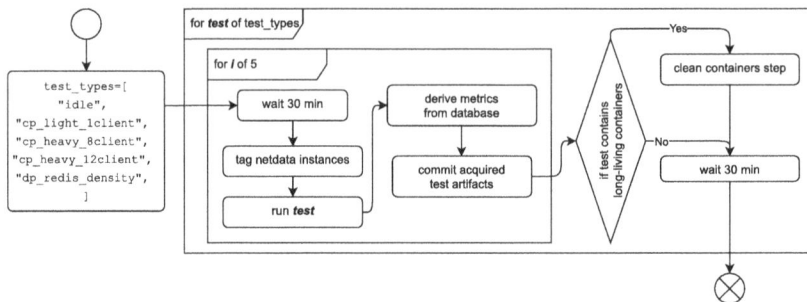

Fig. 2. Test flow diagram

3.2 Test Procedures

The Activity Flow diagram in Fig. 2 illustrates the testing process. Each test type is executed 5 times, with each cycle starting with a 30-minute wait to stabilize the system. The execution tags all Netdata streaming instances for data validation, followed by the test execution using Ansible scripts combined with bash. Data is fetched from the sidecar machine's MongoDB database via an Ansible script, and the results are committed to the git repository to preserve information and signal test completion. Two post-test steps follow: cleaning up containers (for tests with long-running containers) and another 30-minute wait before the next test cycle. Test suites are fully automated and can be run per KD. Table 2 lists all test scenarios, their descriptions, used tools, and collecting metrics.

Table 2. Test scenarios to benchmark performance of a cluster

Test Name - Description	Tools	Collecting Metrics
idle - Gauges how much resources the cluster consumes when there is no workload, in its serenity state within 5 min.	bash, ansible	CPU, RAM, Network bandwidth, disk I/O
cp_light_1client - Executes lifecycle actions (CREATE, LIST, GET, UPDATE, DELETE) on Pods, Deployments, Namespaces, and Services to put a light load. Includes specific sleep intervals post-CREATE for timing analysis, with no cleanup post-test. Deployments feature 5 replicas using k8s.gcr.io/pause:3.1 image; all operations are executed once per resource type.	bash, ansible, k-bench	CPU, RAM, Network bandwidth, disk I/O
cp_heavy_8client - Conducts extensive operations on Pods, Deployments, Namespaces, and Services, executing 8 cycles of CREATE, LIST, GET, UPDATE, DELETE actions to put a considerable load. Pods and Deployments have initial sleep times of 20 and 40 s post-CREATE, respectively, to assess timing dynamics, without cleanup post-execution. Deployments are configured with 5 replicas using k8s.gcr.io/pause:3.1, and all resources undergo the same set of actions 8 times.	bash, ansible, k-bench	CPU, RAM, Network bandwidth, disk I/O
cp_heavy_12client - Performs 12 cycles of CREATE, LIST, GET, UPDATE, DELETE operations on kubernetes Pods, Deployments, Namespaces, and Services to put a stress load. Pods start with a 30-s pause post-CREATE, Deployments with 60 s, aimed at deeper timing analysis, without post-test cleanup. Each Deployment configures 5 replicas using k8s.gcr.io/pause:3.1. The test iterates through each action 12 times for each resource, designed for rigorous performance assessment.	bash, ansible, k-bench	CPU, RAM, Network bandwidth, disk I/O
dp_redis_density - Executes a series of Pod operations within a 1-minute timeframe, focusing on a Redis workload across 3 cycles without cleanup to put a data-heavy load. Initially, 3 Pods with the nginx image and Redis-specific configurations are created, each followed by a 100-s pause. A precondition checks for a specific file in a pod before running Redis server commands in matching Pods, with a 5-s pause post-execution. Another set of operations runs benchmarking commands in Redis worker Pods, also followed by a 5-s pause. Finally, outputs from the Pods are copied locally after a 20-s wait.	bash, ansible, k-bench	CPU, RAM, Network bandwidth, disk I/O, Throughput operations, Latency

3.3 Limitations

While our methodology is comprehensive, certain limitations are acknowledged: *Hardware Constraints*: The use of specific devices (Intel NUCs and Raspberry Pis) may influence performance results; however, they are representative of common edge computing hardware although limited in number. Additionally, homogeneous worker nodes allow for minimizing variables and focus on the KDs themselves. *Network Conditions*: Tests were conducted in a controlled network environment, which may not fully capture the variability of real-world edge networks.

4 Results

While k0s, k3s, and k8s solve common issues of orchestration and distribution, KubeEdge and OpenYurt precisely extend them to the edge devices by providing more IoT-grained features, such as on-device storage, digital twin, etc. Of course, those extra features add overhead to the distributions that might slow down their performances.

4.1 Light Tests

The diagrams in Fig. 3 provide focus on the idle and cp_light_1client tests for testing distributions. It is worth noting that in these two tests, the execution times of systems were considered as well, nevertheless, the time results remain the same across distributions for idle and cp_light_1client tests, exactly 5 min and 4 min respectively. Therefore, a timeline was excluded from the analysis for the light test cases.

It is visible that on a master node, the resource consumption metrics follow the same pattern despite the chosen test case showing a slight increase by approximately 0.3% or 0.5% across resources for the cp_light_1client test. The behavior of worker nodes presents different resource consumption patterns, specifically, the CPU and Disk IO usages increase significantly for all distributions under the cp_light_1client test workload, while the RAM and Network utilizations remain the same. In fact, the increased metrics show double gains in consumption. Thus, adding a lightweight task to an idle cluster shows that KDs

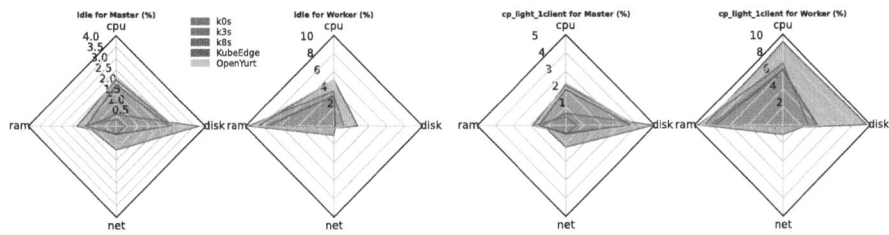

Fig. 3. Light tests: idle and cp_light_1client (Master and Worker nodes, %)

scale their resource consumption differently. For instance, the CPU of k0s, k3s, k8s, and OpenYurt scale up similarly, adding roughly 2% of CPU consumption while KubeEdge adds almost 4%. The Disk usage also resembles the growing pattern for k0s, k3s, k8s, and OpenYurt distributions by representing around 3% of growth when the KubeEdge rockets up by 6% reaching 9% of Disk utilization. Besides that, the only distribution that continuously uses the network is k0s. It can be justified by Konnectivity[7] service that is exploited in k0s for the Controller to Worker communication[8].

In conclusion, the resource efficiency of various lightweight KDs demonstrates notable differences under light load conditions. **(RQ1)** KubeEdge shows significantly higher CPU and Disk usage increases compared to k0s, k3s, k8s, and OpenYurt, indicating potentially lower processing efficiency and higher resource demands. **(RQ2)** Additionally, there are differences in scaling patterns that should be considered for optimized workload scheduling and resource management, particularly for resource-constrained environments.

4.2 Heavy Tests

Adding additional workload significantly alters resource consumption. The most noticeable effects occur on worker nodes, with OpenYurt demonstrating the highest CPU consumption at 26%, followed by KubeEdge at 21%, and the less voracious k0s - 20%, k3s and k8s show 19% and 16% respectively. In terms of disk usage, KubeEdge is the most aggressive, showing Disk IO usage of 25%. Figure 4 presents a heavy test scenario for 12 clients. The results of testing another heavy cp_heavy_8client test could be found in the project's repository though the resource usage pattern is the same.

In the case of light tests, the time measurement is negligible since it doesn't make any differences between distributions. Nevertheless, the time dimension reveals a crucial distinction of kubernetes performances in heavy test scenarios. Particularly, it shows the processing time of the same task could be accomplished

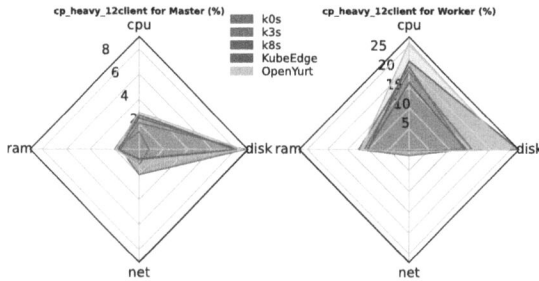

Fig. 4. Heavy tests: cp_heavy_12client (Master and Worker nodes, %)

---

[7] https://kubernetes.io/docs/tasks/extend-kubernetes/setup-konnectivity/.
[8] https://docs.k0sproject.io/v1.21.0+k0s.0/networking/#controllers-worker-communication.

by a specific KD, additionally, it shows the trajectory of a resource consumption. Moreover, the significance of kubernetes's time-based performance evaluation was not fully covered in [6], [12] works. Exemplifying diagram Fig. 5 illustrates CPU usage of worker nodes under heavy load tasks executed on clusters exhibiting the differences in CPU utilization and more importantly the finish time of the workload. The iot-edge[9] project with various other diagrams could be viewed for more precise observations.

It is observable that KubeEdge takes a maximum of 10 min of processing time to accomplish heavy load tasks while OpenYurt and k8s do the same job within 6 min, and the fastest distributions become k0s and k3s with 4 min spent. While in heavy load tests, the most resource-efficient distribution is k8s, it is not the most performant distribution. The k0s and k3s do not demonstrate the most optimal resource usage, but it is clear that these lightweight distributions are more effective performance-wise, presumably due to less overhead compared to the rest.

To conclude, adding additional workload drastically alters resource consumption among the KDs. (**RQ1**) OpenYurt exhibits the highest CPU consumption under heavy loads, followed by KubeEdge, with k0s, k3s, and k8s showing lower CPU usage. (**RQ1**) KubeEdge also demonstrates the highest Disk IO usage, indicating its aggressive resource consumption under heavy load. (**RQ2**) Regarding performance, k0s and k3s complete heavy-load tasks faster than other distributions, despite not being the most resource-efficient. KubeEdge lags tremendously, 4 min from the nearest, indicating the slowest cluster under heavy load. (**RQ3**) These findings illustrate a trade-off between resource efficiency, performance and functionality, suggesting that the optimal choice of distribution depends on specific workload demands and resource availability.

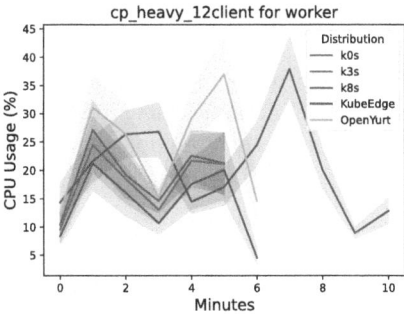

Fig. 5. CPU usage of worker nodes under cp_heavy_12client test

---

[9] https://github.com/DiyazY/iot-edge

4.3 Operational Metrics

Figure 6 illustrates the latency time for KDs scaling from 1 pod to 120 pods. All distributions scale in linear growth, where the pod increase results in pod startup delays gradually climbing from 1 s to 7 s respectively. However, the KubeEdge distributive does not scale as gracefully as others. Its latency for 10 pods already shows a significant gain, reaching almost 3 s of delay. After, the latency rapidly jumps from 3 s to 10 s at 80 pods, which is a notable increase since it has already become the slowest system at 60 pods by overtaking OpenYurt distribution with its worst results at 120 pods. The upward trend is even more dramatic, the latency skyrockets to slightly above 30 s at a point of scaling to 120 pods. If the scaling property is crucial, the KubeEdge is not a good alternative. Presumably, KubeEdge lags scaling by providing feature-rich services that put overheads.

Figure 7 depicts the latency and throughput for Pod Creation(PC) and Deployment (D). It shows relatively similar results for k0s, k3s and k8s, approximately 140 pods per min for PC workload and around 275 pods/min for D with latency between 2–4 ms. This is followed by OpenYurt showing 120 pods per minute for PC and 210 pods per minute for D with 3 ms and 8 ms of latency respectively. The slowest distribution in terms of PC throughput becomes KubeEdge since its maximum throughput is managed at around 60 pods per minute with the highest latency around 46 ms for D.

The throughput (pods/min) and latency (ms) of PC clearly show that the most performant distribution is k0s, which in general has the lowest latency and highest throughput, while for D, the most effective cluster is k8s. Just slightly behind those two is k3s, which in most cases show relatively similar results. Notably, the OpenYurt distribution is less efficacious compared to the previous 3. The worst results are shown by KubeEdge which is overall, 75% less effective (for D 50 pods/min vs 275 pods/min - k3s). It is always worth emphasizing that the latter two distributions are rich feature-wise, hence, it brings extra overhead on their shoulders, consequently, it may result in slower operations.

The performance analysis[10] of namespace, pod, deployment, and service operations reveals that k3s consistently demonstrate the lowest latency, mak-

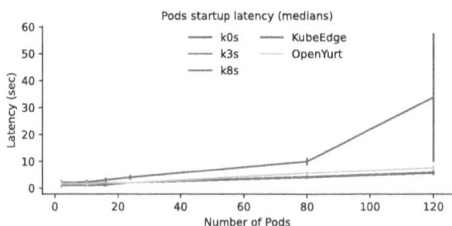

Fig. 6. Pod startup latency (medians)

---

[10] https://github.com/DiyazY/iot-edge/blob/main/src/diagrams/latency-statistics/cp_heavy_12client.pdf.

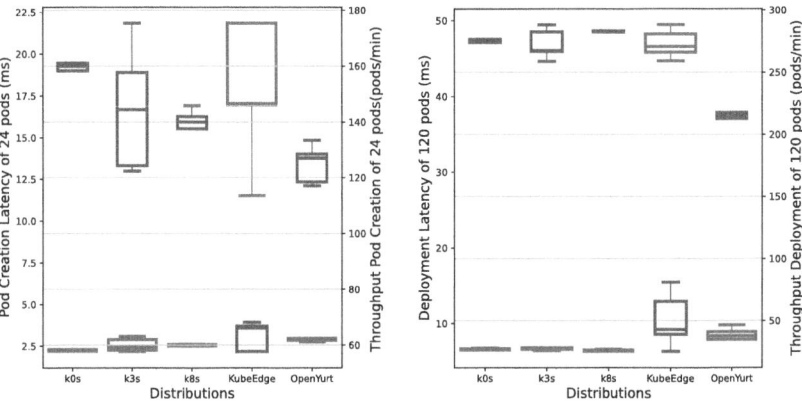

Fig. 7. cp_heavy_12client - Latency (ms) and Throughput (pods/min) for Pod Creation with 24 pods (left) and Deployment(right) with 120 pods (right).

ing it optimal for performance-sensitive applications. In contrast, k0s, k8s, KubeEdge and OpenYurt exhibit higher latencies, suggesting potential inefficiencies likely due to additional overhead in managing operations. Particularly, get and list operations maintain low latencies across all environments, whereas create, update, and delete operations show greater variability, reflecting their complexity. These findings highlight k3s as a superior choice for environments demanding high performance, while k0s, k8s, KubeEdge and OpenYurt may be more suited for specialized use cases where their unique features justify the latency trade-offs.

Finally, operational metrics reveal significant differences in the scalability and performance of clusters. (**RQ2**) All distributions exhibit a linear increase in pod startup delays as they scale from 1 to 120 pods, with KubeEdge showing a notably higher latency increase, making it less suitable for scaling-intensive environments. (**RQ1**) In terms of pod creation throughput, k0s, k3s, and k8s demonstrate the highest performance, with k3s consistently showing the lowest latency for various operations. (**RQ3**) KubeEdge, while feature-rich, shows the worst performance with significantly higher latencies and lower throughputs, suggesting a trade-off between functionality and efficiency. (**RQ3**) These findings suggest that while k3s is optimal for operation performance-sensitive applications, k0s, k8s, KubeEdge, and OpenYurt may be more appropriate for specialized use cases where their unique features justify the latency trade-offs.

4.4 Data Plane

The data plane throughput, measured in operations per second (Ops/sec) using the memtier benchmark[11], is shown in Fig. 8. This metric reflects the system's ability to handle data processing efficiently.

---
[11] https://github.com/RedisLabs/memtier_benchmark/releases/tag/2.0.0.

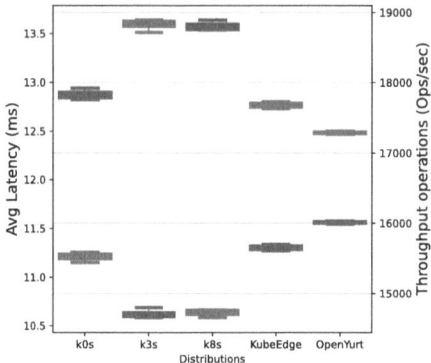

Fig. 8. Data plane - Average Latency (ms) and Throughput operations (Ops/sec)

k8s achieved the highest throughput, nearing 19,000 Ops/sec, followed by k0s at around 18,000 Ops/sec. OpenYurt reached just over 16,000 Ops/sec, while KubeEdge slightly trailed at under 16,000 Ops/sec. k3s had the lowest throughput, below 15,000 Ops/sec.

Latency, depicted in Fig. 8, measures the average response time. k8s had the lowest latency at 10.5 ms, followed by k0s at just above 11.0 ms. OpenYurt and KubeEdge were similar, with latencies slightly under and over 12.5 ms, respectively. k3s recorded the highest latency, around 13.5 ms.

When comparing both throughput and latency, k8s consistently outperforms other distributions, making it the most efficient option for data-heavy high-performance requirements. It achieves the highest throughput and the lowest latency, signifying a robust and responsive data plane. Conversely, k3s shows the least favorable results in both metrics, suggesting potential areas for optimization in data plane throughput and latency.

k0s, while not as performant as k8s, still offers commendable efficiency with high throughput and relatively low latency. OpenYurt maintains a balanced performance but does not excel in either metric compared to the more optimized distributions. KubeEdge, designed for edge computing, shows reduced performance in both throughput and latency, which might be a trade-off for other edge-specific benefits not captured in these metrics.

Resource utilization-wise, clusters' behaviors tangibly differentiate on master machines while remaining almost the same across worker machines (Fig. 9). For master machines, k0s, k3s and OpenYurt show lower CPU usage (0.5%–1.1%) compared to k8s, KubeEdge (1.7%–2%), indicating better efficiency. The RAM consumption, k3s uses the least RAM, followed by k8s, OpenYurt, k0s and KubeEdge, which uses the most. Network utilization is relatively low across all distributions, except k3s being notably more network-heavy. Disk usage adheres to a similar pattern, it is almost the same for k0s, k8s, OpenYurt and KubeEdge, around 2.5%, and significantly higher for k3s by showing 3.5% consumption.

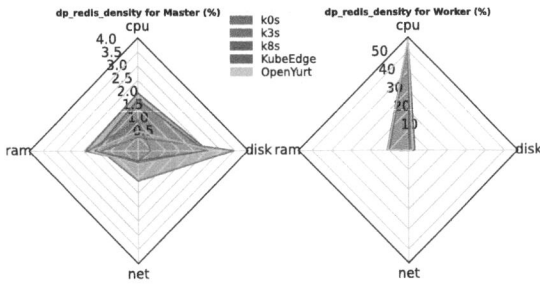

Fig. 9. dp_redis_density - performance metrics (%)

In summary, k8s is the best for high-performance needs **(RQ2)**, while k0s is efficient for resource-constrained environments. k3s and KubeEdge require optimization, and OpenYurt is balanced but not ideal for peak performance. **(RQ3)** These findings emphasize the need to align performance requirements and resource efficiency when choosing the appropriate KD.

5 Discussion

This analysis of KDs reveals a spectrum of resource usage and performance trade-offs. k0s and k8s provide the best balance of throughput and resource efficiency, ideal for demanding applications. k3s, while efficient, requires enhancements for high-throughput environments. KubeEdge and OpenYurt, although feature-rich for edge computing, exhibit higher resource demands, underscoring the need for further refinement to improve their performance and efficiency. **(RQ3)** Table 3 summarizes our findings.

5.1 Future Challenges

While our study provides valuable insights into the performance and resource efficiency of lightweight KDs, several challenges remain to optimize their deployment in edge computing environments. Future work should focus on:

- Optimizing Edge-Specific Distributions: Enhancing the performance and reducing the resource consumption of KubeEdge and OpenYurt without compromising their edge-specific functionalities.
- Scalability Improvements: Investigating methods to improve the scalability of KDs, particularly for KubeEdge, to better handle increased workloads and larger numbers of pods.
- Integration of IoT Features with Efficiency: Developing strategies to integrate IoT-specific features into lightweight KDs like k3s and k0s while maintaining low resource consumption.
- Standardized Benchmarking Tools: Establishing standardized tools and methodologies for benchmarking KDs in edge computing environments to facilitate more consistent and comparable results across studies.

Table 3. Summary Comparison of Kubernetes Distributions

Dist.	Strengths	Weaknesses	Resource Consumption	Suggestion
k0s	High throughput and low latency with minimal resource consumption. Simple installation and management.	Fewer features compared to full Kuernetes distributions. Limited community and enterprise support.	Moderate: efficient in disk usage; moderate CPU and RAM usage.	Highly efficient for resource-constrained environments needing balanced performance and simplicity. Ideal for edge and IoT deployments.
k3s	Extremely lightweight with a small binary size. Low memory and CPU footprint. Simple installation and management.	Lower throughput and higher latency for data-heavy conditions. Limited advanced features and extensions.	Low: lowest utilization on Master node and moderate on Worker nodes.	Optimal for very resource-constrained environments with some compromises in performance under data-heavy load.
k8s	Highest throughput and lowest latency. Robust ecosystem with extensive tools and features. Highly scalable and flexible.	Complex to set up and manage. Overhead can be significant for small-scale deployments.	Low: moderate usage on Master node and low usage on Worker nodes.	Best suited for high-performance, large-scale environments.
OpenYurt	Seamless integration between cloud and edge environments. Enhanced capabilities for managing distributed IoT applications.	Moderate throughput and higher latency. Additional overhead for edge-specific features. Complex to set up and manage.	High: high disk and RAM consumption with the highest CPU utilization.	Well-suited for hybrid cloud-edge environments with IoT applications, balancing performance with advanced features.
KubeEdge	Tailored for edge computing with offline autonomy. Supports IoT device management and communication.	Higher resource consumption compared to other lightweight distributions. Lower throughput and higher latency. Complex to set up and manage.	High: high CPU and RAM utilization with highest disk utilization on Worker nodes.	Best for specialized edge computing scenarios where offline capabilities and IoT integrations are critical, though resource optimization is needed.

6 Conclusion

This paper analyzed the performance and resource utilization of lightweight KDs, focusing on k0s, k3s, k8s, OpenYurt, and KubeEdge. Our findings show that k8s and k0s are the most efficient, balancing performance and resource usage, particularly under both light and heavy loads. KubeEdge, while tailored for edge computing, consumes more CPU and disk resources, making it less ideal for resource-constrained environments. k3s, though resource-efficient, requires optimization for better throughput and latency in data-heavy scenarios.

Selecting the right KD depends on specific deployment needs. k8s and k0s are recommended for high-performance environments, while k3s, with further tuning, could be effective in resource-limited settings. KubeEdge and OpenYurt, although feature-rich, may need additional optimization.

Future research should focus on the unique optimizations of each distribution, particularly those designed for edge computing, to further enhance their efficiency and applicability. By understanding these factors, kubernetes deployments can be better optimized for diverse environments, ensuring efficient resource use and high performance.

Acknowledgement. This work is supported by funding from Business Finland in project Industry X.

References

1. Bahy, M.B., Dwi Riyanto, N.R., Fawwaz Nuruddin Siswantoro, M.Z., Santoso, B.J.: Resource utilization comparison of kubeedge, k3s, and nomad for edge computing. In: 2023 10th International Conference on Electrical Engineering, Computer Science and Informatics (EECSI), pp. 321–327. IEEE (2023)
2. Bhoi, A.K.: 5G IoT and edge computing for smart healthcare. Elsevier, Place of publication not identified, Intelligent Data-Centric Systems (2022)
3. EdgelessSystems: A comparison of kubernetes engines: from basic functionality to security (2024). https://www.edgeless.systems/resource-library/kubernetes-distributions-comparison/
4. Fogli, M., et al.: Performance evaluation of kubernetes distributions (k8s, k3s, kubeedge) in an adaptive and federated cloud infrastructure for disadvantaged tactical networks. In: 2021 International Conference on Military Communication and Information Systems (ICMCIS), pp. 1–7. IEEE (2021)
5. Kjorveziroski, V., Filiposka, S.: Kubernetes distributions for the edge: serverless performance evaluation. J. Supercomput. **78**(11), 13728–13755 (2022)
6. Koziolek, H., Eskandani, N.: Lightweight kubernetes distributions: a performance comparison of microk8s, k3s, k0s, and microshift. In: ICPE 2023 - Proceedings of the 2023 ACM/SPEC International Conference on Performance Engineering, pp. 17–29. ACM, New York, NY, USA (2023)
7. Moreschini, S., Pecorelli, F., Li, X., Naz, S., Hästbacka, D., Taibi, D.: Cloud continuum: the definition. IEEE Access **10**, 131876–131886 (2022). https://doi.org/10.1109/ACCESS.2022.3229185
8. Pereira Ferreira, A., Sinnott, R.: A performance evaluation of containers running on managed kubernetes services. In: 2019 IEEE International Conference on Cloud Computing Technology and Science (CloudCom), pp. 199–208. IEEE (2019)
9. Truyen, E., Kratzke, N., Van Landuyt, D., Lagaisse, B., Joosen, W.: Managing feature compatibility in kubernetes: vendor comparison and analysis. IEEE access **8**, 228420–228439 (2020)
10. Wang, Z., Goudarzi, M., Aryal, J., Buyya, R.: Container orchestration in edge and fog computing environments for real-time IoT applications. In: Buyya, R., Hernandez, S.M., Kovvur, R.M.R., Sarma, T.H. (eds.) Computational Intelligence and Data Analytics. LNDECT, pp. 1–21. Springer, Singapore (2023)
11. Yang, T., et al.: Kubeedge wireless for integrated communication and computing services everywhere. IEEE Wirel. Commun. **29**(2), 140–145 (2022)
12. Čilić, I., Krivić, P., Podnar Žarko, I., Kušek, M.: Performance evaluation of container orchestration tools in edge computing environments. Sensors (Basel, Switzerland) **23**(8), 4008 (2023)

Comparative Analysis of Lightweight Kubernetes Distributions for Edge Computing: Security, Resilience and Maintainability

Diyaz Yakubov(✉) and David Hästbacka

Tampere University, 33014 Tampere, Finland
{diyaz.yakubov,david.hastbacka}@tuni.fi

Abstract. The increasing demand for real-time data processing in Internet of Things (IoT) devices has elevated the importance of edge computing, necessitating efficient and secure deployment of applications on resource-constrained devices. Kubernetes and its lightweight distributions—k0s, k3s, KubeEdge, and OpenYurt—extend container orchestration to edge environments, but their security, reliability, and maintainability have not been comprehensively analyzed. This study compares Kubernetes and these lightweight distributions by evaluating security compliance using kube-bench, simulating network outages to assess resiliency, and documenting maintainability. Results indicate that while k3s and k0s offer superior ease of development due to their simplicity, they have lower security compliance compared to Kubernetes, KubeEdge, and OpenYurt. Kubernetes provides a balanced approach but may be resource-intensive for edge deployments. KubeEdge and OpenYurt enhance security features and reliability under network outages but increase complexity and resource consumption. The findings highlight trade-offs between performance, security, resiliency, and maintainability, offering insights for practitioners deploying Kubernetes in edge environments.

Keywords: Kubernetes · Lightweight Kubernetes · Container orchestration · Resilience testing · Edge Computing · Resource-constrained Devices · Security · Maintainability

1 Introduction

The rapid spreading of Internet of Things (IoT) devices and the increasing demand for real-time data processing have propelled edge computing to the forefront [4,8,9]. By bringing computation and data storage closer to the data sources, edge computing reduces latency, conserves bandwidth, and enables faster decision-making. However, deploying applications at the network edge introduces challenges, particularly concerning security, resilience, and maintainability.

Edge computing environments are often resource-constrained, and the devices are frequently distributed across vast geographical areas, including intermittent network connectivity. Such conditions amplify security vulnerabilities due to increased attack surfaces and physical accessibility. Resilience becomes a concern as network disruptions can lead to service outages, and maintaining operations across distributed nodes adds complexity to system management.

Container orchestration platforms like Kubernetes (k8s) have revolutionized application deployment and management in cloud environments through automation and scalability. Recognizing the potential benefits for edge computing, several lightweight kubernetes distributions (later KD), e.g., k0s, k3s, KubeEdge, and OpenYurt, have been developed to extend k8s functionalities on the edge.

While performance optimization has been a central focus in prior studies comparing lightweight KDs [3,6,7,10], there is a research gap on security, resiliency, and maintainability. This study provides a comparative analysis of selected lightweight KDs focusing on the following research questions: **RQ1:** How do lightweight KDs differ in terms of security compliance, and what are the implications for edge computing applications? **RQ2:** How do these distributions perform under simulated network outage scenarios, and what insights does this provide about their resiliency? **RQ3:** What are the maintainability challenges associated with each distribution when deployed in edge environments?

This study highlights trade-offs between security, resilience and maintainability of different distributions, providing insight to practitioners and researchers aiming to deploy kubernetes in resource-constrained edge environments. The paper concludes with recommendations for selecting the distribution based on specific needs, balancing security, resiliency, and maintainability.

2 Background and Related Work

2.1 Lightweight Kubernetes Distributions for Edge Computing

Kubernetes (k8s)[1] has become the de facto standard for container orchestration, automating deployment, scaling, and management of containerized applications. Various distributions have been developed for different use cases, also focusing on resource-constrained environments such as edge devices and IoT gateways. k3s[2] is a lightweight KD developed by Rancher Labs, now part of SUSE. Designed to have a smaller footprint, k3s is packaged as a single binary (around 100 MB) and requires less memory and CPU than the standard Kubernetes. k0s[3] is another lightweight KD, created by Mirantis. Similar to k3s, k0s aims to provide a streamlined and easy-to-install Kubernetes experience with minimal resource consumption. It combines all necessary components into a single binary and supports various storage options, including etcd and SQLite. OpenYurt[4], by

---

[1] https://kubernetes.io/.
[2] https://k3s.io/.
[3] https://k0sproject.io/.
[4] https://openyurt.io/.

Alibaba Cloud, extends Kubernetes for the edge while retaining standard APIs, and enhancing edge autonomy and cloud-edge synergy. KubeEdge[5], a CNCF project, brings Kubernetes to edge environments by providing infrastructure and APIs to manage applications on edge nodes as if they were in the cloud.

2.2 Related Work

Koziolek et al. [3] conducted a detailed performance comparison of lightweight KDs, including MicroK8s, k3s, k0s, and MicroShift. They focused on resource usage and control plane and data plane performance under stress scenarios. However, they did not address security or reliability aspects.

Cilic et al. [10] evaluated the applicability of Kubernetes, k3s, KubeEdge, and ioFog in edge environments. They analysed deployment complexity, memory footprint, and service startup times. Although they highlighted challenges specific to edge environments, such as resource constraints and service management, their study did not delve deeply into security compliance or maintainability.

Kotopulis Ostinelli et al. [5] focused on performance evaluation and emulation of LTE/5G networks over a lightweight open platform using k3s. They demonstrated the using of lightweight KDs in telecommunications environments, emphasizing scalability, automation, and reliability in 5G deployment scenarios.

Fogli et al. [2] evaluated the performance of k8s, k3s, and KubeEdge in adaptive and federated cloud infrastructures, particularly in disadvantaged tactical networks with limited bandwidth and high latency. They found KubeEdge's performance superior in maintaining cluster stability under degraded network conditions, emphasizing the significance of reliability in such environments.

3 Methodology

Experimental Setup. Test cluster: *Master Node:* Intel NUC (i7-10710U/64 GB DDR4/1 TB NVMe) device serving as the control plane. *Worker Nodes:* Three Raspberry Pi 4 Model B (4 GB) devices acting as resource-constrained edge nodes. *Auxiliary Node:* Intel NUC (i7-10710U/64 GB DDR4/1 TB NVMe) for data collection and storage. To minimize variables and focus on the KDs themselves, all devices were connected via LAN and configured with the same Ubuntu 22.04.2 making a closed system. More details are in the project's repository[6]. The KDs were installed and configured according to their official documentation.

Security Assessment (RQ1). For the security evaluation, we ran *kube-bench* on each distribution to assess compliance with the CIS Kubernetes Benchmark[7].

---

[5] https://kubeedge.io/.
[6] https://github.com/DiyazY/iot-edge/blob/main/src/diagrams/deployment_diagram-full-v3-colored.pdf.
[7] https://github.com/aquasecurity/kube-bench.

We developed a Security Score to quantify the compliance level, assigning criticality weights to each check and applying coefficients based on the test outcomes (PASS, WARN, FAIL).

Security Score: Calculated based on the weighted results from *kube-bench*, reflecting compliance with critical security benchmarks. To each security check a criticality weight[8] from 1 (Informational) to 5 (Critical) was assigned, reflecting the potential impact on the cluster's security. The outcome of each check was assigned a coefficient: PASS (1), WARN (0.5), and FAIL (−1). The Security Score for each distribution was calculated using the formula: Security Score = $(\sum CriticalityWeight * ResultCoefficient)/MaximumPossibleScore * 100\%$

Resiliency Assessment Under Network Outages (RQ2). To simulate network outages and evaluate resiliency, we conducted two types of tests: *1) Master Node Outage*: Temporarily disconnected the master node from the network for a fixed duration while workloads were running, then observed the cluster's behavior and recovery process. *2) Worker Node Outage*: Disconnected a worker node under similar conditions and monitored the impact on workloads and the node's reintegration into the cluster. *k-bench*[9] was used to generate workloads.

We used the following metrics to evaluate: *Recovery Time* - Time taken for the cluster to return to a fully operational state after a simulated outage. *Resource Utilization* - CPU, memory, network bandwidth, and disk I/O during outages and recovery phases. *netdata*[10] was used to monitor resource utilization. To ensure statistical significance, each test was repeated five times, and the results were averaged. Between tests, we allowed sufficient cool-down periods to stabilize the system and avoid carry-over effects. The test flow diagram and other tests results (idle, light and heavy load tests, long Network outage test) can be found in the project's repository[11].

Maintainability Evaluation (RQ3) was assessed by documenting the following: *Installation Complexity*: Recorded the time and steps required to install each distribution, noting any challenges encountered. *Configuration and Updates*: Evaluated the ease of configuring cluster components and performing updates or patches. *Operational Overhead*: Monitored the need for manual interventions during tests, such as node reboots or troubleshooting procedures.

The metrics include: *Setup Time* - Duration and complexity of initial installation. *Update Complexity* - Steps and time to apply updates or patches. *Manual Interventions* - Frequency and nature of required manual maintenance tasks.

---

[8] https://github.com/DiyazY/iot-edge/blob/main/src/kube-bench-results/final-reports/SECURITY.md.
[9] https://github.com/vmware-tanzu/k-bench.
[10] https://www.netdata.cloud/.
[11] https://github.com/DiyazY/iot-edge/blob/main/src/diagrams/test_flow-2nd.pdf.

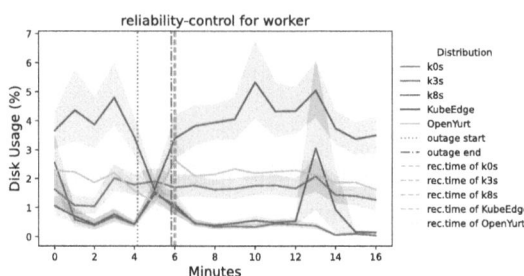

Fig. 1. Disk I/O usage on worker nodes during master node outage

4 Results

4.1 Security Assessment (RQ1)

Using the metrics defined in Sect. 3 the Security Scores for the evaluated distributions are as follows: k0s scored 23.69%, k3s scored 7.21%, and k8s, KubeEdge, and OpenYurt each scored 55.00%.

The results indicate that KDs based on the standard platform - such as k8s, KubeEdge, and OpenYurt—benefit from comprehensive default security configurations, leading to higher security compliance scores. In contrast, k0s and k3s, designed with a minimalist approach to optimize resource efficiency by omitting certain security features, achieve lower scores. Consequently, these lightweight distributions may require additional configuration and hardening to meet security best practices, especially in edge environments.

4.2 Resiliency Assessment (RQ2)

Master Node Outage, during the *reliability_control* test, the master node was disconnected for 100 s while workloads were running. Observations include: *Resource Utilization*: The failed master node exhibited increased network, CPU, and disk I/O usage, but decreased RAM usage. *Worker Nodes*: Network utilization increased, and disk I/O varied among distributions. *Disk I/O Behavior*: KubeEdge and OpenYurt decreased disk I/O usage on worker nodes during the outage, while k0s, k3s, and k8s showed increased disk I/O (Fig. 1).

Worker Node Outage, in the *reliability_worker* test, a random worker node was disconnected for 100 s. Key findings include: *Failed Worker Node*: Showed increased disk I/O and RAM utilization during the outage. *KubeEdge Behavior*: Demonstrated prolonged high disk I/O utilization after recovery and a delayed return to normal network usage compared to other distributions. *Network Utilization*: KubeEdge's network usage decreased during the outage and gradually increased upon recovery, suggesting message preservation and retransmission mechanisms. Figure 2 depicts disk I/O and Network usages in this case.

Additionally, KubeEdge exhibited a delayed completion of the *reliability_worker* test compared to other distributions, potentially due to its edge-specific features. If we examine the recovery times in Fig. 3, it is noticeable that

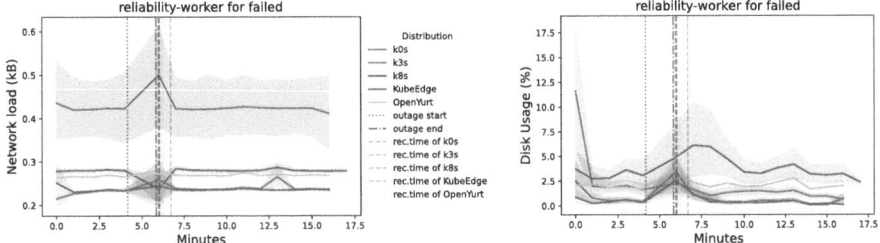

Fig. 2. Disk I/O (left) and Network (right) usages on failed worker node during outage

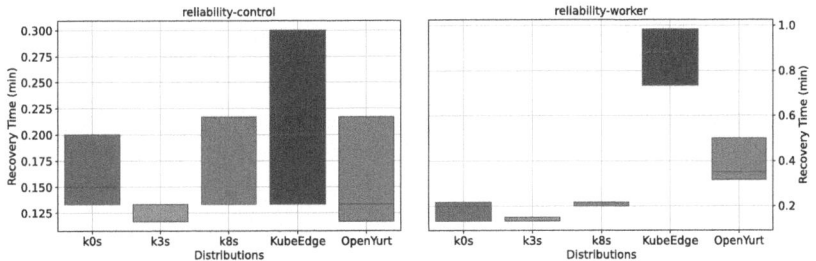

Fig. 3. Recovery Time: Master node unavailable (right), Worker node unavailable (left)

KubeEdge and OpenYurt have prolonged recovery times, which is particularly obvious in worker node outage scenarios since the workloads are running on worker nodes.

Analysis of Resiliency Findings, the observations suggest that KubeEdge and OpenYurt implement mechanisms to preserve messages during network outages, enhancing resiliency at the cost of increased resource consumption and longer recovery times. In contrast, k0s, k3s, and k8s show faster recovery and lower resource usage but may not preserve in-transit messages during outages.

4.3 Maintainability Assessment (RQ3)

Analysis of Maintainability Findings. Our maintainability assessment indicates that k0s and k3s offer superior ease of use and lower maintenance efforts, making them suitable for edge environments. In contrast, KubeEdge and OpenYurt, while providing advanced features for edge computing, introduce additional complexity that may challenge maintainability.

Tables 1 and 2 summarize the maintainability aspects of each distribution. Consistent with our observations, [1] emphasizes that differences in automation capabilities and day-2 operations management significantly impact the maintainability of KDs. These findings support the notion that while advanced features enhance functionality, they may negatively impact maintainability.

Table 1. Maintainability Comparison of Kubernetes Distributions

Distribution	Installation Effort (hours)	Update Process	Operational Overhead
k0s	Easy (3 h)	Simple, manual/automated	Low
k3s	Easy (2 h)	Simple, manual/automated	Low
k8s	Moderate (7 h)	Complex, manual	Moderate
KubeEdge	Difficult (14 h)	Complex, manual	High
OpenYurt	Difficult (14 h)	Complex, manual	High

Table 2. Maintainability Evaluation of Kubernetes Distributions

Installation and Setup	Configuration and Updates	Operational Overhead	Documentation and Community Support
k0s and k3s: Offered the simplest installation processes, with minimal steps and straightforward commands. Single-binary designs simplify deployment. *k8s*: Required more complex setup due to its modular components and configuration options. *KubeEdge and OpenYurt*: KubeEdge required separate installation of cloud and edge components, along with configuration of mesh communication network for node-to-node communication. OpenYurt needed to set up its edge autonomy features carefully.	*k0s and k3s*: Provided ease of configuration with sensible defaults. Updating these distributions was relatively straightforward, often involving simple commands or replacing the binary. *k8s*: Updates and configuration changes required careful planning to avoid disruptions, given its complexity and the potential impact on running services. *KubeEdge and OpenYurt*: Updates were more involved due to the additional components and dependencies. Configuration changes had to account for edge-specific features and potential connectivity issues.	*k0s and k3s*: Demonstrated high maintainability with minimal need for manual interventions during tests. Their resilience to restarts and system reboots reduced operational overhead. *k8s*: Required moderate maintenance efforts. While stable, the complexity of its components occasionally necessitated manual adjustments. *KubeEdge and OpenYurt*: Incurred higher operational overhead. For example, OpenYurt experienced networking issues after several test cycles, necessitating restarts and troubleshooting. KubeEdge's additional features increased the maintenance burden.	*k0s and k3s*: Benefited from active communities and comprehensive documentation, aiding in troubleshooting and maintenance tasks. *k8s*: As the standard KD, it has extensive resources and community support. *KubeEdge and OpenYurt*: While documentation exists, the specialized nature of these distributions means that community support is less extensive, potentially complicating maintenance. Moreover, many pages in the official documentation are marked as TBD (To Be Defined).

5 Discussion

While k3s and k0s demonstrate superior maintainability due to simplicity and ease of setup, they exhibit lower security compliance compared to k8s, KubeEdge, and OpenYurt. k8s and its edge-optimized variants provide better security by default but introduce extra complexity in deployment and maintenance. In terms of network outage resiliency, KubeEdge and OpenYurt exhibit unique behaviors aimed at preserving system state and ensuring message durability. This is evident in their resource utilization patterns during simulated outages, where they consume more disk I/O and exhibit delayed recovery times. These mechanisms enhance resiliency in intermittent network conditions common in edge environments but may impact performance and resource consumption. Maintainability assessments reveal that minimalist designs of k3s and k0s reduce operational overhead. In contrast, the added complexity of KubeEdge and OpenYurt necessitates more extensive maintenance.

6 Conclusion

This study analysed lightweight KDs, namely k0s, k3s, k8s, KubeEdge and OpenYurt, with a focus on security, resilience, and maintainability in edge computing environments. Our findings indicate that k3s and k0s excel in maintainability due to their simplicity and ease of deployment, making them suitable for resource-constrained edge settings where operational overhead must be minimized. However, they exhibit lower security compliance, highlighting the need for additional security configurations to meet best practices. KubeEdge and OpenYurt offer features tailored for edge computing and demonstrate higher security compliance and mechanisms to enhance resiliency under network outages. These benefits come at the cost of increased complexity and resource consumption, impacting maintainability and performance. The standard Kubernetes distribution (k8s) provides a balanced approach but may still be resource-intensive for some edge deployments. Selecting the appropriate distribution depends on the specific requirements and constraints of the deployment scenario, including the priority of security features, tolerance for complexity, and available resources for maintenance. Practitioners must carefully consider the trade-offs between security, resiliency, and maintainability to select a distribution that aligns with their operational needs. Future work on KDs should balance security and resource constraints without compromising maintainability, enhance automation to reduce operational overhead, explore adaptive resiliency mechanisms that balance performance and resource utilization under varying network conditions, standardize edge features to improve interoperability and ease of use, and finally, employ AI-driven agents for predictive maintenance. Likewise, future test suites should cover various outage and network saturation scenarios at a larger scale.

Acknowledgement. This work is supported by funding from Business Finland in project Industry X.

References

1. Kubernetes benchmarking study 2022. Technical report, humanitec (2022)
2. Fogli, M., et al.: Performance evaluation of kubernetes distributions (k8s, k3s, kubeedge) in an adaptive and federated cloud infrastructure for disadvantaged tactical networks. In: 2021 International Conference on Military Communication and Information Systems (ICMCIS), pp. 1–7. IEEE (2021)

3. Koziolek, H., Eskandani, N.: Lightweight kubernetes distributions: a performance comparison of microk8s, k3s, k0s, and microshift. In: ICPE 2023 - Proceedings of the 2023 ACM/SPEC International Conference on Performance Engineering, pp. 17–29. ACM, New York, NY, USA (2023)
4. Moreschini, S., Pecorelli, F., Li, X., Naz, S., Hästbacka, D., Taibi, D.: Cloud continuum: the definition. IEEE Access **10**, 131876–131886 (2022)
5. Ostinelli, N.K., Arzo, S.T., Granelli, F., Devetsikiotis, M.: Emulation of LTE/5G over a lightweight open-platform: re-configuration delay analysis. In: 2021 IEEE Global Communications Conference (GLOBECOM), pp. 01–06. IEEE (2021)
6. Pereira Ferreira, A., Sinnott, R.: A performance evaluation of containers running on managed kubernetes services. In: 2019 IEEE International Conference on Cloud Computing Technology and Science (CloudCom), pp. 199–208. IEEE (2019)
7. Truyen, E., Kratzke, N., Van Landuyt, D., Lagaisse, B., Joosen, W.: Managing feature compatibility in kubernetes: vendor comparison and analysis. IEEE Access **8**, 228420–228439 (2020)
8. Wang, Z., Goudarzi, M., Aryal, J., Buyya, R.: Container orchestration in edge and fog computing environments for real-time IoT applications. In: Buyya, R., Hernandez, S.M., Kovvur, R.M.R., Sarma, T.H. (eds.) Computational Intelligence and Data Analytics. LNDECT, pp. 1–21. Springer, Singapore (2023)
9. Yang, T., et al.: Kubeedge wireless for integrated communication and computing services everywhere. IEEE Wirel. Commun. **29**(2), 140–145 (2022)
10. Čilić, I., Krivić, P., Podnar Žarko, I., Kušek, M.: Performance evaluation of container orchestration tools in edge computing environments. Sensors (Basel, Switzerland) **23**(8), 4008 (2023)

Enhancing Failure Resilience of Cloud-Edge Microservices: The FREEDA Approach

Francisco Ponce[✉], Stefano Forti, Jacopo Soldani, and Antonio Brogi

University of Pisa, Pisa, Italy
francisco.ponce@di.unipi.it,
{stefano.forti,jacopo.soldani,antonio.brogi}@unipi.it

Abstract. FREEDA is an ongoing research project aimed at supporting DevOps engineers in achieving failure-resilient and sustainable deployments of microservice-based applications across the Cloud-Edge computing continuum. This paper first introduces the context and core concept of FREEDA, followed by a focus on how it enhances the failure resilience of microservices deployed across the Cloud-Edge continuum. Specifically, we present a declarative approach for generating deployment constraints designed to enhance the resilience of microservices prior to their deployment. Additionally, we introduce a proof-of-concept implementation and highlight its potential through an illustrative example.

Keywords: failure resilience · application deployment · placement constraints · cloud-edge · microservices

1 Introduction

The evolution of Cloud computing into large-scale, distributed Cloud-Edge environments is driven by the increasing capabilities of IoT devices and the need to reduce latency and fully exploit the capabilities of Edge computing [3]. This infrastructure is highly heterogeneous, with varying devices, protocols, and workloads, and faces dynamic changes and uncertainties like node failures and connectivity issues [9]. Microservice-based applications (MSAs), composed of small, loosely coupled components with specific functional and non-functional requirements, must account for these challenges to ensure QoS when deployed over a Cloud-Edge infrastructure. Additionally, deployment strategies must consider environmental sustainability, aligning with the European Union's goal of reducing carbon emissions of the IT industry.[1]

The FREEDA project [11] aims at enabling the environmentally sustainable and failure-resilient deployment of MSAs across Cloud-Edge infrastructures. To this end, FREEDA is developing the toolchain sketched in Fig. 1. The toolchain

---

[1] https://www.consilium.europa.eu/en/eu-strategic-agenda-2019-2024/.

plans the deployment D of an MSA A over the Cloud-Edge infrastructure I by balancing the services' hardware, software, cost, and sustainability requirements in R. The services forming A are available in multiple *flavours*, namely multiple different versions offering the same functionalities, but with different service quality levels and deployment requirements [4]. With such inputs, the leftmost part of the toolchain enriches the failure resilience and sustainability of the to-be-deployed MSA using historical data (H) from the last deployment of A on I (e.g., logs, node availability). Whilst the original set of requirements, denote hard requirements, the additional failure resilience/sustainability requirements denote soft requirements, meaning that the trade-off step will try to enforce them "best-effort". As a result, DevOps engineers will get a specification of the deployment D, together with an explanation E of why D was chosen as the "best trade-off" among the hard and soft deployment requirements.[2]

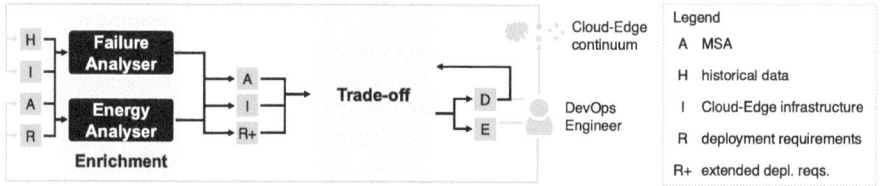

Fig. 1. Overview of FREEDA's approach [11]

In this paper, we focus on the enrichment step of the FREEDA toolchain, specifically on the ongoing research on failure analysis. Existing solutions generally focus on providing guidelines for designing/developing resilient MSAs [5,6] or on configuring deployment scripts to enable self-healing capabilities [2]. However, no existing approach supports analysing an MSA alongside the available Cloud-Edge infrastructure to enforce a failure-resilient deployment. Techniques for analyzing failures in MSAs primarily center on detecting failures and identifying their root causes [1,7,8,12]. While these methods can automatically pinpoint potential root causes of observed failures, they mainly return these causes alone, leaving DevOps engineers to manually inspect logs or monitored metrics to trace how the failure propagated to the observed state [9]. As a result, there remains a lack of automated solutions for analysing and enforcing the failure-resilient deployment of MSAs across the Cloud-Edge computing continuum.

The enrichment step of FREEDA addresses this challenge through the realisation of the failure analyser in Fig. 1, whose approach is presented in this paper. Building on the way in which service failure causalities are identified by root cause analysis tools like yRCA [10], and incorporating insights from infrastructure logs, our failure analyser generates soft constraints designed to enhance the resilience of MSA deployments. Specifically, we present a declarative method for

---

[2] A more detailed introduction to the FREEDA approach can be found in [11].

```
1   suggested(affinity(d(C,FC),d(S,FS))) :-
2       deployedTo(C,FC,N), deployedTo(S,FS,M), dif(C,S), dif(N,M),
3       timeoutEvent(C,S,T),
4       \+( congested(N,M,T); disconnected(N,T); disconnected(M,T) ).

5   suggested(avoid(d(C,FC),N)) :-
6       deployedTo(C,FC,N), deployedTo(S,_,M), dif(C,S), dif(N,M),
7       timeoutEvent(C,S,T),
8       ( congested(N,M,T); disconnected(N,T) ).

9   suggested(antiaffinity(d(C,FC),d(S,FS))) :-
10      deployedTo(C,FC,N),
11      ( unreachable(C,T); internal(C,T) ),
12      overloaded(N,R,T), race(N,R,C,FC,S,FS,T).

13  suggested(avoid(d(C,FC),N)) :-
14      deployedTo(C,FC,N),
15      ( unreachable(C,T); internal(C,T) ),
16      ( (overloaded(N,_,T), \+ race(N,_,C,FC,_,_,T)) ; disconnected(N,T) ).
```

Fig. 2. Example clauses for the suggested/1 predicate

generating these soft constraints, along with a Proof-of-Concept (PoC) implementation[3] and an illustrative example. The proposed approach includes an initial set of common-sense rules aimed at improving failure resilience. However, it is designed to be fully customisable, allowing application administrators to adapt the rules to different policies and contexts based on their specific needs.

The rest of this paper is organised as follows. Section 2 introduces the declarative method for enhancing failure resilience, which is then exemplified in Sect. 3. Section 4 concludes the paper by drawing concluding remarks.

2 Generating Soft Constraints for Failure Resilience

Knowledge Representation. The current MSA deployment information is denoted via facts like deployedTo(C,F,N), indicating that component C is deployed in its flavour F to node N. For instance, deployedTo(backend,medium,n2) states that the backend runs in its medium flavour on node n2. From an MSA failure perspective, we assume that timeout events between components C1 and C2 are denoted via timestamped facts like timeoutEvent(C1,C2,Timestamp). Besides, internal error and unreachability for a component C are denoted via facts like internal(C,Timestamp) and unreachable(C,Timestamp), respectively.

On the other hand, considering infrastructure logging, we assume that the predicate congested(N,M,T) identifies that link congestion between nodes N and M occurred at time T. Likewise, the predicate disconnected(N,T) holds true if node N incurred a network disconnection at time T. Predicate overloaded(N,R,T) denotes the situation in which a specific resource R (e.g., RAM, CPU, HDD) was

---
[3] PoC available at: https://github.com/FREEDA-Project/FailureEnhancer.

subject to overloading at time T. Last, predicate race(N,R,C,FC,S,FS,T) denotes a situation at time T in which components C (flavoured FC) and S (flavoured FS) were racing for resource R on the same node N.

Enhancing Failure Resilience. Based on the above, the reasoner in Fig. 2 is used to generate a set of suggested soft constraints to improve the resilience of the current deployment by embedding rules of thumb to improve placement decisions. Indeed, it finds all distinct suggested constraints by checking which clauses of predicate suggested/1 fire in the considered knowledge base. We here discuss four example clauses of such a predicate, noting, however, that they can be easily extended or refined to account for more MSA failures and/or network conditions as well as for different policies to enforce.

The first clause of suggested/1 (lines 1–4) identifies that an interaction between different components C (flavoured FC) and S (flavoured FS), deployed to two distinct nodes N and M, respectively (line 2), went through a timeout event (line 3), despite no congestion or disconnection events occurred (line 4). To avoid this from happening again, our reasoner suggests deploying C and S closer, by adding an affinity constraint between the two components in their current flavours, viz.,affinity(d(C,FC),d(S,SF)) (line 1). Indeed, timeouts can be mitigated by deploying interacting components on the same node.

The second clause of suggested/1 (lines 5–8) identifies that a timeout event at time T at component C in its flavour FC deployed to node N and involving component S deployed to a distinct node M (line 6), might have been caused by network congestion between N and M or by disconnection of node N (line 8). Our reasoner suggests avoiding placing C (flavoured FC) onto node N by including a node avoidance constraint, viz., avoid(d(C,FC),N) (line 5). Indeed, the link between nodes N and M might be continuously subject to congestion, or faulty. A symmetric clause (not shown) exists to handle the symmetric situation (i.e., congestion or disconnection of node M) by suggesting an avoid(d(S,FS),M) constraint.

The third clause of suggested/1 (lines 9–12) identifies that component C (flavoured FC), deployed to node N (line 10) was either unreachable or experiencing an internal error at time T (line 11). This failure overlapped with node N overloading of resource R, due to another component S (flavoured FS) racing with C for the resource R (line 12). Our reasoner suggests avoiding placing C and S onto the same node through an anti-affinity constraint between the two components in their current flavours, viz., antiaffinity(d(C,FC),d(S,SF)) (line 9). Indeed, this might prevent the components C and S from competing for resources.

The fourth clause of suggested/1 (lines 13–16) identifies component C deployed to N in its flavour FC (line 14) went through a failure event (line 15), which was possibly due to node overloading (in absence of a race) or disconnection (line 16). Our reasoner suggests avoiding to place C (flavoured FC) onto node N by including a node avoidance constraint, viz., avoid(d(C,FC),N) (line 13). Indeed, there might be some incompatibility between the component requirements and the node capabilities, or node hardware might be faulty.

3 Illustrative Example

Consider a sample MSA composed of three components, i.e., Frontend, Backend, and Database, each available in three different flavours, i.e., large, medium, and tiny. The last deployment for the MSA is depicted in Fig. 3a, with the Frontend deployed to node n1 with flavour large, and Backend and Database deployed to node n2 with flavours medium and large, respectively. Suppose now that during the last deployment, we monitored the failures in Fig. 3b. Namely, the Database becomes unreachable at time 6, the Backend experiences an internal failure at time 7, and a timeout expires at time 8 on Frontend while waiting for a reply from Backend. Additionally, node n1 suffers a disconnection in the time slots 4-6, node n2 encounters CPU overload in the time slots 5-9, and the communication between nodes n1 and n2 suffered from network congestion in the time slots 7-9.

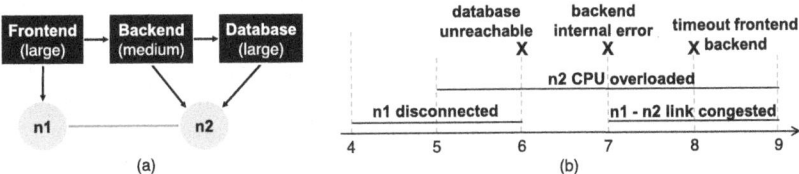

Fig. 3. Example of (a) MSA Deployment and (b) monitored events.

Our PoC identifies that (C1) Backend in medium flavour and Database in large flavour should be deployed to different nodes, to avoid them to race for/overload CPU resources. Constraints (C2) suggests avoiding the deployment of Frontend in flavour large on node n1, and also avoid Backend in flavour medium on node n2:

```
[ antiaffinity(d(backend, medium), d(database, large)),                    % (C1)
  avoid(d(frontend, large), n1), avoid(d(backend, medium), n2)]            % (C2)
```

Akin constraints would have been obtained if reasoning solely at the component level (rather than at the finer level of component flavours). However, this would result in only one possible choice for the new deployment, namely, deploying Frontend and Database to node n2, and deploying Backend to node n1. This limitation reduces the search space in which FREEDA can find the "best tradeoff" between the hard requirements and the newly introduced soft requirements, potentially leading to some soft requirements being dropped. This is because the only available solution may not satisfy all constraints (e.g., the resources available on n1 may not suffice to meet the hard requirements of the Backend).

Instead, by incorporating component flavours into the reasoning process, the soft constraints generated by the reasoner become more fine-grained. For example, the avoidance constraint is tied specifically to the large flavour of Frontend, which makes it possible to keep the Frontend on n1 by deploying it in a different flavour, such as medium or tiny. Such a finer granularity provides more flexibility for FREEDA to identify the "best trade-off" among the hard and soft requirements, yet relying on the latter to narrow the search space and avoid the very same failures from happening again in the upcoming MSA deployment.

4 Conclusions

We have introduced the FREEDA approach for enhancing the failure resilience of MSAs deployed across the Cloud-Edge computing continuum. Specifically, we have presented a declarative approach for generating deployment constraints designed to enhance the resilience of microservices prior to their deployment. We have also introduced a PoC implementation of the proposed approach and showcased it through an illustrative example. Future work includes realising the (overall) FREEDA approach and assessing it through case studies based on benchmarking MSAs and Cloud-Edge testbeds.

Acknowledgements. . This work was partly supported by the projects *FREEDA* (CUP: I53D23003550006), funded by PRIN (MUR, Italy) and Next Generation EU, and by UNIPI PRA 2022 64 "OSMWARE", funded by the University of Pisa.

References

1. Aggarwal, P., et al.: Localization of operational faults in cloud applications by mining causal dependencies in logs using golden signals. In: Hacid, H., et al. (eds.) ICSOC 2020. LNCS, vol. 12632, pp. 137–149. Springer, Cham (2021). https://doi.org/10.1007/978-3-030-76352-7_17
2. Brogi, A., et al.: Self-healing trans-cloud applications. Computing **104**(4), 809–833 (2022). https://doi.org/10.1007/S00607-021-00977-Z
3. Ferrer, A.J., et al.: Towards the decentralised cloud: survey on approaches and challenges for mobile, ad hoc, and edge computing. ACM Comput. Surv. **51**(6), 1–36 (2019). https://doi.org/10.1145/3243929
4. Forti, S., Brogi, A.: Declarative osmotic application placement. In: Polyvyanyy, A., Rinderle-Ma, S. (eds.) CAiSE 2021. LNBIP, vol. 423, pp. 177–190. Springer, Cham (2021). https://doi.org/10.1007/978-3-030-79022-6_15
5. Giedrimas, V., Omanovic, S., Alic, D.: The aspect of resilience in microservices-based software design. In: Mazzara, M., Ober, I., Salaün, G. (eds.) STAF 2018. LNCS, vol. 11176, pp. 589–595. Springer, Cham (2018). https://doi.org/10.1007/978-3-030-04771-9_44
6. Heorhiadi, V., et al.: Gremlin: systematic resilience testing of microservices. In: ICDCS 2016, pp. 57–66. IEEE (2016). https://doi.org/10.1109/ICDCS.2016.11
7. Liu, P., et al.: Unsupervised detection of microservice trace anomalies through service-level deep Bayesian networks. In: ISSRE 2020, pp. 48–58. IEEE (2020). https://doi.org/10.1109/ISSRE5003.2020.00014
8. Meng, Y., et al.: Localizing failure root causes in a microservice through causality inference. In: IWQoS 2020, pp. 1–10. IEEE (2020). https://doi.org/10.1109/IWQOS49365.2020.9213058

9. Soldani, J., Brogi, A.: Anomaly detection and failure root cause analysis in (micro) service-based cloud applications: a survey. ACM Comput. Surv. **55**(3), 59:1–59:39 (2023). https://doi.org/10.1145/3501297
10. Soldani, J., et al.: yRCA: an explainable failure root cause analyser. Sci. Comput. Program. **230**, 102997 (2023). https://doi.org/10.1016/j.scico.2023.102997
11. Soldani, J., et al.: Towards sustainable deployment of microservices over the cloud-IoT continuum, with FREEDA. In: FRAME 2024, pp. 1–4. ACM (2024). https://doi.org/10.1145/3659994.3660311
12. Wu, L., et al.: MicroRCA: root cause localization of performance issues in microservices. In: NOMS 2020, pp. 1–9. IEEE (2020). https://doi.org/10.1109/NOMS47738.2020.9110353

ML-Based Performance Modeling in Edge FaaS Systems

Federica Filippini[✉][iD], Luca Cavenaghi[iD], Nicolas Calmi[iD], Marco Savi[iD], and Michele Ciavotta[iD]

University of Milano-Bicocca, Milan, Italy
{federica.filippini,luca.cavenaghi,nicolas.calmi,
marco.savi,michele.ciavotta}@unimib.it

Abstract. The Function as a Service (FaaS) model is becoming increasingly attractive for both cloud and edge computing scenarios, offering a solution where self-contained functions are executed in response to specific events. In this model, the complexities of load balancing and scaling are handled by the service providers. However, accurate resource consumption estimates are crucial in FaaS-enabled clusters, especially at the edge, to optimize resource efficiency, minimize latency, prevent overloads, and ensure scalability. This work focuses on performance modeling within FaaS-enabled distributed and decentralized edge environments, at both the node and function levels. Using a Machine Learning (ML)-based approach, we propose a framework to predict key performance metrics, such as CPU usage, memory, and energy consumption. Additionally, we forecast potential system overloads based on the incoming load. By introducing a profiling tool that characterizes functions by their resource usage patterns, prediction of node-level resource consumption without needing detailed function-level knowledge is made possible. Experimental results show that our models achieve 97% accuracy in predicting node overloads.

Keywords: Function as a Service · Performance Modeling · Machine Learning · Edge Computing

1 Introduction

Function as a Service (FaaS) [18] constitutes a major innovation in cloud computing, offering a scalable and event-driven model for managing computational resources. In this model, self-contained code units (functions) are triggered by specific events or requests. By offloading complexities such as resource management, load balancing, and automatic scaling to service providers, developers can focus solely on application logic. Consequently, FaaS is becoming an increasingly

---

This work was partially supported by the European Union - Next Generation EU under the Italian National Recovery and Resilience Plan (NRRP), Mission 4, Component 2, Investment 1.3, CUP E83C22004640001, partnership on "Telecommunications of the Future" (PE00000001 - program "RESTART").

ⓒ IFIP International Federation for Information Processing 2025
Published by Springer Nature Switzerland AG 2025
C. Pahl et al. (Eds.): ESOCC 2025, LNCS 15547, pp. 112–127, 2025.
https://doi.org/10.1007/978-3-031-84617-5_10

attractive solution, not only in cloud environments but also in edge computing scenarios [4].

Balancing user expectations for Quality of Service (QoS) with minimizing operational costs remains a complex challenge [20]. While accurate performance models are instrumental in optimizing resource management, they also reduce operational costs and ensure responsiveness, particularly in FaaS-enabled clusters where workload patterns fluctuate dynamically [11]. Furthermore, accurate prediction of system metrics plays a critical role in load-balancing algorithms, which are central to managing decentralized FaaS environments at the edge [5]. This becomes especially relevant in serverless edge platforms, which consist of geo-distributed nodes that need to cooperate to handle user requests efficiently, given their constrained resources [2]. Although extensive benchmarking has characterized the resource consumption of serverless clusters (e.g., [3,4]), effective forecasting methods remain unavailable.

This work proposes a Machine Learning *(ML)-based framework* to predict critical performance metrics (e.g., CPU usage, memory usage, and energy consumption) for functions and computing nodes, with a particular emphasis on deployments in resource-constrained edge environments. Our models forecast the system overload status based on the incoming load at both node and function levels, which is crucial to prevent service interruptions. Additionally, we developed a profiling and classification tool that clusters functions according to their resource usage patterns. Leveraging this, we can train models adopting a group-based approach rather than focusing on individual functions. This significantly enhances generality, as the resource consumption of edge nodes can be predicted without knowing details about the individual deployed functions.

The experimental validation of our models demonstrates high predictive accuracy; in particular, the node overload forecast achieves a global accuracy of 97%. Furthermore, we demonstrate the effectiveness of function profiling on predicting node-level performance.

The remainder of this paper is organized as follows: Sect. 2 reviews the state of the art in performance modeling for FaaS systems. Section 3 presents our proposed framework, covering the data collection process, the development of the profiling and classification tool, and model generation. Finally, Sects. 4 and 5 present experimental validation and conclude the paper.

2 Related Work

The development of analytical or ML-based models to predict the performance of applications running on edge and cloud systems is gaining momentum in the research landscape. However, recent works related to resource usage forecasting in the edge or cloud mostly consider general or microservice workflows [6,15], while those with a specific focus on serverless platforms and FaaS usually target the prediction of the incoming workload or the average latency, or characterize mechanisms related to the containers warm and cold start [8,10,13]. To the best of the authors' knowledge, considerations on the resource usage are mostly left to benchmarking suites [3,4,14,21], often tailoring cloud serverless platform.

In particular, [6] proposes μP, a microservices development framework that enables the prediction of response times and other metrics related to the utilization of microservices *by design*, leveraging Layered Queuing Networks. The work in [15] focuses on both the short- and long-term prediction of resource usage in the cloud, through a self-adapting data-driven system that automatically selects the optimal ML-based prediction algorithm according to a preliminary load analysis, and leverages the usage forecasts to plan the resource provisioning and perform scaling actions. Differently, [7] proposes a framework to predict the performance degradation of microservices based on the type and amount of incoming requests, to be used for a proactive management of cloud-based applications; in particular, the framework supports the adoption of black-box ML models for the regression of general performance metrics.

Authors in [8] exploit the Seasonal Auto Regressive Integrated Moving Average time series forecasting model to predict the arrival time of new requests, used to guide the decisions of a prediction-based autoscaler. The end-to-end response time and the execution costs of serverless functions are targeted by [10], which proposes an analytical model based on the characterization of delays and transition probabilities in a complex workflow, represented as a directed graph including cycles, self-loops, loops and parallel paths. An analytical performance model is developed also in [13] under the assumption of Poisson request arrivals; based on the incoming workload, authors characterize system metrics as, e.g., the rate of cold and warm starts, the probability of rejections, the average response time and the mean utilization of active resources.

3 Proposed Framework

This work aims to improve load management frameworks in decentralized FaaS environments at the edge [2]. In these settings, decision-making agents, utilizing algorithms such as heuristics [5] and Reinforcement Learning [16], dynamically determine the proportion of incoming requests that can be processed locally, offloaded, or rejected based on the predicted state of the computing node.

Load balancing frameworks usually realize a decision pipeline exploiting three integrated modules (see Fig. 1): the first one focuses on forecasting the upcoming workload for each agent; the second one predicts the resource consumption and the overall node operational state based on the expected load, providing essential context for the agent to make informed traffic management decisions. Finally, the third module realizes intelligent workload distribution strategies, using the output of the previous components to optimize performance.

The framework we introduce in this paper, which is openly available on GitHub[1], serves as the second module in this pipeline. Its importance in developing effective load management strategies can be illustrated through an example based on the simple *Static Strategy* proposed in [2], where a fixed threshold is used to determine when the request load exceeds capacity for each function, without considering the overall node state. Imagine, e.g., two functions, f_1 and

---

[1] https://github.com/unimib-datAI/dfaas/tree/main/metrics_predictions.

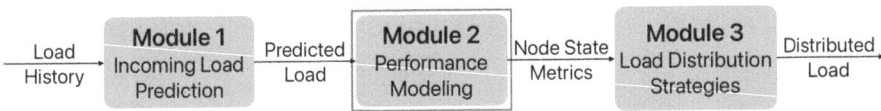

Fig. 1. Decision pipeline for a FaaS workload management framework

f_2, deployed on the same node, with load thresholds of 50 req/s and 60 req/s, respectively. Without appropriate performance models, the node would be seen as capable of handling the load if f_1 and f_2 receive exactly 50 and 60 req/s. However, the system would flag the node as overloaded if f_1 received 51 req/s, even if f_2 is idle at 0 req/s, thus leaving resources unutilized.

This example reveals the limitations of a static approach and suggests that a more advanced load-balancing algorithm could utilize node-wide resource estimation, rather than focusing on individual functions.

3.1 Framework Architecture

As depicted in Fig. 2, our framework carries out three primary operations. The first is *data collection*, in which the *Samples Generator* executes load tests on one or more functions, collecting performance metrics from both individual nodes and functions. The second operation is *model development*, where i) the *Function Profiler* builds an unsupervised clustering model to group functions according to their resource usage patterns; ii) the *System Forecaster* trains and evaluates a range of regression and classification models to predict performance metrics and system overload conditions, either for individual functions or groups identified by the *Function Profiler*. Both operations are typically performed once during the initial deployment of a new function on a node. However, they may also be periodically executed to update and maintain the prediction accuracy of the models. Finally, in the *inference* phase, the *Profile Predictor* component utilizes the classification model developed by the *Function Profiler*. It profiles newly-deployed functions and assigns them to the most appropriate cluster, selecting the relevant prediction models for estimating function performance. The next sections provide a detailed description of the framework components and how the performance models are generated.

3.2 Data Collection

This section outlines our designed process for collecting the data necessary to train our ML-based performance models. The data collection is carried out by the *Samples Generator* component, which generates synthetic traffic directed at the functions deployed on the target node and gathers metrics that characterize the system's state. In the following subsections, we detail the considered performance metrics and provide a detailed breakdown of the data collection process.

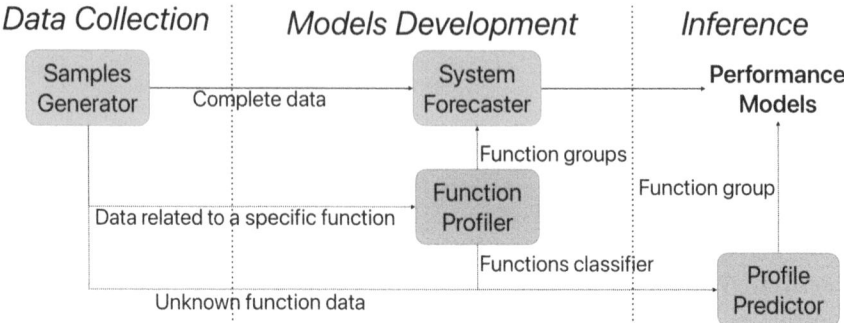

Fig. 2. Architecture of the proposed framework

Performance Metrics. Throughout the load tests, the *Samples Generator* collects relevant metrics at both the node and function levels. The temporal resolution for data collection (scraping) is set through suitable parameters, among which a frequency, denoted by T_{scrape}, whose value must be adequately chosen to avoid increasing the data collection overhead, but at the same time capture important variations in the monitored values. We collect the following metrics:

- *Per-node CPU utilization* (CPU_n): the percentage of used CPU on a node n, obtained as the sum of the percentages used by the individual cores (if, e.g., there are 4 CPU cores on n, CPU_n can vary between 0% and 400%).
- *Per-node memory utilization* (RAM_n): the value (in Bytes) of RAM used on n in the specified time interval, computed as the average difference between the node total memory and the available RAM.
- *Per-node power consumption* (Π_n) : Node energy consumption can be measured by external devices (e.g., wattmeters) or through software exporters. Although the first one provides higher accuracy, we followed the second approach as it allows to monitor also individual functions.
- *Number of function replicas* (ρ_f) *and CPU* (cpu_f), *memory* (ram_f), *and power consumption* (π_f) : To monitor the resource consumption of a function f, we first identify its replicas. Their number ρ_f is an important parameter to characterize the system response to workload changes. Moreover, cpu_f, ram_f and π_f are computed as a sum of utilization values of functions' containers.
- *Functions success rate and average latency* (s_f and l_f) : These metrics express the percentage of requests that receive a positive response and quantify the average time it takes for a request to be served, respectively.

Data Collection Process. The *Samples Generator* designs and runs load tests according to user-specified parameters, that is, the list of functions to consider, the maximum number of requests per second that each function can receive, and the overall duration of the test session. The generated scenarios aim to replicate various traffic conditions.

Each testing configuration defines a specific simulation scenario, which is typically repeated multiple times to ensure consistency of the results and minimize the incidence of anomalies in the collected data. It defines, for each function, the number of requests per second this will receive throughout the simulation. The list of potential traffic volumes is obtained by starting from a load of 0 req/s and incrementing it by a fixed unit until reaching the maximum value.

Baseline values $\overline{CPU}_n$, $\overline{RAM}_n$ and $\overline{\Pi}_n$ are collected while the system is not yet engaged in any activity, to be used as reference in the rest of the analysis. Then, the *Samples Generator* loops over the set of configurations and starts the load testing phase, generating synthetic traffic as each configuration specifies.

After each iteration of load testing is completed, the *Samples Generator* assesses the state of the target node and its functions. Accurately identifying when a computing node is overloaded enables resource optimization and the maintenance of high system performance, thereby preventing potential bottlenecks and service degradation. This is particularly important in distributed Function as a Service (FaaS) contexts, where the system state significantly influences critical decisions, such as load balancing among nodes [5].

Assessing the overload state Σ_n of a node n requires analyzing a set of key metrics that overall reflect the health of the system. In particular, we assign $\Sigma_n = 1$ (overloaded state) when one or more of the following conditions are met:

- $\frac{1}{|F_n|} \sum_{f \in F_n} s_f < 95\%$, where F_n is the set of functions deployed on n. This indicates that the functions struggle in handling incoming requests, potentially due to resource constraints or configuration issues.
- $CPU_n > 80\%$. This threshold is chosen to leave enough processing power to handle sudden spikes in load without degrading performance.
- $RAM_n > 80\%$. As for the CPU, this guarantees a buffer for peak demand and for caching and process management operations.
- At least one function deployed on the node is *overloaded*. We define a function f as overloaded if $s_f < 90\%$.[2] This condition recognizes that even a single function can have a significant impact on the overall node performance and the offered QoS.

These threshold values result from an empirical experimentation: we observed that exceeding them correlates with a significant performance decay (e.g., $RAM_n > 80\%$ may lead to swapping and potential service interruptions).

At the conclusion of each test iteration, a cool-down period is initiated to allow the system to return to its *baseline* state before additional load tests are performed. This process guarantees that subsequent measurements are obtained under standardized and comparable conditions. The duration of the cool-down period, denoted as $T_{cooldown}$, is determined based on the following criteria: i) the current CPU, RAM, and power consumption metrics must differ from their

---

[2] The threshold is chosen to ensure a high standard of reliability; while its value can be easily adjusted in different scenarios, we considered that the success rate of a functions workflow in AWS drops below 70% if the average s_f is 85%, and below 20% if it is 75% [19].

baseline values, recorded before the start of the experiments, by no more than 15%; ii) the number of replicas per function in the cluster must remain fewer than 2. These threshold values were derived empirically to ensure that the system fully returns to baseline conditions while avoiding unnecessary extensions to the overall simulation time.

3.3 Function Profiling and Clustering

Function profiling plays a critical role in the framework by enabling performance models that consider function classes, rather than individual functions, to estimate system states. The rationale is that when a new function is deployed on a node, it only needs to be profiled by the *Function Profiler* and assigned to the most appropriate class by the *Profile Predictor* component, eliminating the need to retrain the models.

The *Function Profiler* component leverages collected metrics to profile individual functions by encoding their patterns of resources consumption as vectors of real numbers. These function profiles are then analyzed to identify clusters of similar behavior. In more detail, the *Function Profiler* performs a linear rescaling of each metric to the [0, 1] range using the *MinMax* technique, then calculates a triplet of statistics—average, minimum, and maximum—for each metric and load value assessed during testing. These triplets are concatenated to construct a feature vector, denoted as v. The dimensionality of v is subsequently reduced via Principal Component Analysis (PCA) [12], which performs a linear transformation to project the input data into a latent space, capturing the directions of maximum variance[3]. As a result, a compact and representative feature vector v' is obtained, retaining all significant characteristics of the original metrics.

To automatically define performance classes, an unsupervised clustering model is then trained using the components of the dense vector v' as features, leveraging the K-Means algorithm[4]. The optimal number of clusters k is initially estimated using the *elbow* method. However, while informative, this heuristic does not guarantee the selection of the optimal k in all scenarios. To improve the selection process, our framework refines k by evaluating the performance of models trained on function groups derived from values near k_e (e.g., $k_e + 1$ or the subsequent elbow). Limiting this analysis to a narrow range of k values ensures a balance between model accuracy and the computational efficiency of the process.

---

[3] In the experiments detailed here, the variance threshold was set at 95%, a value selected to balance the retention of pertinent information with computational efficiency.

[4] We note that other implementations of the proposed framework are possible, e.g., PCA could be easily replaced by neural manifold fitting techniques and K-means by Density Based Clustering.

3.4 Model Development

This section describes the *System Forecaster*, which is responsible for training and comparing machine learning (ML) models to predict the performance of functions and computing nodes. The main features that are considered in the process are the incoming load of each individual function (or functions class), and the node type where the functions are deployed, which depends on its hardware characteristics (see Sect. 4.1). The target variables to predict are the performance metrics outlined in Sect. 3.2, such as CPU_n, RAM_n, Π_n, cpu_f, ram_f, π_f, Σ_n, and l_f. A distinct model is created for each target variable, as detailed below; these independent models can then be assembled into a coherent system that, as a whole, works as a single holistic model.

With minimal adjustments to data preparation, the *System Forecaster* follows basically the same approach for both individual functions and function classes. The only difference consists in an initial data aggregation step performed for each metric when considering function classes: the *System Forecaster* i) computes the total incoming load, CPU_g, RAM_g, and Π_g, summing corresponding values (e.g., cpu_f) across all functions in the group g; ii) assigns $\Sigma_g = 1$ if at least one function is overloaded; and iii) calculates the latency L_g as the average l_f across all functions in g. Metrics at the node level (e.g., CPU_n) remain unchanged since the total number of deployed functions per node does not vary.

Data are always preprocessed to remove outliers, and the Synthetic Minority Over-sampling Technique (SMOTE) [1] is applied to imbalanced target variables, generating synthetic data for minority classes. Then, data are normalized using the *MinMax* technique and randomly split into training and test sets.

An initial model selection phase can be performed by the *System Forecaster* exploiting AutoGluon[5], an open-source AutoML tool that automates the search for optimal ML algorithms and hyperparameters. In our context, AutoGluon identified Gradient Boosting, implemented through LightGBM (LGBM) [9], as the most efficient model due to its decision tree-based structure. Therefore, in this study we adopted LGBM-Classifier for discrete variables (e.g., the node state Σ_n) and LGBM-Regressor for continuous variables.

Gradient Boosting supports both standard and quantile regression [22], the latter being a statistical method that estimates the α-quantile of a dependent variable. Quantile regression is particularly relevant in performance prediction, as it allows for more robust interpretation in critical scenarios. For instance, by using the 0.95-quantile, we estimate a resource consumption threshold such that 95% of actual values are expected to fall below it. This is highly beneficial in cases where overestimating resource usage can help mitigate the risk of forwarding requests to overloaded nodes, thereby enhancing overall system efficiency.

The quantile regression model uses the *quantile loss function*, denoted as $\mathcal{L}_Q$, to adjust model weights, unlike standard regression, which uses Mean Squared Error (MSE). In, e.g., 0.95-quantile regression, errors where observations exceed the forecast are penalized less than those below the forecast.

---

[5] https://auto.gluon.ai/stable/index.html

4 Experimental Analysis

This section details the setup (see Sect. 4.1) and results (see Sect. 4.2) of the experiments carried out to evaluate the accuracy of the trained models and the impact of the function clustering approach.

4.1 Experimental Setup

The framework was tested using OpenFaaS[6] platform and Prometheus[7] as the metrics collection system. NodeExporter[8], cAdvisor[9] and Scaphandre[10] exporters were integrated to collect performance metrics, both at the node and individual function level. Load is injected through Vegeta[11], a tool that can generate a configurable flow of HTTP requests targeting specific endpoints. Note that, despite the choice of exploiting OpenFaaS for our experiments, the framework we propose is agnostic to the specific platform, as long as they enable the integration with the aforementioned metrics exporters.

We selected six functions with diverse resource requirements for our study. Five of these functions—`figlet`, `shasum`, `env`, `nmap`, and `curl`—were sourced from OpenFaaS's function repository, with no access to their source code. The remaining function, `eat-memory`, was specifically developed for this research, allowing us to investigate the cluster's behavior using a function with well-known internal characteristics. Specifically, `eat-memory` allocates 1 MB of memory and induces a 1-second delay.

Finally, we evaluated three distinct types of computing nodes, selected to align with common configurations used in edge network architectures [17]. Specifically, we instantiated three virtual machines (VMs) as follows: a *light* node with 2 CPUs and 8 GB of RAM, a *mid* node with 4 CPUs and 16 GB of RAM, and a *heavy* node with 6 CPUs and 24 GB of RAM. These configurations were designed to provide a comprehensive perspective on potential edge network setups, facilitating an assessment of architectural efficiency relative to the available computational resources. All VMs were hosted on a server running Linux Ubuntu 22.04, equipped with 8 CPUs and 32 GB of RAM. However, each VM was instantiated and tested in isolation to avoid interferences that could compromise the accuracy of the experimental results.

4.2 Experimental Results

This section presents the experimental results of our study. Specifically, we provide a preliminary comparison of performance metrics measured across various functions to uncover distinct patterns that motivate our work.

---

[6] https://docs.openfaas.com/.
[7] https://prometheus.io/.
[8] https://github.com/prometheus/node_exporter.
[9] https://github.com/google/cadvisor.
[10] https://hubblo-org.github.io/scaphandre-documentation/index.html.
[11] https://github.com/tsenart/vegeta.

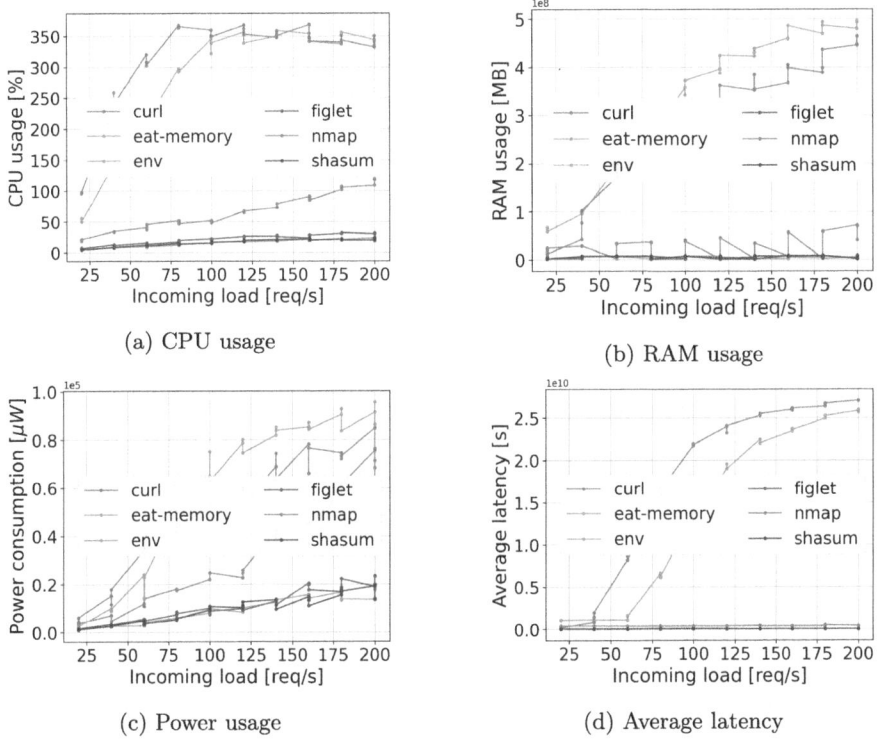

Fig. 3. Performance metrics of different functions

We then analyze the impact of the number of function clusters k. With $k = 3$ determined as the optimal value, we assess the accuracy of our performance models. Regression models are evaluated using Mean Squared Error (MSE), Root Mean Squared Error (RMSE), R^2 score, and standard deviation, while classification models are assessed in terms of precision, recall, and F1-score. We considered both standard and quantile regression, with α set to 0.05 and 0.95. Finally, we assess how training ML models on function classes allows to effectively predict node-level performance metrics, even without knowing details on the individual deployed functions.

Preliminary Comparison of Per-Function Performance Metrics. This section provides a preliminary overview of the resource usage and latency patterns for the different functions listed in Sect. 4.1. Observing the plots in Fig. 3, an initial intuitive subdivision into three distinct clusters emerges.

In particular, the eat-memory and nmap functions show similar behaviors for all metrics, as do figlet, shasum and env. On the other hand, the curl function is characterized by metric patterns that are clearly different from the others, with the only exception of the average latency in Fig. 3d.

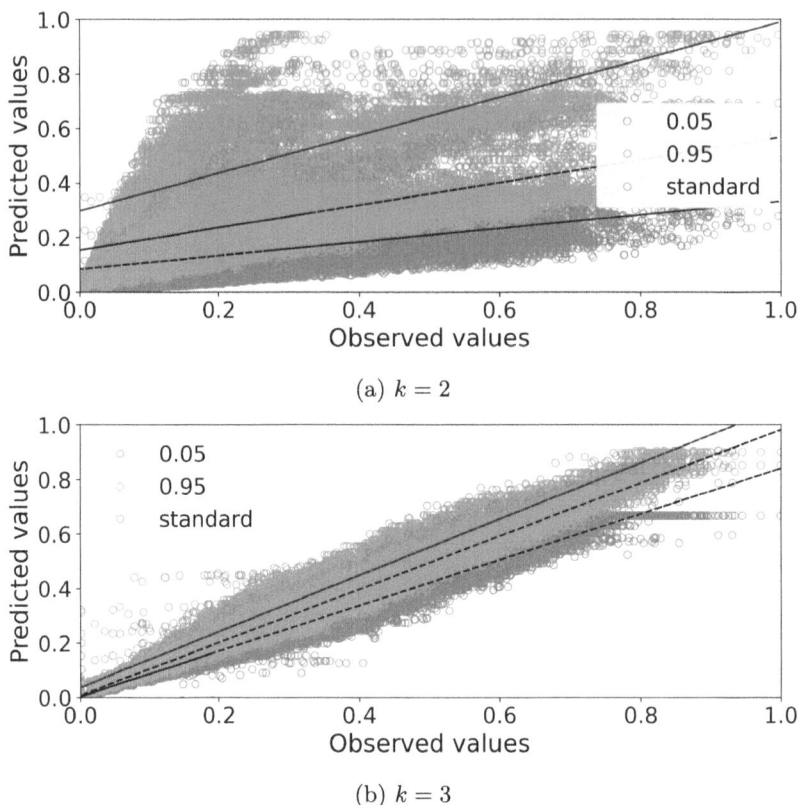

Fig. 4. Prediction results for the CPU usage in the *lu* cluster

This behavioral variety suggests that it is not possible to define a clear and univocal separation into function classes through a purely visual analysis, which motivates the development of an automated clustering model. Moreover, the unexpected behavior of eat-memory in consuming significant CPU resources and energy underscores the importance of developing performance prediction models, even for functions where static analysis of available source code could potentially be used to estimate resource consumption.

Optimal Cluster Selection (k). Due to the limited number of functions we considered in this analysis, the choice of the most appropriate number of classes k was made by directly evaluating the predictive performance of our models on the classes identified by varying k between 2 and 6.

The best results are obtained for $k = 2$ and $k = 3$. When setting $k = 2$ or $k = 3$, the clustering process identified: i) a *high-usage* (hu) functions class, which includes eat-memory and nmap, and ii) a *low-usage* (lu) functions class consistently containing env, figlet, and shasum. Additionally, for $k = 2$, the

Table 1. Prediction results for different metrics and regression models

	Metric	Model type	MSE	RMSE	stddev.	R^2	$\mathcal{L}_Q$	$P > R$	$R \leq P$
function class	$CPU_h u$	standard regression	0.0004	0.0208	0.1880	0.99	-	-	-
		0.05-quantile regression	0.0023	0.0478	0.1570	0.94	0.0012	1.80%	98.2%
		0.95-quantile regression	0.0011	0.0334	0.2064	0.97	0.0009	96.75%	3.25%
	$CPU_m u$	standard regression	0.0002	0.0149	0.2004	0.99	-	-	-
		0.05-quantile regression	0.0023	0.0481	0.1672	0.94	0.0011	2.06%	97.94%
		0.95-quantile regression	0.0009	0.0294	0.2197	0.98	0.0009	97.64%	2.36%
	$CPU_l u$	standard regression	0.0009	0.0305	0.1938	0.98	-	-	-
		0.05-quantile regression	0.0040	0.0632	0.1675	0.90	0.0027	8.14%	91.86%
		0.95-quantile regression	0.0035	0.0589	0.2052	0.91	0.0027	95.52%	4.48%
node	CPU_n	standard regression	0.0008	0.0288	0.1808	0.98	-	-	-
		0.05-quantile regression	0.0048	0.0689	0.1467	0.86	0.0027	4.64%	95.36%
		0.95-quantile regression	0.0033	0.0574	0.1952	0.90	0.0027	95.11%	4.89%
function class	$RAM_h u$	standard regression	0.0076	0.0874	0.1122	0.62	-	-	-
		0.05-quantile regression	0.0193	0.1390	0.0391	0.03	0.0029	1.94%	98.06%
		0.95-quantile regression	0.0307	0.1753	0.2182	−0.55	0.0042	98.01%	1.99%
	$RAM_m u$	standard regression	0.0231	0.1519	0.1609	0.53	-	-	-
		0.05-quantile regression	0.0610	0.2469	0.0107	−0.23	0.0056	2.38%	97.62%
		0.95-quantile regression	0.0688	0.2623	0.3115	−0.39	0.0075	97.70%	2.30%
	$RAM_l u$	standard regression	0.0073	0.0856	0.0947	0.55	-	-	-
		0.05-quantile regression	0.0180	0.1340	0.0432	−0.11	0.0042	8.38%	91.62%
		0.95-quantile regression	0.0304	0.1742	0.1662	−0.88	0.0095	94.70%	5.30%
node	RAM_n	standard regression	0.0042	0.0649	0.1159	0.76	-	-	-
		0.05-quantile regression	0.0225	0.1499	0.1171	−0.27	0.0069	5.05%	94.95%
		0.95-quantile regression	0.0102	0.1010	0.1237	0.43	0.0045	94.86%	5.14%
function class	$\Pi_h u$	standard regression	0.0004	0.0203	0.1498	0.98	-	-	-
		0.05-quantile regression	0.0019	0.0432	0.1205	0.92	0.0011	1.81%	98.19%
		0.95-quantile regression	0.0013	0.0367	0.1737	0.94	0.0011	96.27%	3.73%
	$\Pi_m u$	standard regression	0.0006	0.0237	0.15160	0.98	-	-	-
		0.05-quantile regression	0.0022	0.0464	0.1197	0.91	0.0013	2.34%	97.66%
		0.95-quantile regression	0.0020	0.0453	0.1835	0.91	0.0014	97.61%	2.39%
	$\Pi_l u$	standard regression	0.0018	0.0427	0.1683	0.94	-	-	-
		0.05-quantile regression	0.0064	0.0797	0.1310	0.79	0.0033	8.77%	91.23%
		0.95-quantile regression	0.0081	0.0900	0.2116	0.73	0.0039	95.04%	4.96%
node	Π_n	standard regression	0.0015	0.0388	0.1391	0.93	-	-	-
		0.05-quantile regression	0.0057	0.0754	0.1113	0.73	0.0033	5.34%	94.66%
		0.95-quantile regression	0.0055	0.0743	0.1633	0.74	0.0035	95.34%	4.66%
function class	$L_h u$	standard regression	0.0022	0.0464	0.1923	0.95	-	-	-
		0.05-quantile regression	0.0139	0.1179	0.1136	0.65	0.0024	1.62%	98.38%
		0.95-quantile regression	0.0090	0.0951	0.2394	0.77	0.0023	98.30%	1.70%
	$L_m u$	standard regression	0.0004	0.0192	0.1677	0.99	-	-	-
		0.05-quantile regression	0.0154	0.1239	0.0631	0.46	0.0021	2.14%	97.86%
		0.95-quantile regression	0.0030	0.0548	0.1895	0.89	0.0014	98.26%	1.74%
	$L_l u$	standard regression	0.0004	0.0212	0.0380	0.76	-	-	-
		0.05-quantile regression	0.0018	0.0427	0.0020	0.03	0.0003	8.40%	91.60%
		0.95-quantile regression	0.0015	0.0386	0.0629	0.21	0.0011	95.31%	4.69%

Table 2. Node state prediction results

Σ_n	Precision	Recall	f1-score	Number of instances
0 (not overloaded)	0.99	0.96	0.97	22654
1 (overloaded)	0.96	0.99	0.97	22716

Overall model accuracy: 97% over 45370 test instances

curl function is assigned to the lu class, whereas for $k = 3$, it forms part of a separate *medium-usage* (mu) class. Although the clusters identified are very similar, results indicate that $k = 3$ yields substantially improved predictive performance, particularly in the CPU usage metric, as illustrated in Figs. 4a and 4b. These plots compare the observed and predicted values for the lu class (i.e., CPU_{lu}), where predictions aligning more closely with the observed data indicate higher accuracy (points nearer to the line). In particular, the best results are obtained for $k = 2$ and $k = 3$, but in the transition from 2 to 3 the MSE drops from 0.0401 to 0.0028 and while R^2 increases from -0.46 to 0.98, demonstrating a significant improvement in the fit of the model. This trend is consistently observed across all models and target variables.

Prediction Results of the Regression Models. The models developed to predict performance metrics at the node and class level show promising results for both standard and quantile regression approaches. Table 1 presents the values of MSE, RMSE, standard deviation, R^2, and, for quantile-based models, the quantile loss $\mathcal{L}_Q$. To assess the effectiveness of quantile regression models, we analyzed the percentage of *predicted* values (P) that exceed the *observed* values (R) in the test set and vice versa.

We observe that the predictions of CPU utilization (CPU_n) align well with the specified quantiles, indicating an accurate estimate of resource consumption. However, predictions for all function groups tend to be slightly conservative.

RAM consumption is generally more difficult to predict due to its high variability. As a result, some performance metrics (e.g., R^2) show slight degradation, although $\mathcal{L}_Q$ remains reasonably close to the values observed for CPU usage. The last two columns of Table 1 further demonstrate the overall effectiveness of the quantile-based models, showing predictions aligned with the specified α for RAM_n, and slightly conservative estimates for RAM_g.

The results achieved for the power consumption and for the latency in the three function groups are in line with those related to the CPU usage; for the former, standard regression yields good performance both for node-level and groups-level predictions. Similarly, L_g is predicted with reasonable accuracy both considering standard and quantile regression.

Node State Classification. As reported in Table 2, the node state prediction model demonstrates high accuracy in distinguishing overloaded from non-

Table 3. Comparison between per-class and per-function models for node-level metrics

	Metric	Model type	MSE	RMSE	stddev.	R^2	$\mathcal{L}_Q$	$P > R$	$R \leq P$
Classes	CPU_n	standard regression	0.000853	0.029204	0.181582	0.97	-	-	-
		0.05-quantile regression	0.004812	0.069368	0.146946	0.86	0.002668	4.92%	95.08%
		0.95-quantile regression	0.003421	0.058485	0.195683	0.9	0.002804	95.24%	4.76%
	RAM_n	standard regression	0.004204	0.064837	0.11684	0.77	-	-	-
		0.05-quantile regression	0.022446	0.14982	0.119375	−0.25	0.006838	5.26%	94.74%
		0.95-quantile regression	0.010242	0.101204	0.124444	0.43	0.004592	94.79%	5.21%
	Π_n	standard regression	0.001587	0.039831	0.139838	0.93	-	-	-
		0.05-quantile regression	0.005675	0.07533	0.112316	0.73	0.003358	5.19%	94.81%
		0.95-quantile regression	0.005623	0.074986	0.163428	0.73	0.003556	94.83%	5.17%
Functions	CPU_n	standard regression	0.000555	0.023557	0.18178	0.98	-	-	-
		0.05-quantile regression	0.007153	0.084576	0.135259	0.79	0.002985	4.76%	95.24%
		0.95-quantile regression	0.003434	0.058603	0.191214	0.9	0.002876	95.14%	4.86%
	RAM_n	standard regression	0.000837	0.028932	0.127305	0.95	-	-	-
		0.05-quantile regression	0.006141	0.078366	0.120091	0.65	0.003253	5.14%	94.86%
		0.95-quantile regression	0.006116	0.078205	0.112274	0.66	0.003379	94.89%	5.11%
	Π_n	standard regression	0.000968	0.031119	0.14191	0.95	-	-	-
		0.05-quantile regression	0.004766	0.069039	0.112647	0.78	0.003011	4.95%	95.05%
		0.95-quantile regression	0.00419	0.064732	0.158349	0.8	0.003167	95.14%	4.86%

overloaded conditions. Notably, it performs marginally better in detecting overloads, as reflected in the slightly higher recall for the overloaded class. This improved sensitivity to overloaded states reduces the risk of unaddressed performance issues, which is crucial to mitigate service disruptions. At the same time, the model balances this sensitivity with low false-positive rates, preventing unnecessary alarms in operational settings where maintaining system stability and availability is essential.

Node-Level Predictions. This section compares the prediction capabilities of node-level performance models trained considering individual functions or the three aforementioned function classes. The results are reported in Table 3. We can observe that the values obtained in the two cases are quite similar both for standard and quantile regression, with the only exception of the RAM usage prediction. As mentioned, this is characterized by a high variability, therefore considering more detailed features specific for the individual functions is of great help in producing accurate estimates.

5 Conclusion

Modeling the performance of serverless functions and the states of the computing nodes where they are executed enables service providers to design intelligent strategies that ensure the operational efficiency and sustainability of FaaS-enabled systems.

In this paper, we present an integrated framework for profiling serverless functions, gathering key performance metrics, and training machine learning models to forecast resource consumption and operational states at both the function and node levels under various load scenarios.

The trained models exhibited high accuracy, achieving a 97% success rate in predicting node states, underscoring the potential of these predictions to inform strategic decision-making and optimization operations. This, in turn, can greatly enhance the resilience and performance of FaaS-based edge environments.

Future work may explore intelligent methods, such as Bayesian Optimization, to improve the data collection process by efficiently identifying optimal configurations for load testing, as well as consider a deeper experimental validation including more complex functions, multi-component applications and the comparison with state-of-the-art methods.

References

1. Chawla, N.V., Bowyer, K.W., et al.: SMOTE: synthetic minority over-sampling technique. J. Artif. Intell. Res. **16**, 321–357 (2002)
2. Ciavotta, M., Motterlini, D., et al.: DFaaS: decentralized function-as-a-service for federated edge computing. In: IEEE CloudNet, pp. 1–4 (2021)
3. Copik, M., Kwasniewski, G., et al.: Sebs: a serverless benchmark suite for function-as-a-service computing. In: ACM Middleware Proceedings, pp. 64–78 (2021)
4. Das, A., Patterson, S., Wittie, M.: Edgebench: benchmarking edge computing platforms. In: IEEE UCC, pp. 175–180 (2018)
5. Filippini, F., Calmi, N., et al.: Analysis and evaluation of load management strategies in a decentralized FaaS environment: a simulation-based framework. In: ACM SEATED Proceedings, pp. 1–8 (2024)
6. Garbi, G., Incerto, E., Tribastone, M.: MP: a development framework for predicting performance of microservices by design. In: IEEE CLOUD, pp. 178–188 (2023)
7. Grohmann, J., Straesser, M., et al.: SuanMing: explainable prediction of performance degradations in microservice applications. In: ACM/SPEC ICPE Proceedings, pp. 165–176 (2021)
8. Jegannathan, A.P., Saha, R., Addya, S.K.: A time series forecasting approach to minimize cold start time in cloud-serverless platform. In: IEEE BlackSeaCom, pp. 325–330 (2022)
9. Ke, G., Meng, Q., et al.: Lightgbm: a highly efficient gradient boosting decision tree. In: Advances in Neural Information Processing Systems, vol. 30 (2017)
10. Kumari, A., Sahoo, B., Behera, R.K.: Workflow aware analytical model to predict performance and cost of serverless execution. Concurrency Comput. Pract. Experience **35**(22), e7743 (2023)
11. Ma, R., Zhan, Y., et al.: Interless: interference-aware deep resource prediction for serverless computing. In: CCDC, pp. 3783–3788 (2024)
12. Maćkiewicz, A., Ratajczak, W.: Principal components analysis (PCA). Comput. Geosci. **19**(3), 303–342 (1993)
13. Mahmoudi, N., Khazaei, H.: Performance modeling of serverless computing platforms. IEEE Trans. Cloud Comput. **10**(04), 2834–2847 (2022)
14. Maissen, P., Felber, P., et al.: FaaSdom: a benchmark suite for serverless computing. In: ACM DEBS Proceedings, pp. 73–84 (2020)

15. Nawrocki, P., Osypanka, P., Posluszny, B.: Data-driven adaptive prediction of cloud resource usage. J. Grid Comput. **21** (2023)
16. Petriglia, E., Filippini, F., et al.: Comparing actor-critic and neuroevolution approaches for traffic offloading in FaaS-powered edge systems. In: ACM SEATED Proceedings, pp. 17–24 (2024)
17. Premsankar, G., Di Francesco, M., Taleb, T.: Edge computing for the Internet of Things: a case study. IEEE Internet Things J. **5**(2), 1275–1284 (2018)
18. Rajan, A.P.: A review on serverless architectures-function as a service (FaaS) in cloud computing. Telkomnika (Telecommun. Comput. Electron. Control) **18**(1), 530–537 (2020)
19. Ristov, S., Kimovski, D., Fahringer, T.: FaaScinating resilience for serverless function choreographies in federated clouds. IEEE Trans. Netw. Serv. Manage. **19**(3), 2440–2452 (2022)
20. Sheshadri, K., Lakshmi, J.: QoS aware FaaS platform. In: 2021 IEEE/ACM 21st International Symposium on Cluster, Cloud and Internet Computing (CCGrid), pp. 812–819. IEEE (2021)
21. Somu, N., Daw, N., et al.: PanOpticon: a comprehensive benchmarking tool for serverless applications. In: COMSNETS, pp. 144–151 (2020)
22. Waldmann, E.: Quantile regression: a short story on how and why. Stat. Model. **18**(3-4), 203–218 (2018)

Privacy and Trust Management

A Quantitative Privacy Evaluation Method Based on Tsallis Entropy for Trustworthy Data Sharing

Shudan Yang[✉] and Pierluigi Plebani

Politecnico di Milano, Piazza Leonardo Da Vinci, 32, 20133 Milan, Italy
{shudan.yang,pierluigi.plebani}@polimi.it

Abstract. Data sharing has become a key factor in data analytics, as it allows organizations to operate on others' data for secondary usages. At the same time, when sharing datasets, it is essential to transform the data to protect sensitive information while still providing data consumers with high-quality access. This balance between privacy and visibility highlights the importance of quantifying privacy to ensure effective data sharing. Entropy, a key measure in information theory, is a natural fit for addressing the challenges of privacy quantification. However, current methods for measuring privacy, particularly those involving temporal and subjective data, face limitations in adaptability and scope. To address these issues, this paper proposes a Quantitative Privacy Evaluation Method Based on Tsallis Entropy for Trustworthy Data Sharing. This approach unifies existing entropy-based privacy models under a single Tsallis entropy framework, improving generalization across various datasets through an adjustable parameter. Building on this model, the paper introduces a method for quantifying the strength of privacy protection, providing theoretical support for assessing the degree of data sharing. Finally, the effectiveness of the proposed Tsallis entropy model in quantifying privacy is analyzed in the context of a multi-center clinical trial scenario.

Keywords: Data Sharing · Privacy Protection · Privacy Evaluation · Tsallis Entropy

1 Introduction

Research on privacy protection to enable trust data sharing dates back to the 1970s, when statistician Dalenius [2] provided a rigorous definition of data privacy. However, with the rapid development of emerging technologies such as the Internet of Things, artificial intelligence, and cloud computing—many of which are based on big data—privacy protection to enable effective data sharing has become areas of heightened interest in both academia and industry [10]. In particular, the pressing demand for privacy protection in government and corporate data-sharing initiatives forces us to reconcile the differences between privacy protection and data availability, striking a balance between usability and privacy risks. In this context, privacy risk analysis and assessment offer a feasible solution. However, privacy risk analysis, especially in quantifying privacy risks, necessarily involves the issue of privacy measurement. From this perspective, research on privacy measurement holds substantial theoretical and practical value.

As a tool for quantifying information, entropy [12] has proven effective in communication theory [7], and privacy, being a form of information, can similarly be quantified using entropy. Several scholars have explored this idea, employing concepts such as event entropy, anonymity set entropy, and conditional entropy [4]. However, these studies are often fragmented and show poor adaptability across different types of data, limiting its application primarily to specific domains, such as location privacy protection [8,13]. As a result, a unified model or framework has yet to be developed.

Tsallis entropy [15] was initially developed to address non-extensive (nonadditive) systems. It extends the principles of information processing beyond traditional additive systems, offering greater flexibility and adaptability to the diverse nature of different datasets.

Building on this analysis, this paper proposes a Quantitative Privacy Evaluation Method Based on Tsallis Entropy for Trustworthy Data Sharing. It integrates existing information theoretic privacy metric models based on Shannon entropy, information gain, etc., into a unified Tsallis entropy framework, introducing a tunable parameter to improve its generalization across diverse datasets while taking into account the individual privacy requirements of different sensitive values. In this model, the data provider is considered the sender, the privacy customer the receiver, and the privacy sharing channel the communication medium. Based on this framework, we introduce measures such as Tsallis-based privacy entropy, Tsallis-based average mutual information, Tsallis-based conditional entropy, and Tsallis-based conditional mutual information to quantify key aspects of the privacy protection system: privacy measurement at the information source, privacy sharing, privacy with background knowledge, and shared information. Furthermore, we propose a method to quantify both the strength of privacy protection and the degree of unauthorized access by data consumers, providing theoretical support for the quantitative risk assessment of privacy sharing. To validate the effectiveness of our approach, we apply it to data sharing in multi-center clinical trials and analyze its performance.

The remainder of this paper is structured as follows: Sect. 2 reviews related work. Section 3 introduces Reference Scenario. Section 4 and 5 introduce Quantitative Privacy Evaluation Method Based on Tsallis Entropy for Trustworthy Data Sharing. Section 6 applies the privacy measurement method and evaluation system to multi-center clinical trials and analyzes the results. Finally, Sect. 7 concludes the paper.

2 Related Work

One of the earliest studies to apply information theory to privacy measurement was conducted by Diaz et al. [3] and Serjantov et al. [11], who used Shannon entropy to quantify anonymity in communication systems.

Following this, other researchers applied entropy to privacy measurement in specific domains requiring trusted data sharing, such as location services, social networks, and healthcare systems. The representation of the random variable's probability and the method for handling entropy vary across different schemes.

In more recent research on privacy quantification using information theory, Yang et al. [18] proposed a method based on information gain to quantify privacy. In this method, the higher the information gain, the greater the risk of revealing the user's identity. Rodriguez et al. [9] extended the entropy-based privacy metric by incorporating the entropy rate to evaluate user mobility profiles. Peng et al. [1] developed an information entropy model for privacy protection, providing a quantitative analysis of privacy issues in location services. Wagner et al. [16] conducted a review of major privacy measurement methods, categorizing them into eight types based on system output. In the "uncertainty" category, entropy was used as the primary measure. Li et al. [6] introduced an efficient feature scoring protocol based on Gini impurity, demonstrating that secure feature selection can improve classifier accuracy on real-world datasets without revealing sensitive information. More recently, Guo et al. [5] designed a privacy measurement algorithm that combines information entropy with user privacy preferences, addressing privacy quantification issues in data-sharing scenarios.

In summary, existing theoretical frameworks for privacy measurement based on information theory remain fragmented and lack a unified model that consistently performs well across diverse datasets. To address this issue, this paper aims to treat privacy protection systems as communication models and explore adaptive entropy models for privacy measurement, with the goal of improving adaptability across various datasets.

3 Reference Scenario

In this section, we define the reference scenario with the relevant elements as depicted in Fig. 1:

- Data provider (DP): The entity responsible for providing the data set.
- Data set (X): The original data that may be shared with multiple consumers. This data is referred to as the *privacy source*, represented by the random variable X, consisting of a set of discrete events. These events form the privacy message space $x_1, x_2, \ldots, x_n$, where each x_i ($i = 1, 2, \ldots, n$) represents a specific private message within the shared events.
- Shared data set (Y): A transformed version of X obtained by applying privacy-preserving techniques. This transformed data is referred to as the *privacy target*, represented by the random variable Y, which consists of the private messages that data consumer can access. The privacy target is expressed as $y_1, y_2, \ldots, y_m$, where each y_j ($j = 1, 2, \ldots, m$) represents a specific private message available to the consumer.
- Data consumer (DC): The entity with the right to consume Y. Depending on the consumers' permissions, the accessible private messages may vary.

– Background knowledge (K): The pre-existing information available to DC. This knowledge could come from previous interaction with other data products from the same data provider and could be used in combination with the shared data set Y to potentially infer additional private information from the original data set X, which may not be visible directly in Y.

To better illustrate the method, we use COVID-19 data sharing as a case study. Suppose a hospital (DP) collects a dataset X of patient information during the pandemic. In this context, X refers to the entire dataset of patients, and each patient is described by specific attributes such as: x_1: Name, x_2: Patient Location, x_3: medical history, x_4: Test Results. Each x_i represents an attribute, with attribute values varying across patients. This data is transformed into different shared datasets (Y) depending on the type of data consumer, such as government officials and researchers from multiple trial centers (DC). **Government officials:** They are granted full access to the dataset, including all attributes such as hospital location, patient information, medical records, and treatment details. **Trial center researchers:** They are granted partial access, allowing them to view all patient data except sensitive information, such as hospital location. While safeguarding the rights of data consumers is crucial, it is equally important to protect the rights of data providers. A key risk in information systems is *overreach risk*, generally defined as the potential loss of information value due to unauthorized data access. This risk often arises from unclear data access permissions, enabling data consumers to inadvertently or deliberately access sensitive information beyond their authorized scope using their background knowledge K. Moreover, inadequate privacy protection measures may allow data consumers access to unauthorized information. This not only increases the risk of sensitive information leakage but also leads to the potential misuse of data. To address these challenges, as will be discussed in the next section.

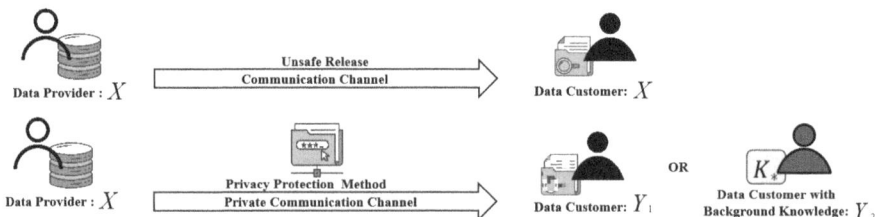

Fig. 1. Reference Scenario for Data Sharing

4 Quantitative Privacy Assessment Model Based on Tsallis Entropy

The general setting reported in Fig. 1 is suitable in a federated setting, where organizations share some data governance regulation and could act as data providers or data consumers. For this reason, our primary concern is to ensure the proper allocation of access permissions within the federated system. To achieve this goal, this section introduces a Quantitative Privacy Evaluation Method Based on Tsallis Entropy for Trustworthy Data Sharing using the information-theoretic communication framework from [12]. This model considers varying levels of privacy sensitivity, overreach risk in the federated system. Privacy is quantified by introducing Tsallis-based privacy entropy, Tsallis-based mutual information, Tsallis-based conditional entropy, and Tsallis-based conditional mutual information.

4.1 Sensitivity Weighting for Privacy Values

In privacy-preserving communication models with multiple discrete sources, applying uniform protection to all sensitive values can reduce the effectiveness of privacy measures. For example, in a study analyzing long-term COVID-19 health data, various attributes—such as Symptoms, Medical History, and Pathology—are used to describe each patient's condition. For example, the attribute medical history could require stronger privacy protection due to the potential long-term health risks and their impact on insurability or employment. In contrast, another attribute like symptoms is less sensitive and may not need the same level of protection. Applying the same level of protection to less sensitive data could result in overprotection, potentially reducing the accuracy of statistical analysis. Privacy needs are subjective, and the sensitivity of data reflects the level of protection required. Therefore, in practice, not all private information is equally sensitive, and privacy protection should vary accordingly [17]. Providing higher protection for more sensitive values while offering lower protection for less sensitive ones can encourage data providers to share protected data more willingly, fostering a balance between data usability and privacy.

In this work, we address the personalized privacy needs of different sensitive values by introducing **sensitivity weights**. These weights enable customized protection and are integrated into our Quantitative Privacy Evaluation Model based on Tsallis entropy.

The attribute x_i, (e.g., a patient's name, location, medical history) is considered sensitive in terms of privacy, the sensitivity weight w_i $(i = 1, 2, \ldots, n)$ reflects the data provider's subjective perception of its privacy sensitivity, often referred to as subjective sensitivity. The sensitivity of private information can depend on factors such as the specific application scenario, individual perception, personal preferences, and economic value. Sensitivity weights are generally determined by adhering to four key principles:

- *Non-negativity*: the sensitivity weight for a sensitive value must be greater than or equal to 0. Zero sensitivity means no privacy protection is required.
- *Monotonicity*: higher sensitivity corresponds to a larger weight. More sensitive data requires stronger privacy protection.
- *Continuity*: small changes in the probability of a privacy event should result in continuous changes in the weighted entropy, reflecting gradual shifts in privacy sources.

– *Inverse Proportionality*: less frequent sensitive values have higher weights, as rare events carry more information and require stronger privacy protection.

To ensure that the sensitivity weights are realistic and adaptable, we propose a user scoring strategy based on a dynamic sliding window mechanism, which allows for the adaptive calculation of these weights. The steps for sensitivity weight design are as follows:

Step 1: Sensitivity Scoring. Define the sensitivity score range for each attribute as $[D_0, D_{max}]$, where higher scores indicate greater sensitivity, with $D_{max} > D_0 \geq 0$. The value of D_{max} is set by the data provider and is used as a benchmark to gauge the relative sensitivity of different attributes. For instance, Patient Location might have a maximum score $D_{max} = 10$, medical history $D_2 = 5$, and Test Results $D_1 = 2$.

Step 2: Determining Sensitivity Levels. Sensitivity levels are categorized into L distinct groups. Data providers assign scores to each sensitive attribute. Following outlier removal, each attribute is assigned a sensitivity level l, such as: Patient Location: Level 3, Medical History: Level 2, and Test Results: Level 1. To capture both long-term and short-term variations in data sensitivity, a sliding window mechanism employing time-based decay or gain factors is utilized. This mechanism adjusts the sensitivity level of data attributes dynamically, reflecting changes such as a decrease in the access frequency of Medical History over time, which result in a decrease in its sensitivity level from Level 2 to Level 1.

Step 3: Adaptive Sensitivity Weight Calculation. Higher sensitivity levels are associated with higher weights. The weight for a value at sensitivity level l is calculated as:

$$W_l = \frac{l-1}{L-1} \qquad (1)$$

For the given sensitivity levels: Patient Location: $W_3 = 1$, Medical History: ($W_2 = 0.5$, Test Results: $W_1 = 0$. As per the non-negativity principle in privacy weighting, the Test Results attribute is deemed not to require privacy protection due to its zero weight.

To account for dynamic changes, a decay function $\alpha(t)$ is introduced to adjust the weight over time:

$$w_i(t) = W_l \cdot \alpha(t) \qquad (2)$$

The decay function $\alpha(t)$ is expressed as: $\alpha(t) = e^{-\beta t}$. where β represents the decay rate, influencing how quickly the weight diminishes over time, and Δt signifies the time elapsed since the last data evaluation. For instance, a sensitivity level initially set at 2 might have a weight of $W_2 = 0.5$. At $t = 10$, the decay function reduces the weight to $w_2(10) = W_2 \cdot \alpha(10) \approx 0.184$, reflecting a significant reduction in sensitivity due to decreased access frequency or relevance.

By integrating these time-dependent adjustments, the proposed model ensures that sensitivity weights are dynamic, providing a more accurate and real-time reflection of data sensitivity. This methodology not only enhances privacy protections but also facilitates secure and efficient data sharing.

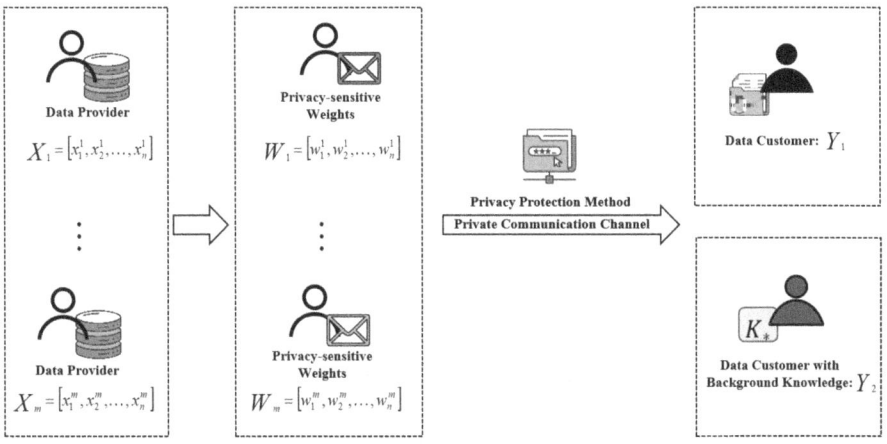

Fig. 2. Context-Aware Data Sharing Model Based on Tsallis Entropy

Therefore, for privacy messages x_i ($i = 1, 2, \ldots, n$) in the communication model shown in Fig. 2, the weight space for a single privacy source X can be represented as:

$$\begin{pmatrix} X \\ W(X) \\ P(X) \end{pmatrix} = \begin{pmatrix} x_1 & x_2 & \ldots & x_i & \ldots & x_n \\ w_1 & w_2 & \ldots & w_i & \ldots & w_n \\ p(x_1) & p(x_2) & \ldots & p(x_i) & \ldots & p(x_n) \end{pmatrix}, \quad w_i \geq 0, \ i = 1, 2, \ldots, n \quad (3)$$

where $P(X)$ represents the probability distribution over the privacy messages x_i for a given privacy source X. Each probability $p(x_i)$ corresponds to the likelihood of occurrence for the respective privacy message x_i, constrained such that $0 \leq p(x_i) \leq 1$, and the sum of all probabilities $\sum_{i=1}^{n} p(x_i) = 1$, ensuring a valid and complete probability distribution across all considered privacy messages. Similarly, the privacy target Y (the shared dataset) can be modeled as:

$$\begin{pmatrix} Y \\ P(Y) \end{pmatrix} = \begin{pmatrix} y_1 & y_2 & \cdots & y_m \\ p(y_1) & p(y_2) & \cdots & p(y_m) \end{pmatrix}, \quad (4)$$

where $0 \leq p(y_j) \leq 1$, and $\sum_{j=1}^{m} p(y_j) = 1$. So the privacy-weighted Tsallis entropy $S_{q_w}(X)$, is defined as:

$$S_{q_w}(X) = -\sum_{i=1}^{n} w_i p(x_i)^q \ln_q p(x_i) \quad (5)$$

where $S_q(X)$ quantifies the average uncertainty within data privacy, considering different sensitivities to privacy breaches represented by weights w_i. A greater $S_{q_w}(X)$ value signifies a higher level of privacy, indicating a lower likelihood of privacy leakage. The parameter q is adapted to reflect the characteristics of different datasets, affecting the entropy measurement:

- For $q < 1$, Tsallis entropy places more weight on low-probability events, making it suitable for analyzing datasets where rare events hold significant importance.
- For $q = 1$, Tsallis entropy simplifies to Shannon entropy, providing a general measure of uncertainty applicable to any type of data.
- For $q > 1$, Tsallis entropy emphasizes high-probability events, making it appropriate for long-tail distributions, such as those in internet traffic and social network data.

When DC gains access to some shared data (Y), the remaining uncertainty about the dataset X held by the DP can be quantified using the privacy-weighted Tsallis conditional entropy, denoted as $S_{q_w}(X|Y)$.

$$S_{q_w}(X|Y) = -\sum_{i=1}^{n} w_i \sum_{j=1}^{m} p(x_i, y_j)^q \ln_q p(x_i|y_j) \tag{6}$$

This metric captures the level of uncertainty about X, considering the information already available to DC through DP. This uncertainty arises from the interference (privacy protection) introduced by the privacy-sharing channel. Due to the privacy protection mechanisms in place, DC face a degree of uncertainty about the DP's X while accessing it. This privacy entropy satisfies the fundamental properties of Tsallis entropy, including non-negativity, symmetry, extensibility, determinism, additivity, extremality, and convexity, adhering to the principles outlined by the maximum entropy theorem [14]. The degree of privacy sharing during the transmission of private information can be measured by the weighted average of Tsallis mutual privacy information, defined as follows:

$$I_w(X;Y) = \sum_{i=1}^{n} w_i \sum_{j=1}^{m} p(x_i, y_j)^q \ln_q \frac{p(x_i, y_j)}{p(x_i)p(y_j)} \tag{7}$$

$I_w(X;Y)$ represents the average amount of privacy information shared between the DP and DC, effectively measuring the severity of privacy sharing.

4.2 Overreach Risk

To account for potential overreach risk by data consumer DC due to insufficient protection, our model incorporates the background knowledge space K of the DC, which may include historical log records as illustrated in Fig. 1. This background knowledge space is mathematically defined as:

$$\binom{K}{P(K)} = \binom{k_1 \quad k_2 \quad \cdots \quad k_c}{p(k_1) \quad p(k_2) \quad \cdots \quad p(k_c)} \tag{8}$$

where $0 \leq p(k_c) \leq 1, \sum_{c=1}^{l} p(k_c) = 1$, $c = 1, 2, ..., l$, ensuring a valid probability distribution across the elements of K. By combining information from the privacy target Y with background knowledge K, DC may potentially access private data beyond the authorized limits. This introduces the concept of conditional overreach entropy:

$$S_q(X|YK) = -\sum_{i=1}^{n}\sum_{j=1}^{m}\sum_{c=1}^{l} p(x_i, y_j, k_c)^q \ln_q p(x_i|y_j, k_c) \tag{9}$$

The conditional entropy $S_q(X|YK)$ quantifies the remaining uncertainty about X after DC obtains information from both privacy target Y and background knowledge K. This measure can serve as an indicator of the level of privacy protection under scenarios of potential overreach risk.

Taking into account the data provider's subjective sensitivity or preferences regarding their information, we define the weighted conditional overreach entropy $S_{q_w}(X|YK)$. This metric reflects the extent of overreach concerning the privacy target Y, supported by background knowledge K, while considering privacy weights. It can be used to quantify the strength of privacy protection mechanisms under overreach risk conditions:

$$S_{q_w}(X|YK) = -\sum_{i=1}^{n} w_i \sum_{j=1}^{m}\sum_{c=1}^{l} p(x_i, y_j, k_c)^q \ln_q p(x_i|y_j, k_c) \tag{10}$$

Furthermore, we define the privacy overreach mutual information $I_w(X;Y|K)$, which quantifies the average mutual information between X and Y given the background knowledge K. This measure captures the extent of privacy information that DC gains and indicates potential privacy leakage facilitated by K:

$$I_w(X;Y|K) = \sum_{i=1}^{n} w_i \sum_{j=1}^{m}\sum_{c=1}^{l} p(x_i, y_j, k_c)^q \ln_q \frac{p(x_i, k_c|y_j)}{p(x_i|k_c)p(y_j|k_c)} \tag{11}$$

5 Privacy Metrics and Evaluation of Privacy Protection Mechanisms and Overreach Risk

Tsallis entropy and Tsallis mutual information can be used to measure the privacy of information. Based on these metrics, we can develop a method to evaluate the robustness of privacy protection mechanisms against overreach risk.

5.1 Privacy Measurement Methods

In the Quantitative Privacy Evaluation Method Based on Tsallis Entropy, privacy metrics revolve around several core components: the inherent amount of private information in the source, the potential for overreach risk by the data consumer DC, the effectiveness of privacy protection algorithms, and the degree of privacy leakage. The inherent private information in a data source is quantified by the source entropy $S_{q_w}(X)$, representing the initial amount of private information held. This measure remains constant once the source and its characteristics are defined.

The potential overreach risk by DC and the effectiveness of privacy protection algorithms are assessed using $S_{q_w}(X \mid YK)$. This metric reflects the uncertainty DC faces when attempting to access information beyond approved limits using background knowledge K, providing an indicator of the algorithm's strength in protecting privacy.

The relationship between privacy conditional entropy $S_q(X|Y)$ and privacy mutual information $I(X;Y)$ is consistent in measuring privacy, offers insights into the balance of information exposure and retention. These metrics, when extended to include background knowledge K, form the basis for measuring the degree of privacy leakage and the capability of DC to exploit data beyond intended bounds. We define the average privacy mutual information $I_w(X;Y \mid K)$ to evaluate both DC's ability to overreach risk and the effectiveness of the privacy protection algorithm. Let O_r represent a specific overreach risk utilizing K, and P_i denote a particular protection algorithm. Then, the metrics $I_{wP_i,O_r}(X \mid YK)$ and $I_{wP_i,O_r}(X;Y \mid K)$ are utilized to assess the robustness of the overreach risk O_r, the effectiveness of the protection algorithm P_i, and the extent of privacy leakage under the defensive measures of P_i against O_r.

Property 1. Complementarity of Privacy Conditional Entropy and Mutual Information. **Proof:** Based on the formulation of Tsallis entropy, we analyze the relationship between privacy conditional entropy $S_q(X|Y)$ and privacy mutual information $I(X;Y)$ as follows:

$$I(X;Y) = \sum_{i=1}^{n}\sum_{j=1}^{m} p(x_i, y_j)^q \ln_q \frac{p(x_i|y_j)}{p(x_i)}$$

$$= \sum_{i=1}^{n}\sum_{j=1}^{m} p(x_i, y_j)^q \ln_q \frac{1}{p(x_i)} - \sum_{i=1}^{n}\sum_{j=1}^{m} p(x_i, y_j)^q \ln_q \frac{1}{p(x_i|y_j)}$$

$$= S_q(X) - S_q(X|Y) \tag{12}$$

This relationship indicates that as privacy conditional entropy $S_q(X|Y)$ increases, indicating greater uncertainty or better privacy preservation after observing Y, the mutual information $I(X;Y)$ decreases. This inverse relationship demonstrates while $S_q(X|Y)$ measures the residual uncertainty about X given Y, $I(X;Y)$ quantifies the reduction in uncertainty about X due to knowledge of Y. Thus, they provide complementary perspectives on the information dynamics between X and Y, reflecting their consistent roles in privacy assessment.

5.2 Evaluation and Analysis of Privacy Protection Mechanisms and Overreach Risk

In real systems, the primary objective of privacy protection mechanisms is to maximize the privacy of the data provider DP while ensuring that the data consumer DC access only the legitimate amount of private information, even under varying degrees of overreach risk. Our goal is to minimize the amount of unauthorized private information that DC can obtain through overreach risk. Ideally, $I_w(X;Y \mid K)$ should be as close to zero as possible, even when DC possess background knowledge K.

Definition 1 (Comparative Effectiveness of Protection Mechanisms): When evaluating privacy protection systems under potential overreach risk by consumers, represented by an overreach risk O_r, and comparing two different protection mechanisms P_i and P_j:

If $S_{q_{wP_i,O_r}}(X \mid YK) < S_{q_{wP_j,O_r}}(X \mid YK)$ or $I_{wP_i,O_r}(X;Y \mid K) > I_{wP_j,O_r}(X;Y \mid K)$, then mechanism P_j is more effective than P_i, denoted as $P_i(O_r) < P_j(O_r)$. This indicates that P_j leads to higher uncertainty for DC or lower information gain from X given Y and K, which is desirable for stronger privacy protection.

If $S_{q_{wP_i,O_r}}(X \mid YK) = S_{q_{wP_j,O_r}}(X \mid YK)$ or $I_{wP_i,O_r}(X;Y \mid K) = I_{wP_j,O_r}(X;Y \mid K)$, then the two mechanisms are equally effective, denoted as $P_i(O_r) = P_j(O_r)$.

Where the partial order relation of the privacy-preserving mechanism is transitive, and the equivalence relation is reflexive and symmetric.

Definition 2 (Effectiveness Distance): In the context of privacy protection methods under overreach risk condition, let protection methods P_i and P_j result in DC obtaining $I_{wP_i,O_r}(X;Y \mid K)$ and $I_{wP_j,O_r}(X;Y \mid K)$, respectively. The effectiveness distance between these two methods is defined as:

$$d_I(O_r) = I_{wP_j,O_r}(X;Y \mid K) - I_{wP_i,O_r}(X;Y \mid K) \tag{13}$$

where a positive $d_I(O_r)$ implies that P_j is more effective than P_i at preventing overreach risk because it results in lower mutual information, indicative of better privacy protection.

Similarly, under the same privacy protection method P_i, when different DC use their respective overreach risk strategy O_r and O_q to access shared data, the effectiveness distance between these two consumers' overreach risk behaviors is defined as: $d_I(P_i) = I_{wP_i,O_r}(X;Y \mid K) - I_{wP_i,O_q}(X;Y \mid K)$.

6 Case Study

The Quantitative Privacy Assessment Model Based on Tsallis Entropy and its measurement methods introduced earlier are applicable to a variety of scenarios. Here, we analyze the effectiveness of the proposed model in a clinical trial privacy protection scenario, which is simplified for illustrative purposes.

A pharmaceutical company is developing a new drug to treat post-COVID-19 syndrome and plans to assess its safety and efficacy through a multi-center randomized controlled trial conducted across several medical institutions in Europe. **Trial centers:** The trial involves M hospitals or medical institutions, denoted by the set $B = \{b_1, b_2, \ldots, b_M\}$, with each b_i representing a trial center. **Participant allocation:** Participants, represented by set A, are randomly assigned to one of these centers for treatment.

The objective during the clinical trials is to ensure trusted data sharing while preventing unauthorized access or privilege escalation. In this scenario, each participating hospital serves as a data provider, and data consumers include government officials, who have full access to the shared data, and researchers at various trial centers, who have restricted access—specifically, they do not have access to the provider's location information.

The potential risk for the data providers arises from authorized researchers within the federated system who, either intentionally or unintentionally, gain access to sensitive information beyond their authorized scope due to improper permission settings. To balance data security with the legitimate access needs of data consumers, we implement a strict permission allocation mechanism, ensuring both the protection of patient privacy and the confidentiality of sensitive information. An overview of this case study is illustrated in Fig. 3.

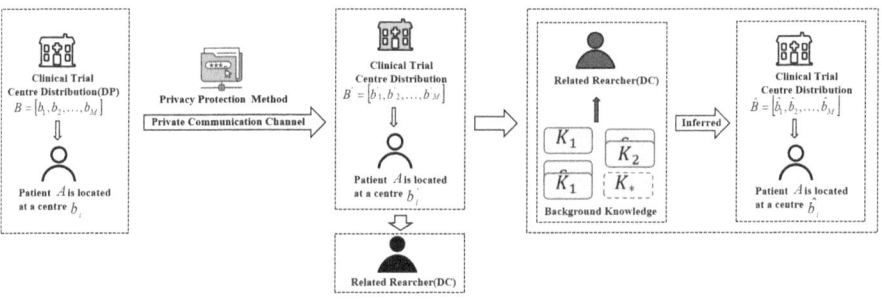

Fig. 3. Data sharing model Based on Tsallis Entropy in clinical trial

To protect the privacy of the patient's location and prevent researchers from directly accessing this sensitive data, the patient's location distribution B must be secured. After applying a clinical trial privacy protection mechanism (which may include anonymization, generalization, or noise), the protected patient's location distribution becomes B', which can be observed by researchers.

Let $B' = \{b'_1, b'_2, \ldots, b'_M\}$, where b'_i represents the trial center of patient A after privacy protection, as observed by the researcher. The probability of patient A being located at a given trial center b_i is denoted as $p(b_i)$, where $0 \leq p(b_i) \leq 1$ and $\sum_{i=1}^{M} p(b_i) = 1$. When a researcher accesses the protected distribution B', they may combine this information with background knowledge to infer patient A's actual location. This inferred location is denoted by $\hat{B}$, where $\hat{B} = \{\hat{b}_1, \hat{b}_2, \ldots, \hat{b}_M\}$, and $\hat{b}_i$ represents the researcher's estimated location of patient A in relation to their true location.

6.1 Quantitative Analysis

Since the clinical trial center location distribution data is neither characterized by rare or anomalous events nor by high-probability events, we set $q = 1$. At this point, the privacy source entropy, which reflects the distribution of clinical trial center locations B, is given by $S_q(B) = - \sum_{i=1}^{M} p(b_i)^q \ln_q p(b_i) = 0$.

If generalization is used as the privacy protection mechanism for patient A's clinical trial center, and the published location of A is generalized from region b_i to b'_i, the observable distribution of the clinical trial center is shown in the Initial Privacy Protection B' row in Table 1. At this point, using the Quantitative Privacy Evaluation Method Based on Tsallis Entropy as designed in this paper, the privacy status of the patient's clinical trial center can be calculated as: $S_q(B') = - \sum_{i=1}^{M} p(b'_i)^q \ln_q p(b'_i) = 2.322$.

When researchers try to access location information that has been protected by generalization, they can combine this information with background knowledge, such as historical logs. As shown in Table 1, suppose researchers increased the probability of patient A being located at b_i from $\frac{1}{5}$ to $\frac{1}{2}$ by combining background knowledge, while decreasing the inferred probabilities for other regions, making it easier to infer the location information of patient A. At this point, we can calculate the entropy: $S_q(\hat{B}) = - \sum_{i=1}^{M} p(\hat{b}_i)^q \ln_q p(\hat{b}_i) = 1.961$. This represents the uncertainty faced by a researcher when using background knowledge to determine the patient's clinical trial center. It is evident that the measured privacy protection entropy significantly decreases: $S_q(\hat{B}) < S_q(B')$. This reduction indicates a privacy threat to the patient when data consumers have access to such background knowledge. This aligns with the theoretical framework we propose, highlighting the need for robust privacy protection that can withstand the integration of external knowledge by data consumers, namely overreach risk.

Table 1. Inferred Distribution under Initial Protection and Overreach risk

Distribution Stage	$p(b_1)$	...	$p(b_{i-2})$	$p(b_{i-1})$	$p(b_i)$	$p(b_{i+1})$	$p(b_{i+2})$	...	$p(b_M)$
Initial Privacy Protection B'	0	...	$\frac{1}{5}$	$\frac{1}{5}$	$\frac{1}{5}$	$\frac{1}{5}$	$\frac{1}{5}$	...	0
Overreach Risk ($\hat{B}$)	0	...	$\frac{1}{5}$	$\frac{1}{10}$	$\frac{1}{2}$	$\frac{1}{10}$	$\frac{1}{10}$	...	0

6.2 Mitigation Strategies

To mitigate this privacy threat effectively, it is essential to implement stronger privacy measures to further generalize patient A's location data. By expanding the geographic generalization from a small cluster of centers, b_{i-2} to b_{i+2}, to a broader area encompassing b_{i-2} to b_{i+7}, we distribute the observation of potential locations more widely, significantly enhancing privacy. This adjustment in the spatial distribution in Table 2, where the observable distribution of locations after this enhancement of privacy protections is analyzed. The $S_q(B')$, from an earlier value of 2.322 6.1 to 3.322, demonstrating an effective rise in privacy levels. This improvement is consistent with the principles outlined in Definition 1 5.2. The more distributed the observed locations, the less precise any inference from the data consumer can be, hence increasing the uncertainty or entropy.

Table 2. Stronger Protection and Overreach Risk Distributions

Distribution Stage	$p(b'_1)$	...	$p(b'_{i-2})$	$p(b'_{i-1})$	$p(b'_i)$	$p(b'_{i+1})$	$p(b'_{i+2})$	$p(b'_{i+3})$	...	$p(b'_{i+7})$	...	$p(b'_M)$
Stronger Privacy Protection B'	0	...	$\frac{1}{10}$	$\frac{1}{10}$	$\frac{1}{10}$	$\frac{1}{10}$	$\frac{1}{10}$	$\frac{1}{10}$	...	$\frac{1}{10}$	...	0
The Same Overreach Risk ($\hat{B}$)	0	...	$\frac{1}{6}$	$\frac{1}{4}$	$\frac{1}{4}$	$\frac{1}{12}$	$\frac{1}{12}$	$\frac{1}{30}$	...	$\frac{1}{30}$	...	0

Further analysis shows that even when researchers equipped with similar levels of background knowledge attempt to infer the distribution of patient A's actual location, as illustrated in Table 2, the entropy of this inferred distribution, $S_q(\hat{B})$, is calculated to be 2.846. This value indicates a reduction in the effectiveness of background knowledge in breaching privacy due to the enhanced protection measures, rising from the previously observed 1.961 6.1. This finding corroborates with Definition 2 5.2, confirming that Quantitative Privacy Evaluation Method Based on Tsallis Entropy is both consistent and effective.

7 Conclusion

This paper introduces a Quantitative Privacy Evaluation Method Based on Tsallis Entropy for Trustworthy Data Sharing. The key approach is to model the privacy protection system for secure data sharing as a communication model. By defining the source, destination, and channel, and introducing concepts such as Tsallis-based entropy, average Tsallis-based mutual information, Tsallis-based conditional entropy, and Tsallis-based conditional mutual information, we integrate existing privacy protection entropy models into a unified Tsallis entropy framework. Through an adjustable parameter, this framework enhances generalization across various datasets. We have also provided initial methods for measuring privacy information, evaluating the strength of privacy protection, and assessing the customer's overreach degree in different scenarios.

Although this work presents only the fundamental methods for quantifying privacy using Tsallis entropy, it lays the groundwork for a comprehensive framework to address the challenges of privacy quantification. In future work, we plan to apply this privacy evaluation tool to real-world access control scenarios. Our goal is to develop an automated, real-time mechanism to measure the privacy level of data providers and the maximum visibility of data accessible to data consumers. This will help assess whether shared data aligns with data-sharing protocols as large-scale data sharing occurs, ultimately balancing the trade-offs between data sharing and privacy protection.

Acknowledgments. This work has been partially supported by the project LLC-Network funded by Fondazione CARIPLO.

References

1. Changgen, P., Hongfa, D., Yijie, Z., Youliang, T., Zufeng, F.: Information entropy models and privacy metrics methods for privacy protection. J. Softw. **27**(8), 1891–1903 (2016)
2. Dalenius, T.: Towards a methodology for statistical disclosure control (1977)
3. Diaz, C., Seys, S., Claessens, J., Preneel, B.: Towards measuring anonymity. In: International Workshop on Privacy Enhancing Technologies, pp. 54–68. Springer (2002)
4. Freudiger, J., Manshaei, M.H., Hubaux, J.P., Parkes, D.C.: On non-cooperative location privacy: a game-theoretic analysis. In: Proceedings of the 16th ACM Conference on Computer and Communications Security, pp. 324–337 (2009)
5. Guo, Y., Zuo, J., Guo, Z., Qi, J., Lu, Y.: Data sharing privacy metrics model based on information entropy and group privacy preference. Cryptography **7**(1), 11 (2023)
6. Li, X., Dowsley, R., De Cock, M.: Privacy-preserving feature selection with secure multiparty computation. In: International Conference on Machine Learning, pp. 6326–6336. PMLR (2021)
7. Machanavajjhala, A., Kifer, D., Gehrke, J., Venkitasubramaniam, M.: l-diversity: privacy beyond k-anonymity. ACM Trans. Knowl. Discov. Data (TKDD) **1**(1), 3–es (2007)
8. Pan, X., Zhang, M., Ji, S., Yang, M.: Privacy risks of general-purpose language models. In: 2020 IEEE Symposium on Security and Privacy (SP), pp. 1314–1331. IEEE (2020)
9. Rodriguez-Carrion, A., et al.: Entropy-based privacy against profiling of user mobility. Entropy **17**(6), 3913–3946 (2015)
10. Samaraweera, G.D., Chang, J.M.: Security and privacy implications on database systems in big data era: a survey. IEEE Trans. Knowl. Data Eng. **33**(1), 239–258 (2019)
11. Serjantov, A., Danezis, G.: Towards an information theoretic metric for anonymity. In: International Workshop on Privacy Enhancing Technologies, pp. 41–53. Springer (2002)
12. Shannon, C.E.: A mathematical theory of communication. Bell Syst. Tech. J. **27**(3), 379–423 (1948)
13. Shokri, R., Theodorakopoulos, G., Le Boudec, J.Y., Hubaux, J.P.: Quantifying location privacy. In: 2011 IEEE Symposium on Security and Privacy, pp. 247–262. IEEE (2011)
14. Tsallis, C.: Possible generalization of Boltzmann-Gibbs statistics. J. Stat. Phys. **52**, 479–487 (1988)
15. Tsallis, C.: Nonadditive entropy and nonextensive statistical mechanics-an overview after 20 years. Braz. J. Phys. **39**, 337–356 (2009)
16. Wagner, I., Eckhoff, D.: Technical privacy metrics: a systematic survey. ACM Comput. Surv. (CSUR) **51**(3), 1–38 (2018)
17. Xiao, X., Tao, Y.: Personalized privacy preservation. In: Proceedings of the 2006 ACM SIGMOD International Conference on Management of Data, pp. 229–240 (2006)
18. Yang, Y., Lutes, J., Li, F., Luo, B., Liu, P.: Stalking online: on user privacy in social networks. In: Proceedings of the Second ACM Conference on Data and Application Security and Privacy, pp. 37–48 (2012)

SafeAR: Privacy-Maintenance in Augmented Reality Applications

Rogério Luís de C. Costa(✉)[iD], Anabela Marto[iD], Leonel Santos[iD], Alexandrino Gonçalves[iD], and Carlos Rabadão[iD]

CIIC, ESTG, Polytechnic University of Leiria, Leiria, Portugal
{rogerio.l.costa,anabela.marto,leonel.santos,alex,
carlos.rabadao}@ipleiria.pt

Abstract. Augmented Reality (AR) experiences combining real-world and virtual objects have been applied in several areas, such as entertainment, manufacturing, and training. Such experiences commonly use devices that collect data about users and their surrounding environment, which may be shared and disseminated through the Internet. This leads to increased concerns about maintaining the privacy and confidentiality of individuals and companies. However, identifying and mitigating the risks of data breaches in AR applications is an open challenge.

In this paper, we present SafeAR, a project aimed at creating automatic tools to ensure the privacy and confidentiality of sensitive data while maintaining seamless, real-time, and persistent physical-digital AR experiences. In SafeAR, we apply machine learning to automatically identify the occurrences of privacy risks in raw data captured by AR applications. We study different risk identification and data sanitization methods and architectural solutions for an ecosystem that processes the raw data captured by AR applications and makes sanitized data available, considering the usual specific requirements (e.g., response time) and resource limitations of AR applications. The proposals are validated on a location-based AR game and a headset application for training and manufacturing.

Keywords: Augmented Reality · Privacy protection · Machine Learning · Cloud-based Services · Mobile game

1 Introduction

Augmented Reality (AR) technologies are currently being successfully used with intelligent devices in several domains. These technologies combine real and virtual content, enabling real-time user interaction within a three-dimensional environment [1]. Usually, AR applications need to identify user movements and interactions with objects to apply them to the virtual environment. Applications scan and map the 3D surroundings, performing object identification and tracking. However, while acquiring data about the surroundings, AR applications can capture sensitive and confidential data (e.g., e-mails and facial images) of the

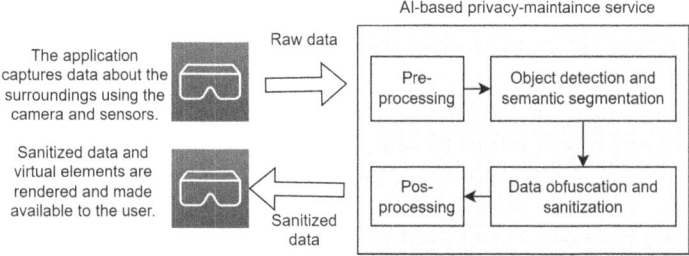

Fig. 1. The AI-based service processes the data captured by AR applications before rendering and applies sanitization methods to protect sensitive data. Sanitized data is sent back to applications and rendered together with virtual elements.

user or bystanders, leading to security problems related to maintaining privacy and confidentiality [4].

In this work, we present SafeAR, a project to create tools for the scalable development of privacy- and confidentiality-preserving AR applications. We aim to develop an ecosystem platform that provides services that AR applications may consume. The applications would pass raw data to the ecosystem and receive sanitized data with enhanced privacy and confidentiality protection. We use artificial intelligence to identify sensitive entities in raw data. Due to the characteristics of AR applications related to the recognition of entities in 3D environments in real-time and the usual resource constraints in AR devices, chosen solutions must have recognition accuracy, inference speed characteristics, and be lightweight. Then, distributed (e.g., cloud-based) architectures are an alternative that we are exploring. Figure 1 presents an overview of the SafeAR service.

We have chosen two use cases from distinct application areas to validate our proposals. The first is on a location-based AR game (LBARG) that runs on a smartphone and on which virtual content is added on top of real-world representations and tied to the player's geographical location. The second assessment scenario uses a headset-based AR application to aid training and manufacturing.

2 Background and Related Work

AR technologies and experiences have applications in several domains. AR devices have integrated hardware (like multiple cameras, microphones, and screens) to capture information. Data may be collected through pictures, video, voice recording, movement identification, and metadata (e.g., about the device's IP and geographical location). Due to resource constraints, many of these devices rely on cloud-based processing [6]. Meanwhile, cybersecurity issues in AR applications commonly rely on input processing, data access and sharing, and output rendering [3,9]. AR applications capture and store information about the user (e.g., what the user sees and the user's actions) and about bystanders without their knowledge, leading to specific privacy concerns [10], as attackers may exploit AR applications lacking confidentiality-maintenance capabilities to provide relevant knowledge of a real-world system [2]. Indeed, maintaining security and privacy in AR is an open issue [7], and protections that must be enforced include guaranteeing anonymity, undetectability, and unlinkability [3].

SafeAR focuses on input protection, whose main threats are the unauthorized or unintended disclosure of information [3]. Sanitization policies (e.g., input and video) are the most common defence. DARKLY [5] is a solution integrated with OpenCV that deploys privacy protection mechanisms (such as access control) based on user-defined policies. Users may impose degrees of sensitivity and limit the detail provided to applications. However, these policies do not consider the context in which information and objects are present. Zarepour et al. [13] discuss using context-based privacy in wearable visual life loggers using data on the ambient environment as contextual clues to trigger recognition methods that identify possible sensitive subjects in images. PlaceAvoider [11] also deals with image sanitization, and the final decision on deletion depends on the user. However, AR applications usually require real-time videos. RTFace [12] applies face recognition to perform video sanitization using a near-the-edge system.

3 Research Methodology

Figure 2 presents a summary of the main tasks of our research work. Initially, we identify several classes of objects that can lead to privacy and confidentiality risks in AR applications and possible countermeasures. We also point out the usual requirements (e.g., response time) in AR applications, as one should consider them when evaluating the appropriate countermeasure for each type of threat.

Then, we research the application of machine learning techniques to process the data streams generated by AR applications and identify privacy and confidentiality risks. We evaluate object detection and segmentation algorithms and context-aware object identifiers. The selection of the countermeasures considers performance, effectiveness, and user interaction with AR applications.

The next step is to develop an ecosystem to support the maintenance of privacy and confidentiality in AR applications. This ecosystem incorporates the machine learning methods and the countermeasures developed and makes them accessible through services to exchange raw and processed data between AR applications and the platform. Considering resource limitations on devices and performance requirements of AR applications, we evaluate using distributed architectures based on edge and cloud when defining the ecosystem architecture.

We consider two scenarios to validate our proposals. The first is a mobile AR game that uses the smartphone's camera and location, used to assess our proposals impacts on application performance and user experience. The second application is a virtual guide to assemble desktops. The popularity of smartphone usage motivated the first application, and the advantages of using AR (particularly AR headsets) in the industry led to the choice of the second application. Evaluation metrics include response time and accuracy in identifying threats. We are also studying users' perceptions on how the different countermeasures impact their experience when using AR applications.

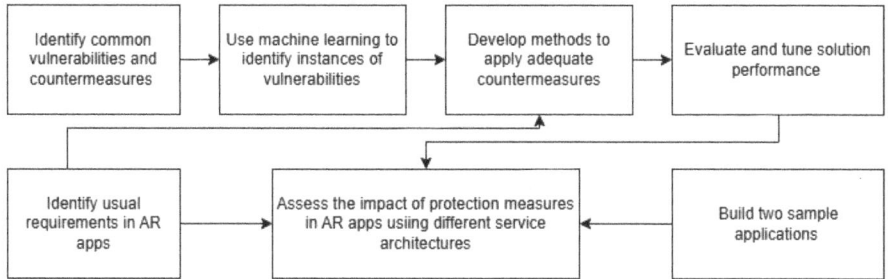

Fig. 2. Main research tasks

4 Current Stage and Discussion

Our work started by focusing on data captured by AR applications through the device's cameras. We developed several methods and prototypes, as described in the following, and made source code available in repositories that may be accessed through the project's website at https://safear.ipleiria.pt/.

Ofuscation Service Prototype: We prototyped the service Fig. 1 outlines using YOLO for object detection and segmentation and providing different image obfuscation strategies, namely blurring, masking, and pixelation. Implementations using YOLOv5, YOLOv8, and YOLOv9 are available. We chose these versions based on their performance and resource usage characteristics. Our service consumes raw image data and sanitizes them based on a set of class identifiers and corresponding obfuscation methods provided as parameters. The server executes required preprocessing, identifies and segments instances of the specified classes and applies the chosen obfuscation strategy. We executed several experiments using data from ten classes of the COCO dataset [8]. On average, instance identification and segmentation tasks took 35.7% of the elapsed time, data transfer took 63.9% of the execution time, and object obfuscation took only 0.4% of the elapsed time. Figure 3 presents masking performs best among evaluated obfuscation methods, pixelation performs worst, and processing time depends on the number of objects to be obfuscated in the image. The number of objects does not impact the performance of instance segmentation and data transfer.

Location-Based AR Game: We developed a prototype of an LBARG on which players can collect items in a specific area in the real world. To assess an alternative solution that might improve the service's performance, we developed a local library (named SafeARUnity) in Unity using Sentis to execute object recognition, segmentation, and obfuscation. Performance limitations rely on resource availability on the mobile phone where the application is running.

Ongoing Research: Based on the experimental results, we envision some research directions to explore. Employing a hybrid architecture (Fig. 4) with a middleware that runs on the AR device may improve the solution performance, as

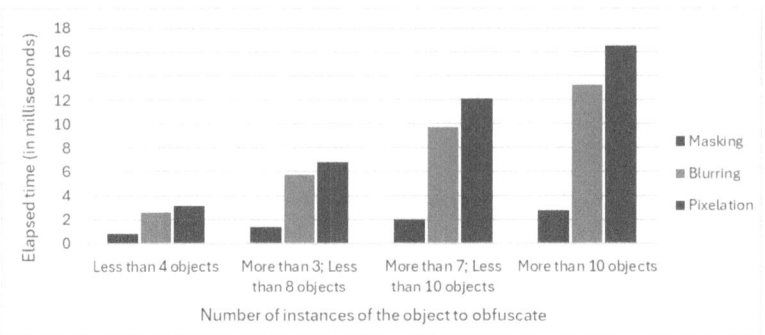

Fig. 3. Elapsed times (in ms) per obfuscation type and number of objects to obfuscate

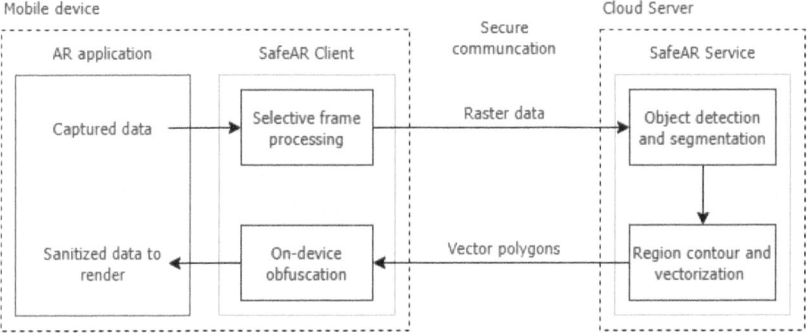

Fig. 4. Distributed architecture for sensitive data identification and obfuscation

the middleware would filter the data to be sanitized, reducing data transmission from the device to the service, and execute obfuscation based in coordinates defined by the service, reducing the amount of data transmitted from the server to the AR device. Developing a single deep model to perform segmentation and inpainting is another research direction we are exploring. We are also working on questionnaires to evaluate how privacy measures impact user experience and immersion.

5 Conclusions

AR applications are currently highly used in several contexts, but dealing with privacy and confidentiality issues in AR applications is an open issue. In this paper, we describe the work currently done at SafeAR to create tools to protect privacy and confidentiality in AR applications.

We evaluated using deep learning models to segment sensitive object instances and then apply data protection measures. Performance requirements and resource limitations common in AR applications make it challenging to create feasible solutions, leading to the need to evaluate highly distributed architectures. Future research directions also include creating a single specialized deep model that performs risk identification and the application of countermeasures.

Acknowledgements. This work is funded by national funds through FCT - Fundação para a Ciência e a Tecnologia, I.P., in the context of the projects SafeAR - 2022.09235.PTDC - and UIDB/04524/2020 and under the Scientific Employment Stimulus - CEECINS/00051/2018.

References

1. Azuma, R.: A survey of augmented reality. Presence: Teleoperators Virtual Environ. **6**, 355–385 (1997)
2. Böhm, F., Dietz, M., Preindl, T., Pernul, G.: Augmented reality and the digital twin: state-of-the-art and perspectives for cybersecurity. J. Cybersecur. Priv. **1**(3), 519–538 (2021)
3. De Guzman, J.A., Thilakarathna, K., Seneviratne, A.: Security and privacy approaches in mixed reality: a literature survey. ACM Comput. Surv. (CSUR) **52**(6), 1–37 (2019)
4. Harborth, D., Pape, S.: Investigating privacy concerns related to mobile augmented reality apps - a vignette based online experiment. Comput. Hum. Behav. **122**, 106833 (2021)
5. Jana, S., Narayanan, A., Shmatikov, V.: A scanner darkly: protecting user privacy from perceptual applications. In: 2013 IEEE Symposium on Security and Privacy, pp. 349–363. IEEE (2013)
6. King, A., Kaleem, F., Rabieh, K.: A survey on privacy issues of augmented reality applications. In: 2020 IEEE Conference on Application, Information and Network Security (AINS), pp. 32–40. IEEE (2020)
7. Lebeck, K., Ruth, K., Kohno, T., Roesner, F.: Towards security and privacy for multi-user augmented reality: foundations with end users. In: 2018 IEEE Symposium on Security and Privacy (SP), pp. 392–408. IEEE (2018)
8. Lin, T.Y., et al.: Microsoft coco: common objects in context (2015). https://doi.org/10.48550/arXiv.1405.0312
9. Roesner, F., Kohno, T., Molnar, D.: Security and privacy for augmented reality systems. Commun. ACM **57**(4), 88–96 (2014)
10. Siriwardhana, Y., Porambage, P., Liyanage, M., Ylianttila, M.: A survey on mobile augmented reality with 5G mobile edge computing: architectures, applications, and technical aspects. IEEE Commun. Surv. Tutorials **23**(2), 1160–1192 (2021)
11. Templeman, R., Korayem, M., Crandall, D.J., Kapadia, A.: Placeavoider: steering first-person cameras away from sensitive spaces. In: NDSS, vol. 14, pp. 23–26 (2014)
12. Wang, J., Amos, B., Das, A., Pillai, P., Sadeh, N., Satyanarayanan, M.: A scalable and privacy-aware IoT service for live video analytics. In: Proceedings of the 8th ACM on Multimedia Systems Conference, pp. 38–49 (2017)
13. Zarepour, E., Hosseini, M., Kanhere, S.S., Sowmya, A.: A context-based privacy preserving framework for wearable visual lifeloggers. In: 2016 IEEE International Conference on Pervasive Computing and Communication Workshops (PerCom Workshops), pp. 1–4. IEEE (2016)

Serverless and Cloud Systems

Deep Surrogate Models of Serverless Batch Processing Services

Yicheng Gao[1]($\boxtimes$), Roberto Sala[2], Danilo Ardagna[2], and Giuliano Casale[1]

[1] Department of Computing, Imperial College London, London, UK
{y.gao20,g.casale}@imperial.ac.uk
[2] DEIB, Politecnico di Milano, Milan, Italy
{roberto.sala,danilo.ardagna}@polimi.it

Abstract. Serverless computing breaks down applications into workflows of stateless functions, where the output of each function serves as the input for the next. When these workflows are distributed across multiple processing nodes, managing the interactions between nodes is crucial to maintaining overall system performance. However, existing analytical performance models do not cope well with the dependencies involved in distributed workflows when the offloaded jobs arrive in batches. In this paper, we study the problem for two processing resources in tandem and develop a scalable surrogate modeling approach based on neural networks that can be used for serverless resource management purposes. We validate our performance model with both synthetic and real-world AI application traces, demonstrating that our surrogate model achieves a mean average percentage error of about 5%.

Keywords: Batch processing · Function-as-a-service · Stochastic model · Performance measures

1 Introduction

Edge computing has emerged in recent years as a key paradigm for distributing computing. Recently, Function as a Service (FaaS) has garnered significant attention and current research often focuses on designing platforms and architectures that adapt serverless computing to edge scenarios [15]. In this paper, we focus instead on the problem of performance characterization of serverless solutions for prediction tasks in resource management. Many studies adopt learning-based approaches to analyze and predict the performance of applications running in edge computing systems [2,9,13,20,23]. For example, in [23], a neural network model, built with denoising auto-encoder and fuzzy clustering for QoS prediction in mobile edge environments, is designed to improve the prediction accuracy while addressing the overfitting problem. In [2], five widely used machine learning models, such as support vector regression and random forest, are considered for predicting CNN inference execution time on edge GPUs. However, when applying learning-based methods in the design phase of serverless edge computing systems, extensive large-scale profiling experiments are required to collect sufficient training data, leading to significant operational costs. Additionally, gathering adequate data in the design phase may be particularly challenging due to the limited availability of system performance metrics at this stage.

Alternatively, some researchers consider analytical performance models for FaaS platforms, allowing application developers and serverless operators to perform capacity planning and system analysis rapidly, without the need for costly and large-scale experimental setups [11]. The authors in [12] and [11] develop transient and steady-state analytical performance models based on M/G/m/m queueing systems to make capacity predictions for serverless computing platforms. The authors in [5] present a sizing method, called COCOA, leveraging the layered queueing network (LQN) model and $M/M/k$ setup models to derive performance estimates for provisioning FaaS systems that meet service-level agreements.

While these existing analytical models are well-suited for performance prediction of serverless computing, they overlook the fact that offloaded jobs often arrive in batches [8], leading to significant challenges due to the limited computational resources available at the edge. These batch arrivals complicate resource allocation and queueing dynamics, often resulting in performance bottlenecks. Therefore, efficient performance models are crucial to capture the constraints and operational dynamics of serverless edge computing systems.

To address these issues, we propose a surrogate modeling approach for predicting the performance of serverless edge computing systems. We first model the system as a tandem queueing network, where tasks visit sequentially the resources, and apply the decomposition technique to break down the workflow into individual components. Each component is then analyzed in isolation using BMMPP/GI/c queues to capture the effects of batch arrivals. Due to the complexity of solving such tandem models analytically, we further develop a Deep Neural Network (DNN)-based surrogate model to approximate the performance metrics. Finally, extensive simulations validate the accuracy and robustness of our proposed model. Overall, the contributions are as follows:

- We investigate the workflow characteristics of application traces from AI-SPRINT, a real-world serverless platform, offering an in-depth analysis of its batch arrival patterns [4,15].
- We formulate a performance model based on tandem queueing networks with batch arrivals to capture the impacts of batch job patterns and distributed workflow dependencies.
- To address the computational overhead of analytical methods, we propose a DNN-based surrogate model, henceforth referred to as a deep surrogate model, to approximate the performance metrics of tandem workflows.
- We validate our performance model through extensive simulations with both synthetic workloads and real-world traces, demonstrating that our surrogate model achieves strong alignment with actual performance data, yielding a mean average percentage error of 5.33%.

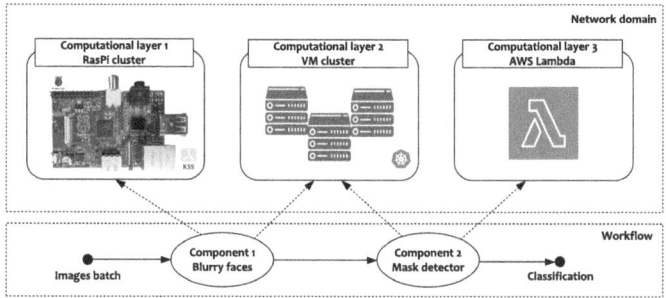

Fig. 1. An example of an AI-SPRINT application for mask detection. Edge nodes are managed through minified Kubernetes distributions (*e.g.,* K3s). Containers deployed in private and public VMs are orchestrated by K8s.

The rest of the paper is organized as follows. Section 2 introduces the AI-SPRINT applications and presents a detailed trace analysis. Section 3 gives the motivation for modeling with tandem queueing networks and outlines the approach for their approximation. Section 4 presents the performance model and deep surrogate modeling approach. Experimental results are discussed in Sect. 5 prior to conclusions.

2 System Characteristics

2.1 AI-SPRINT Applications and Profiling

AI-SPRINT ("Artificial Intelligence in Secure PRIvacy-preserving computing coNTinuum") is a comprehensive framework designed to facilitate the development and deployment of AI applications across a distributed computing continuum, encompassing both edge devices and cloud infrastructures [3,18]. The framework addresses the critical need to balance performance, accuracy, and security within AI-driven workflows.

An AI-SPRINT application consists of multiple interconnected Python components, each performing a specific task within the workflow. The execution of these components is event-driven and orchestrated by OSCAR [14], an open-source platform that supports the FaaS model. Each component is triggered by file uploads, and the output of one component triggers the next in the sequence.

To ensure execution consistency and reliability, each component is encapsulated within a Docker container. The architecture supports a diverse range of computational resources, from edge devices like Raspberry Pis to cloud-based virtual machines and AWS Lambda, allowing for optimized resource allocation tailored to the computational demands of each component.

An example of an AI-SPRINT application is depicted in Fig. 1, which features a two-component workflow for mask detection executed across multiple computing layers. The first component, *Blurry Faces*, processes video input by extracting frames every five seconds, detecting faces using a neural network, and anonymizing them through pixel modification. The anonymized frames are then

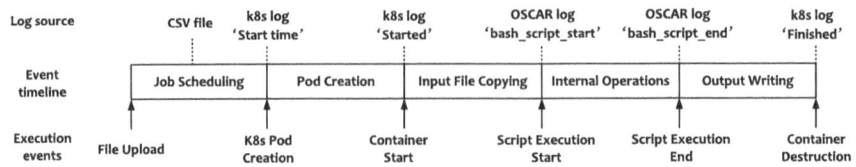

Fig. 2. Detailed logging process of OSCAR-P with execution stages and timestamps

passed to the second component, *Mask Detector*, which detects the presence of masks on the faces and annotates the images with corresponding labels and confidence scores. This application exemplifies the use of edge computing, where video preprocessing is performed on a cluster of Raspberry Pi devices to ensure data privacy by keeping sensitive information at the edge. The anonymized frames are then uploaded and analyzed in the cloud, allowing for efficient and secure mask detection across various urban areas.

To systematically profile AI-SPRINT applications across diverse hardware configurations, an advanced auto-profiling tool integrated with the OSCAR framework named OSCAR-P is further employed [4]. The profiling process begins with specifying detailed hardware parameters and application requirements, including node configurations, memory capacity, processing power, Docker images, and levels of parallelism. OSCAR-P then conducts experiments by dynamically adjusting parameters and executing the application under various scenarios. After each run, it retrieves and processes execution logs, capturing timing, resource usage, and overall performance for each component.

Figure 2 provides the detailed logging process managed by OSCAR-P, highlighting the execution stages and their corresponding timestamps. The logs, collected from both K8s and OSCAR, provide in-depth insights into the application performance across the different stages.

For such AI-SPRINT applications, predicting performance during the design phase is crucial, particularly when estimating the response time across various configurations, as it enables effective capacity planning, resource management, while maintaining quality of service. However, this task is challenging due to the complexity of distributed, multi-component workflows. Accurately predicting execution time for components across a computing continuum and understanding their complex interactions is inherently difficult. Moreover, the design phase often lacks sufficient data, making data-driven approaches both time-consuming and costly to implement [10]. To address these challenges, we propose an analytical approach that captures system performance. To reduce the computational overhead of the specific analytical method, we develop a deep surrogate model for efficient performance metric prediction.

2.2 Trace Collection and Analysis

In this section, we analyse the mask detection application execution traces collected through OSCAR-P. As depicted in Fig. 1, the components are profiled using multiple configurations on AWS EC2. The trace spans six days, during

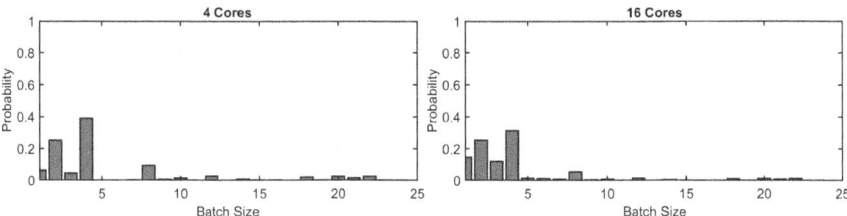

Fig. 3. Probability mass function of batch sizes across different core configurations

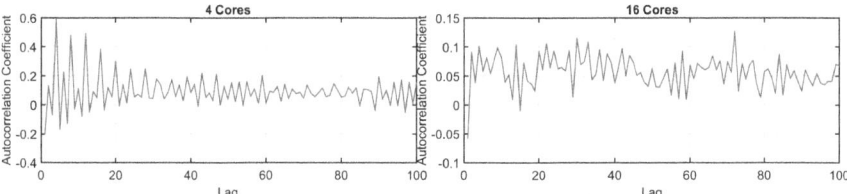

Fig. 4. Autocorrelation function of batch sizes across different core configurations

which a series of experiments are conducted to comprehensively assess the system under a wide range of operational conditions.

Input Traffic Configuration: The experiments consider different numbers of 5-s videos as input. Each set of input data is processed three times on VMs to ensure robust and consistent results. To simulate diverse real-world usage scenarios, the input traffic is configured to arrive in batches, with varying throughput rates ranging from 0.02 to 1.86 requests per second. This variability is achieved by maintaining a batch size of four files and altering the inter-arrival time between batches, allowing for a detailed analysis of the system performance under various load conditions.

VMs Configuration: The configuration of the VM cluster is critical for understanding how the number of cores affects the performance of the mask-detection application. In this context, each node refers to an individual VM within the cluster. For simplicity, we profiled the application on homogeneous AWS EC2 m4.large VMs, equipped with Intel Xeon processors, each featuring two cores and 8 GB of memory. This configuration allows a maximum of two instances of the application to run concurrently on each node. Each application component operates within an isolated, single-core container, requiring one core to function. Thus, the level of parallelism-the maximum number of concurrent containers that can run on a node-is directly determined by the number of available cores. In this setup, the VMs scale horizontally to configurations with 2, 4, 8, and 16 cores for profiling the application. Notably, the service times for all components remain relatively stable across these configurations.

With these predefined configurations, AI-SPRINT application traces are collected from logs across a varying number of cores. Both the full workflow and its

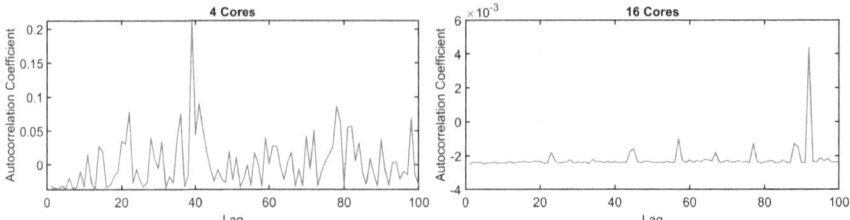

Fig. 5. Autocorrelation function of inter-arrival times between batches

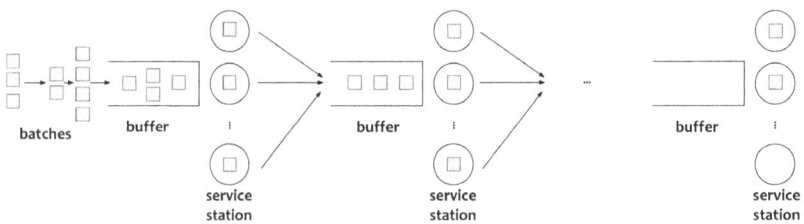

Fig. 6. An example of a tandem queueing network with batch arrivals

individual components are profiled. Each log file records essential information about the jobs, including creation and completion times, as well as the parallelism level. To capture these characteristics, we analyze each single component by its probability distribution and temporal dependencies, enabling accurate performance predictions. Specifically, we utilize the Autocorrelation Function (ACF) to analyze the temporal dependencies within the traces.

For each individual component, Fig. 3 illustrates that the probability mass function (PMF) spans batch sizes from 1 to 25, with a notable concentration around 4. Although the system is configured for batches of 4 jobs, Kubernetes scheduling policies (which determine resource allocation, pod distribution, and job queueing) led to variations in the actual batch sizes. These factors can create discrepancies between the intended batch size and the one observed during execution. Furthermore, Fig. 4 shows that the autocorrelation of batch sizes is weak and diminishes rapidly, implying that the sizes of consecutive batches are independent. In Fig. 5, the periodic spikes observed in the ACF of the inter-arrival times suggest the presence of recurring scheduling patterns. However, these periodic spikes diminish rapidly, indicating that the inter-arrival times between batches are close to independent over lags.

3 Motivation

Given the characteristics of the AI-SPRINT application workflow, we propose modeling the system as a tandem queueing network, where each component operates as a sequential queueing system, an example is given in Fig. 6.

3.1 Traffic Decomposition Methods

To address state spaces explosion and complex interactions within such tandem networks, we apply the traffic decomposition approach [21]. This technique enables the analysis of each node in isolation by treating the output from one queue as the arrival process for the next. Each output is characterized in terms of its statistical moments, and in some works also its autocorrelation function [7], and then fit to a simplified stochastic process to describe arrivals. Within the traffic decomposition approach, we propose to capture the dynamics of each component by employing the BMMPP/GI/c model that we approximate by means of a neural surrogate. A BMMPP is a Batched Marked Modulated process that can be used to describe non-i.i.d. point processes with batch arrivals [22]. BMMPP/GI/c queueing systems have general independent service and c servers. They are typically classified as M/G/c-type models and their underlying (infinite) continuous-time Markov chain is characterized by an upper block Hessenberg structure in their infinitesimal generator $Q_{M/G/c\text{-type}}$, where only the first block below the main diagonal contains non-zero elements, while all subsequent lower blocks are zero matrices.

To approximate the BMMPP/GI/c model, which is difficult to analyze due to state-space explosion driven by its multiserver parameter c, we initially focus on the response time and model the system as an equivalent single-server BMMPP/GI/1 queue with an adjusted service rate to account for c. Our proposal is to adapt for the first time an approximation method in [19] proposed in the context of product-form queueing network theory to multiserver matrix analytic queueing systems.

Specifically, we first model the BMMPP/GI/c system as a single-server queue with a service rate of $c\mu$, where μ is the service rate of each individual server and c is the number of parallel servers. This represents an equivalent rate of service of the station when all its servers are busy. The response time R_s for this single-server system can be obtained using matrix analytic methods for the BMMPP/GI/1 queue. Second, an adjustment is needed to account that in certain periods of time the server will not be fully loaded. The correction factor is expressed as $\alpha = \frac{c-1}{c} \times \frac{1}{\mu}$. This factor ensures that for a job that arrives when the station is idle, the total response time will be

$$\frac{1}{c\mu} + \frac{c-1}{c} \times \frac{1}{\mu} = \frac{1}{\mu}$$

as intended. Summarizing, the response time $\widetilde{R_m}$ can be approximated as [19]

$$\widetilde{R_m} = R_s + \frac{c-1}{c} \times \frac{1}{\mu}. \tag{1}$$

The merit of our proposal to apply this approach for the first time to matrix analytic queues is that it allows for an efficient approximation of the response time of the BMMPP/GI/c system by resorting to analytical methods that are available for BMMPP/GI/1 queues.

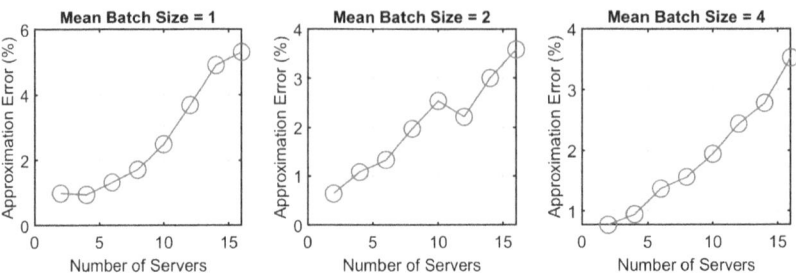

Fig. 7. Approximation error for multiserver scenarios

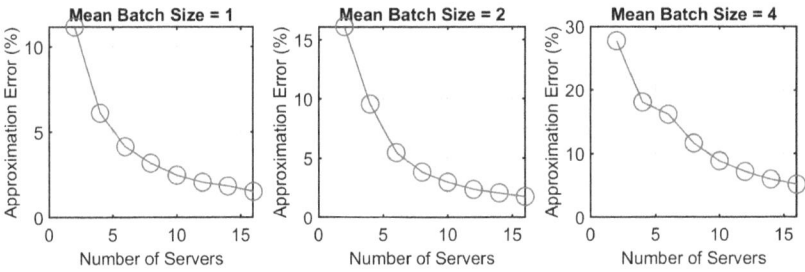

Fig. 8. Approximation error for complete tandem workflows

To determine the accuracy of the proposed approximations in a way that abstracts the accuracy of the associated single-server solver, we test the proposed method first using simulation. The approximation error σ is evaluated as

$$\sigma = \frac{|\widetilde{R_m} - R_m|}{R_m} \times 100\%, \qquad (2)$$

where R_m is the response time obtained through a BMMPP/GI/c simulator.

As illustrated in Fig. 7, the approximation error remains minimal across different numbers of servers and mean batch sizes. For scenarios with a small number of servers (e.g., $c \leq 5$), the error is consistently below 2%, demonstrating that the approximation is highly accurate in these settings. As the number of servers increases, the error gradually escalates but the deviation remains limited to 4–6%. These results indicate that the approximation provides a precise solution for a BMMPP/GI/c system.

3.2 Tandem Workflow Approximation

In the full application workflow modeled as a tandem queueing network, the departure process of one component directly serves as the arrival process for the subsequent component. To approximate the performance of the full tandem workflow, we initially leverage MAMsolver [16,17] to solve each individual component within the network. MAMsolver integrates the ETAQA technique

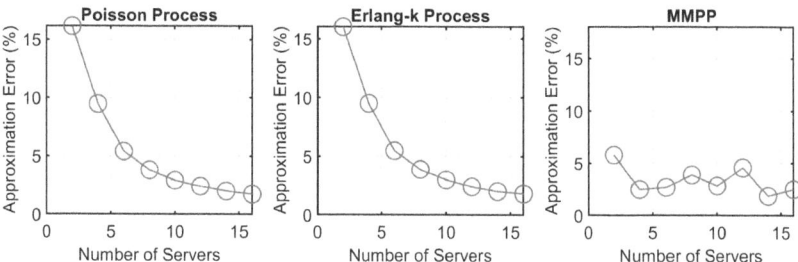

Fig. 9. Approximation error for tandem workflows with different arrival process fitting methods in the subsequent queues

to enhance computational efficiency in computing key stationary performance metrics M/G/1-type, GI/M/1-type, and QBD processes. In this initial evaluation, the departure process of each component is derived with simulation to analyze moments and ACF of the inter-departure times, and then passed as the arrival process for the subsequent component in the tandem workflow. For all subsequent components, the arrival process is defined by the departure process of the preceding component. This sequential analysis allows us to approximate the performance of the entire tandem workflow, despite the challenges posed by inter-component dependencies. Later on, our methodology will not require using simulation anymore, which is considered here only to illustrate the level of accuracy that could be achieved through moment-based traffic decomposition when the values of the moments are accurately estimated.

To simplify the analysis, we first approximate the inter-departure times by fitting them to an Erlang-k distribution, which captures the first two moments. The results in Fig. 8 show that the approximation error for the complete workflow remains below 27.73% across all configurations. As the mean batch size increases, the error tends to rise, particularly in scenarios with fewer servers. For smaller batch sizes, the error decreases rapidly, falling below 5% as the number of servers increases, indicating a high level of accuracy. However, as the batch size grows, the error increases to around 30%, reflecting the increased difficulty in modeling more complex batch dynamics.

Further, we compare different methods of fitting the arrival process for the subsequent queues within the tandem workflow, specifically under a batch size of 2. The results in Fig. 9 compare the approximation errors across tandem workflows modeled with three different types of arrival processes for the subsequent queues: Poisson, Erlang-k, and MMPP. The MMPP model, which accounts for the first three moments and the lag-1 ACF, demonstrates higher performance, with the approximation error consistently staying below 5.8% across different configurations. This enhanced accuracy highlights the capability of MMPP to capture the more complex dynamics of the departure process of batch queues compared to the Erlang-k and Poisson models, which ignore dependence between inter-departure times.

Issues with Approximation Methods. While existing BMMPP/GI/1 solvers provide accurate approximations of multiserver systems, they suffer from high computational complexity when applied to low variability arrivals as in the AI-SPRINT system. To demonstrate this, we employ MAMsolver as a case study for analyzing the BMMPP/GI/1 model. Specifically, we examine the time complexity associated with varying numbers of phases in the arrival process, averaging 1,000 samples for each configuration. Running experimental tests, we find that if both the arrival and service processes are considered, the computational burden can exceed 10^6 s, further illustrating the limitations of this approach in handling complex systems. This approach becomes particularly costly in design studies, where thousands of models may need to be solved. To address this issue, we propose leveraging surrogate models as discussed in the next section.

4 Deep Surrogate Model

4.1 Performance Model

Since we apply the decomposition technique to the entire application workflow, this section provides a detailed performance modeling of each individual component. Specifically, we utilize a two-state Batch Markov Modulated Poisson Process, denoted as BMMPP(2), to model the batch arrival process of each component. The intensity matrices of BMMPP(2) can be characterized by $\mathbf{D}_b$, $b = 0, 1, \ldots, B$, where B is the maximum batch size, as follows.

The intensity matrix $\mathbf{D}_0$ governs transitions without arrivals:

$$\mathbf{D}_0 = \begin{bmatrix} -\lambda_1 & \lambda_{12} \\ \lambda_{21} & -\lambda_2 \end{bmatrix}, \tag{3}$$

where λ_{12} and λ_{21} represent the transition rates between the two states. The states map to different arrival rates for the incoming jobs. The intensity matrices $\mathbf{D}_b$, $b = 1, \ldots, B-1$, describe transitions associated with batch arrivals of size b and are given by $\mathbf{D}_b = \mathrm{diag}(\lambda_1 p_{11b}, \lambda_2 p_{22b})$, where p_{11b} and p_{22b} are the probabilities of observing a batch arrival of size b in states 1 and 2, respectively. The intensity matrix $\mathbf{D}_B$ is defined as:

$$\mathbf{D}_B = \begin{bmatrix} -\lambda_1 - \lambda_{12} - \sum_{i=1}^{B-1} \lambda_1 p_{11i} & 0 \\ 0 & -\lambda_2 - \lambda_{21} - \sum_{i=1}^{B-1} \lambda_2 p_{22i} \end{bmatrix}. \tag{4}$$

Thus, the infinitesimal generator $\mathbf{Q}_{BMMPP(2)}$ of the underlying Markov process is given by $\mathbf{Q}_{BMMPP(2)} = \sum_{b=0}^{B} \mathbf{D}_b$.

Given the negligible correlation in the trace data, we consider a variant of the BMMPP(2) where the batch size probabilities are assumed to be identical across states, *i.e.*, $p_{iib} = p_{jjb}$, for any $i \neq j$. Under this assumption, the intensity matrices can be expressed as [22] $\mathbf{D}_0 = \mathbf{Q} - \mathbf{\Delta}(\boldsymbol{\delta})$, $\mathbf{D}_b = \mathbf{\Delta}(\boldsymbol{\delta}) \cdot \mathbf{\Delta}(p_b)$, $b \geq 1$, where $\mathbf{\Delta}(\boldsymbol{\delta})$ is a diagonal matrix with $\boldsymbol{\delta} = [\lambda_1, \lambda_2]^T$, and $\boldsymbol{\delta}(p_b)$ is a diagonal matrix with the batch probabilities p_b as its diagonal elements, satisfying $\sum_{b=1}^{B} p_b = 1$.

By assuming no correlation between inter-arrival times and batch sizes, this variant, denoted as $\text{BMMPP}_v(2)$ and also known as a MAP with independent and identically distributed (i.i.d.) batch arrivals, provides a tractable approach for modeling the batch arrival process of each application component. Additionally, the service time distribution is modeled using a General Independent (GI) distribution, offering flexibility to capture a wide range of service behaviors, and the model incorporates c servers to account for the parallel processing capabilities of each component.

Regarding the embedded Markov chain of the $\text{BMMPP}_v(2)/\text{GI}/c$ queue we study, each state in the chain is represented by three elements: the number of jobs in the system, the phase of the arrival process, and the phase of the service process. Both the arrival process and service process consist of multiple exponential phases in series. Due to the structural characteristics of this Markov chain, the state space can be partitioned into boundary and repetitive blocks. Consequently, the infinitesimal generator matrix $\boldsymbol{Q}$ can be constructed as follows:

$$\boldsymbol{Q}_{\text{BMMPP}_v(2)/\text{GI}/c} = \begin{bmatrix} \boldsymbol{B}_0 & \boldsymbol{B}_1 & \boldsymbol{B}_2 & \boldsymbol{B}_3 & \cdots \\ \boldsymbol{C}_0 & \boldsymbol{A}_1 & \boldsymbol{A}_2 & \boldsymbol{A}_3 & \cdots \\ 0 & \boldsymbol{A}_0 & \boldsymbol{A}_1 & \boldsymbol{A}_2 & \cdots \\ 0 & 0 & \boldsymbol{A}_0 & \boldsymbol{A}_1 & \ddots \\ \vdots & \vdots & \vdots & \vdots & \ddots \end{bmatrix} \tag{5}$$

where $\boldsymbol{A}_k$, $k = 0, 1, 2, \ldots$, and $\boldsymbol{C}_0$ denote the transitions for repetitive states, and $\boldsymbol{B}_k$, $k = 0, 1, 2, \ldots$, represent the transitions for boundary states.

Specifically, $\boldsymbol{A}_0$, $\boldsymbol{A}_1$, $\boldsymbol{A}_k$, $k \geq 2$, represent the backward, local, and forward transitions, respectively, as follows:

$$\boldsymbol{A}_0 = \begin{bmatrix} 0 & \cdots & 0 \\ \vdots & \ddots & \vdots \\ r\mu & \cdots & 0 \end{bmatrix}, \boldsymbol{A}_1 = \begin{bmatrix} -k\lambda + r\mu & r\mu & \cdots & 0 \\ 0 & -k\lambda + r\mu & r\mu & \cdots \\ 0 & 0 & -k\lambda + r\mu & r\mu & \cdots \\ \vdots & \vdots & & \ddots & \ddots & \ddots \end{bmatrix} \tag{6}$$

$$\boldsymbol{A}_k = \begin{bmatrix} P_x\lambda & 0 & 0 & \cdots \\ 0 & P_x\lambda & 0 & 0 & \cdots \\ 0 & 0 & P_x\lambda & 0 & 0 & \cdots \\ \vdots & \vdots & \vdots & \ddots & \ddots & \ddots \end{bmatrix} \tag{7}$$

where P_x denotes the probability mass function of the batch size. $\boldsymbol{C}_0 = [0, 0, \ldots, r\mu]^T$ represents the backward transition for the first repetitive block. Moreover, $\boldsymbol{B}_0$ and $\boldsymbol{B}_k$ denote the local and forward transitions for the boundary states, where $\boldsymbol{B}_0 = -\lambda$ and $\boldsymbol{B}_k = [\cdots 0, 0, P_k\lambda, 0, 0, \cdots]$.

4.2 Deep Surrogate Model

To solve the $\text{BMMPP}_v(2)/\text{GI}/c$ queue in a more efficient way than with traditional matrix analytic methods, we further propose a Deep Neural Network

Table 1. Parameters for training data generation

Parameter	Range/Set
Mean inter-arrival time (E_1)	[50, 100] (unit steps)
SCV	{1, 2, 4, 8, 16, 32, 64}
Second central moment (E_2)	$E_2 = (1 + \text{SCV}) \times E_1^2$
Lag-2 autocorrelation (γ_2)	{0.0, 0.75, 0.9, 0.95, 0.99}
Batch size (S)	{2, 4, 8, 16, 32, 64}
Service rate (μ)	Erlang distribution with shape parameter μ_p (1–5) and scale parameter μ_a (0.1–0.5)
Number of cores (c)	{1, 2, 4, 8, 16}

(DNN)-based surrogate model. This model is tailored to learn the system behavior and approximate the performance metrics of each component in multiserver systems. Specifically, it employs a feedforward neural network architecture with multiple hidden layers of fully connected neurons. Each hidden layer applies Rectified Linear Unit (ReLU) activation functions to introduce nonlinearity, enhancing the capability to learn complex mappings between input features and performance metrics.

Training data for the proposed deep surrogate model is generated from simulations of BMMPP/PH/c systems. The dataset includes critical features such as the statistical moments of arrival processes E_{a1}, E_{a2}, E_{a3}, the PMF of batch arrival sizes P_{bs}, service process parameters E_{s1}, E_{s2}, and the number of servers c. The target outputs are performance metrics, including moments of response times. To ensure effective training and enhance model performance, both the input features and output targets are normalized using min-max scaling. The training process focuses on minimizing the Mean Absolute Percentage Error (MAPE) between the predicted and actual performance metrics. An adaptive optimization algorithm adjusts the learning rate dynamically to ensure efficient convergence. The network undergoes training for a specified number of epochs, with a batch size optimized for both computational efficiency and memory management, facilitating robust learning and accurate approximation of the performance metrics.

5 Experimental Results

5.1 Simulation-Based Evaluation

In this section, we evaluate our proposed deep surrogate model for full tandem workflows using data simulated by the JMT tool [1]. For each component in the tandem workflow, we model it as a BMAP/GI/c system, where BMAP generalizes BMMPP for more complex dynamics.

BMAP Sample Generation. First, we generate samples of BMAP to simulate the arrival process for each component in the tandem queueing network. For

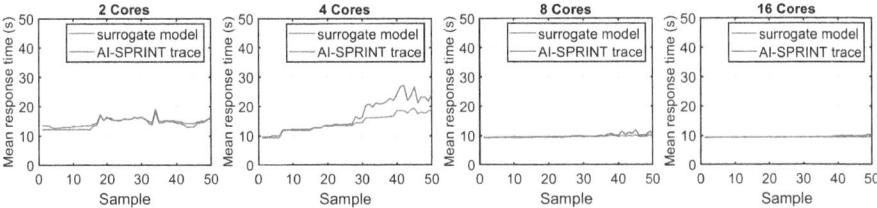

Fig. 10. Comparison of the response time between trace-based simulations and deep surrogate model

the first component, by configuring the mean inter-arrival time between batches and the squared coefficient of variation (SCV), we characterize the BMAP using the following parameters: the mean inter-arrival time E_1, which is the average time between consecutive batch arrivals; the second central moment $E_2 = (1 + \text{SCV}) \times E_1^2$; and the lag-2 autocorrelation γ_2. The third moment E_3 is set to the minimum value possible for the underlying MAP using the formulas in [6].

Given these parameters, we generate BMAP samples, each consisting of 10^6 requests. For each subsequent component in the tandem workflow, we use the JMT tool to log the departure times of each request from the preceding component. These logged departure times are then used to model the arrival process for the next component in the tandem network.

Training Data Generation. With the input of BMAP samples for each component, we further simulate the mean response time of each queue with the JMT tool. In parallel, we perform a full workflow simulation using the JMT tool, with the arrival process of the first component as input, allowing for assessing the overall system performance. To generate the training data for the deep surrogate model, we further detail the configuration by simulating a range of scenarios using the JMT tool in Table 1.

Training Process. We train the deep surrogate model using the following architecture and configurations. The DNN consists of four hidden layers with 128, 64, 32, and 16 neurons respectively, using ReLU activation functions for non-linearity. The final layer outputs the moments of response time prediction for each component of the tandem workflow. We implement the model using PyTorch and optimize it using the Adam optimizer. The learning rate is 0.001, the batch size is 512, and the number of epochs is 100.

Experimental Evaluation. The effectiveness of our proposed deep surrogate model is evaluated by comparing its aggregated predictions with the response times obtained from the full tandem workflow simulations conducted in the JMT tool. The evaluation results present an average MAPE of 19.04% across all samples, demonstrating the accuracy of our proposed surrogate model in predicting the performance of tandem queueing systems.

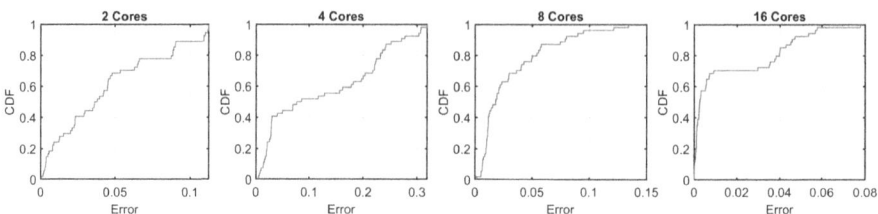

Fig. 11. CDF of the prediction error of the deep surrogate model

5.2 Mask Detection Application Trace

To evaluate the effectiveness of our proposed deep surrogate model for real-world tandem workflows, we compare its performance against the trace-driven simulation using traces collected from the mask detection applications operating within serverless edge computing systems. The experimental setup includes 216 different configurations, varying by the number of cores and job arrival rates. The trace data collected under each configuration spans a range of 32 to 3,968 requests. The inter-arrival times between batches within these traces exhibit low variability, allowing us to approximate them using an Erlang distribution. This approximation is well-suited for time-to-event random variables with low variability in Markovian modeling, as the Erlang distribution accurately captures the first two moments, $i.e.$, the mean and the variance, effectively in this context.

For both the trace-driven simulation and our proposed deep surrogate model, the input parameters include the number of cores, the first two moments of the inter-arrival and service time distributions, and the PMF of batch sizes. In the trace-driven simulation, the complete response time for each sample is simulated based on the trace data, providing a comprehensive measure of response times for the entire tandem workflow. In the deep surrogate model, it predicts the moments of response time for each component in the tandem workflow. These component-level moments are then aggregated to estimate the overall response time for the entire system.

Figure 10 presents the comparison of response times between the surrogate model and the AI-SPRINT trace across four core configurations. The surrogate model demonstrates a strong alignment with the mask detection trace, achieving an overall MAPE of 5.33%, indicating its effectiveness in capturing the system behavior. For the 2-core, 8-core, and 16-core configurations, response times are consistently below 20 s showing minimal deviation. In the 4-core configuration, a slight fluctuation is observed, where the application trace shows an increase in response times to around 20–25 s, while the surrogate model captures the overall trend but with a degree of error. This discrepancy is likely due to sudden bursts of high load in the real system, managed by Kubernetes, leading to temporary resource contention and scheduling delays.

We conjecture that during the 4-core experiments, the system may have entered an unusual state midway through the test, differing from the typical conditions observed in other tests. However, we could not firmly confirm this as we did not have direct access to the internals. Indeed, the strong alignment in the first half of the experiment with 4 cores shows that under normal conditions this case can also be matched fairly accurately. The overall alignment underscores the robustness of the model and its ability to generalize across diverse configurations, accurately predicting system performance in real-world scenarios.

Figure 11 shows the CDF of the prediction error of the proposed surrogate model under different core configurations. The CDF of the error across 2, 8, and 16-core configurations demonstrates that the surrogate model consistently achieves high accuracy, with most errors remaining below 0.1. These cases reflect strong alignment with the AI-SPRINT trace, indicating the robustness of the model under dynamic environments. The 4-core configuration stands out as an outlier, with maximum errors extending up to 30%, which are still acceptable from a practical standpoint. Nevertheless, the median error is far lower and equal to 10%. Overall, the CDF analysis demonstrates that our proposed surrogate model achieves high accuracy across different configurations.

6 Conclusion

In this paper, we propose a surrogate modeling approach for performance prediction in serverless edge computing systems. Focusing on real application traces, we show the need for capturing batch arrival patterns and propose a tandem BMMPP/GI/c performance model. Extensive simulations to validate the surrogate model, using both synthetic workloads and real-world traces, demonstrate that our proposed deep neural surrogate achieves high accuracy against real traces. Future work may look at extending our surrogate models to non-tandem topologies and multiclass batch arrivals.

References

1. Bertoli, M., et al.: JMT: performance engineering tools for system modeling. ACM SIGMETRICS PER **36**(4), 10–15 (2009)
2. Bouzidi, H., et al.: Performance prediction for convolutional neural networks on edge GPUs. In: ACM CF, pp. 54–62 (2021)
3. Filippini, F., et al.: SPACE4AI-R: a runtime management tool for AI applications component placement and resource scaling in computing continua. In: IEEE/ACM UCC, pp. 1–7 (2023)
4. Galimberti, E., et al.: OSCAR-P and amllibrary: performance profiling and prediction of computing continua applications. In: ACM/SPEC ICPE, pp. 139–146 (2023)
5. Gias, A.U., Casale, G.: COCOA: cold start aware capacity planning for function-as-a-service platforms. In: IEEE MASCOTS, pp. 1–8 (2020)
6. Heindl, A., et al.: Explicit inverse characterizations of acyclic maps of second order. In: EPEW 2006, pp. 108–122. Springer (2006)
7. Horváth, A., Telek, M.: A joint moments based analysis of networks of MAP/MAP/1 queues. PEVA **67**(9), 759–778 (2010)

8. Huang, J., et al.: Revenue-optimal task scheduling and resource management for IoT batch jobs in mobile edge computing. Peer-to-Peer Netw. Appl. **13**(5), 1776–1787 (2020)
9. Liu, Z., et al.: Context-aware and adaptive QoS prediction for mobile edge computing services. IEEE TSC **15**(1), 400–413 (2019)
10. Madougou, S., et al.: The landscape of GPGPU performance modeling tools. Parallel Comput. **56**, 18–33 (2016)
11. Mahmoudi, N., Khazaei, H.: Performance modeling of serverless computing platforms. IEEE Trans. Cloud Comput. **10**(4), 2834–2847 (2020)
12. Mahmoudi, N., Khazaei, H.: Temporal performance modeling of serverless computing platforms. In: WoSC, pp. 1–6 (2020)
13. Miao, Y., et al.: Intelligent task prediction and computation offloading based on mobile-edge cloud computing. FGCS **102**, 925–931 (2020)
14. Pérez, A., et al.: On-premises serverless computing for event-driven data processing applications. In: IEEE CLOUD, pp. 414–421 (2019)
15. Risco, S., et al.: Serverless workflows for containerised applications in the cloud continuum. J. Grid Comput. **19**, 1–18 (2021)
16. Riska, A., Smirni, E.: MAMsolver: a matrix analytic methods tool. In: International Conference on Modelling Techniques and Tools for Computer Performance Evaluation, pp. 205–211 (2002)
17. Riska, A., Smirni, E.: ETAQA solutions for infinite Markov processes with repetitive structure. INFORMS J. Comput. **19**(2), 215–228 (2007)
18. Sedghani, H., et al.: Advancing design and runtime management of AI applications with AI-sprint (position paper). In: IEEE COMPSAC, pp. 1455–1462 (2021)
19. Seidmann, A., et al.: Computerized closed queueing network models of flexible manufacturing systems: a comparative evaluation. Large Scale Syst. **12**(2), 91–107 (1987)
20. Tang, Q., et al.: Distributed task scheduling in serverless edge computing networks for the IoT: a learning approach. IEEE IoT J. **9**(20), 19634–19648 (2022)
21. Whitt, W.: The queueing network analyzer. Bell Syst. Tech. J. **62**(9), 2779–2815 (1983)
22. Yera, Y., et al.: Fitting procedure for the two-state batch Markov modulated Poisson process. EJOR **279**(1), 79–92 (2019)
23. Yin, Y., et al.: QoS prediction for service recommendation with features learning in mobile edge computing. IEEE TCCN **6**(4), 1136–1145 (2020)

pyStorageLess: Leveraging Von Neumann's Architecture to Abstract Storage Heterogeneity in Serverless Applications

Sashko Ristov[1(✉)], Mika Hautz[1], Philipp Gritsch[1], Isabella Schmut[1], Peter Koll[1], and Michael Felderer[1,2,3]

[1] University of Innsbruck, Innsbruck, Austria
sashko.ristov@uibk.ac.at
[2] Institute of Software Technology, German Aerospace Center (DLR), Cologne, Germany
[3] University of Cologne, Cologne, Germany

Abstract. A novel approach PYSTORAGELESS introduces storage interoperability for serverless functions in federated serverless infrastructures. The serverless functions are deployed only once, and the storage can be dynamically linked to the functions at runtime by the user through control data inputs while invoking the serverless functions. PYSTORAGELESS uses the Von Neumann approach to abstract the function to have computing resources, memory, storage, and input/output data, regardless of the provider that hosts each part. PYSTORAGELESS splits data inputs into value and control, allowing users to dynamically attach the storage at runtime. With such extreme flexibility, users may distribute parts of the function across different providers to improve performance.

Keywords: Federated clouds · FaaS · storage interoperability · serverless

1 Introduction

Function-as-a-Service (FaaS) is a widely used serveless computing model that allows the execution of serverless applications without maintaining the underlying cloud infrastructure. Recent approaches, such as federated Faas [14] and Sky computing [18], offer more cost-effective and faster execution of serverless applications. Various techniques exist to FaaSify a method [1,2,15] or a code block [9] and deploy it as a serverless function across multiple providers. Despite achieving a high level of abstraction in terms of FaaS portability, interoperability remains a challenge. Functions are not pure computing units and are not isolated [6]. The stateless nature of serverless computing necessitates storing state in persistent storage, or functions call other managed cloud services [3]. Migrating such non-isolated code from on-premises to the cloud or between cloud providers often requires migrating the associated storage due to data locality [17], thereby adapting the SDKs to the target storage.

Unfortunately, the existing approaches for storage interoperability lag significantly behind solutions for function portability. For example, while the libraries, such as Apache Libcloud or jclouds, offer a common interface for storages of different providers, their abstraction is at the low level because developers still need to recode the function to change the provider and redeploy the updated function. Therefore, in this paper, we first investigate the weaknesses of the current storage interoperability methods, which motivate our novel approach for achieving storage interoperability at a high level of abstraction. We introduce a publicly available storage interoperability library PYSTORAGELESS[1], which we used to develop several serverless workflows[2] utilizing our Abstract Function Choreography Language (AFCL) [4,13].

2 Von Neumann's Abstraction of the Serverless Function in PyStorageLess

The state-of-the-art approaches include open-source libraries such as Apache Libcloud or jclouds, or the Lithops storage API [16], which provide a single interface for accessing storages like AWS S3 or GCP Cloud Storage. Developers specify the driver for the respective storage, allowing for interoperable storage access without changing the interface. Figure 1 (left) presents the semi-dynamic, two-layered approach of Apache Libcloud. At the top layer, developers must select the driver (provider), and at the second layer, they use developer APIs for access and provisioning. While this approach allows developers to choose the specific driver, they must recode and redeploy functions if they want to change the driver. PYSTORAGELESS (Fig. 1, right), on the other side, employs a different approach. At the top, PYSTORAGELESS abstracts all providers and their regions, enabling developers to focus on their APIs instead of selecting the appropriate driver first. This approach allows for the dynamic selection of buckets from specific cloud providers at runtime without requiring recoding and redeployment of the functions.

Fig. 1. Apache Libcloud 2-layers vs. pyStorageLess dynamic 3-layers.

---

[1] https://github.com/FaaSTools/pyStorage.
[2] https://github.com/AFCLWorkflows/.

We leverage Von Neumann's architecture to represent an abstract view of a serverless function that persist the state, i.e., accesses an abstract persistent storage, as depicted in Fig. 2. A serverless function comprises portable computing code that utilizes host memory, CPU, and the file system where it's deployed. During the deployment, the user selects the memory assigned to the function. Cloud providers often scale CPUs accordingly; for instance, AWS Lambda can utilize up to six CPUs when assigned the maximum allowed memory of 10 GB [8]. GCP, on the other side, allows developers to configure CPU resources of a function. The default hard drive is 512 MB, which is configurable during deployment. We denote all these portable and re-configurable computing resources with the gray lambda function in Fig. 2.

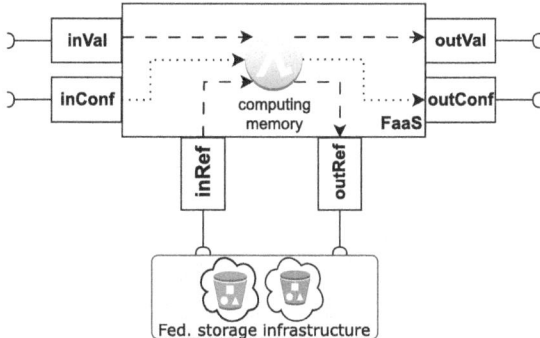

Fig. 2. Abstraction based on the Von Neumann's architecture.

Users invoke serverless functions with a payload, which is a key-value structure in JSON. Typically, functions receive small data explicitly *by value* through the payload when invoked. We denote this data port as `inVal`. Additionally, users pass large data implicitly *by reference* to files, which is provided in the payload. Unfortunately, existing libraries like Apache Libcloud restrict the storage to the provider whose driver is hardcoded in the function code. To address this limitation, we introduce an additional input data port `inConf`. Through `inConf`, users implicitly *configure* the driver that the function uses to access the referenced file. PYSTORAGELESS parses the given URI in the `inConf` and automatically detects the required driver and the location of the target data (e.g., files). It's important to note that `inConf` is not only used for URIs for downloading large data but also to specify the drivers and locations for large data outputs. Based on the extracted drivers and locations, PYSTORAGELESS uses a third data port, `inRef`, to access the given data *by reference*. This setup allows for more flexible and dynamic management of storage resources within serverless functions.

Once all data is placed in the file system or memory of the function, the processing begins. After processing finishes, the small data outputs of the computing are explicitly delivered to the output port `outVal` of the function. On the other hand, large data outputs are first stored via the `outRef` data port at the location that was received from the `inConf` data port. Once the large output data is stored, references to the stored output data are implicitly delivered to the output port `outPort`. This final step enables other functions within the serverless application (e.g., serverless workflow) to use the data through their `inConf` data port. Cloud providers often restrict direct message passing between functions, and serverless workflows typically exchange large data through cloud object storage to overcome this limitation [7].

3 pyStorageLess Architecture and Implementation

PYSTORAGELESS introduces an interoperable library that supports dynamic selection of storage attachments in serverless functions through control data inputs, as presented in Fig. 3. Developers can send bucket URL parameters as function data inputs and dynamically choose the bucket of the specific FaaS provider at runtime, rather than at the design phase (as in state-of-the-art Apache Libcloud and jclouds approaches). For example, if the function is invoked with source and destination URLs that refer to AWS S3 and GCP storages, respectively, the function will download the input data from AWS S3 and upload the results on GCP storage. Without any change in the function, the function can be now invoked with source and destination URLs that refer to GCP and AWS S3 storages, respectively, to download the input data from GCP storage and store the results in AWS S3.

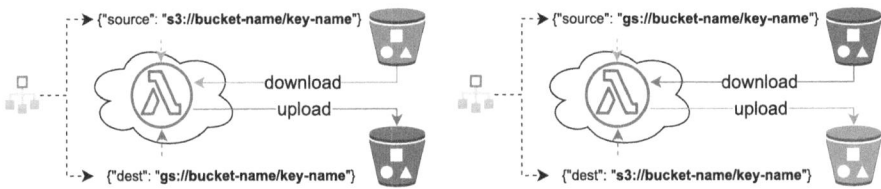

Fig. 3. Dynamic storage selection through the data inputs to the function.

Moreover, developers use a single `copy(source, dest)` method to download files from the bucket `source` to the function's local file system, upload results to the `dest` bucket, or copy from one storage to another, even across different providers. For the latter case, developers need to create two objects of Apache Libcloud, while PYSTORAGELESS handles copies files with a single object.

Figure 4 presents an example of a function written in Python that downloads the file with the reference `source` and uploads it to a set of destinations `targets`. The developer imports the PYSTORAGELESS as a library and codes the function to load the source and destination URLs (lines 6–7). In line 11, developer uses the copy interface to download the file from the source location. Further on, for each given target URL, developers code the function to upload the downloaded file (line 14), with the same object and copy method. Note that developers simply read values from the event (function's payload) and pass the source and destination to the copy method, which enables dynamic selection of the storages.

```
1   import json
2   from storage.pyStorage import pyStorage
3
4   def lambda_handler(event, context):
5
6       source_url = event['source']
7       targets = event['dest']
8
9       response = []
10      local_filename = source.split('/')[-1]
11      pyStorage.copy(source, local_filename)
12
13      for t in targets:
14          x = pyStorage.copy(local_filename, t)
15          response.append(x)
16
17      return {
18          'statusCode': 200,
19          'body': json.dumps(response)
20      }
```

Fig. 4. An example of a serverless function written in Python that downloads a file from the source and uploads it to multiple destination buckets dest. source and dest are provided at runtime and can span across various cloud providers.

3.1 Overview of Developer APIs

Figure 5 presents the high-level overview of the PYSTORAGELESS architecture. PYSTORAGELESS provides various APIs for dynamically attaching storage to serverless functions. For simplicity, Fig. 5 presents two APIs only. The interface downloadFile(srcStorage, destLocal) is used to download a file from the srcStorage and stores the file in the local file system of the function in the local file path destLocal. Unlike Apache Libcloud, where the developer needs to change the driver and change and redeploy the function, PYSTORAGELESS allows the developer to pass the input data to the srcStorage at design time and then simply invoke the function with the URL of another provider at runtime. With this approach, downloadFile() attaches one or multiple abstract storage backends and dynamically selects the URIs of the files to be downloaded.

Similarly, the interface uploadFile(srcLocal, destStorage) uploads a file from the local file path srcLocal to an abstract storage destStorage that is attached to the function. The target storage is determined dynamically by the input data that is passed to destStorage at runtime, using the same procedure that was already explained for downloadFile(srcStorage, destLocal). PYSTORAGELESS supports three other interfaces for an entire bucket, such as copy_bucket(source, target), create_bucket(bucket_name, region), and delete_bucket(bucket, delete_if_not_empty).

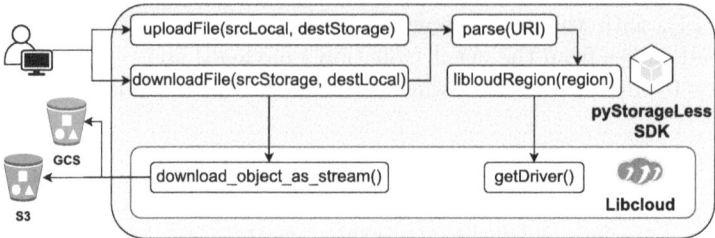

Fig. 5. pyStorageLess overview (partial view).

PYSTORAGELESS extends Apache Libcloud with a mechanism to dynamically switch between different storage backends without impacting function execution. Figure 5 shows the main components and APIs of PYSTORAGELESS. The PYSTORAGELESS interfaces `downloadFile(srcStorage, destLocal)` and `uploadFile(srcLocal, destStorage)` call the `parse(URI)` with the respective parameters `srcStorage` and `destStorage`. Then, `parse(URI)` parses the given URI and determines the provider and its region. Since Apache Libcloud uses a separate driver for each AWS region, while GCP has only one driver for all regions, `get_driver()` is invoked with the translated Apache Libcloud region from the method `libloudRegion(region)`. This method takes an AWS region label as input and returns an Apache Libcloud region label. Finally, for uploading and downloading a file, PYSTORAGELESS uses the Apache Libcloud methods, e.g., the `download_object_as_stream()` for downloading a file.

3.2 pyStorageLess in AFCL Workflows

The input data in the AFCL workflow json file can specify the location of input data (AWS S3 or GCP), that is, by replacing the field `<bucket>` from Fig. 6 with either AWS S3 or GCP cloud storage URI. Additionally, inside the workflow json, one can update the respective locations of the functions that should be invoked, either on AWS or GCP. With this approach, users can dynamically attach storages to workflow functions each time the AFCL workflow is invoked.

```
{
    "key_input": "<bucket>/input/ALL.chr22.80000.vcf.gz",
    "key_columnsfile": "<bucket>/input/columns.txt",
    "output_bucket": "<bucket>",
    "AFR": "<bucket>/input/AFR",
    "ALL": "<bucket>/input/ALL",
    "AMR": "<bucket>/input/AMR",
    "EAS": "<bucket>/input/EAS",
    "EUR": "<bucket>/input/EUR",
    "GBR": "<bucket>/input/GBR",
    "SAS": "<bucket>/input/SAS"
}
```

Fig. 6. Example of the workflow input that is sent to the xAFCL serverless workflow management system to attach the storages dynamically during runtime.

4 Conclusion and Future Work

The contributions of PYSTORAGELESS's approach, enabling users to manage storage dynamically at runtime, are manifold. Firstly, it facilitates the development of portable functions with interoperable storage, enhancing flexibility and reducing vendor lock-in. Secondly, it expands data access capabilities with an interoperable method, `copy(source, dest)`, which simplifies file operations by requiring only a single object, regardless of whether it involves downloading, uploading, or copying files between storage providers. Thirdly, PYSTORAGELESS allows users to deploy identical functions across both AWS and GCP, enabling dynamic selection of storage drivers and data input/output locations. Users can choose between AWS S3 or GCP Cloud Storage for their data inputs and outputs, enhancing flexibility and interoperability across multiple cloud providers. Lastly, community can utilize other serverless workflows (Montage, BWA, Genome1000, celebrityCollage [10], etc.), whose functions are coded with PYSTORAGELESS and allow interoperable storage in federated FaaS.

We will extend our work into several directions. First, we will introduce runtime mechanisms in PYSTORAGELESS to dynamically select the provider of the destination target storage by considering data locality. Second, we will develop a multi-objective scheduler (e.g., as an extension of our FaaSt scheduler [11]) to optimize the conflicting objectives cost and performance. Third, we will consider dynamic bandwidth between functions and storage, which depends on the assigned memory to the functions [5]. Finally, we will extend our SimLess mathematical model [12] to reuse data from not only computing part of a function, but also data access to storages in federated FaaS.

Acknowledgments. This work was supported by Land Tirol under the contract F.35499 (TIM) and KDT JU (grant agreement 101140216, MATISSE).

References

1. Carvalho, L., de Araújo., A.P.F.: Remote procedure call approach using the Node2FaaS framework with terraform for Function as a Service. In: International Conference on Cloud Computing and Services Science - CLOSER. SciTePress (2020)
2. Cordingly, R., et al.: The serverless application analytics framework: enabling design trade-off evaluation for serverless software. In: International Workshop on Serverless Computing (WoSC 2020), pp. 67–72 (2020)
3. Eismann, S., et al.: The state of serverless applications: collection, characterization, and community consensus. IEEE Trans. Softw. Eng. **48**(10), 4152–4166 (2022)
4. Hautz, M., Ristov, S., Felderer, M.: Characterizing AFCL serverless scientific workflows in federated FaaS. In: International Workshop on Serverless Computing, WoSC 2023, pp. 24–29. ACM, Bologna (2023)
5. Klimovic, A., Wang, Y., Stuedi, P., Trivedi, A., Pfefferle, J., Kozyrakis, C.: Pocket: elastic ephemeral storage for serverless analytics. In: Symposium on Operating Systems Design and Implementation (OSDI 2018), pp. 427–444. USENIX Association, Carlsbad (2018)

6. Larcher, T., Gritsch, P., Nastic, S., Ristov, S.: BaaSLess: backend-as-a-service (baas)-enabled workflows in federated serverless infrastructures. IEEE Trans. Cloud Comput. 1–15 (2024)
7. Mahgoub, A., Shankar, K., Mitra, S., Klimovic, A., Chaterji, S., Bagchi, S.: SONIC: application-aware data passing for chained serverless applications. In: Annual Technical Conference (ATC 21), pp. 285–301. USENIX Association (2021)
8. Mahgoub, A., Yi, E.B., Shankar, K., Elnikety, S., Chaterji, S., Bagchi, S.: ORION and the three rights: sizing, bundling, and prewarming for serverless DAGs. In: Symposium on Operating Systems Design and Implementation (OSDI 2022), pp. 303–320. USENIX Association, Carlsbad (2022)
9. Pedratscher, S., Ristov, S., Fahringer, T.: M2FaaS: transparent and fault tolerant FaaSification of node.js monolith code blocks. Future Gener. Comput. Syst. **135**, 57–71 (2022)
10. Ristov, S., Brandacher, S., Hautz, M., Felderer, M., Breu, R.: CODE: code once, deploy everywhere serverless functions in federated FaaS. Futur. Gener. Comput. Syst. **160**, 442–456 (2024)
11. Ristov, S., Gritsch, P.: FaaSt: optimize makespan of serverless workflows in federated commercial FaaS. In: International Conference on Cluster Computing, CLUSTER 2022, pp. 182–194. IEEE, Heidelberg (2022)
12. Ristov, S., Hautz, M., Hollaus, C., Prodan, R.: SimLess: simulate serverless workflows and their twins and siblings in federated FaaS. In: Symposium on Cloud Computing, SoCC 2022, pp. 323–339. ACM, San Francisco (2022)
13. Ristov, S., Pedratscher, S., Fahringer, T.: AFCL: an abstract function choreography language for serverless workflow specification. Fut. Gen. Comp. Syst. **114**, 368–382 (2021)
14. Ristov, S., Pedratscher, S., Fahringer, T.: xAFCL: run scalable function choreographies across multiple FaaS systems. IEEE Trans. Serv. Comput. **16**(1), 711–723 (2023)
15. Ristov, S., Pedratscher, S., Wallnoefer, J., Fahringer, T.: DAF: dependency-aware FaaSifier for node.js monolithic applications. IEEE Softw. **38**(1), 48–53 (2021)
16. Sampé, J., Sánchez-Artigas, M., Vernik, G., Yehekzel, I., García-López, P.: Outsourcing data processing jobs with lithops. IEEE Trans. Cloud Comput. **11**(1), 1026–1037 (2023)
17. Sethi, B., Addya, S.K., Bhutada, J., Ghosh, S.K.: Shipping code towards data in an inter-region serverless environment to leverage latency. J. Supercomput. **79**(10), 11585–11610 (2023)
18. Yang, Z., et al.: SkyPilot: an intercloud broker for sky computing. In: Symposium on Networked Systems Design and Implementation (NSDI 23), pp. 437–455. USENIX Association, Boston (2023)

Software Architecture

A Conceptual Framework for API Refactoring in Service-Oriented Architectures

Fabrizio Montesi[1], Marco Peressotti[1], Valentino Picotti[1(✉)], and Olaf Zimmermann[2]

[1] University of Southern Denmark, Odense, Denmark
{fmontesi,peressotti,picotti}@imada.sdu.dk
[2] Eastern Switzerland University of Applied Sciences (OST), Rapperswil, Switzerland
olaf.zimmermann@ost.ch

Abstract. In the lifetime of a service-oriented architecture, the Application Programming Interfaces (APIs) offered by services may need to be refactored in order to adapt to changing business and technical requirements. Previous studies focused on the effects that such API refactorings have on API definitions, with general considerations on related forces and smells. By contrast, the development strategies for realising these refactorings have received little attention. This paper addresses this aspect.

We introduce EMI, a conceptual framework for the implementation of API refactorings. Our framework is designed to elicit the trade-offs and choices that significantly affect the efficiency, maintainability, and isolation of the resulting architecture. We evaluate our framework by evolving a use case through the implementation of several refactorings, illustrating the different implementation choices that can be made. Based on our experience, we illustrate how to derive mechanical recipes for API refactoring that can follow different strategies in our framework.

1 Introduction

In service-oriented architectures, individual (micro)services perform specific functions and interact through well-defined Application Programming Interfaces (APIs) [4]. Over time, service APIs evolve because of changing requirements [5–8]. This prompted the study of *API refactoring*: the modification of interfaces to improve quality attributes, such as efficiency [18,19].

Recently, a catalogue of API patterns provided a basis for API refactorings [19,25]. Previous studies focused on the high-level forces (e.g., modifiability) and smells (e.g., high latency) that motivate and guide these refactorings. Conversely, it is yet unexplored how developers are supposed to implement an API refactoring and assess its quality; a research gap that we aim to address.

In this paper we introduce EMI (efficiency, maintainability and isolation), a conceptual framework for assessing the implementation of API refactoring in service architectures (Sect. 3). EMI centres around two dimensions: 1) *generality*, which assesses the degree of abstraction of the refactored API source code; 2) *distribution*, which elicits where the refactored API source code resides. Realising the combination of both dimensions results in six development strategies, each representing design choices for the implementation with respective trade-offs. The trade-offs pertain the quality aspects of *efficiency* (E), *maintainability* (M), and *isolation* (I) of the resulting architecture. We score each of these three aspects from 1 to 3 for our strategies, yielding the EMI score for API refactoring. There is no silver bullet: no strategy scores perfectly (9), emphasising the importance of making conscious implementation decisions.

We validate the applicability of our framework by carrying out several API refactorings on an illustrative publication catalogue service (Sect. 4). Specifically, we apply our six development strategies to the same refactoring: the introduction of the API KEY pattern – which rejects requests without a valid key – to a service that offers a catalogue of scientific publications (Sect. 4.1). We then broaden our study to patterns that do not require behavioural changes, MERGE ENDPOINTS and VERSION IDENTIFIER, reaching modular solutions (Sect. 4.2). Our development is available as a benchmark for future research [12]. A main finding is that our framework can be used to distill systematic recipes for API refactoring, which developers can mechanically apply step by step to achieve an implementation with a declared EMI score (Sect. 5). As examples, we provide recipes for the introduction of API KEY and PAGINATION patterns.

In summary, we contribute the EMI framework (Sect. 3), a scheme to guide and assess the implementation of API refactorings, we validate EMI by applying API refactorings to (micro)service architectures (Sect. 4), and provide canonical recipes to obtain certain EMI scores for architecture evolution (Sect. 5). We also discuss related work in Sect. 2, elicit threats to validity in Sect. 6, and conclude with an outlook on future work in Sect. 7.

2 Related Work

Our study builds on the reference catalogue of patterns for API design [25], which addresses the challenge of remote API design [23] through peer-reviewed patterns published in the period 2017–2020 [10,20–22,24].

API refactoring was previously investigated based on the same catalogue [18, 19]. Those studies focus on architectural considerations and especially *why* and *when* an API pattern should be introduced, considering forces and smells. Differently, our work is the first to investigate *how* an API pattern is implemented. Specifically, we are interested in the different choices regarding the code of a refactoring, and the quality trade-offs that they yield. Another difference is that we study how to refactor both the definition and implementation of an API, whereas previous work focuses only on the definition. Our frameworks can be seen as a refinement of Attribute-Driven Design and Architecture Trade-off Analysis Method, which are concerned with informing and assessing architectural decisions in light of quality attribute requirements [1].

The two axes of generality and distribution in EMI can be seen as systematic organisations of various considerations made in the literature of programming languages and microservices. Methods for high generality include aspect-oriented programming [9] and linguistic abstractions for implementing reusable decorators (e.g., couriers in Jolie and delegation in Kotlin). The importance of distribution was already partially observed in [13] for the development of circuit breaker – a pattern for increasing resilience [14] – and later acknowledged in security recommendations [3]. The developments in [13] fall under Parametric/Adjacent and Parametric/External in our framework (Sect. 3). Our interest in the present work is much more general: rather than focusing on a specific use case, we formulate a framework that can be used to reason about any API refactoring. Furthermore, the quality aspects considered here are not considered in [13].

The code in our validation of EMI is written in the service-oriented programming language Jolie [11], for reasons of exposition: Jolie provides native abstractions for the key concerns of API definition and refactoring, like API endpoints and the definition of APIs polymorphic on other APIs (which we use to achieve reusable refactorings) [11,17]. However, our findings are not tied to Jolie. We refer to alternative technologies in Sect. 6.

3 The EMI Framework for API Refactoring

We now present our conceptual framework for API refactoring – the EMI framework. It is depicted in Table 1. We explain it in the rest of this section.

API refactoring changes both an interface and its implementation, while improving at least one quality attribute [18,19]. This may affect the external behaviour of an API observed by clients, without altering its capabilities.

		Distribution		
		Internal	Adjacent	External
Generality	Parametric	E ★★☆ M ★★☆ I ★☆☆	E ★★☆ M ★★★ I ★★☆	E ★☆☆ M ★★★ I ★★★
	Ad-hoc	E ★★★ M ★☆☆ I ★☆☆	E ★★☆ M ★★☆ I ★★☆	E ★☆☆ M ★★☆ I ★★★

Table 1. The EMI framework.

We introduce some terminology. In the remainder, we refer to the changes introduced by an API refactoring as the *new functionality*, bearing in mind that such functionality does not alter the feature set of the API [19]. In line with the API domain model of [25], we consider an API to be a collection of operations that can be invoked by clients. Services can offer APIs through *endpoints*, which expose operations at a designated location according to a given transport protocol. We call such services *API providers*. We distinguish the API and implementation that we start from and then end up with after a refactoring with the prefixes *original* and *refactored*.

3.1 Generality and Distribution

The EMI framework focuses on two dimensions to assess the quality attributes of the implementation of an API refactoring: *generality* and *distribution*.

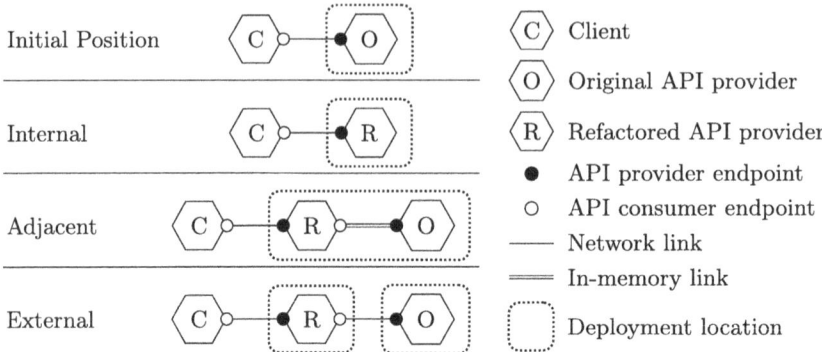

Fig. 1. Possible choices for distribution.

The *generality* dimension concerns whether the implementation of the new functionality depends on or abstracts from the definition of the original API. We identify two possibilities.

Ad-hoc The code of the new functionality depends on hardcoded information on the names, types, or behaviours of the operations in the original API.
Parametric The code of the new functionality abstracts from the names, types, or behaviours of the operations in the original API.

Generality serves as an indicator of the logical coupling between the new code and the old. It is significant because API patterns provide, at least conceptually, reusable solutions to recurring problems. Thus, in a way, generality indicates how much this reusability is achieved in real code.

The *distribution* dimension concerns where the code for the new functionality is located in relation to the original API provider and its clients. There are three possibilities, depicted in Fig. 1.

Internal The code of the new functionality is mixed with the code of the original API provider. Thus, they share state. After the refactoring, the original API provider becomes the refactored API provider.
Adjacent The refactored API provider is a separate service. They have separate state and are executed independently, but they are deployed such that they can communicate efficiently through local resources (local memory channels, inter-process communication, loopback network interfaces, etc.).
External The refactored API provider is a separate service. It is deployed remotely from the original, and thus can communicate with it only through network communication.

3.2 EMI scores

The combination of the axes of generality and distribution gives rise to six possible development strategies, each presenting different trade-offs. To help in navigating these trade-offs, we score each strategy on three quality attributes using a three-level scale (★☆☆, ★★☆, or ★★★): efficiency (E), maintainability (M), and isolation (I). We explain each score next.

Efficiency (E)
   E ★★★ The new functionality is implemented optimally, with no extra overhead caused by design choices.
   E ★★☆ Design choices cause extra overhead in terms of local resources (memory, local communication, etc.).
   E ★☆☆ Design choices cause extra overhead in terms of remote resources (e.g., network communication).

Maintainability (M)
   M ★★★ The original and refactored API providers can be maintained independently.
   M ★★☆ The implementations of the new functionality and the original API provider are separate but tightly coupled.
   M ★☆☆ The implementations of the new functionality and the original API provider are completely mixed.

Isolation (I)
   I ★★★ The original and refactored API providers do not share any local resources for their execution.
   I ★★☆ The original and refactored API providers share execution resources (e.g., CPUs, memory), but do not share state and interact purely by means of the original API.
   I ★☆☆ The new functionality and the original API implementation share internal program state (e.g., stack, variables, heap).

The levels of these scales are intentionally broad, in order to avoid being tied up by very specific technological details. This is in line with the technology-agnosticism of microservices [4].

3.3 Scoring Development Strategies

We end the presentation of our framework with an analysis that justifies the EMI scores of each development strategy, referring also to examples of API patterns and technologies where relevant.

Ad-hoc/Internal (E ★★★ M ★☆☆ I ★☆☆) This is the most efficient strategy, because the new functionality is implemented directly by changing the behaviour of the original API provider. Thus, the code of the new functionality encounters no unnecessary overhead in integrating with the original implementation. For example, introducing the PAGINATION pattern to an implementation that queries a database gives the possibility to modify the query in order to retrieve fewer results – those for the page being requested. For the very same reasons, however, this is also the least maintainable and isolated choice, since the new code is mixed and shares all resources with the old code. Examples of this strategy are shown in Sect. 4.1 and 5.

Parametric/Internal (E★★☆ M★★☆ I★☆☆) This strategy trades some efficiency for maintainability by abstracting from the operation names and behaviours of the original API. The code of the new functionality can be reused across different APIs, but has limited access to changing their behaviour: the new functionality can only intercept, modify, and conditionally forward request and response message to and from the original implementation. Examples of this strategy are implementations adopting Java Servelet Filters or Express middleware functions.

Ad-hoc/Adjacent (E★★☆ M★★☆ I★★☆) Compared to Ad-hoc/Internal, implementing the new functionality in a separate component trades some efficiency for partially improved maintainability and isolation. However, the new functionality remains coupled with the original API (ad-hoc), so changes to the original API require updating the refactored API provider, too. Thus, maintainability is still not ideal. Improved isolation comes at the cost of some overhead in the interaction between the refactored and original API providers. Efficiency is further affected by the new functionality not having access to changing the internal behaviour of the original API provider. This strategy can be implemented with, for example, the sidecar pattern, the ambassador pattern, or Jolie's embedded services (see Sect. 4.1).

Parametric/Adjacent (E★★☆ M★★★ I★★☆) This strategy has the same efficiency and isolation characteristics as the previous one, but greatly improved maintainability by decoupling the implementation of the new functionality from the operation names and message types of the original API. The sidecar and ambassador patterns are again useful to implement this strategy. Jolie's embedded services combined with couriers and interface extenders (see Sect. 4.1) offer an interesting solution, because the refactored API can be automatically and statically computed.

Ad-hoc/External (E★☆☆ M★★☆ I★★★) The strategy with the highest level of isolation, since the new functionality interacts with the original API provider only via remote access and for this reason, this is the least efficient one. This strategy does not achieve the highest maintainability score due to the coupling between the new functionality and the original API. This strategy can be implemented by developing a proxy service offering the refactored API and forwarding each invocation to the original API provider when appropriate.

Parametric/External (E★☆☆ M★★★ I★★★) This strategy has the same efficiency and isolation scores as the previous one, but also the highest maintainability score for the same reason given for Parametric/Adjacent.

No strategy scores a perfect nine. The reason lies in the unavoidable tension between efficiency and isolation: optimal efficiency requires sharing resources, which prevents achieving optimal isolation.

4 EMI at Work

In this section, we validate our framework by applying it in depth – exploring all our strategies for a single pattern – and in breadth – applying selected strategies to other patterns. The code of our examples is available online [12].

4.1 API Key in Jolie

We illustrate the use of our framework by applying each strategy to a concrete use case: the introduction of the API KEY pattern to a service managing a catalogue of scientific publications. API KEY identifies clients through respective unique keys, which must be included in requests.

We code our examples in Jolie [11]. In Jolie, the operations and message types of an API are defined as an **interface**. The next interface defines the API of our publication catalogue service.

```
1  type Publications: { publications*: Publication }
2  type Publication: Proceeding | InProceeding | Article
3  interface PubCatInterface {
4    RequestResponse: getAuthorPubs( {authorId: string} )( Publications )
5                     getConfPubs( {confId: string} )( Publications )      }
```

PubCatInterface comprises two operations: getAuthorPubs, which expects the unique identifier of an author (as the field authorId of the request message) and returns all their publications (message type Publications); and getConfPubs, which given a conference identifier (confId) returns the publications of that conference. The type Publications describes a record with a field publications containing zero or more (*) values of type Publication. Publication is the union of three types (omitted) corresponding to proceedings (Proceeding), papers in proceedings (InProceeding), and journal articles (Article).

Interfaces are offered to clients by defining an **inputPort**, Jolie for an endpoint that accepts remote invocations. An input port is defined inside of its enclosing **service** and commits to a concrete **location** and transport **protocol** (HTTP, SOAP, binary protocols, etc.). The definition of our publication catalogue service is given next (abstracting some internal implementation details).

Listing 1. Original API Provider.
```
1  /* Service definition */
2  service PubCat {
3    /* API Endpoint */
4    inputPort ip { location: "socket://localhost:8080"
5      protocol: http { format = "json" } interfaces: PubCatInterface }
6    /* Behaviour */
7    main {
8      [ getAuthorPubs( request )( response ) { /* fetch the data from db */ } ]
9      [ getConfPubs( request )( response ) { /* fetch the data from db */ } ] } }
```

In Lines 4 to 5, service PubCat exposes PubCatInterface on TCP port 8080 over the HTTP protocol with message payloads in JSON format. Its implementation (Lines 7 to 9) consists of an *input choice* that can react to any invocation of the operations it lists. Each branch in the choice has the form B [op(req)(resp)] where op is the name of the operation, req and resp are the input and output parameters, and B is the code block computing the response.

Introducing the API KEY pattern requires extending request message types with an additional field apiKey (storing the key as a string) and declaring a faulty response message NotAuthorised for invocations with invalid keys. The refactored API is given next.

Listing 2. Refactored API.

```
1  interface PubCatInterfaceWithAPIKey {
2    RequestResponse:
3      getAuthorPubs( {authorId: string, apiKey: string} )( Publications )
4        throws NotAuthorised
5      getConfPubs( {confId: string, apiKey: string} )( Publications )
6        throws NotAuthorised }
```

The refactoring of service PubCat and its interface PubCatInterface to obtain a service exposing the refactored API PubCatInterfaceWithAPIKey can be accomplished following any of the strategies outlined in Sect. 3. We discuss the most interesting aspects of these applications. To see how the code looks in detail for each strategy, the reader can consult our benchmark [12].

Ad-hoc/Internal. We directly modify the code of both the original interface PubCatInterface and the service PubCat. PubCatInterface becomes the refactored API PubCatInterfaceWithAPIKey above. In PubCat, instead, the implementation of each operation is edited to validate the API key in the request message.

```
1  service PubCat {
2    inputPort ip { /* ... */ interfaces: PubCatInterfaceWithAPIKey }
3    main {
4      [ getAuthorPubs( request )( response ) {
5        /* check validity of request.apiKey */
6        if( isKeyValid ) { /* fetch the data from db */ }
7        else { throw NotAuthorised( /* fault data */ ) } } ]
8      [ getConfPubs( request )( response ){ /* as for getAuthorPubs */ } ] } }
```

Ad-hoc/External. We introduce a new service, PubCatWithAPIKey, with an endpoint exposing the interface PubCatInterfaceWithAPIKey. This service acts as an adapter for the original API provider, PubCat, which remains unchanged. The implementation of the API KEY pattern is entirely confined to the new service, which forwards valid invocations to PubCat. This requires the service PubCatWithAPIKey to declare an *output port* (Line 2) pointing to the API endpoint of PubCat. Its implementation (Lines 4 to 11) consists of an input choice where each operation checks the validity of the key in the request (request.apiKey). If the key is valid, then the key is erased from request (Line 8) before invoking the original operation getAuthorPubs@pc to obtain the intended response. Otherwise, the service replies with a faulty NotAuthorised message. Although the implementations of refactored and original API providers are separate, they must be kept in sync wrt future changes to the API, resulting in a negative impact to maintainability.

Listing 3. Ad-hoc/External refactored API provider.
```
1  service PubCatWithAPIKey {
2    outputPort pc { /* PubCat endpoint */ }
3    inputPort ip { /* ... */ interfaces: PubCatInterfaceWithAPIKey }
4    main {
5      [ getAuthorPubs( request )( response ) {
6        /* check validity of request.apiKey */
7        if( isKeyValid ) {
8          undef( request.apiKey ) /* remove API key before forwarding */
9          getAuthorPubs@pc( request )( response ) /* forward call */
10       } else { throw NotAuthorised( /* fault data */ ) } } ]
11     [ getConfPubs( request )( response ) { /* as for getAuthorPubs */ } ] } }
```

Parametric/External. To eliminate the coupling between refactored and original API providers, we leverage the Jolie language construct of an *interface extender*, which uniformly extends the types of all operations in an API. The extender APIKeyExtender defined in Listing 4 adds the apiKey field to all (*) request messages and NotAuthorised as a new potential faulty response. APIKeyExtender precisely describes the changes we have to apply to PubCatInterface in order to obtain PubCatInterfaceWithAPIKey.

Listing 4. Parametric/External refactored API provider.
```
1  interface extender APIKeyExtender {
2    RequestResponse: *( {apiKey:string} )( void ) throws NotAuthorised
3  }
4  service PubCatWithAPIKey {
5    outputPort pc { /* PubCat endpoint */ }
6    inputPort ip { /* ... */ aggregates: pc with APIKeyExtender }
7    courier ip {
8      [ interface PubCatInterface( request )( response ) {
9        if( isKeyValid ) { forward( request )( response ) }
10       else { throw NotAuthorised( /* fault data */ ) } } ] } }
```

Service PubCatWithAPIKey now uses the interface extender to define its API: input port ip **aggregates** pc **with** APIKeyExtender ((Line 6), which instructs Jolie to forward messages for the API of pc, extended with APIKeyExtender, to pc.

Messages forwarded by means of aggregation (applications of **aggregates**) can be intercepted by means of a **courier** block. A courier is a piece of code attached to an input port, which gets executed whenever one of the input port's operations is invoked. The courier at Lines 7 to 10 implements the API KEY pattern for all operations of the interface PubCatInterface. Unlike a regular input choice, a courier can be parametric over the operation names of an interface:

[**interface** PubCatInterface(request)(response){ B }]

where B is the code that is executed on each invocation of an operation of PubCatInterface on input port ip, and which can then decide whether to **forward** the request to the `PubCat` service, or return the error message `NotAuthorised`. The **forward** primitive automatically removes fields added by any interface extenders, so messages to `pc` are well-typed.

Adjacent Strategies. Jolie supports running separate services in the same application with its native **embed** primitive: services `PubCat` and `PubCatWithAPIKey` can be implemented as Adjacent by simply changing their deployment configuration. First, the service `PubCat` is promoted to an in-memory service by changing its location to `"local"` (Listing 1, Line 4). Then, we make the refactored API provider, `PubCatWithAPIKey` (Listings 3 and 4), embed the original `PubCat`: replacing the **outputPort** declaration (Lines 2 and 5) by the statement **embed** `PubCat` **as** `pc` instructs the Jolie runtime to load the service `PubCat` alongside `PubCatWithAPIKey` and make it reachable via an in-memory channel through the output port `pc`. These linguistic features allow for easily switching Jolie codebases between the Adjacent and External columns of the EMI framework, changing the deployment strategy based on performance considerations (*i.e.*, trade network overhead for CPU and memory consumption).

4.2 Other Patterns: MERGE ENDPOINTS and VERSION IDENTIFIER

We now illustrate how to introduce two other patterns: MERGE ENDPOINTS and VERSION IDENTIFIER. Differently from API KEY, these patterns are fully architectural, in the sense that they do not introduce behavioural changes but rather affect only how APIs are accessed. We apply the Parametric/External strategy for both cases.

MERGE ENDPOINTS exposes the operations of two endpoints through a single endpoint. Suppose, for example, that we have a `PubCat` service for a publication catalogue and a `CitInd` service for citation indexing. We develop a new service, `PublicationIndex`, that merges their APIs by using aggregation.

```
1  service PublicationIndex {
2    outputPort pc { // publication catalogue
3      location: /* ... */ protocol: /* ... */ interfaces: PubCatInterface }
4    outputPort ci { // citation index
5      location: /* ... */ protocol: /* ... */ interfaces: CitIndInterface }
6    inputPort ip { location: /* ... */ protocol: /* ... */    aggregates: pc, ci
          } }
```

Note that aggregation requires the operations of the aggregated ports to have distinct names, which is in line with the pattern here. If this is not the case, one can use the other Jolie feature of redirection, explained in the next case.

VERSION IDENTIFIER exposes two (or more) different versions of the same API under a single endpoint. Here aggregation does not work, because the operation names in two versions of the same API likely overlap. Jolie solves this problem by offering the APIs under different *resource paths* at the same physical endpoint. In the next example, input port `ip` offers `PubCatInterfaceV1` under path `v1` and `PubCatInterfaceV2` under path `v2`. Assuming that a client reaches the refactored API provider at location `pubcat.com`, this means that version 1 will be accessible at location `pubcat.com/v1` and version 2 at location `pubcat.com/v2`.

```
1  service PubCatWithAPIKey {
2    outputPort pcv1 { location: /* ... */ protocol: /* ... */
3      interfaces: PubCatInterfaceV1 }
4    outputPort pcv2 { location: /* ... */ protocol: /* ... */
5      interfaces: PubCatInterfaceV2 }
6    inputPort ip { location: /* ... */ protocol: /* ... */
7      redirects: v1 => pcv1, v2 => pcv2 } }
```

This approach does not alter the original (versions of) the APIs, by distinguishing between versions based on the accessed location. Therefore, clients just need to be connected to the right location. An alternative to this approach is to extend the request types of all operations with a version identifier. However, this would require updating the clients to include this information. Furthermore, response types would become less precise, since they would need to accommodate the possible responses across all versions.

5 API Refactoring Recipes

In this section, we illustrate how our framework can be used to distill recipes that can be followed mechanically by programmers to apply an API refactoring. We cover a parametric implementation of the API KEY pattern and an ad-hoc implementation of the PAGINATION pattern. The latter is representative of situations where efficiency requires big sacrifices in maintainability and isolation.

We start with our recipe for API KEY.

Refactoring recipe: Introduce API KEY (Parametric)

Intent. Introduce the API KEY pattern by means of a dedicated service that is parametric on the original API.

Participants and Preconditions.

1. Participant: A Jolie *service*, say Original, exposing the API subject to refactoring as an interface, say OriginalAPI.
2. Precondition: Original offers OriginalAPI through an *input port* OriginalInputPort.

Refactoring steps.

1. Introduce an *interface extender* APIKeyExtender that:
   (a) Extends the request message with a field apiKey holding an API Key.
   (b) Adds a faulty response message NotAuthorised.
2. Introduce a new *service* OriginalWithAPIKey:
   (a) Introduce a new *output port* original.
   (b) Choose between:
      Choice 1 (External): Configure output port original (at OriginalWithAPIKey) and input port OriginalInputPort (at Original) so that they communicate via the network.

Choice 2 (Adjacent): Configure output port original (at Original-WithAPIKey) and input port OriginalInputPort (at Original) so that they communicate via local memory.
(c) Introduce an *input port* ip that aggregates the output port original and extends it with APIKeyExtender.
(d) Introduce a *courier* for ip that intercepts all operations of OriginalAPI and:
  i. Checks the validity of the API Key.
  ii. If the key is valid, forwards the request to original.
  iii. Otherwise, if the key is invalid, replies with the NotAuthorised response.

Postconditions.

1. Invoking any operation op at OriginalWithAPIKey with a valid API Key gives the same response message as invoking op at Original without an API Key.
2. Invoking any operation op at service OriginalWithAPIKey with an invalid API Key results into an NotAuthorised message.
3. Service OriginalWithAPIKey becomes the only client of service Original.

Discussion and EMI Scoring. This recipe yields a parametric implementation, giving maintainability score M★★★. Choice 1 introduces network overhead, giving E★☆☆ and I★★★, while Choice 2 does not, yielding E★★☆ and I★★☆. We get the following possible EMI scores:

Choice 1 (External): E★☆☆ M★★★ I★★★.
Choice 2 (Adjacent): E★★☆ M★★★ I★★☆.

We now present a recipe for the PAGINATION pattern. PAGINATION allows clients to retrieve smaller portions ('pages') of large data sets. The aim is to improve network and memory utilisation; this also addresses the stability antipattern of providing responses of unbounded size [14]. There are four variants of this pattern, corresponding to four different ways of identifying the page that the client wants [24,25]. Here, we implement the offset-based version.

Refactoring recipe: Introduce PAGINATION (Ad-hoc/Internal)

Intent. Introduce the offset-based PAGINATION pattern for an operation.

Participants and Preconditions.

1. Participant: A Jolie *service*, say Original, exposing the operation subject to refactoring, say op, as part of an interface, say OriginalAPI.
2. Precondition: op is a retrieval operation whose response type contains an ordered collection of items to be paginated.

Refactoring Steps.

1. Change the definition of op in OriginalAPI to:
   (a) Extend the *request type* with metadata fields specifying the offset of the requested page, the limit of items per page, and the sort-criterion, if more than one order exists for items in the collection;
   (b) Extend the *response type* with fields describing the response page such as the page number offset, items per page limit, sort-criterion, and total number of pages.
   (c) Add a faulty response message InvalidPageRequest in case of invalid page metadata.
2. Change the implementation of op to:
   (a) Validate the page metadata fields (and reply immediately with Invalid-PageRequest in case of failure).
   (b) Paginate the requested data, possibly by leveraging features of the database query language (like OFFSET and LIMIT for SQL).
   (c) Reply with the requested page and its metadata.

Postconditions.

1. Calling op to request page with a given offset and size limit results into the items of the collection returned by the original op from position offset * limit to position offset * limit + limit.

Discussion. Delegating the pagination to the query language of the database in use achieves efficiency score E★★★. However, since it also modifies the implementation of the specific operation, we obtain maintainability M★☆☆ and isolation I★☆☆. The overall EMI score is therefore E★★★ M★☆☆ I★☆☆.

Considerations on Alternative Implementations. The design smells that motivate the introduction of the PAGINATION pattern are about poor efficiency and thus the Ad-hoc/Internal strategy is a natural choice. If Ad-hoc/Internal is undesirable, other strategies can still be adopted at the cost of high decreases in efficiency. The key problem is distribution. Choosing an Adjacent strategy would still imply that the original API provider fetches all data from its database, but at least this would be 'cut' by the refactored API provider before it is sent back to clients. The same holds for an External strategy, but in this case we would pay also the cost of network communication (of the whole data set) between the refactored and original API providers.

6 Threats to Validity

Our validation of EMI has two main limitations, discussed next.

1. We have explored the application of EMI through a single language (Jolie). There are many other languages and frameworks for programming service-oriented systems, including Spring Boot, Express for Node.js, Ballerina [16], and WS-BPEL [15]. The mechanics and behaviours offered by Jolie's primitives can be achieved in these technologies, sometimes requiring the use of a framework. For example, aggregation and redirection – Jolie for merging and redirecting endpoints – can be implemented via the routing mechanism in Express. We are thus confident that our validation can be reproduced beyond Jolie. However, this requires a dedicated and systematic study, which our benchmark offers a good starting point for.
2. Our validation consists of a sample of four refactoring patterns out of the 22 identified by the Interface Refactoring Catalogue. We have selected this sample because of two main reasons: (i) the API design patterns that they introduce are widely known, and (ii) they are illustrative of the trade-offs between the EMI quality aspects since they do not have a clearly optimal implementation strategy. Nonetheless, the selection remains in part subjective and thus it calls for an exhaustive study of the remaining 18 patterns.

7 Conclusion

We have introduced the EMI framework, the first conceptual framework for navigating the implementation aspects of API refactorings. While broad and technology-agnostic, our scores are informative when it comes to key design decisions on the implementation of API patterns.

Our study opens up at least three interesting lines of future work.

First, in line with previous work [19], we have focused on presenting API refactorings that *add* a pattern. However, our Adjacent and External strategies make it immediate to *remove* a pattern later on. We think that enabling the modular activation and deactivation of patterns is an interesting direction.

The second line of future work deals with exploring additional aspects on top of efficiency, maintainability, and isolation. These aspects are in line with a previous survey on what qualities are important in practice, but there are also others that merit consideration, like scalability and usability [2,18]. We think that scalability would be a first natural extension of our framework, as it is closely related to efficiency and isolation but not completely captured by them.

Lastly, it would be interesting to extend our evaluation – which focuses on applicability – to a systematic user study, involving practitioners in the field of API design and implementation. This would allow us to better understand how easy it is to use EMI for (i) communicating the trade-offs between different strategies, (ii) choosing appropriate strategies, and (iii) facilitating the implementation of API refactorings (possibly for people with different skill levels).

Acknowledgements. We thank Sandra Greiner for the useful discussions. This work is partially supported by Independent Research Fund Denmark (grant no. 0135-00219), Villum Fonden (grant no. 50079) and by the European Union (ERC, CHORDS, 101124225). Views and opinions expressed are however those of the authors only and do not necessarily reflect those of the European Union or the European Research Council. Neither the European Union nor the granting authority can be held responsible for them.

References

1. Bass, L., Clements, P., Kazman, R.: Software Architecture in Practice, 3rd edn. Addison-Wesley (2012)
2. Bogner, J., Wójcik, P., Zimmermann, O.: How do microservice API patterns impact understandability? A controlled experiment (2024)
3. Chandramouli, R.: Security strategies for microservices-based application systems. National Institute of Standards and Technology (2019)
4. Dragoni, N., et al.: Microservices: yesterday, today, and tomorrow. In: Mazzara, M., Meyer, B. (eds.) Present and Ulterior Software Engineering, pp. 195–216. Springer (2017)
5. Erder, M., Pureur, P.: Continuous Architecture: Sustainable Architecture in an Agile and Cloud-Centric World. Elsevier Science (2015)
6. Erder, M., Pureur, P., Woods, E., Safari, O.M.C.A.: Continuous Architecture in Practice: Software Architecture in the Age of Agility and DevOps. Addison-Wesley (2021)
7. Ford, N., Parsons, R., Kua, P.: Building Evolutionary Architectures: Support Constant Change. O'Reilly Media (2017)
8. Fowler, M.: Patterns of Enterprise Application Architecture. Addison-Wesley (2012)
9. Kiczales, G., et al.: Aspect-oriented programming. In: Akşit, M., Matsuoka, S. (eds.) ECOOP'97 - Object-Oriented Programming, 11th European Conference, Jyväskylä, Finland, 9–13 June 1997, Proceedings. LNCS, vol. 1241, pp. 220–242. Springer (1997)
10. Lübke, D., Zimmermann, O., Pautasso, C., Zdun, U., Stocker, M.: Interface evolution patterns: balancing compatibility and extensibility across service life cycles. In: EuroPLoP, pp. 15:1–15:24. ACM (2019)
11. Montesi, F., Guidi, C., Zavattaro, G.: Service-oriented programming with Jolie. In: Web Services Foundations, pp. 81–107. Springer (2014)
12. Montesi, F., Peressotti, M., Picotti, V., Zimmermann, O.: EMI framework benchmark (2024). https://github.com/xpicox/emi-benchmark/tree/main
13. Montesi, F., Weber, J.: From the decorator pattern to circuit breakers in microservices. In: SAC, pp. 1733–1735. ACM (2018)
14. Nygard, M.: Release it!: design and deploy production-ready software (2007)
15. OASIS. Web services business process execution language version 2.0 (2007). http://docs.oasis-open.org/wsbpel/2.0/OS/wsbpel-v2.0-OS.html
16. Oram, A.: Ballerina: A Language for Network-Distributed Applications. O'Reilly (2019)
17. Preda, M.D., Gabbrielli, M., Guidi, C., Mauro, J., Montesi, F.: Service integration via target-transparent mediation. In: 2012 Fifth IEEE International Conference on Service-Oriented Computing and Applications (SOCA), Taipei, Taiwan, 17–19 December 2012, pp. 1–5. IEEE Computer Society (2012)

18. Stocker, M., Zimmermann, O.: From code refactoring to API refactoring: agile service design and evolution. In: Barzen, J. (ed.) Service-Oriented Computing, pp. 174–193. Springer (2021)
19. Stocker, M., Zimmermann, O.: API refactoring to patterns: catalog, template and tools for remote interface evolution. In: EuroPLoP, pp. 2:1–2:32. ACM (2023)
20. Stocker, M., Zimmermann, O., Zdun, U., Lübke, D., Pautasso, C.: Interface quality patterns: communicating and improving the quality of microservices APIs. In: EuroPLoP, pp. 10:1–10:16. ACM (2018)
21. Zimmermann, O., Lübke, D., Zdun, U., Pautasso, C., Stocker, M.: Interface responsibility patterns: processing resources and operation responsibilities. In: EuroPLoP, pp. 9:1–9:24. ACM (2020)
22. Zimmermann, O., Pautasso, C., Lübke, D., Zdun, U., Stocker, M.: Data-oriented interface responsibility patterns: types of information holder resources. In: EuroPLoP, pp. 11:1–11:25. ACM (2020)
23. Zimmermann, O., Stocker, M., Lübke, D., Pautasso, C., Zdun, U.: Introduction to microservice API patterns (MAP). In: Microservices. OASIcs, vol. 78, pp. 4:1–4:17 (2019)
24. Zimmermann, O., Stocker, M., Lübke, D., Zdun, U.: Interface representation patterns: crafting and consuming message-based remote APIs. In: EuroPLoP, pp. 27:1–27:36. ACM (2017)
25. Zimmermann, O., Stocker, M., Lübke, D., Zdun, U., Pautasso, C.: Patterns for API Design: Simplifying Integration with Loosely Coupled Message Exchanges. Addison-Wesley (2022)

A Survey Study About the Impacts of Introducing a Microservices Cataloging Tool in a Large Software Development Unit

Matheus C. Leite[1](✉)[iD], André A. S. Ivo[2][iD], João F. L. Daniel[3][iD], and Eduardo Guerra[3][iD]

[1] Institute of Technological Research (IPT), São Paulo, Brazil
matheus.chaves@ensino.ipt.br
[2] National Institute for Space Research (INPE), São José dos Campos, Brazil
andre.ivo@inpe.br
[3] Free University of Bozen-Bolzano (unibz), Bolzano, Italy
joao.daniel@student.unibz.it, eduardo.guerra@unibz.it

Abstract. Many large companies have recently embraced a micro services-based architecture for their systems. Besides the benefits, this strategy also comes with particular challenges that require careful attention, such as managing a high number of services. Several tools propose to solve this problem through a catalog of services, which has features to categorize and organize them. However, to the best of our knowledge, no work in the literature has investigated the impact of introducing this type of tool, especially when the services are maintained by several teams. In this paper, we conducted a survey study based on UTAUT2 in a large software development unit that recently adopted a service catalog tool, investigating the technology acceptance of such a solution. As a result, the answers showed that the professionals generally considered the tool's introduction positive, pointing to a higher microservice reuse as one of the benefits. On the other hand, the participants also pointed out that promoting the tool to all developers is important for it to work effectively.

Keywords: Software Architecture · Microservices Architecture · Software Governance · Microservices Cataloging Tool · UTAUT2

1 Introduction

The software industry is continuously changing to meet the demands of modern applications. Microservices architecture (MSA) became a popular architectural style that favors scalability and flexibility since a single application is broken down into several smaller, loosely coupled components or services [24]. These services and components operate independently, with their own technology stack, database, and data management model, promoting a high degree of autonomy for each one [4]. REST APIs, event streaming, and message brokers are the most common choices for communication between microservices. Major companies like

Amazon, Netflix, Spotify, and Twitter have already adopted MSA for their core businesses.

Especially when there is a large number of services, there are several difficulties that might arise from their management. For instance, it might be hard to investigate if a service with a given functionality already exists. As a consequence, when developers do not find an existing service, they might create a duplicated one, increasing unnecessarily the complexity and creating problems for maintenance. As another example, a lack of knowledge about how another API represents a domain entity might result in APIs with different representations. That also represents a problem for the system evolution since the domain representation is not standardized.

One solution that contributes to service management is adopting a tool that can catalog the services of a system. It provides a centralized place to search and visualize existing services and their APIs. This kind of tool usually also has features to automate the process of gathering the metadata from each microservice. However, to the best of our knowledge, no previous study in the literature has investigated the impacts of adopting a service catalog tool in the context of developing a software system that uses a microservices architecture.

The notion of making microservices discoverable and reusable has been widely discussed and is supported by various tools. However, there are several compelling reasons to justify a renewed investigation into this topic, particularly with a focus on microservices cataloging tools. The diversity in tool capabilities and compatibility necessitates guidance for organizations to select the appropriate solutions tailored to their specific needs. Each organization possesses unique structures and objectives that influence the effectiveness of cataloging solutions.

Additionally, empirical studies are essential to evaluate how cataloging tools enhance service discoverability and reusability. Many organizations encounter obstacles when adopting microservices architectures, and understanding these challenges can provide strategies for successful implementation. While the concept of discoverable and reusable microservices is well established, ongoing research remains crucial to address the nuanced challenges, technological advancements, and organizational requirements that continue to shape this vital area of software development.

In this paper, we conducted a survey study in a large software development unit of a Brazilian company in the financial sector. When the survey was conducted, this development unit had around 100 professionals and had introduced a service catalog tool in their development environment six months before. The introduced tool was developed internally but had the same features as other commercial ones with the same purpose. The survey was designed based on the extension of the Unified Theory of Acceptance and Use of Technology (UTAUT2) [37] and received 65 answers.

As a result, this work fills the existing gap in the literature regarding the consequences and motivations for the usage of service catalog tools. The quantitative results showed that Habit, Learning Value and Hedonic Motivation had influence in the intention to use the technology, and the qualitative analysis of the open questions answers pointed a better reuse of existing microservices as a positive consequence. On the other hand, the participants also pointed to the tool automation and the promotion of the tool to the entire team as important factors for the tool's effectiveness.

The following sections will provide a clear structure for this paper. Section 2 presents the background. Section 3 provides an in-depth analysis of papers related to the topic. Section 4 outlines the survey questions and comprehensively explains the survey design, sampling strategy, and data collection process. Section 5 presents the survey results and analyzes the data collected. Finally, Sects. 6 and 7 conclude and discuss the study's limitations and future research directions.

2 Service Catalog Tools

The main functionality of a service catalog tool is to keep the register of the existing services in a given system. It also contains features that allow users to search and browse the existing services. For each service, the tool should provide information regarding the service API, sometimes providing additional documentation. Another important feature is automation in the capture of service data.

The following are expected benefits in the usage of this kind of toll: (a) better service management [19]; (b) service documentation [14]; (c) broader view of the software architecture [11]. A service catalog can also aid developers in different types of tasks, such as when searching for an existing service to reuse [35], composing services [3], and mocking and testing services [26].

2.1 Existing Tools

Considering the academic literature and sources used by professionals, several tools that display the capacity to successfully address the essential elements required for the effective cataloging and management of microservices were identified. The following contains a few representative examples:

- **Microservice-Dashboard:** "A dashboard for microservice monitoring and management, which can be configured to stakeholder needs and which supports the integration of different backend systems." [22]
- **Backstage:** "Powered by a centralized software catalog, Backstage restores order to your infrastructure and enables your product teams to ship high-quality code quickly - without compromising autonomy." [2]
- **Leanix:** "LeanIX Value Stream Management automates service documentation, freeing up your DevOps teams so they can resolve incidents faster, conduct thorough impact analysis, and avoid architecture drift. VSM increases cross-team visibility, fosters an culture of ownership and accelerates the onboarding experience of your new joiners." [10]
- **Configure8:** "A complete and accurate software catalog is the foundation of your portal. It should organize your entire ecosystem – all your services and their dependencies, environments, clusters, resources, pipelines, metrics, owners, and more – and automatically reflect changes. Use it to improve your developers' experience and lay the foundation to achieve high standards." [5]

– **Deployhub:** "DeployHub's microservice catalog is a breakthrough in supply chain security. It gathers security and DevOps evidence providing a comprehensive, end-to-end view of your organization's security profile from SBOMs to deployed inventory." [6]

An alternative to the commercial tools is the internal development of a proprietary service catalog tool. One benefit of this alternative is better integration with specific components of the company software development environment. Since, in this case, the tool is made considering more specific company needs, it might fulfill requirements that would not be supported by more general tools. The company where this study was conducted chose to develop its own service catalog tool, and it has all the expected features, as described in this section.

2.2 Related Works

According to Indrasiri and Siriwardena [17], when managing and organizing microservices, several factors need to be considered. These include service naming conventions, the location of the source code repository, the domain to which the service belongs, which team is responsible for it, the API contracts, and the available mode of communication. From a technical standpoint, it is crucial to consider the data modeling techniques used, the deployment process for artifacts, and the packaging type implemented [13].

To address all these topics efficiently, one solution is the adoption of a central website tool accessible to all software architects and developers for cataloging and publishing microservice-related information [22]. Neglecting to automate this process can be a time-consuming and error-prone task for developers, considering the many steps involved. Hence, automation is indispensable in streamlining, creating, or updating microservices' information [17].

Mayer and Weinreich [22] conducted research that presented an innovative dashboard for effectively monitoring and managing microservices. The dashboard includes a comprehensive set of metrics covering runtime and static information, such as API version and request/response schemas. This study also examines the impact of utilizing a tool on software developer teams, recognizing both benefits and difficulties encountered in their daily work.

Another study conducted by Kleehaus and Matthes [19] delves into the challenges of documenting microservices in the IT landscape. According to the researchers, microservices are highly complex and pose new documentation challenges. To understand how organizations are adapting to microservices and documenting their systems and architecture, they surveyed fifty-eight IT professionals in the German market. This research is valuable for understanding development teams' challenges in documenting microservices. However, it is essential to consider how to address these challenges, including choosing the right tools and work models. The study should also examine how the proposed solutions handle these issues.

After thoroughly analyzing the existing literature on microservices architecture, it was discovered that only a few studies have focused on microservices organization and cataloging. To address this gap, this research was conducted to gain insights into the current state of practice and propose recommendations for future research. Upon reviewing various studies, it becomes clear that most of the research in microservices management and organization concentrates on providing technical solutions for visualizing and managing microservices, as demonstrated in Mayer and Weinreich [22], or presenting empirical approaches to documentation and managing obstacles, as in Kleehaus and Matthes [19]. These studies have highlighted the necessity of a tool or framework for cataloging microservices. However, the efficacy of the tool for cataloging microservices has yet to be assessed within a complex business environment characterized by numerous development teams and hundreds of microservices. This study, therefore, aims to evaluate the tool's impact in such an environment.

3 Research Method

To evaluate the adoption of a service catalog tool, we conducted a survey in a development unit that works on a system with a large number of microservices. The survey protocol was based on UTAUT2 [37], a unified theory that offers a comprehensive framework for examining individual technology adoption behavior. This theory represents an advanced iteration of the original Unified Theory of Acceptance and Use of Technology (UTAUT). UTAUT2, as presented in Fig. 1, expands and refines the foundational concepts of UTAUT, providing a more nuanced understanding of the factors that shape individual technology consumption.

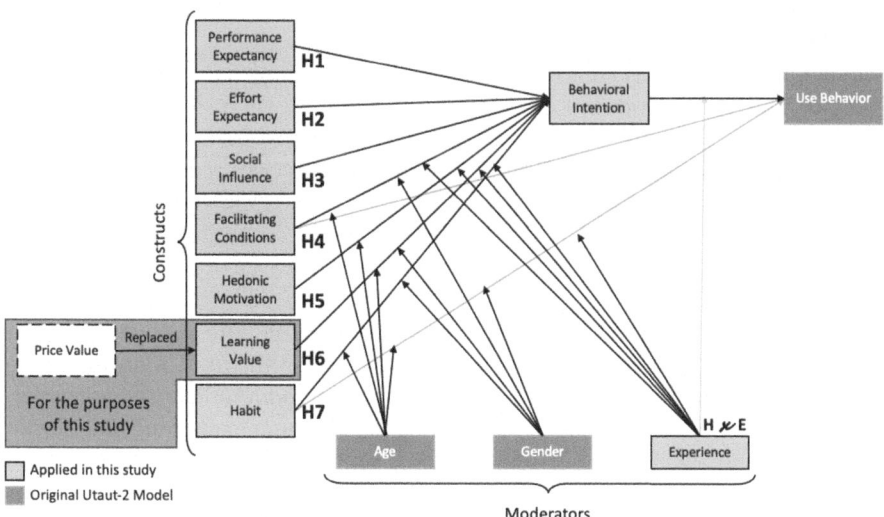

Fig. 1. UTAUT2 Model

3.1 Objective

The research study aims to evaluate the impact of the microservices cataloging tool on software development processes. Through these results, we also expect insights related to practices and tools for microservice governance. In addition to evaluating the consequences of tool adoption, the study also explored subjective aspects such as how developers have integrated the tool into their workflow and the potential impact on their productivity. The data collected from participants was analyzed qualitatively and qualitatively.

3.2 Study Context

We applied the survey study in the context of a large software development unit of a Brazilian company in the financial sector. The company had conducted a migration to replace legacy systems with cloud-native architectures and infrastructures, mainly adopting microservice-based solutions. In this process, professionals reported significant challenges in the management of a large number of services.

After analyzing the available commercial tools for the service catalog, the company decided to create a tailor-made solution. The two main reasons claimed were security and to better fit specific needs. However, the company's decision to develop its own tool was not the focus of our analysis, and it is out of the scope of this study. The tool is web-based and allows users to browse the existing services and operations based on different criteria, such as domain entity and keyword. The service documentation provides the link to the source code and the schema for the API operations parameters and return. The tool has features to read service information from a swagger descriptor.

When the survey was conducted, this development unit had around 100 professionals and had introduced a service catalog tool in their development environment six months before. By that time, the tool covered 70% of the system services, which represent more than two hundred microservices registered, together with more than a thousand API methods.

3.3 Survey Design

The survey was conducted as a comprehensive questionnaire with open-ended and closed-ended questions. It aimed to assess the acceptance and adoption of the microservices cataloging tool that had been recently adopted by the company. The questionnaire consisted of five modules, the first one explaining the aim of the research and asking the participants for informed consent and agreement to the survey's terms.

Subsequently, in the second module, participants were requested to provide information regarding their roles, professional experience, and technical knowledge. No personal information that allowed the identification of the participant was requested. Moving forward to the third module, the questions aimed to capture how developers did their daily work before the tool was introduced. This part of the questionnaire aims to capture how the tasks that were supported by the repository had been executed before its adoption.

The fourth module of the survey was created based on the UTAUT2 constructs, where closed-ended questions were utilized. The questions were presented as declarative statements and a Linkert scale was used for the response options. Participants were asked to indicate their level of agreement on a scale ranging from "Strongly Agree" (denoted as 5) to "Strongly Disagree" (represented as 1). In the context of this study, **Price Value** was replaced by **Learning Value** [1] since from the perspective of the participants, in this case, the consumption of technology does not involve monetary acquisition and the microservices cataloging tool can contribute to the learning process. Table 1 present the 22 questions used to represent the UTAUT2 constructs in the context of this study.

Table 1. Experimental observed parameters

#	Declarative statements	UTAUT-2
01	Helps organize and centralize the information needed to optimize the adoption and reuse of microservices.	Performance Expectancy
02	Guides and assists development teams in discussions about which business domain each microservice belongs to.	Performance Expectancy
03	Automatically and centrally updates the information of all new or already built microservices.	Performance Expectancy
04	It has segregations by API's visibility (public, private, sync, async)	Effort Expectancy
05	It has a friendly interface (user interface).	Effort Expectancy
06	It has friendly navigation (user experience).	Effort Expectancy
07	Use by one team member influences other team members to use it.	Social Influence
08	The use by a collaborator with a high hierarchical level influences other team members to use it.	Social Influence
09	For greater adoption, the organization should encourage its use	Social Influence
10	It has the necessary infrastructure for its day-to-day use	Facilitating Conditions
11	It remained stable (Uptime) most of the time.	Facilitating Conditions
12	It has segmentation by user profiles.	Facilitating Conditions
13	Team members are curious to use it.	Hedonic Motivation
14	There is some type of gratuity for any member of the organization who uses it. Usage generates satisfaction in team members.	Hedonic Motivation
15	Usage generates satisfaction in team members.	Hedonic Motivation
16	Helps in learning about which domains (DDD) exist in the system.	Learning Value
17	Helps in querying which API's (endpoints) each microservice has.	Learning Value
18	Helps in querying which is the current version of each microservice.	Learning Value
19	Usage can become an effective habit in the daily lives of development teams	Habit
20	The habit of using it helps to reduce the need for interaction between members of the development teams.	Habit
21	The habit of use helps in the reuse and adoption of microservices among development teams.	Habit
22	The habit of using it increases the productivity of development teams.	Habit

In the fifth module, participants were allowed to express additional perceptions and opinions through one open-ended question: *"Given your experience with the microservices cataloging tool, evaluate the positives and negatives and make suggestions for improvements."* The question was optional and aimed to elicit overall impressions regarding the experience with the microservices cataloging tool. Participants were free to express their points of view, including recommendations, evaluations, and observations.

To ensure the protection of participants, necessary measures were taken to maintain anonymity, safeguard data, and uphold confidentiality. Informed consent was obtained from all participants, emphasizing their voluntary and anonymous involvement. Furthermore, the study was designed in such a way that it did not pose any potential harm to the participants.

3.4 Dissemination

The survey was disseminated by email and other company communication channels to professionals working in the development unit where the microservices cataloging tool had been utilized. The survey was conducted through an online form. Respondents were also encouraged to share the survey link within their professional network within the same development team. The participation in the study was voluntary and anonymous.

3.5 Data Analysis

The data from the closed-ended questions was evaluated quantitatively. To analyze the data, the UTAUT-2 model (Unified Theory of Acceptance and Use of Technology) was adapted to evaluate the microservices cataloging tool's usage. The model was used to quantitatively assess the survey results obtained from implementing this methodology, including the instrument described in Sect. 3.3. The hypotheses formulated for this study are as follows:

- **H1:** The performance expectation positively influences the intention to use the Microservices Cataloging Tool.
- **H2:** The expectation of effort positively influences the intention to use the Microservices Cataloging Tool.
- **H3:** Social influence positively influences the intention to use the Microservices Cataloging Tool.
- **H4:** The facilitating conditions positively influence the intention to use the Microservices Cataloging Tool.
  - **H4E:** The facilitating conditions are moderated by experience.
- **H5:** Hedonic motivation positively influences the intention to use the Microservices Cataloging Tool.
  - **H5E:** The Hedonic motivation are moderated by experience.
- **H6:** Learning positively influences the intention to use the Microservices Cataloging Tool.
  - **H6E:** The value they place on education are moderated by experience.

– **H7:** Habit positively influences the intention to use he Microservices Cataloging Tool.
  • **H7E:** The habit are moderated by experience.

The model's evaluation involved several metrics: Cronbach's Alpha (A.C.) for reliability, Composite Reliability (C.R.) for internal consistency, Average Variance Extracted (A.V.E.) for convergent validity, and cross-loading criterion for discriminant validity [15]. The UTAUT-2 model was applied and evaluated for each of the 22 surveyed questions. The collected data was analyzed using SmartPLS software, both descriptively and through the analysis of structural equations, to identify the most relevant characteristics of the usage intention of the Microservices Cataloging tool.

The answers to the open-ended questions were used in a qualitative analysis using a coding methodology. This involves assigning codes to individual responses systematically, examining each line of gathered data sequentially [34], and allowing for the emergence of codes and themes organically from the collected responses. We followed the recommendation for software engineering studies to execute a series of steps such as data extraction, coding of data, and transformation of codes into categorization of codes as **strengths** or **weaknesses**. This systematic process helped us to understand qualitative insights better and identify underlying patterns and recurring themes that may not have been previously defined.

4 Survey Results

The survey was distributed via email and included a link to a questionnaire that lasted for three months. A total of 65 individuals responded. Considering that this number is more than half of the number of professionals in the target development unit, the number of participants can be considered representative.

4.1 Participants Profile

The survey asked respondents about their roles in the software development industry over the past five years, making it possible to signalize more than one. The majority of respondents (50.8%) identified as Software Engineers, followed by Developers (46.2%), Operations/DevOps Engineers (40%), Site Reliability Engineers (27.7%), and Software Architects (21.5%). Other roles were mentioned but had fewer responses than these pre-established ones.

The second question asked respondents how long they had worked in software development. The majority (27.7%) had worked in this field for four to six years, while the next largest group (23.1%) had worked for fifteen years or more. Respondents who had worked for one to three years, ten to twelve years, thirteen to fifteen years, seven to nine years, and less than one year were fewer in number.

Upon analyzing the gathered data, it has become evident that most participants have a good grasp of the subject matter being studied. Additionally, the organization's software development teams exhibit varying experience levels, which is critical in understanding how different groups adapt to the tool and its impact on their daily work processes.

It is worth highlighting that most respondents in the analyzed data are either current or former software developers and engineers. This information holds significant importance since it indicates that while all development team members may feel the effects of software catalog microservices, developers and engineers will likely have more extensive knowledge and skills in recognizing and addressing these impacts.

4.2 Scenario Before Tool Implementation

To better understand the context before the tool adoption, this section reports the answers of the participants to the questions from the third module of the questionnaire. Regarding how team members identified a microservice with specific functionality, 75.4% used direct conversations with other teams, while 67.7% searched code repositories, and 56.9% utilized Teams and Confluence for messaging and documentation. Respondents also suggested using Governance spreadsheets, ProttoBuffers, Thanos/Prometheus metrics, calling endpoints, and Github Pages for identification purposes.

Regarding identifying API contracts of microservices used in business rules, 64.6% of the respondents selected direct conversations with other teams and searching in code repositories. Additionally, 55.4% used documentation in Confluence, and 46.2% sent messages to groups via Teams. Respondents also mentioned using the Developer Portal, documentation in the code repository, email, testing with support, testing in error and success, searching for Swagger in applications, or Postman/Insomnia, and Github Pages collections.

In terms of identifying business rules implemented in microservices across different versions, 78.5% of respondents preferred direct conversations with other teams. At the same time, 53.8% used documentation in Confluence and searching in code repositories, and 43.1% sent messages to groups via Teams. Respondents also suggested email, testing with support, testing on trial and error, crash on integrations, Swagger, Github Pages, and practical tests with APIs in dev/home environments. When questioned about identifying the particular business domain to which the microservice belonged, 64.6% of respondents preferred direct conversations with other teams, while 47.7% used documentation in Confluence, and 41.5% sent messages to groups or searched code repositories. Respondents also suggested holding meetings, relying on architectural documentation maintained by the teams, Swagger, and Github Pages.

4.3 Overview of UTAUT2 Constructs

After investigating the given situations, a common trend of reliable scores can be observed when using Linkert's one-dimensional scale. The participants were required to rate their level of agreement on a scale that ranged from "Strongly Agree" (represented as 5) to "Strongly Disagree" (represented as 1). Figure 2 presents the distribution of the answers for the questions related to the UTAUT2 constructs.

The tables were analyzed in terms of the constructs proposed by UTAUT-2:

- **PE:** Performance Expectancy
- **EE:** Effort Expectancy
- **SI:** Social Influence
- **FC:** Facilitanting Conditions
- **LV:** Leaning Value
- **HM:** Hedonic Motivation
- **HB:** Habit

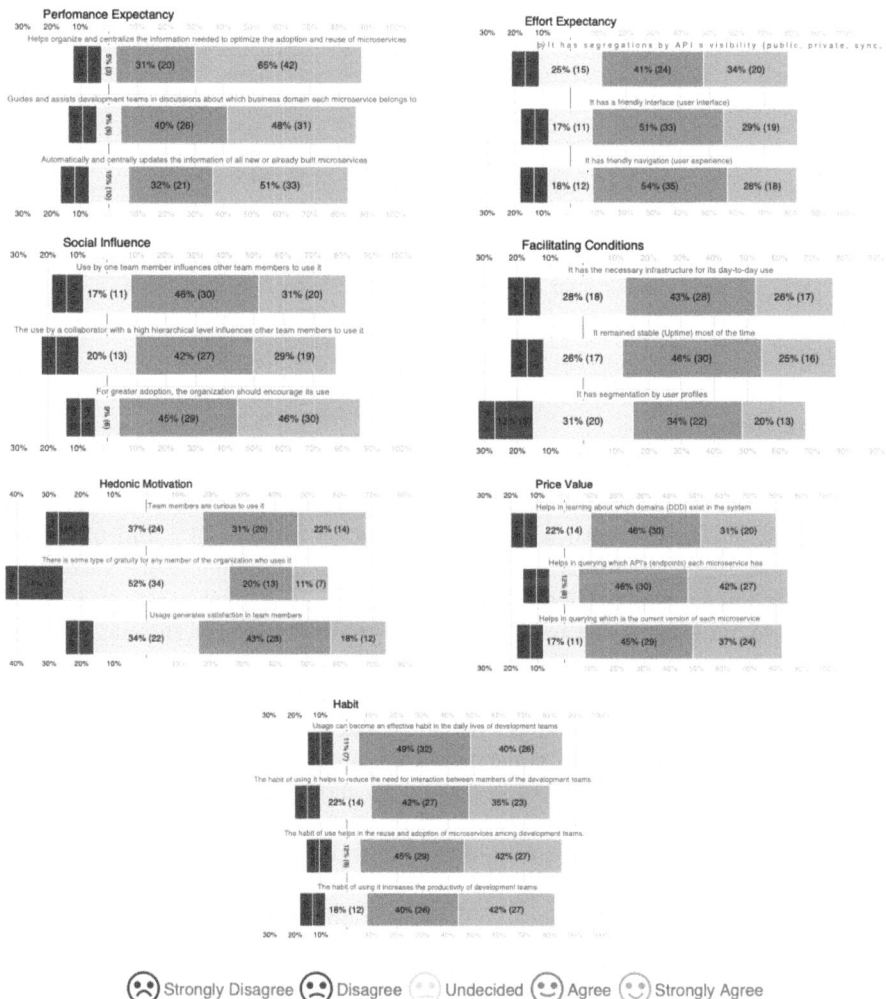

Fig. 2. Distribution of the answers for for the questions related to the UTAUT2 constructs

Table 2. UTAUT-2 Construct descriptive statistics.

Construct	Mean	StDev	Min	Median	Max
PE	4.4	0.7	1.0	3.0	5.0
EE	4.0	0.8	1.0	3.0	5.0
SI	4.0	0.8	1.0	3.0	5.0
FC	3.8	0.9	1.0	3.0	5.0
LV	4.1	0.7	1.0	3.0	5.0
HM	3.5	0.9	1.0	3.0	5.0
HB	4.2	0.7	2.0	3.0	5.0

Table 3. Contingency table.

Construct	Strongly Agree (5)	Agree (4)	Don't agree or disagree (3)	Disagree (2)	Strongly disagree (1)
PE	106 (54.3%)	067 (34.3%)	19 (09.7%)	02 (1.0%)	1 (0.5%)
EE	057 (29.2%)	092 (47.1%)	38 (19.4%)	05 (2.5%)	3 (1.5%)
SI	069 (35.3%)	086 (44.1%)	30 (15.3%)	09 (4.6%)	1 (0.5%)
FC	046 (23.5%)	080 (41.0%)	55 (28.2%)	12 (6.1%)	2 (1.0%)
LV	071 (36.4%)	089 (45.6%)	33 (16.9%)	01 (0.5%)	1 (0.5%)
HM	033 (16.9%)	061 (31.2%)	80 (41.0%)	19 (9.7%)	2 (1.0%)
HB	103 (39.6%)	114 (43.8%)	41 (15.7%)	02 (0.7%)	0 (0.0%)
Total	485 (33.9%)	589 (41.1%)	296 (20.6%)	50 (3.4%)	10 (0.6%)

Based on the data presented in Table 2, the average scores for all situations ranged from 3.5 to 4.2, with a standard deviation between 0.7 and 0.9. This suggests that the evaluations were consistent and individual score variations were not significant. Furthermore, the median score remained constant at 3 for all constructs, indicating that most ratings were centered around this mean value.

The statistical analysis of contingency Table 3 reveals significant patterns regarding utilizing the microservices cataloging tool.

The data indicates a clear trend towards high levels of agreement across all constructs. For instance, in the construct (PE), a majority of participants either "Strongly Agree" (54.3%) or "Agree" (34.3%), indicating a significant level of agreement. Similarly, in other constructs, the categories of "Strongly Agree" and "Agree" prevail, pointing towards an overall agreement among the participants.

In constructs (HM) and (FC), the category of "Don't Agree nor Disagree" with (41.0%) and (28.2%), respectively, stands out from the other constructs. This reflects the subtle differences in participants' perspectives regarding these two constructs, possibly due to a need for more clarity in their positions. Although the "Disagree" and "Strongly Disagree" categories are included in variable proportions across different scenarios, their occurrence emphasizes the existence of opposing opinions, particularly in specific contexts.

The constancy of "Strongly Agree" and "Agree" responses, along with uniform standard deviations across scenarios, suggests that participants' opinions are stable. However, the fluctuation in the percentage distribution of each construct demonstrates the complexities of individual perceptions in diverse contexts.

In summary, despite the occurrence of disagreements in some instances, the data shows a consistent pattern of strong agreement. This highlights the importance of considering subtle differences in interpretations while acknowledging the overall degree of consensus among participants.

4.4 Structural Equation Modeling SEM

Structural Equation Modeling (SEM) is a sophisticated statistical technique for investigating a model's complex interplay between observed and unobserved variables [7]. It has applications in various research domains such as social sciences, psychology, education, and economics to test complex theories or hypotheses [7].

SEM enables the assessment of both direct and indirect causal relationships between variables, as well as the model's suitability for the observed data. It aids in understanding the interrelationships between variables, identifying latent factors (unobserved) that may affect observed variables, and evaluating the strength and direction of their relationships [18].

Based on the UTAUT-2 model presented in Sect. 3, the analysis was constructed for each of the seven constructs. For an experience moderator variable to be properly examined and have a meaningful impact on the model, the sample size for each moderator category must be sufficiently broad and diverse. The model evaluation was carried out by examining Cronbach's Alpha (A.C.) for internal consistency, followed by Composite Reliability (C.R.) as a measure of internal consistency. Convergent validity was assessed through Average Variance Extracted (A.V.E), and discriminant validity was estimated using the cross-loadings criterion. [15].

Based on the information shown in Table 4, it can be concluded that the Average Variance Extracted (A.V.E) tests with values of 0.5 [8] and Cronbach's Alpha 0.6 [16] produced results that meet the appropriate standards. Like Cronbach's Alpha, Composite Reliability is also a measure of reliability, and all constructs achieved coefficients that exceeded the acceptable threshold of 0.8 [21].

The study's measurements are highly reliable, as evidenced by the consistent Composite Reliability and A.V.E values across various scenarios. This consistency reinforces the accuracy and consistency of the survey items in measuring the intended constructs. Discriminant validity is an essential concept in research construct analysis. By adhering to the widely accepted Fornell and Larcker criterion (1981), which ensures that the measures employed to gauge various constructs are separate and not highly correlated, this research reinforces the reliability and validity of the interpretations drawn from the conducted analyses. The discriminant validity test assesses indicators to verify whether they differ

Table 4. Reliability Testing.

Construct	A.C.	C.R.	A.V.E.
PE	0.791	0.878	0.705
EE	0.737	0.856	0.673
SI	0.627	0.800	0.572
FC	0.752	0.859	0.671
LV	0.803	0.884	0.717
HM	0.840	0.901	0.753
HB	0.928	0.948	0.821

from one another. The correlation matrix and the square root of the average extracted variance from constructs are evaluated. In this study, the discriminant validity data adhere to Fornell and Larcker's criterion (1981), in which the value in each column is more significant than those below it, representing the correlation between constructs [12,29].

Table 5 presents the estimated correlation matrix and the square root of the average extracted variance from constructs, the **Experience** moderator, and **Behavioral Intention**.

Table 5. Discriminant validity.

	BI[1]	EE	EX[2]	FC	HB	HM	PE	LV	SI
BI[1]	**1.00**								
EE	0.67	**0.82**							
EX[2]	0.09	0.03	**1.00**						
FC	0.75	0.65	0.16	**0.81**					
HB	0.78	0.57	0.22	0.69	**0.90**				
HM	0.60	0.58	0.01	0.67	0.39	**0.86**			
PE	0.59	0.50	−0.08	0.49	0.61	0.33	**0.84**		
LV	0.76	0.55	0.13	0.60	0.71	0.39	0.62	**0.84**	
SI	0.58	0.49	0.04	0.60	0.41	0.53	0.46	0.37	**0.75**

1 - Behavioral Intention
2 - Experience Moderator

In this study, the bootstrapping technique was used to analyze the correlations between the constructs related to the hypotheses. Multiple samples were created from the original data for a more precise and dependable analysis. Hypotheses accepted using the Student's t-test had reference values of T-Value 1.96 and P-Value < 0.05 [12].

Bootstrapping is a statistical method that calculates crucial statistics, creates confidence intervals, and thoroughly tests hypotheses without making strict assumptions about data distribution [12].

Table 6 presents the results of the bootstrapping analysis, which confirmed some of the hypotheses.

According to the results obtained, the construct **Habit** had the greatest influence on the intention to use Technology. Followed by **Learning Value**, **Hedonic Motivation**, and **Experience** when related to **Facilitating Condition**. According to the adjusted R^2 value obtained in this study, the constructs explain 80.1% of its variance.

Table 6. Bootstrapping analysis

	Hypothesis	T-Values	P-Values	
PE → BI[1]	H1	0.319	0.750	
EE → BI[1]	H2	0.359	0.719	
SI → BI[1]	H3	1.323	0.186	
FC → BI[1]	H4	1.332	0.183	
LV → BI[1]	H5	2.619	0.009	C
HM → BI[1]	H6	2.285	0.022	C
HB → BI[1]	H7	2.839	0.005	C
MODERATORS				
EX[2] → BI[1]		0.573	0.567	
EX[2] x FC → BI[1]	H4E	2.267	0.023	C
EX[2] x LV → BI[1]	H5E	1.011	0.312	
EX[2] x HM → BI[1]	H6E	0.883	0.377	
EX[2] x HB → BI[1]	H7E	1.477	0.140	

1 - Behavioral Intention

2 - Experience Moderator

C - Hypothesis Confirmed

4.5 Qualitative Analysis

During the qualitative analysis phase, the data extraction procedure was conducted. It is important to highlight that participation in the open-ended statement was optional. We received responses from 15 individuals marked as P1 to P15, of which 14 were considered valid and included in the analysis.

The responses to a survey statement were recorded in a spreadsheet. Each response was allocated to a row, with participants identified as P1 through P14. Next, the data encoding process was carried out, assigning one or more codes to each response. To exemplify the process, see some notable samples of response text: From participant P7 - "The tool is useful but requires more promotion within the organization to increase its visibility." adds the code **"Needs More Promotion of the Tool"**. Participant P12, "Cataloging microservices is an essential aspect that significantly assists in software planning and development.", adds the code **"Assists in Software Development"**.

The categorization of codes as **strengths** or **weaknesses** of the microservices cataloging tool resulted from a rigorous translation process. The resulting Table 7 presents the reduction of overlap achieved.

Table 7. The categorization of codes.

	Codes	Total
Strenghts	Assists in Software Development Process	06
	Microservices Centralized Information	11
	Microservice Reuse	08
	Microservice API's Knowledge	13
Weaknesses	Needs More Promotion of the Tool	07
	Needs More Automation	02

The following table displays the results of a qualitative analysis to understand participants' perceptions of the microservices cataloging tool. The analysis identified the strengths and weaknesses of various aspects of this approach. The numbers in the table indicate the total number of individuals expressing each specific perception.

5 Discussion

This section presents the discussions and general findings obtained from analyzing the responses collected in the survey study. While the hypothesis evaluation is performed through descriptive and inferential statistics, including Structural Equation Modeling (SEM), the results taken from the qualitative analysis were based on the codes extracted from the participants' answers.

Based on the descriptive statistics of Sect. 4.3, the analyzed scenarios showed that participants generally agreed with the proposed constructs. Most participants either agreed or had a neutral stance towards them. Response averages consistently ranged between 3.5 and 4.2, indicating that opinions remained closely aligned and positively assessed. The distribution of responses, with a standard deviation generally ranging from 0.7 to 0.9, demonstrates a certain level of variability in opinions, which is typical in surveys of this nature. However, it is worth highlighting that the responses did not exhibit excessive dispersion concerning the means. This further underscores the consistency of the evaluations.

Most participants tended to select the response options "Don't agree or disagree" or "Agree" as seen in the consistently observed medians. This suggests a level of consensus in their opinions, increasing confidence in the outcomes. The distribution of response categories also highlights the positive sentiment of the assessments, with the "Agree" category being the most prominent. The lower proportions in extreme categories like "Strongly Agree" and "Strongly Disagree" further indicate a sense of balance and significance in the conveyed opinions.

Using inferential statistics (SEM), analyzing the constructs and the **Experience** moderator through statistical methods provides insights into the factors influencing users' intentions to utilize the microservices cataloging tool. The results showed that the hypotheses were confirmed for **Habit, Learning Value, Hedonic Motivation**, and **Experience** when related to **Facilitating Conditions**, all of which influence the intention to use the technology.

The qualitative analysis shows the overall perception of the microservices cataloging tool is positive. Many participants highlighted its benefits regarding centralized information on microservices, microservice reuse, the microservice API's knowledge, and assistance in the software development process. However, some concerns were raised regarding the need for more promotion of the tool by the company and more automation in its use. These insights provide a comprehensive view of the pros and cons of the microservices cataloging tool and can guide decision-making regarding its adoption in software engineering practices.

5.1 Hypothesis Confirmed

In the previous section, the bootstrapping analysis technique was used to investigate the hypotheses for the intention to utilize the microservices cataloging tool. The investigation revealed that the **Habit** construct was validated, meaning that individuals tend to use the technology automatically in their daily jobs. This discovery is significant for adopting the tool, as the development team may begin to use it habitually, making it easier to integrate a microservices cataloging tool into the software development process.

One of the most significant influences on development teams is the **Learning Value** construct. This construct represents the total value that tools bring to the table. It is vital because it enables software developers to identify APIs for each microservice in a productive environment, along with their current version. Additionally, the tool facilitates learning of functional domains that are part of the system. This knowledge is essential in enabling software developers and architects to make strategic decisions about how the system will grow and support business rules and non-functional requirements.

Hedonic motivation refers to the pleasure and enjoyment derived from using technology. It has been identified as a significant determinant of technology acceptance and use. Its significance lies in the fact that it reflects the potential of the microservice cataloging tool to be utilized in a manner that could inspire delight among software developers, as opposed to being perceived as tedious or exhausting by team members. Hedonic motivation is an important driver in determining whether the tool will be adopted and integrated into the team's daily software development processes.

The latest confirmed hypothesis concerns the concept of **Facilitating Conditions**. It refers to the extent to which an individual believes that an organization's technical infrastructure is available to support the use of the system. This construct highlights the fact that the overall infrastructure is suitable for supporting the tool usage by software development teams. It is crucial to pay attention to this point because the technology must have good availability and scalability; otherwise, the teams will not be able to utilize it in their software development process.

As previously mentioned, more research is needed regarding the actual effects of incorporating a cataloging tool for microservices in the governance procedures of businesses that utilize a microservices-based architecture. Also, identify the impacts on its utilization, including difficulties encountered and recognized benefits. Companies must exercise caution in today's rapidly evolving microservices landscape when introducing new features into their systems, which require careful consideration and planning.

5.2 Threats to Validity

Empirical studies face certain validity threats, which can be of construct, internal validity, external validity, and reliability [39]. Below, we describe the threats for this study according to this classification and how we mitigated them.

Construct validity refers to ensuring correct operational measures for the concepts (constructs) under study [39]. Since the survey protocol was based on the constructs of UTAUT2, threats in this regard are limited. However, there is still a threat that respondents will not understand the responses in the same way as the authors. This threat is also reduced since the participants were, in general, experienced in the field and work with the target tool in their routine.

Internal validity is associated with causal inference and happens when it is believed that a certain condition is a consequence of a second condition when, in reality, they are a consequence of a third condition not considered in the study [39]. To mitigate this threat, we included open-ended and close-ended questions, allowing us to combine a quantitative and a qualitative analysis.

External validity is about generalizing the results to a large population [39]. In this regard, studies that focus on one project do not rely on external generalization but rather on analytical generalization [30,40], i.e., "the results are extended to cases that have common characteristics [to the studied case]" [30]. Based on that, we argue that other large development units that manage a large number of services might have similar results. However, it remains a threat related to the influence of other factors.

Reliability is related to the dependence of the data and results on the researchers who performed the study [39]. To improve this aspect, we defined a protocol based on a well-known technique, including a questionnaire and data analysis procedures.

6 Study Limitations and Future Research

One significant consideration identified in the analysis is the restricted scope of the sample, which encompasses only a single company. While this provides insight into broader architectural challenges in selecting a toolset for cataloging various tools, it does not effectively explore why some other tools may have been unsuitable. A more comprehensive analysis should consider the organization's specific needs, compatibility and integration issues, and any functionality limitations that influenced the decision-making process.

Future research could address these limitations by examining the factors that guided toolset selection and investigating the compatibility, integration challenges, and functional constraints of the other tools mentioned. This deeper exploration aims to enhance understanding of the architectural issues involved in selecting the ideal toolset for cataloging and supporting microservices.

7 Conclusions

This study investigated the introduction of a microservices cataloging tool in a large software development unit that manages a high number of services. Given the absence of studies that evaluate the impact of this kind of tool, this paper fills an existing gap in the literature. Through evaluating various scenarios and hypotheses, valuable insights have emerged that influence how developers perceive and adopt the tool.

Based on the findings, the tool being considered has been met with a high number of positive responses. The tool's ability to centralize and organize information, facilitate discussions on business domains for each microservice, and automatically publish its most important data has been particularly praised for enhancing job performance.

Participants have also expressed their belief that the tool can help cultivate productive habits, reduce unnecessary team interactions, improve the reuse of existing microservices, and ultimately increase overall productivity. It shows that the decision to use the microservices cataloging tool is mainly driven by the habitual behavior of the user. Learning value, hedonic motivation, and experience also play a significant role when considering the enabling conditions for technology use.

There is a pressing need for a tool or framework that can effectively organize and catalog microservices, especially in cases with a high number of operations and services. The findings of this research strongly indicate that large development units looking to optimize their service management can significantly benefit from incorporating this tool into their workflow. To this end, this study offers valuable assistance by examining the potential benefits of this kind of tool and identifying obstacles that need to be overcome in their implementation. By doing so, we hope to provide businesses with the knowledge they need to make informed decisions and maximize the benefits of microservices cataloging.

Future works might perform similar studies in other companies from different sectors and with other characteristics to verify if these results can be further generalized. Moreover, the users' interaction with the catalog can also be used as a source of information to identify emerging patterns and best practices.

References

1. Ain, N., Kaur, K., Waheed, M.: The influence of learning value on learning management system use: an extension of utaut2. Inf. Dev. **32**(5), 1306–1321 (2016)
2. Backstage: Backstage/backstage: Backstage is an open platform for building developer portals (2023). https://github.com/backstage/backstage
3. Baresi, L., Garriga, M.: Microservices: the evolution and extinction of web services? In: Microservices, pp. 3–28. Springer International Publishing, Cham (2020)
4. Bonér, J., Bonâer, J.: Reactive Microservices Architecture: Design Principles for Distributed Systems. O'Reilly Media, O'Reilly, UK (2016)
5. configure8: Homepage (2023). https://www.configure8.io/
6. DeployHub: Microservice catalog tool (June 2023). https://www.deployhub.com/
7. English, F.: Encyclopedia of educational leadership and administration (2006). https://doi.org/10.4135/9781412939584, http://dx.doi.org/10.4135/9781412939584
8. Fornell, C., Larcker, D.F.: Evaluating structural equation models with unobservable variables and measurement error. J. Mark. Res. **18**(1), 39 (1981). https://doi.org/10.2307/3151312
9. Fowler, M., Lewis, J.: Microservices (2014). https://martinfowler.com/articles/microservices.html
10. GmbH, L.: Use case: Service & amp; api catalog: Value stream management (vsm) (2023). https://www.leanix.net/en/use-cases/service-and-api-catalog
11. Gortney, M.E., et al.: Visualizing microservice architecture in the dynamic perspective: a systematic mapping study. IEEE Access **10**, 119999–120012 (2022)
12. Hair, J.: A Primer on Partial Least Squares Structural Equation Modeling (PLS-SEM). SAGE Publications, Singapore (2014). https://books.google.com.br/books?id=IFiarYXE1PoC
13. Haselbock, S., Weinreich, R., Buchgeher, G., Kriechbaum, T.: Microservice design space analysis and decision documentation: a case study on api management (November 2018). https://doi.org/10.1109/soca.2018.00008, http://dx.doi.org/10.1109/SOCA.2018.00008
14. Hassan, S., Bahsoon, R.: Microservices and their design trade-offs: a self-adaptive roadmap (2016). https://doi.org/10.1109/SCC.2016.113
15. Henseler, J., Ringle, C.M., Sinkovics, R.R.: The use of partial least squares path modeling in international marketing (January 2009). https://doi.org/10.1108/s1474-7979(2009)0000020014, http://dx.doi.org/10.1108/s1474-7979(2009)0000020014
16. Hill, M., Hill, A.: Investigação por questionário. Sílabo, Lisbon (2002). https://books.google.com.br/books?id=-6neOwAACAAJ
17. Indrasiri, K., Siriwardena, P.: Microservices Governance, pp. 151–166. Apress, Berkeley, CA (2018). https://doi.org/10.1007/978-1-4842-3858-56
18. Kaplan, D.: Structural Equation Modeling: Foundations and Extensions. SAGE, London (2009)

19. Kleehaus, M., Matthes, F.: Challenges in documenting microservice-based it landscape: a survey from an enterprise architecture management perspective (October 2019). https://doi.org/10.1109/edoc.2019.00012, http://dx.doi.org/10.1109/EDOC.2019.00012
20. Lindblom, E.: What is a microservice catalog and why do you need one? (March 2023). https://thenewstack.io/microservices/what-is-a-microservice-catalog-and-why-do-you-need-one
21. Marcoulides, G.A.: Modern Methods for Business Research. Lawrence Erlbaum, Mahwah (1998)
22. Mayer, B., Weinreich, R.: An approach to extract the architecture of microservice-based software systems (March 2018). https://doi.org/10.1109/sose.2018.00012, http://dx.doi.org/10.1109/SOSE.2018.00012
23. Nadareishvili, I., Mitra, R., McLarty, M., Amundsen, M.: Microservice architecture: aligning principles, practices, and culture (2016)
24. Newman, S.: Building Microservices: Designing Fine-Grained Systems, 1st edn. O'Reilly Media, Chicago, February 2015
25. Newman, S.: Monolith to Microservices. O'Reilly Media, Sebastopol, CA, November 2019
26. Peralta, J.H.: Microservice apis: using python, flask, fastapi, openapi and more (2023)
27. Pinheiro, C., Vasconcelos, A., Guerreiro, S.: Microservice architecture from enterprise architecture management perspective. In: Shishkov, B. (ed.) Business Modeling and Software Design, pp. 236–245. Springer International Publishing, Cham (2019)
28. Richardson, C.: Microservice Patterns. Manning Publications, New York, NY (February 2019)
29. Ringle, C.M., Da Silva, D., Bido, D.D.: Modelagem de equações estruturais com utilização do smartpls. Revista Brasileira de Marketing **13**(2), 56–73 (2014). https://doi.org/10.5585/remark.v13i2.2717
30. Runeson, P., Höst, M.: Guidelines for conducting and reporting case study research in software engineering. Empir. Softw. Eng. **14**(2), 131–164 (2009)
31. Sill, A.: The design and architecture of microservices. IEEE Cloud Comput. **3**(5), 76–80 (2016)
32. Soni, A., Ranga, V., Jadhav, S.: MockRest—a generic approach for automated mock framework for REST APIs generation. In: Lecture Notes in Networks and Systems, pp. 237–255. Springer, Singapore (2020)
33. Subramanian, S., Inozemtseva, L., Holmes, R.: Live API Documentation. ACM, New York, NY, USA (May 2014)
34. Sulír, M., Bačíková, M., Chodarev, S., Porubän, J.: Visual augmentation of source code editors: a systematic mapping study. J. Vis. Lang. Comput. **49**, 46–59 (2018). https://doi.org/10.1016/j.jvlc.2018.10.001
35. Söylemez, M., Tekinerdogan, B., Kolukısa Tarhan, A.: Challenges and solution directions of microservice architectures: a systematic literature review (2022). https://doi.org/10.3390/app12115507, https://www.mdpi.com/2076-3417/12/11/5507
36. Usman, M., Badampudi, D., Smith, C., Nayak, H.: An ecosystem for the large-scale reuse of microservices in a cloud-native context. IEEE Softw. **39**(5), 68–75 (2022). https://doi.org/10.1109/MS.2022.3167447
37. Venkatesh, M.: Davis, Davis: User acceptance of information technology: toward a unified view. MIS Q. **27**(3), 425 (2003). https://doi.org/10.2307/30036540

38. Wang, Y., Kadiyala, H., Rubin, J.: Promises and challenges of microservices: an exploratory study (2021). https://doi.org/10.1007/s10664-020-09910-y
39. Wohlin, C., Runeson, P., Höst, M., Ohlsson, M.C., Regnell, B., Wesslén, A.: Planning. In: Experimentation in Software Engineering, vol. 9783642290, pp. 89–116. Springer, Berlin, Heidelberg (2012)
40. Yin, R.: Case Study Research: Design and Methods. Applied Social Research Methods. SAGE Publications, New York (2003)

TOSCARISMA: Modeling CARISMA-Based Service Communication Using TOSCA

Kevin Klein[1,2], Pascal Hirmer[1], Alexander Walz[1], and Steffen Becker[2]

[1] Mercedes-Benz AG, Sindelfingen, Germany
{kevin.klein,pascal.hirme,alexander.walz}@mercedes-benz.com
[2] Institute of Software Engineering, University of Stuttgart, Stuttgart, Germany
steffen.becker@iste.uni-stuttgart.de

Abstract. Nowadays, the amount of software in modern cars as well as its complexity increases rapidly due to applications such as autonomous driving. Consequently, more powerful computing platforms are employed and software applications are developed in a distributed manner, e.g., by applying the widely established microservice pattern. Microservices introduce additional complexity regarding the communication between the individual services. Solutions that address these challenges have been developed. One of these solutions that is specifically designed for an application to the automotive domain is the CARISMA approach. The main idea of CARISMA is to employ a service mesh architecture that is adapted to the design of future electric/electronic (E/E) architectures. In this paper, we present an approach to describing a topology of services deployed based on CARISMA including their relationships regarding service-to-service-communication using the Topology and Orchestration Specification for Cloud Applications (TOSCA). This way, a complex CARISMA topology can be described using a model-based approach relying on abstract and reusable components. This increases the understandability of the modeled topology and enables an automated deployment and management. Furthermore, because only desired service-to-service communication paths are established, the complexity of the resulting CARISMA configuration is reduced.

Keywords: Service Meshes · CARISMA · TOSCA · Automotive Software Architecture

1 Introduction

The automotive industry is experiencing an impactful transformation towards Software-defined Vehicles (SDV) characterized by a transition from hardware to software regarding the primary driver of functionality and innovation. Consequently, the amount of software components in modern cars will continue its rapid growth, which on the one hand drives new features but on the other hand comes with a high complexity and the need for new software architectures. Traditional car architectures, which are based on a multitude of dedicated Electronic Control Units (ECUs) are not suitable anymore to support complex software-driven applications, such as autonomous driving. In newer architectures, a large number of these individual ECUs will be replaced with more powerful ones, referred to as High-Performance Computers (HPCs). HPCs offer more computational resources and decrease the complexity of the E/E architecture in general by transitioning from a great number of individual ECUs to fewer HPCs connected to smaller ECUs for sensors and actors [14]. These HPCs will be connected by modern communication technologies, such as Automotive Ethernet [11], enabling the design of in-car applications in a distributed manner. Consequently, a large number of software components will be designed as microservices [15] – some of them will even communicate with cloud backends.

Since the aforementioned development introduces challenges, e.g., additional complexity regarding networking and inter-service communication, solutions that cope with these challenges have been developed. One of these solutions is the CAR-Integrated Service Mesh Architecture (CARISMA) that we introduced in our previous work [8]. We adapted the traditional service mesh architecture [9] such that it meets the specific requirements of a car. The previously presented version of CARISMA is designed so that every service is made available to every other service within the service mesh. Although this design enables very flexible service-to-service communication, it also introduces a rapid increase regarding the complexity of the service mesh configuration, as our evaluation results suggest. One reason for this is that communication paths between software components that are not intended to communicate are established.

In this paper, we present an approach to cope with this issue by extending the CARISMA approach to support an automated orchestration and provisioning of the involved components and services. To this end, we rely on a model-based approach not only because it enables us to reduce the consumption of computational resources by establishing only the required communication paths but also because it allows us to provide the foundation for a CARISMA-based setup as templates that can be instantiated for concrete deployments. Changes to these templates can be rolled out and applied in an automated fashion via Continuous Integration/Continuous Delivery (CI/CD) pipelines. One model-based approach to automated deployment and management of cloud applications that gained interest within the research community is the Topology and Orchestration Specification for Cloud Applications (TOSCA) [12]. We decided to use TOSCA as basis for our method because it offers a generic approach to automated software provisioning in the cloud that promises to be applicable to CARISMA and because it is not limited to certain technologies or providers.

The remainder of this paper is structured as follows: in Sect. 2 we introduce basic concepts, including CARISMA and TOSCA. Section 3 describes the main contribution of this paper: we present TOSCARISMA – a method for orchestration and provisioning of CARISMA-based setups using TOSCA. In Sect. 4, our prototypical implementation is described. After that, in Sect. 5, we present related work. Finally, Sect. 6 summarizes the paper and gives an outlook on future work.

2 Foundations

This section introduces the necessary fundamentals of the method presented in this paper: the CARISMA approach [8] and TOSCA [12].

2.1 CARISMA

The rapidly growing amount of software in modern cars demands for a more flexible software platform that supports a dynamic deployment of applications. Some of these applications will be microservices (see [15] for more details) consumed by other applications or services. Hence, there will the need to support a flexible deployment of services while maintaining their ability to communicate among themselves as well as for an easy integration of services that run in the cloud. As a possible solution to these challenges, in our previous work [8] we introduced CARISMA – an architecture that enables in-car applications to run distributed across a cluster of HPCs and, furthermore, to incorporate software components that run in the cloud. To this end, we adapted the traditional service mesh architecture (see [9] for more details) such that it meets the specific requirements of a car, e.g., limited availability of computational resources. Figure 1 depicts an example that is based on our approach. It consists of the following main components: (i) a Control Plane hosting a configuration service as well as a node and service registry service storing meta-information about the nodes and services, (ii) at least one Data Plane, and (iii) exactly one Side-Car Proxy per Data Plane. Compared to the traditional service mesh architecture, we decided against the traditional Side-Car Proxy pattern, where a Side-Car Proxy accompanies every service. Contrary to the cloud, for an in-car application, resource consumption is crucial. Also, additional Side-Car Proxies within one HPC would not differ in terms of the configuration and, therefore, are an avoidable resource consumption. Hence, we reduced the number of Side-Car Proxies to exactly one per HPC. Furthermore, we do not run the Control Plane on a dedicated node. Instead, we differentiate between a central HPC that receives a coordinative role and hosts the Control Plane next to a Data Plane and satellite nodes, which are Data Planes only.

In a first step, every HPC has to register with the node registry service. As a result of this step, every HPC receives a unique node identifier which can then be used for service registration. In a second step, the services must be registered with the service registry service. As soon as a service is registered, it will become available through the Side-Car Proxies.

Based on the information that is stored as part of the node registry, a per-node configuration can be generated and transmitted to the connected Side-Car Proxies of the nodes whenever the service registry is updated.

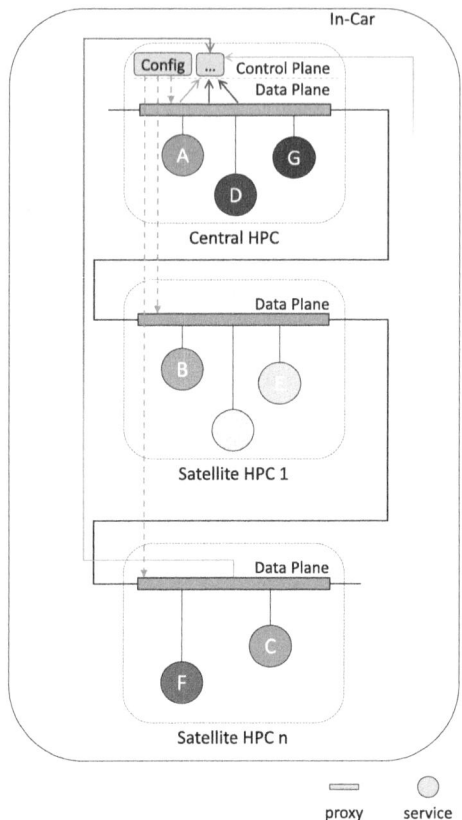

Fig. 1. Example applying the CARISMA approach. Note that the color of the arrows refers to the service the data originates from. Figure adapted from [8].

Every Side-Car Proxy comprises two listeners: (i) the *ingress listener* routing incoming traffic from other nodes to the desired local service and (ii) the *egress listener* routing outgoing traffic initiated by local applications to their desired target service on the same or another node.

As soon as the nodes and services are registered, the inter-service communication becomes possible through the egress listener of the corresponding Side-Car Proxy. In case the desired service is located on the same node, the request is routed to the local port on which the service listens. If, on the other hand, the service is located on a different node, the request is routed through the ingress listener of the Side-Car Proxy that belongs to the corresponding target node. Even if the configuration changes and the desired target service is moved to another node, the configuration is updated instantly by the Control Plane and the caller can continue sending requests to the desired target service through the egress listener of the corresponding Side-Car Proxy. It is important to note, that before registering a new service instance followed by a configuration update, it must be ensured that the new instance is running and can receive requests in order to avoid failing requests.

Furthermore, CARISMA supports integrating services that run in a cloud backend in the same fashion as with services running within the HPC cluster.

2.2 TOSCA

In this section, we describe the key concepts behind TOSCA. This section is mainly based on [6,12].

The manual deployment of large cloud applications turned out to be complex and error-prone. One possible solution to cope with this problem is TOSCA. TOSCA is an approved OASIS standard that aims at automating the orchestration and management of cloud applications in a portable manner by describing the structure and the management functionalities of these cloud applications in a YAML-based modeling language. The metamodel behind TOSCA allows the representation of a cloud application as a *service template* that consists of a *topology template* and zero or more *management plans*.

The topology template is a typed, directed graph of so called *node templates*. These node templates, that form the vertices of the graph, are connected by so called *relationship templates*. The node templates represent the components that are necessary to provision the application. The relationship templates, however, represent how these components are connected and, therefore, form the graph's edges. Moreover, TOSCA introduces a set of *node types* and *relationship types* as the available building blocks. Furthermore, TOSCA supports introducing custom types for both node and relationship types by extending existing ones as known from object-oriented programming. This mechanism can be used to implement custom behavior. To this end, they may define lifecycle operations that can be invoked by an orchestration engine when instantiating a service template. For example, a database node type might define a "create" operation that implements the creation of an instance of the component at runtime. This operation might involve executing some custom installation scripts. Moreover, this node type might also define a custom "start" or "stop" operation that implements how to correctly start or stop the instance when requested by an orchestration engine. Those lifecycle operations are typically represented by implementation artifacts such as scripts or Ansible[1] playbooks that implement the actual behavior.

Finally, management plans describe the applications deployment and management aspects. There are essentially two types of plans: the *build plan* and the *termination plan*. Plans of the build plan type are responsible for the creation of a new instance of a service template whereas plans of the termination plan type are responsible for the termination of an existing instance of a service template. To this end, each plan is essentially a workflow, i.e., a combination of lifecycle operations of the nodes of a topology. TOSCA supports two kinds of workflows:

---

[1] Ansible: https://www.ansible.com.

declarative workflows and *imperative workflows*. Declarative workflows are generated by the orchestration engine based on the nodes and relationships in the topology whereas imperative workflows need to be manually specified by the author of the topology. Imperative workflows are typically being used when there is the need to implement a specific use-case that has not been considered when defining the node and relationship types.

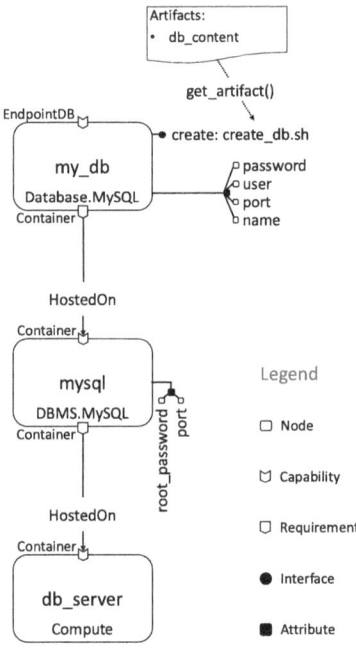

Fig. 2. Example of a TOSCA service template. Figure based on [12].

For an overall example, consider the service template depicted in Fig. 2. The visual notation used is based on Vino4TOSCA [5]. The shown topology comprises the following three nodes: (i) *db_server* of the node type *Compute*, (ii) *mysql* of the node type *DBMS.MySQL*, and (iii) *my_db* of the node type *Database.MySQL*. Node (i) offers the "Container" capability and, therefore, indicates that the node can act as a container or host for one or more other nodes. Moreover, this capability is defined as a valid target type for the relationship type "HostedOn" and can, therefore, be connected to other nodes exposing the "Container" requirement via a relationship of that type. Node (ii) represents a mysql database server through the custom node type and comprises specific attributes. In contrast to node (i), it exposes a requirement for the "Container" capability and, therefore, needs to be connected to a node that offers it through a relationship of a proper type. In this example, it is, therefore, connected via a relationship of type "HostedOn" to node (i). Additionally, node (ii) also offers the "Container" capability and can, therefore, act as a container or host for other nodes as well. Node (iii) constitutes a mysql database via the associated custom node type and also comprises specific attributes. Analogously to node (ii), it exposes a requirement for the "Container" capability that needs to be satisfied and is, therefore, connected to node (ii). Furthermore, it offers the "EndpointDB" capability. Moreover, it redefines the standard lifecycle operation "create" to execute a custom shell script in order to create the database. This script receives a custom artifact containing the default database content as input. The topology could be deployed, e.g., with the orchestrator provided by OpenTOSCA [3].

3 TOSCARISMA

This section contains the main contribution of our paper: TOSCARISMA – a method for modeling CARISMA-based service-to-service communication using TOSCA. To this end, our method comprises three custom node types as well as one custom relationship type. Figure 3 shows an example of a CARISMA-based topology that has been modeled based on TOSCARISMA: two services (Service A and Service B) that are deployed onto two different HPCs, with Service A sending requests to Service B.

According to the CARISMA approach, the request routing is handled by the respective Side-Car Proxy of the HPC on which the service is running, thus justifying a dependency of the services on the respective Side-Car Proxy instance on the same HPC. In accordance with our previous paper [8], we chose Envoy[2] as Side-Car Proxy technology for our examples, but of course, TOSCARIMA is also compatible with other solutions.

The Side-Car Proxies, in turn, receive their configuration from the CARISMA Control Plane deployed onto one of the HPCs through an API, thus justifying a dependency of the Side-Car Proxy instances on the CARISMA instance. According to the CARISMA approach, that instance would run on the central HPC. But because there are no further differences between the central HPC and other HPC nodes in the context of CARISMA, we do not explicitly differentiate between a central and a non-central HPC within TOSCARISMA.

Altogether, the services, the CARISMA instance, and the Side-Car Proxy instances run on an HPC, thus justifying a corresponding dependency. Consequently, the HPCs represent the only nodes within the depicted topology that do not depend on other nodes.

Concerning the build plan that would be generated and executed when deploying the depicted topology using an orchestration engine, refer to Fig. 4. As the first step, the HPCs as the only nodes without a dependency on other nodes would be started. This step could be executed in parallel. Secondly, the CARISMA instance would represent the only node that other nodes depend on but, in turn, has no unsatisfied dependencies and, therefore, would be created. Since all Envoy instances depend on that CARISMA instance, their deployment

---

[2] Envoy: https://www.envoyproxy.io.

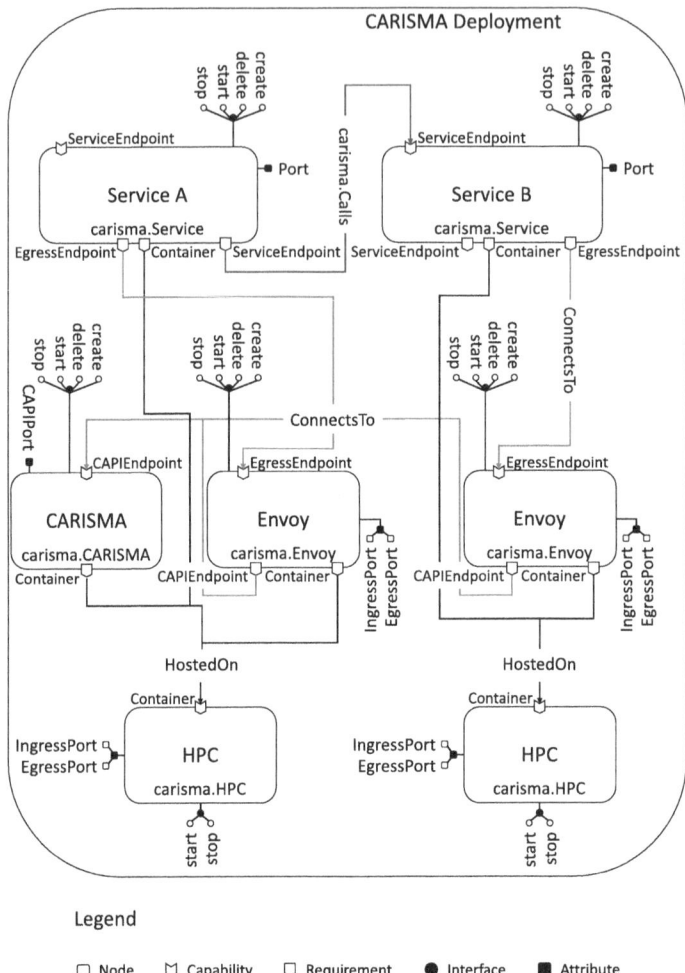

Fig. 3. Example of a TOSCARISMA-based service template. The relationships are depicted in different colors for better readability.

would need to wait for this step to complete. Following this step, both Envoy instances represent nodes that other nodes within the topology depend on but, in turn, do not have any unsatisfied dependencies and, therefore, are being created next. As the last step, the service instances need to be deployed. The deployment of the Envoy instances followed by the deployment of the service instances can again happen in parallel on a per-node basis.

Please note that we deliberately did not include one aspect as part of the figure to improve its readability: technically, when constructing the relationship between two services, the service registry would need to be updated, thus justifying a dependency on the CARISMA instance. To this end, the custom node type carisma.Service would need to expose an additional requirement for the "Endpoint" capability which has to be used to connect an instance of it to an instance of carisma.CARISMA via the "ConnectsTo" relationship.

In the following, we explain the custom node and relationship types of the TOSCARISMA method in more detail.

carisma.HPC: This custom node type is derived from the standard TOSCA node type "Compute" and represents an HPC. Additionally to the attributes inherited from "Compute", we defined two attributes representing the ingress port and the egress port of the Side-Car Proxy running on that HPC. Since there is exactly one Side-Car Proxy instance per HPC, these attributes do not only belong to the Side-Car Proxy instance but instead to the overall HPC. Attaching these attributes to the HPC enables passing these attributes as input to lifecycle operations of dependent nodes. For example, the egress port is not only required to configure the Side-Car Proxy properly but also as a configuration parameter for the services running on that HPC. Moreover, HPCs cannot simply be provisioned on demand concerning an in-car setup. Instead, they can be started and stopped as needed. Consequently, we defined these two standard lifecycle operations. To reduce the complexity of our approach, we decided to refrain from implementing the node registration process as described in Sect. 2.1. Instead, we propose to encode the HPC's IP address in an appropriate derived attribute and use its value as unique node identifier for updating the service registry.

carisma.CARISMA: This custom node type is derived from the standard TOSCA node type "SoftwareComponent" and represents a CARISMA instance. For this custom node type, we defined an attribute representing the CARISMA API port. Because other nodes need to connect to the CARISMA instance, e.g., the Envoy instances, to receive their configuration, this custom node type offers an "Endpoint" capability representing the CARISMA API (CAPI) endpoint. This capability can be used to connect instances of carisma.Envoy to it via the "ConnectsTo" relationship. Furthermore, because this custom node type is inherited from "SoftwareComponent" it exposes a requirement for the "Container" capability which has to be used to connect an instance of it to an instance of carisma.HPC via the "HostedOn" relationship. Moreover, we redefined the standard lifecycle operations for this custom node type accordingly.

carisma.Envoy: This custom node type is derived from the standard TOSCA node type "SoftwareComponent" and represents an Envoy instance. For this custom node type, we defined two attributes representing the ingress port as well as the egress port. Because this custom node type is inherited from "SoftwareComponent" it exposes a requirement for the "Container" capability which has to be used to connect an instance of it to an instance of carisma.HPC via the "HostedOn" relationship. This relationship is used to retrieve the attribute values for the ingress port and egress port from the corresponding carisma.HPC instance. These attribute values are then used to initialize the instance's attributes accordingly. Since instances of carisma.Service running on the same HPC need to route their traffic through its egress port, this custom node type offers an "Endpoint" capability representing the egress endpoint. This capability can be used to connect instances of carisma.Service to it via the "ConnectsTo" relationship. The ingress port of an Envoy instance is used to receive traffic originating from other Envoy instances. Consequently, this dependency is not relevant at deployment time. Furthermore, the Envoy instances will need to connect to the ingress port of the Envoy instances running on the other HPCs that host connected services. This can potentially result in cyclic dependencies and stop the orchestrating engine from deploying the topology. For this reason, we decided not to model that dependency as part of TOSCARISMA. Also, we redefined the standard lifecycle operations for this custom node type accordingly.

carisma.Service: This custom node type is derived from the standard node type "SoftwareComponent" and represents a service. Currently, we assume that a service within this setup exposes all APIs through one port. To this end, we defined an attributes representing the service port. Because this custom node type is inherited from "SoftwareComponent" it exposes a requirement for the "Container" capability which has to be used to connect an instance of it to an instance of carisma.HPC via the "HostedOn" relationship. Additionally, this custom node type exposes a requirement for the "Endpoint" capability which has to be used to connect an instance of it to an instance of carisma.Envoy via the "ConnectsTo" relationship. This relationship is used to retrieve the attribute value for the egress port from the corresponding carisma.Envoy instance. This attribute value can then used by the service to initiate an outgoing connection to another service through the egress endpoint of the Envoy instance running on the same HPC as the service. Furthermore, this custom node type offers an "Endpoint" capability and exposes a requirement for the "Endpoint" capability. This requirement and capability can together with the custom relationship type carisma.Calls be used to indicate a communication path between two services.

carisma.Calls: This custom relationship type is derived from the standard TOSCA relationship type "ConnectsTo" and is intended to represent a communication path between two services and therefore should only be used with instances of the carisma.Service type. Moreover, it relies on CARISMA-specific attributes of the source and target node, which it passes to a custom implementation artifact that has been assigned to the "pre_configure_source" operation of the default "Configure" interface. This custom implementation artifact registers the service with the service registry of the CARISMA Control Plane.

4 Prototypical Implementation

This section describes the prototypical implementation of our method. First, we implemented the custom node and relationship types as described in the previous section. Second, we implemented an echo service and client with debugging output for verification purposes comparable to the echo service and client presented in the evaluation section of our previous work [8]. Third, we modeled the topology as depicted in Figure 4 and deployed it using xOpera[3] in version 0.7.0 as orchestration engine. We chose xOpera because it is open-source and supports the features that we needed for our validation. All software components that were deployed as part of our evaluation were deployed in the form of Linux containers using podman[4] in version 4.9.3. The implementation of our prototype is described in more detail in the following subsections.

4.1 High-Performance Computer

For our validation we did not employ actual HPCs. Instead, we simulated two distinct machines by defining two instances of the carisma.HPC type with `localhost` assigned as hostname and set different values for the ingress and egress port properties. This way we were able to model two distinct machines while keeping the Ansible scripts intact. We then redefined the standard lifecycle operations "start" and "stop" for these instances in our topology template to add debugging output that lets us verify whether the machines are started and stopped correctly. Furthermore, the debugging output allowed us to verify that the service registration with the CARISMA Control Plane functioned as expected and was based on correct host information.

4.2 CARISMA

In our topology template we defined an instance of the carisma.CARISMA type and, furthermore, defined an additional attribute that holds the id of the CARISMA container. Moreover, we redefined the standard lifecycle operations as follows:

Create: This operation uses podman to create a container based on the CARISMA image and stores the id of the created container in the corresponding instance attribute.

Start: This operation uses podman to start the CARISMA container using the container id stored in the corresponding instance attribute.

Stop: This operation uses podman to stop the CARISMA container using the container id stored in the corresponding instance attribute.

Delete: This operation uses podman to remove the CARISMA container using the container id stored in the corresponding instance attribute.

Concerning the CARISMA API port, we sticked to default port used by the CARISMA implementation and used that as the value for the corresponding instance attribute.

---

[3] xOpera: https://github.com/xlab-si/xopera-opera.
[4] podman: https://podman.io.

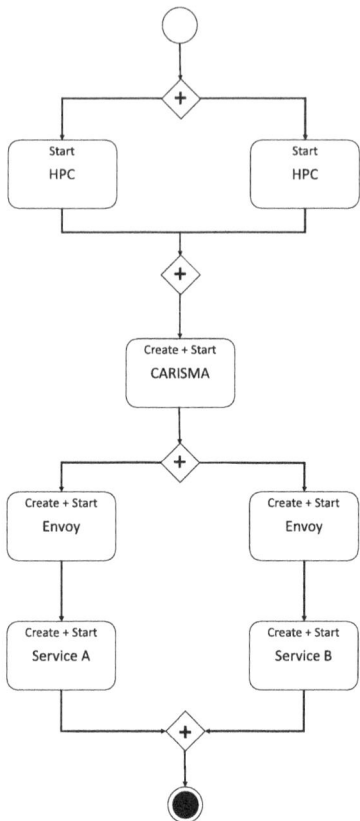

Fig. 4. Example of a TOSCA build plan that could be generate from a TOSCARISMA-based service template.

4.3 Envoy

Within our topology template we defined the instances of the carisma.Envoy type in a very similar fashion as for the carisma.CARISMA type described in Sect. 4.2. To this end, we defined an additional attribute that holds the id of the Envoy container and deployed Envoy based on the official container image[5]. Also, we redefined the standard lifecycle operations in the same way as we did for CARISMA.

4.4 Service

In our topology template we defined two additional attributes for the instances of the carisma.Service type: one that holds the id of corresponding container

---

[5] Envoy container image: https://hub.docker.com/r/envoyproxy/envoy/tags?name=v1.31-latest.

and another one that holds the image name of the service. The first one was, again, filled by and passed to the implementation artifacts of the standard lifecycle operations for container management as described in Sect. 4.2. The latter was passed to the implementation artifact for the standard lifecycle operation "create" to specify whether the echo service or client has to be deployed for the concrete instance of the carisma.Service type.

In order to enable the communication path from the echo client to the echo service, we furthermore defined a relationship of the type carisma.Calls connecting the requirement for the "Endpoint" capability exposed by the echo client to the "Endpoint" capability offered by the echo service.

Finally, we deployed our topology by instantiating the service template with xOpera and verified: (i) the correct deployment of the modeled components based on the output of podman, (ii) the correct configuration of the side-car proxies using the information provided through the Envoy administration interface, and (iii) the successful service-to-service communication based on debugging output.

5 Related Work

Service-Oriented Architectures (SOA) [10] are not new to automotive software platforms. AUTOSAR[6] Adaptive as well as COVESA[7] implement this paradigm as part of their platforms (see [1,2,7] for details), with AUTOSAR being the de facto standard among the big automotive vendors. Typically, concerning SOA these platforms operate in a very similar fashion: based on a service interface definition they generate code that is then used to interact with the communication facilities of the platform. Unfortunately, this approach introduces a strong dependency on the platform and is very inflexible w.r.t. a re-deployment of an in-car service to a different car computer or the integration of services that run in cloud backends.

In our previous work [8] we addressed these issues by proposing the CARISMA approach. To this end, we looked into the field of cloud application development where lots of services are designed as microservices [15]. However, they come with additional complexity, e.g., regarding networking and inter-service communication. To tackle these issues, service meshes have been developed and widely adopted, enabling developers to separate and implement any infrastructure-related concerns, e.g., service-to-service communication, into a dedicated layer [9]. Hence, we adapted the service mesh architecture to become suitable for an integration in an in-car software platform, resulting in the CARISMA approach.

One drawback of our approach is, that it currently does not employ any automated orchestration approach and therefore cannot construct communication paths between in-car applications on-demand. Instead, every possible communication path is established which leads to a rapid increase concerning the memory

---

[6] AUTOSAR: https://autosar.org.
[7] COVESA: https://covesa.global.

consumption of their service mesh configuration. Therefore, in this paper, we further improve CARISMA by enabling automated orchestration and provisioning of services for within CARISMA-based setups.

Automated orchestration and provisioning is an important aspect of cloud application development. In consequence, there are many approaches and technologies available, that are able to automatically set up applications. Prominent examples are, e.g., Puppet[8] Terraform[9] CloudFormation[10] Chef[11] or TOSCA [12]. These tools are usually based on models describing the steps that are required to set up the application and they typically offer the possibility to implement custom behaviour by incorporating scripts. Many of these technologies and tools share the same drawback: they dependent on specific software or cloud providers and, therefore, introduce the risk of vendor lock-ins.

We decided to use TOSCA as basis for our approach, because the format used by TOSCA is standardized and there are several open-source orchestration engines available providing different functionalities as recent research by Stötzner et al. [13] showed. Moreover, TOSCA is not limited to certain technologies, tools, or cloud providers. This is an important aspect since our goal was to extend an approach that is designed to be applied to the automotive domain. To this end, the underlying orchestration technology must be able to incorporate, e.g., automotive specific hardware like HPCs. Furthermore, it should be possible to customize and extend the implementation to support custom use-cases. Additionally, TOSCA supports both imperative and declarative provisioning approaches and even a combination of both [4].

6 Conclusion

In this paper, we present TOSCARISMA, a method for automated orchestration and provisioning of components and services for CARISMA-based setups. By extending the existing CARISMA approach with the concepts of TOSCA, we enable an automated deployment of the CARISMA base components as well as services and applications running within a CARISMA-based environment.

An essential advantage of our method is that it also supports modeling communication paths between applications deployed in CARISMA-based environments. Consequently, unlike the original approach, not every possible communication path has to be established; instead, only the desired communication paths need to be supported. This helps to reduce the memory footprint because it reduces the complexity of the configuration transmitted to the Side-Car Proxies.

By building upon the TOSCA standard, we introduce a generic approach that does not depend on specific technologies and software providers, rendering a vendor lock-in nearly impossible. Furthermore, we implement our method based on reusable custom node and relationship types. In combination with a CI/CD

---

[8] Puppet: https://www.puppet.com.
[9] Terraform: https://www.terraform.io.
[10] CloudFormation: https://aws.amazon.com/cloudformation/.
[11] Chef: https://www.chef.io.

pipeline, these types could be published via a public repository and referenced by topology authors.

For future work, we will extend the custom TOSCA node and relationship types of our prototypical implementation to support more components that can potentially be integrated with CARISMA. Additionally, we want to evaluate our method using different orchestration engines as well.

Acknowledgments. This publication was partially funded by the German Federal Ministry for Economic Affairs and Climate Action (BMWK) as part of the Software-Defined Car (SofDCar) project (19S21002).

References

1. AUTOSAR: Explanation of ara::com API. https://www.autosar.org/fileadmin/standards/R23-11/AP/AUTOSAR_AP_EXP_ARAComAPI.pdf
2. AUTOSAR: Specification of Communication Management. https://www.autosar.org/fileadmin/standards/R23-11/AP/AUTOSAR_AP_SWS_CommunicationManagement.pdf
3. Binz, T., et al.: OpenTOSCA - a runtime for TOSCA-based cloud applications. In: Basu, S., Pautasso, C., Zhang, L., Fu, X. (eds.) Service-Oriented Computing. ICSOC 2013. LNCS, vol. 8274, pp. 692–695. Springer, Berlin, Heidelberg (2013). https://doi.org/10.1007/978-3-642-45005-1_62
4. Breitenbucher, U., Binz, T., Kepes, K., Kopp, O., Leymann, F., Wettinger, J.: Combining declarative and imperative cloud application provisioning based on TOSCA. In: 2014 IEEE International Conference on Cloud Engineering. IEEE (2014). https://doi.org/10.1109/ic2e.2014.56
5. Breitenbücher, U., Binz, T., Kopp, O., Leymann, F., Schumm, D.: Vino4TOSCA: a visual notation for application topologies based on TOSCA. In: Meersman, R., et al. (eds) On the Move to Meaningful Internet Systems: OTM 2012. OTM 2012. LNCS, vol. 7565, pp. 416–424. Springer, Berlin, Heidelberg (2012). https://doi.org/10.1007/978-3-642-33606-5_25
6. Brogi, A., Soldani, J., Wang, P.: TOSCA in a nutshell: promises and perspectives. In: Villari, M., Zimmermann, W., Lau, K.K. (eds.) Service-Oriented and Cloud Computing. ESOCC 2014. LNCS, vol. 8745, pp. 171–186. Springer, Berlin, Heidelberg (2014). https://doi.org/10.1007/978-3-662-44879-3_13
7. COVESA: CommonAPI C++ User Guide. https://github.com/COVESA/capicxx-core-tools/releases/download/3.1.12/CommonAPICppUserGuide.pdf
8. Klein, K., Hirmer, P., Walz, A., Becker, S.: Applying service meshes to in-car architectures: the CARISMA approach. In: Proceedings of the 18th ACM International Conference on Distributed and Event-Based Systems, pp. 159–170. DEBS '24, Association for Computing Machinery, New York, NY, USA (2024). https://doi.org/10.1145/3629104.3669938, https://doi.org/10.1007/s38314-022-0779-z
9. Koschel, A., Bertram, M., Bischof, R., Schulze, K., Schaaf, M., Astrova, I.: A look at service meshes. In: 2021 12th International Conference on Information, Intelligence, Systems & Applications (IISA). IEEE (2021). https://doi.org/10.1109/iisa52424.2021.9555536
10. Lawler, J.P., Howell-Barber, H.: Service-Oriented Architecture. Taylor & Francis Group

11. Matheus, K., Königseder, T.: Automotive Ethernet. Cambridge University Press, Cambridge. https://doi.org/10.1017/9781108895248
12. OASIS: Topology and Orchestration Specification for Cloud Applications (2020). https://docs.oasis-open.org/tosca/TOSCA-Simple-Profile-YAML/v1.3/os/TOSCA-Simple-Profile-YAML-v1.3-os.html. Accessed 22 July 2024
13. Stötzner, M., et al.: A systematic technology review of general-purpose open-source TOSCA orchestrators. In: Proceedings of the IEEE/ACM 16th International Conference on Utility and Cloud Computing. UCC '23, ACM (2016). https://doi.org/10.1145/3603166.3632130
14. Windpassinger, H.: On the Way to a Software-defined Vehicle **17**(7-8), 48–51. https://doi.org/10.1007/s38314-022-0779-z
15. Zimmermann, O.: Microservices tenets: agile approach to service development and deployment **32**(3-4), 301–310. https://doi.org/10.1007/s00450-016-0337-0

Workflow Net Compositions for the Analysis of Service-Oriented Systems

Mandy Weißbach[(✉)], Wolf Zimmermann, and Thomas Kühn

Martin-Luther-Universität Halle-Wittenberg, Institut für Informatik,
Von-Seckendorff-Platz 1, 06120 Halle, Germany
{mandy.weissbach,wolf.zimmermann,thomas.kuehn}@informatik.uni-halle.de

Abstract. Current service-oriented systems rely on asynchronous and recursive service calls. Still when analyzing the behavior of software-oriented systems the calling context of a service call is rarely considered. In earlier work, we could show that common workflow net-based analyses fail to detect deadlocks in a service-oriented system, if they are caused by recursive service calls. To investigate this issue, this work proposes different kinds of service compositions based on the context-sensitivity of recursive service calls and the concept of calling depth. Within this framework, we highlight that context-insensitive deadlock analyses fail, as they ignore the calling context. However, we could show that a context-sensitive deadlock analysis only needs to consider a calling depth of two to be successful. Our key insight is, that context-sensitivity of service composition might impact the correctness of a behavioral analysis.

Keywords: Process Rewrite Systems · Deadlock · Workflow Nets · Petri Nets · Context-Sensitive Composition

1 Introduction

Nowadays, it is common to build service-oriented systems based on numerous microservices and/or serverless functions. These services are tightly coupled, yet easily interchangeable. However, their composition might lead to undesired behavior, such as, deadlocks or contract violations. Thus before composing services, performing a static analysis is necessary to avoid such undesired behavior. Due to the large number of services, recursive service calls – no matter whether intended or not – are likely in such systems. We distinguish between *synchronous* and *asynchronous* service calls. While the former are blocking, i.e., the caller waits until the callee returns, that latter are non-blocking, i.e., the caller and callee are executed concurrently. Consequently, static analysis must consider both synchronous and asynchronous as well as recursive service calls.

A typical approach for the static analysis of service-oriented systems is to describe the behavior of each service with a formal model. These abstract descriptions are composed to a formal description of the whole service-oriented system.

Using this formal description, the absence of undesired behavior in the whole system can be verified. In general, a static analysis should be *conservative*, i.e., if no undesired behavior is found, the system will not exhibit the undesired behavior at runtime. Notably though, false positives might be detected. Considering, for instance, workflow nets [14], each service including its interfaces and service calls is abstracted to a Petri net. These Petri nets are composed by adding transitions to capture the calls and returns of services. Although this composition completely abstracts from the data being processed, the resulting Petri net can be statically analyzed to prove the absence of, among others, deadlocks, reachability of states, or validity of invariants. It is of particular interest whether this analysis is conservative. In [17], we already showed that such a composition may lead to deadlock-free Petri nets, although the service-oriented system contains a deadlock. Likewise, in [18], we showed a similar result for protocol violations. In both cases, we found that a static analysis fails, if the composition ignored the calling context of service calls. To further investigate the role of the calling context in conservative static analysis, we investigate different compositions of abstract service descriptions focusing on deadlock analysis. Consequently, in this paper, our main contributions are:

- We introduce context-sensitive and context-insensitve composition, similar to the notions used in interprocedural program analysis [1].
- Furthermore, we propose a k-context-sensitive composition that limits the context-sensitive composition to a fixed calling depth k.
- We show that if a context-sensitive composition contains a deadlock then a 2-context-sensitive composition contains a deadlock.

In particular, our last contribution implies that for deadlock analysis a Petri-net-based approach can still be employed, if for each service call a context-sensitive composition is done once.

The paper is organized as follows: In Sect. 2, we introduce our formal model of services and their abstraction to process rewrite systems. In Sect. 3, we outline the notion of context-sensitivity of workflow compositions. Based on this notion, we prove our main results for deadlock analysis (Sect. 4). Finally, in Sect. 5, we discuss relevant related work and conclude the paper, in Sect. 6.

2 Background on Service Abstraction and Composition

2.1 Formalization of Services and Service-Oriented Systems

We assume that a service S is an implementation with a provided interface I_P^S and a required interface I_R^S, whereas an interface is a set of procedure signatures. Moreover, we consider that the implementation of S only contain service calls to procedures of the required interface. A service-oriented system, as illustrated in Fig. 1, is composed of two or more services which communicate only via a required and provided interface. Procedures of an interface can be either called synchronously or asynchronously. If a synchronous procedure is called, e.g., if a is called in main, it blocks the caller until the callee has been completed. If an asynchronous procedure is called, e.g., if b is called from main, then the callee and the caller continue their execution in parallel. They are either synchronized by an explicit **sync** statement, on the caller site or when both, caller and callee reach a **return** statement, cf. Service A in Fig. 1. Henceforth, the illustrated service-oriented system will serve as our running example.

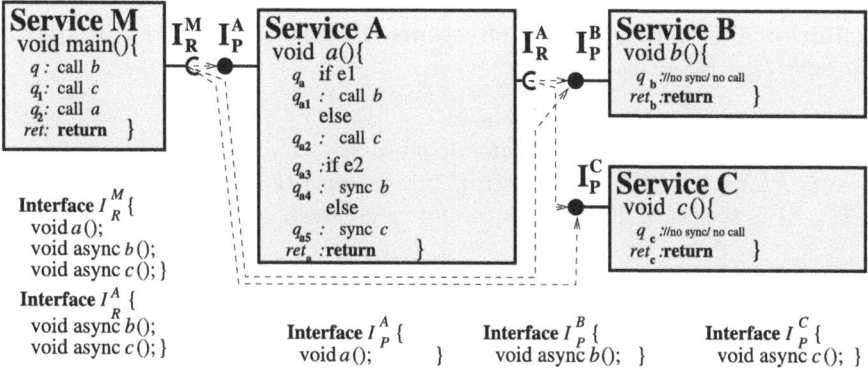

Fig. 1. A service-oriented system comprising four services, whereas a main service calls the services B, C, and A. Here, both synchronous and asynchronous as well as recursive calls to b and c are illustrated.

2.2 Generalization to Process Rewrite Systems

In [10], Mayr presented a unified view of Petri nets and several simple process algebras by representing them as subclasses of the general rewriting formalism *Process Rewrite Systems*. It is based on rewrite rules over process-algebraic expressions. The set of process-algebraic expressions $PEX(Q)$ over a finite set of *atomic processes* Q is the smallest set satisfying:

- $\varepsilon \in PEX(Q)$ is the *empty process*,
- if $q \in Q$ is an *atomic process*, then $q \in PEX(Q)$, and
- if $e_1, e_2 \in PEX(Q)$, then $e_1.e_2 \in PEX(Q)$ is the *sequential composition* and $e_1 \parallel e_2 \in PEX(Q)$ is the *parallel composition*.

Both compositions are associative and have the empty process ε as identity; $\parallel$ is commutative; (.) has priority over $\parallel$ composition. We omit brackets accordingly.

According to Mayr, process-algebraic expressions can be classified as follows:

i. $\mathbf{1} \triangleq Q \cup \{\varepsilon\}$
ii. $\mathbf{P} \subseteq PEX(Q)$ is the smallest set satisfying $\mathbf{P} = \mathbf{1} \cup \{e_1 \parallel e_2 \bullet e_1 \in \mathbf{P} \wedge e_2 \in \mathbf{P}\}$
iii. $\mathbf{S} \subseteq PEX(Q)$ is the smallest set satisfying $\mathbf{S} = \mathbf{1} \cup \{e_1.e_2 \bullet e_1 \in \mathbf{S} \wedge e_2 \in \mathbf{S}\}$
iv. $\mathbf{G} \triangleq PEX(Q)$

$$\frac{e_1 \to e_2}{e_1 \Rightarrow e_2} \text{ (R)} \qquad \frac{e_1 \Rightarrow e_2}{e_1.e \Rightarrow e_2.e} \text{ (S)} \qquad \frac{e_1 \Rightarrow e \quad e \Rightarrow e_2}{e_1 \Rightarrow e_2} \text{ (T)}$$

$$\frac{e}{e \Rightarrow e} \text{ (L)} \qquad \frac{e_1 \Rightarrow e_2}{e_1 \parallel e \Rightarrow e_2 \parallel e} \text{ (P1)} \qquad \frac{e_1 \Rightarrow e_2}{e \parallel e_1 \Rightarrow e \parallel e_1} \text{ (P2)}$$

$$e, e_1, e_2 \in PEX(Q)$$

Fig. 2. Inference rules for the definition of the derivation relation in PRS [10]

Definition 1 (Process Rewrite Systems (PRS)). *A process rewrite system is a tuple $\Pi \triangleq (Q, \to, q_0, F)$ where*

- *Q is a finite set of atomic processes,*
- *$q_0 \in Q$ is the initial state (an atomic process),*
- *$\to \subseteq PEX(Q) \times PEX(Q)$ is a set of process-rewrite rules,*
- *$F \subseteq Q$ is the set of final states (atomic processes).*

Using the inference rules in Fig. 2, the PRS Π defines a reflexive transitive derivation relation $\Rightarrow \subseteq PEX(Q) \times PEX(Q)$.

A process-rewrite rule $e_1 \to e_2$ is of class (C_1, C_2) with $C_1, C_2 \in \{\mathbf{1}, \mathbf{P}, \mathbf{S}, \mathbf{G}\}$, iff $e_1 \in C_1$ and $e_2 \in C_2$. A PRS is of class (C_1, C_2), iff each process-rewrite rule is of class (C_1, C_2).

In [10], Mayr introduced the hierarchy of PRS classes and showed their correspondences to other formalisms specifying transition systems. In particular, he showed that (**P**,**P**)-PRS are equivalent to Petri nets [9] and that (**S**,**S**)-PRS are equivalent to pushdown systems [10].

Definition 2. *Let $\Pi = (Q, \to, q_0, F)$ be a PRS. A process-algebraic expression $e \in PEX(Q)$ is reachable iff $q_0 \Rightarrow e$. A reachable $d \in PEX(Q)$ is a deadlock iff there exist no $e \in PEX(Q) \setminus F$ with $e \neq d$ such that $d \Rightarrow e$.*

The execution of a PRS is defined by the application of process-rewrite rules starting from q_0. Any process-algebraic expression e derivable from $q_0 \Rightarrow e$ is reachable. A deadlock occurs in a PRS, if a process-algebraic expression d is reached, for which inference rule (R) is not applicable. For general (**G**, **G**)-PRS, Mayr [10] already showed that reachability and, consequently, the reachability of a deadlock is decidable.

2.3 Formalizations of Service Abstractions and Service Compostion

In this paper, we focus on service abstractions and the composition process. In particular, we consider synchronous and asynchronous service calls, synchronizations, and service returns. The synchronizations are connected with futures, i.e., it synchronizes with specific asynchronous service calls. For simplicity, we assume that there are no service-internal calls and synchronizations, since they can be easily replaced by external calls to the same service.

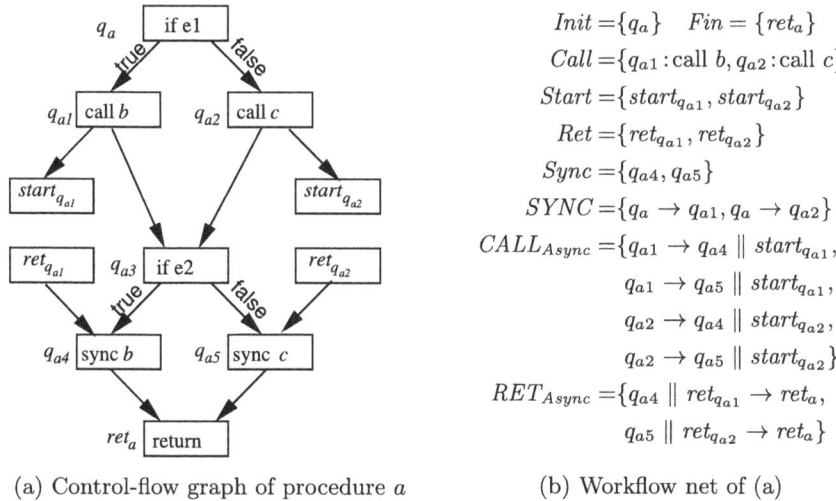

Fig. 3. Control-flow graph of Service A's procedure a and resulting workflow net.

Without loss of generality, our service abstraction focuses on the control-flow of the service's implementation. Figure 3(a) shows the control-flow graph of procedure a of Service A from Fig. 1. We denote the nodes of the control-flow graph *program points*, whereas each point is associated with the corresponding state and instruction, e.g., q_{a1} : call b. Consequently, the edges represent the control flow from one instruction to the next [1], for example, from q_{a1} : call b to q_{a3} : if e2. In particular, we distinguish between *interaction* and *interaction-free* nodes. Interaction nodes are those instructions of a service that interact with other services, i.e., service calls, synchronization instructions, return instructions. Interaction-free nodes, in contrast, are instructions that do not interact with other services, e.g., conditionals or computations. Moreover, we introduce two additional nodes to represent a *request* to a service, e.g., $start_{q_{a1}}$, and the corresponding *response*, e.g., $ret_{q_{a1}}$. For simplicity, we maintain that the following assumptions hold for the control-flow graph of a procedure:

1. For each procedure f in the provided interface, there is a unique initial node q_f without predecessors and a unique return node ret_f without successors.
2. For each call instruction q : call f, there is a request node $start_q$ and a response node ret_q with an edge $q \to start_q$ and $ret_q \to q'$, but **no** path from $start_q$ to ret_q. If the call was asynchronous, there is an addition edge $q \to q'$ to the successor node q'.
3. Each explicit synchronization of an asynchronous call $q : sync_f$ has two predecessors. One of them is a response node ret_q and the other one shall not be a response node.
4. If the control-flow graph is augmented by edges $start_{q_i} \to ret_{q_i}$ for each call node q_i, then for each reachable asynchronous call q : call g there must be at least one path from q to ret_f containing a synchronization q' : sync g.

As is typical of control-flow graphs [1], Assumption 1 ensures that a control-flow graph of a procedure has a unique entry and exit point. Assumption 2 guarantees that each service call has a request and a response node. Thus, the execution continues if the service call returns. Assumption 3 maintains that an asynchronous call always synchronizes with the corresponding response node and another node of the control-flow graph. Assumption 4 ensures that all asynchronous calls can be synchronized before returning from the procedure.

We denote a path $\langle q_0, \ldots, q_n \rangle$, $n \geq 1$ *interaction-free*, iff q_0 is an initial node or an interaction node, q_n is an interaction node, and all nodes q_i, with $0 < i < n$, are interaction-free nodes. An interaction-free path from q_0 to q_n is denoted by $q_0 \hookrightarrow q_n$. For example, the control-flow graph in Fig. 3a has the following interaction-free paths: $q_a \hookrightarrow q_{a1}$, $q_a \hookrightarrow q_{a2}$, $q_{a1} \hookrightarrow q_{a4}$, $q_{a1} \hookrightarrow q_{a5}$, $q_{a2} \hookrightarrow q_{a4}$, $q_{a2} \hookrightarrow q_{a5}$, $ret_{q_{a1}} \hookrightarrow q_{a4}$, $ret_{q_{a2}} \hookrightarrow q_{a5}$, $q_{a4} \hookrightarrow ret_a$, and $q_{a5} \hookrightarrow ret_a$.

Our service abstraction abstracts from arguments passed by calls, return values, and internal nodes of a service's control-flow graph.

Definition 3 (Service Abstraction). *Let S be a service with the provided interfaces I_P and the required interfaces I_R. The service abstraction of S with control-flow graph CFG is a tuple $\mathcal{S} \triangleq (A, R)$ where $A \triangleq Init \uplus Fin \uplus Call \uplus Start \uplus Ret \uplus Sync$ is the set of atomic processes (respectively states) of $\mathcal{S}$ and:*

i. $Init \triangleq \{q_f \bullet f \in I_P\}$ is the set of initial program points of each procedure in the provided interface.
ii. $Fin \triangleq \{ret_f \bullet f \in I_P\}$ is the set of return nodes of each procedure in the provided interface.
iii. $Call \triangleq \{q : \text{call } f \in CFG\}$ is the set of service call program points in f.
iv. $Start \triangleq \{start_q \bullet q : \text{call } f \in CFG\}$ is the set of request nodes of each service call in f.
v. $Ret \triangleq \{ret_q \bullet q : \text{call } f \in CFG\}$ is the set of response nodes corresponding to each service call in f.
vi. $Sync \triangleq \{q \bullet q : \text{sync } f \in CFG\}$ is the set of synchronization program points.

Note that both $Call \triangleq Call_{Sync} \uplus Call_{Async}$ and $Ret \triangleq Ret_{Sync} \uplus Ret_{Async}$ can be separated into disjoint sets for either synchronous or asynchronous calls.

Finally, the set of process-rewrite rules of $\mathcal{S}$ is defined as $R \triangleq SYNC \cup CALL_{Async} \cup RET_{Async}$ where:

$SYNC \triangleq \{q_1 \to q_2$
$CALL_{Async} \triangleq \{q_1 \to q_2 \parallel start_{q_1}$
$RET_{Async} \triangleq \{q_1 \parallel ret_q \to q_2$

- $q_1 \in A \setminus (Call_{Async} \cup Ret_{Async} \cup Sync) \wedge q_2 \in A \setminus Sync \wedge q_1 \hookrightarrow q_2\}$
- $q_2 \in A \wedge start_{q_1} \in Call_{Async} \wedge q_1 \hookrightarrow q_2\}$
- $\exists q_1 \in Sync : (ret_q, q_1) \in CFG \wedge q_1 \hookrightarrow q_2\}$

For simplicity, we add the class of the corresponding instruction, if the node's name is not unique, i.e., $q : \text{call } f$ denotes the program point of a call of f and $q : \text{sync } f$ denotes the program point of a synchronization with f. Notably though, $start_q$ and ret_q are unambiguous since they are created for each program point q of a call instruction.

Remark 1. Figure 3b illustrates the workflow net that corresponds to the control-flow graph in Fig. 3a. The nodes in *Init* and *Fin* are used to connect the service to its clients. Conversely, the nodes in *Call* and *Ret* are used to connect workflow nets of a service to the required services. Notably, $Call_{Sync}$ and Ret_{Sync} are empty, as both call b and call c are asynchronous service calls. All transition rules in R abstract from interaction-free inner nodes by only considering interaction-free paths. Simply put, the workflow net introduces a single transition for an interaction-free path. In particular, the interaction-free node q_{a3} is skipped, when constructing the transition rules in $CALL_{Async}$. In detail, $SNYC$ captures the synchronous execution, whereas $CALL_{Async}$ models the concurrent execution of asynchronous calls introducing the parallel composition and RET_{Async} the synchronization of a concurrent execution removing a parallel composition.

As Definition 3 only introduces transition rules of class (**P**,**P**), our service abstraction is equivalent to workflow nets, as defined in [14].

3 Towards Context-Sensitivity in Service Composition

As the interaction nodes of our service abstraction are only connected by a service-internal control-flow, connections between services must be composed according to the architecture of the service-oriented system. To this end, service composition connects request nodes of a caller to the initial nodes of a called service as well as the return nodes of the callee to the corresponding response node of the caller. While this composition seems trivial, we show that there are different possibilities for service composition that have very different properties. Given the similarities between these possibilities and interprocedural program analysis [1], we adopt the same terminology. Simply put, a *context-insensitive composition* ignores the calling context when connecting service calls to the called service. In contrast, a *context-sensitive composition* considers each calling context during the service composition. In addition, we introduce *k-context-sensitive composition* to cover the calling context up to the calling depth k and employs the context-insensitive composition from this calling depth on. These notions are defined by adding process-rewrite rules to the corresponding compositions. Note that the notion of calling depth differs from recursion depth, as it tracks the maximum number of times a procedure f occurs on the stack during execution.

The context-insensitive composition simply maps each call node to the initial node of the called procedure. For service calls the return nodes of the callees are mapped to the corresponding response node of the caller.

Definition 4 (Context-Insensitive Composition). *Given a service-oriented system $\mathfrak{S}$ with services $S_1, \ldots, S_n$ and the abstractions $\mathcal{S}_i \triangleq (A_i, R_i)$ of service S_i with $i = 1, \ldots, n$. The context-insensitive composition of $\mathcal{S}_1, \ldots, \mathcal{S}_n$ is a PRS $\Pi_{\mathfrak{S}}^{(ins)} \triangleq (Q, R)$ where $Q \triangleq \biguplus_{i=1}^{n} A_i$ and $R \triangleq (\biguplus_{i=1}^{n} R_i) \uplus R_{Call} \uplus R_{Ret}$ with:*

$R_{Call} \triangleq \{ start_{q'} \to q_f \bullet q' : \text{call } f \in \overline{Call} \}$ $R_{Ret} \triangleq \{ ret_f \to ret_{q'} \bullet q' : \text{call } f \in \overline{Call} \}$

Henceforth, $\overline{Call} \triangleq \biguplus_{i=1}^{n} Call_i$ collects the call nodes of all service abstractions.

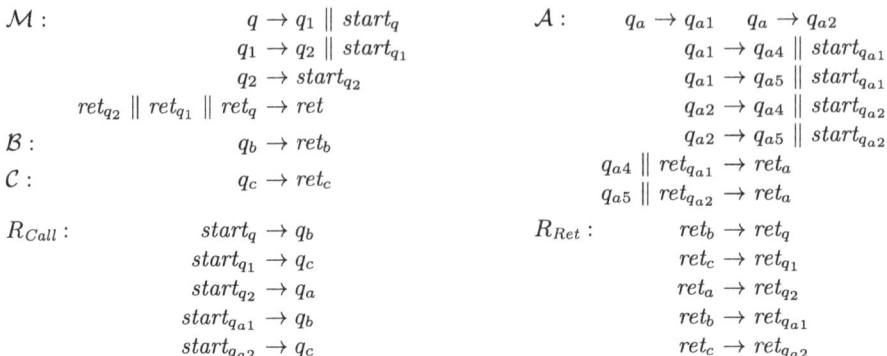

Fig. 4. Context-insensitive composition of the service-oriented system of Fig. 1

Figure 4 illustrates the context-insensitive composition of the service-oriented system introduced in Fig. 1. It shows the process-rewrite rules of the four workflow nets abstracting from Services M, Service A, Service B, and Service C. Moreover, it depicts the added context-insensitive process-rewrite rules binding each request node to the corresponding initial node R_{Call} and return nodes to the corresponding response node R_{Ret}.

Remark 2. Just like the commonly used workflow net composition [14], Definition 4 gives rise to a PRS of class (**P**,**P**), which is equivalent to Petri nets, cf. Sect. 2.2. If no service abstraction features the parallel composition ∥, e.g., if there are no asynchronous service calls, the resulting PRS is of class (**1**, **1**) and thus equivalent to finite state machines.

As shown in [17], the context-insensitive composition is not conservative, because it abstracts from the stack's behavior when modeling service calls. During the service execution, a synchronous service call q : call f replaces the top most program point by ret_q and pushes the initial program point of the called procedure f onto the stack. When returning from f, the ret_f is popped from the stack and ret_q is replaced by its successors. For asynchronous calls, the execution q : call f forks to $start_q$ and the successor of q. This creates a tree-structured stack, where parallel processes maintain their own part of the stack [7]. Thus, when an asynchronous call is synchronized with q' : sync f, the top program point on the sibling stack must be ret_q. Then both program point q' and the sibling stack are popped and the successor of q' is pushed on the stack. In essence, the *context-insensitive composition* do not capture this behavior in R_{Call} and R_{Ret}. Consequently, to create a context-sensitive composition, it must take the stack's behavior into account. To this end, we introduce *futures* to keep track of the different active asynchronous calls to asynchronous procedures. In particular, whenever a service is called the corresponding response node is maintained throughout the callees execution. As a result, however, the resulting states are not representable as Petri net markings anymore.

Definition 5 (Context-Sensitive Composition). *Given a service-oriented system $\mathfrak{S}$ with services $S_1, \ldots, S_n$ and the abstractions $\mathcal{S}_i \triangleq (A_i, R_i)$ of service S_i with $i = 1, \ldots, n$. The context-sensitive composition of $\mathcal{S}_1, \ldots, \mathcal{S}_n$ is a PRS $\Pi_{\mathfrak{S}}^{(sen)} \triangleq (Q, R)$ where $Q \triangleq \biguplus_{i=1}^{n} A_i$ and $R \triangleq (\biguplus_{i=1}^{n} R_i) \uplus R_{Call} \uplus R_{Ret}$ with:*

$$R_{Call} \triangleq \{start_{q'} \to q_f.ret_{q'} \bullet q' : \text{call } f \in \overline{Call}\}$$
$$R_{Ret} \triangleq \{ret_f.ret_{q'} \to ret_{q'} \bullet q' : \text{call } f \in \overline{Call}\}$$

$$R_{Call}:\quad start_q \to q_b.ret_q \qquad\qquad R_{Ret}:\quad ret_b.ret_q \to ret_q$$
$$start_{q_1} \to q_c.ret_{q_1} \qquad\qquad\qquad ret_c.ret_{q_1} \to ret_{q_1}$$
$$start_{q_2} \to q_a.ret_{q_2} \qquad\qquad\qquad ret_a.ret_{q_2} \to ret_{q_2}$$
$$start_{q_{a1}} \to q_b.ret_{q_{a1}} \qquad\qquad\qquad ret_b.ret_{q_{a1}} \to ret_{q_{a1}}$$
$$start_{q_{a2}} \to q_c.ret_{q_{a2}} \qquad\qquad\qquad ret_c.ret_{q_{a2}} \to ret_{q_{a2}}$$

Fig. 5. Context-sensitive composition of the service-oriented system in Fig. 1 only focusing on the process-rewrite rules added by the composition. The service abstractions shown in Fig. 4 are unchanged

Figure 5 illustrates the resulting process-rewrite rules for the context-sensitive composition of the example service-oriented system (Fig. 1). In contrast to the context-insensitive composition, the resulting context-sensitive composition elicits the deadlock, as the following derivation shows:

$q \Rightarrow q_1 \parallel start_q \Rightarrow q_1 \parallel q_b.ret_q \Rightarrow q_1 \parallel ret_b.ret_q \Rightarrow q_1 \parallel ret_q \Rightarrow q_2 \parallel start_{q_1} \parallel ret_q$
$\Rightarrow q_2 \parallel q_c.ret_{q_1} \parallel ret_q \quad \Rightarrow q_2 \parallel ret_c.ret_{q_1} \parallel ret_q \quad \Rightarrow q_2 \parallel ret_{q_1} \parallel ret_q$
$\Rightarrow start_{q_2} \parallel ret_{q_1} \parallel ret_q \quad \Rightarrow q_a.ret_{q_2} \parallel ret_{q_1} \parallel ret_q \quad \Rightarrow q_{a1}.ret_{q_2} \parallel ret_{q_1} \parallel ret_q$
$\Rightarrow (q_{a5} \parallel start_{q_{a1}}).ret_{q_2} \parallel ret_{q_1} \parallel ret_q \Rightarrow (q_{a5} \parallel q_b.ret_{q_{a1}}).ret_{q_2} \parallel ret_{q_1} \parallel ret_q$
$\Rightarrow (q_{a5} \parallel ret_b.ret_{q_{a1}}).ret_{q_2} \parallel ret_{q_1} \parallel ret_q \Rightarrow (q_{a5} \parallel ret_{q_{a1}}).ret_{q_2} \parallel ret_{q_1} \parallel ret_q$

Remark 3. It is easy to see, that the stack's behavior is precisely modeled. Consider a call program point $q : \text{call } f$ of an asynchronous call with successors q_1 and $start_q$, and a synchronization node $q_2 : \text{sync } f$ with a predecessor ret_q. If there is a path from q_1 to q_2, the following derivation is possible:

$$q \Rightarrow_{\Pi_{\mathfrak{S}}^{(sen)}} q_1 \parallel start_q \qquad \text{Def. 3, } CALL_{Async}$$
$$\Rightarrow_{\Pi_{\mathfrak{S}}^{(sen)}} q_2 \parallel start_q \qquad \text{as there is a path } q_1 \Rightarrow_{\Pi_{\mathfrak{S}}^{(sen)}} q_2$$
$$\Rightarrow_{\Pi_{\mathfrak{S}}^{(sen)}} q_2 \parallel (q_f.ret_q) \qquad \text{Def. 5(ii), } R_{Call}$$
$$\Rightarrow_{\Pi_{\mathfrak{S}}^{(sen)}} q_2 \parallel (ret_f.ret_q) \qquad \text{Assumption 1 and Def. 3, } Fin$$
$$\Rightarrow_{\Pi_{\mathfrak{S}}^{(sen)}} q_2 \parallel ret_q \qquad \text{Def. 5, } R_{Ret}$$
$$\Rightarrow_{\Pi_{\mathfrak{S}}^{(sen)}} q_3 \qquad \text{Def. 3, } RET_{Async} \text{ and } q_2 \hookrightarrow q_3$$

Thus, the response node ret_q represents the future of the program point $q : \text{call } f$. If f is called recursively, then the recursive calls must be synchronized before the current call can be synchronized, because synchronizations can only be executed on the top of the stack.

Although context-sensitive compositions model recursions to arbitrary calling depth, following the ideas of interprocedural program analysis [1], we henceforth consider limiting the calling depth to a fixed k. In general, our k-context-sensitive composition is context-sensitive up to a calling depth of k and context-insensitive once the calling depth is exceeded. Thus, our composition must keep track of the number of times each procedure f is recursively called, i.e., if a procedure f is called, its calling depth is increased by one until k is reached.

Definition 6 (k-Context-Sensitive Composition). *Given a service-oriented system $\mathfrak{S}$ with services $S_1, \ldots, S_n$ corresponding provided interfaces $I_P^1, \ldots, I_P^n$, the abstractions $\mathcal{S}_i \triangleq (A_i, R_i)$ of service S_i with $i = 1, \ldots, n$ and a fixed calling depth $k \in \mathbb{N} \cup \{\infty\}$. Let $\mathbb{K} \triangleq \{0, 1, \ldots, k\}$ be the set of calling depth and $I_P \triangleq \biguplus_{i=1}^{n} I_P^i$ the set of all provided procedures. Then the function $\delta : I_P \to \mathbb{K}$ maps each procedure to its current calling depth and Δ denotes the set of all possible mappings.*

The k-context-sensitive composition of $\mathcal{S}_1, \ldots, \mathcal{S}_n$ is a PRS $\Pi_{\mathfrak{S}}^{(k)} \triangleq (Q, R)$ where $Q \triangleq (\biguplus_{i=1}^{n} A_i) \times \Delta$ and $R \triangleq R_{Intern} \uplus R_{Call} \uplus R_{Ret}$ with:

$R_{Intern} \triangleq \{(q_1, \delta) \to (q_2, \delta)\}$ • $q_1 \to q_2 \in \overline{R}\}$

$\uplus \{(q_1, \delta) \to (q_2, \delta) \parallel (q_3, \delta)\}$ • $q_1 \to q_2 \parallel q_3 \in \overline{R}\}$

$\uplus \{(q_1, \delta) \parallel (q_2, \delta) \to (q_3, \delta)\}$ • $q_1 \parallel q_2 \to q_3 \in \overline{R}\}$

$R_{Call} \triangleq R_{Call}^{<k} \uplus R_{Call}^{=k}$

$R_{Call}^{<k} \triangleq \{(start_q, \delta) \to (q_f, \delta').(ret_q, \delta)$ • $q : \text{call } f \in \overline{Call} \wedge \delta(f) < k \wedge \delta' = \delta|_f^{\delta(f)+1}\}$

$R_{Call}^{=k} \triangleq \{(start_q, \delta) \to (q_f, \delta)$ • $q : \text{call } f \in \overline{Call} \wedge \delta(f) = k\}$

$R_{Ret} \triangleq R_{Ret}^{<k} \cup R_{Ret}^{=k}$

$R_{Ret}^{<k} \triangleq \{(ret_f, \delta).(ret_q, \delta') \to (ret_q, \delta')$ • $q : \text{call } f \in \overline{Call} \wedge \delta'(f) < k\}$

$R_{Ret}^{=0} \triangleq \{(ret_f, \delta) \to (ret_q, \delta)$ • $q : \text{call } f \in \overline{Call} \wedge \delta(f) = 0 \wedge k = 0\}$

$R_{Ret}^{=k} \triangleq \{(ret_f, \delta).(q', \delta') \to (ret_q, \delta).(q', \delta')$ • $q : \text{call } f \in \overline{Call} \wedge \delta'(f) = k \wedge k > 0\}$

$\cup \{(ret_f, \delta) \parallel (q', \delta') \to (ret_q, \delta) \parallel (q', \delta')$ • $q : \text{call } f \in \overline{Call} \wedge \delta'(f) = k \wedge k > 0\}$

Here, $\overline{R} \triangleq \biguplus_{i=1}^{n} R_i$ collects the process-rewrite rules of all service abstractions and $\delta|_f^i$ creates a new function δ' where $\delta'(f) = i$ and $\delta'(g) = \delta(g)$ for $g \in I_P \setminus \{f\}$.

The process-rewrite rules in R_{Intern} are copies of the roles of each service abstraction for each possible $\delta \in \Delta$, maintaining the calling within service internal execution. In essence, the calling depth δ within a call remains the same. In contrast, the process-rewrite rules in $R_{Call}^{<k}$ denote service calls with calling depth less than k. These rules mirror the context-sensitive composition (Definition 5), yet increase the calling depth of the callee by one. Conversely, the rules in $R_{Call}^{=k}$ denote service calls with a calling depth of at least k. These now mirror the context-insensitive composition (Definition 4) and do not further increase the calling depth. Analogously, the process-rewrite rules in $R_{Ret}^{<k}$ handle the return of calls with a calling depth of at most k. Like in the context-sensitive composition

(Definition 5), (ret_q, δ') represents the future keeping track of the caller's context. The rules in $R_{Ret}^{=k}$ cover the return of calls with a calling depth larger than k. In contrast to the context-insensitive composition, the caller's context must be determined by investigating the second stack element (q', δ') unless $k = 0$. Consequently, if $k = 0$ this composition becomes context-insensitive, such that $R_{Call}^{<k} = \emptyset$ and the set $R_{Ret}^{=0}$ is used.

In addition, Definition 6 gives raise to the general notion of calling depth for reachable process algebraic expressions e of a k-context-sensitive composition.

$$cd(e) \triangleq \max_{(q,\delta) \in atoms(e)} \max_{f \in I_P} \delta(f)$$

Above, $atoms(e)$ denotes the set of atoms of e, i.e., atomic processes of the PRS.

Lemma 1. *Let $\mathfrak{S}$ be a service-oriented system, then*

1. *the 0-context-sensitive composition $\Pi_\mathfrak{S}^{(0)}$ is equivalent to $\Pi_\mathfrak{S}^{(ins)}$,*
2. *the ∞-context-sensitive composition $\Pi_\mathfrak{S}^{(\infty)}$ is equivalent to $\Pi_\mathfrak{S}^{(sen)}$, and*
3. *if $e_1 \Rightarrow_{\Pi_\mathfrak{S}^{(\infty)}} e_2$ and $cd(e_1) \leq k$ and $cd(e_2) \leq k$, then $e_1 \Rightarrow_{\Pi_\mathfrak{S}^{(k)}} e_2$*

Proof (Sketch). The proof of (i) is straightforward. The proof of (ii) is based on a bijective mapping $\alpha : State_\infty \to State_{sen}$ where $State_\infty$ and $State_{sen}$ are the sets of reachable states of $\Pi_\mathfrak{S}^{(\infty)}$ and $\Pi_\mathfrak{S}^{(sen)}$, respectively. In short, α *forgets* δ. Based on this function a 1-1-bisimulation can be proven. Finally, (iii) can be proven by induction on the derivation of $e_1 \Rightarrow_{\Pi_\mathfrak{S}^{(k)}} e_2$

4 Impact of Context-Sensitivity for Deadlock Analysis

In this section we examine the deadlock analysis. As we already showed in [17], the context-insensitive composition depicted in Fig. 4 is deadlock-free, although the composed service-oriented system in Fig. 1 contains a deadlock. In detail, the deadlock occurs, because the synchronization in q_{a5} tries to synchronize with the wrong call, i.e., the first call of c from Service M. On a closer look, the context-insensitive composition mixes the two calls, hence missing both deadlocks. In contrast, the context-sensitive composition distinguishes all calls and thus captures the deadlock. Surprisingly, we can show that it is not necessary to employ a context-sensitive composition for detecting deadlocks. Instead, we show that a 2-context-sensitive composition will suffice:

Theorem 1 (Recursion-Depth in Deadlock Analysis). *Let $\mathfrak{S}$ be a service-oriented system. If the context-sensitive composition of $\Pi_\mathfrak{S}^{(sen)}$ has a deadlock, then $\Pi_\mathfrak{S}^{(2)}$ has a deadlock.*

To proof this theorem, we need to proof the following two properties:

Lemma 2 (Deadlock Detection with k-Context-Sensitive Composition). *Let $\mathfrak{S}$ be a service-oriented system and I_P the set of provided interfaces. If $\Pi_\mathfrak{S}^{(\infty)}$ has a deadlock e with calling depth $cd(e) = k$, then $\Pi_\mathfrak{S}^{(k+1)}$ also has deadlock e.*

Proof (Sketch). It must be shown that (i) $q_0 \Rightarrow_{\Pi_{\mathfrak{S}}^{(k+1)}} e$ and (ii) e is a deadlock in $\Pi_{\mathfrak{S}}^{(k+1)}$.

(i) follows directly from Lemma 1(iii).

(ii) Let e be a deadlock with $cd(e) = k$. Hence, no process-rewrite rule of $\Pi_{\mathfrak{S}}^{(\infty)}$ can be applied. Suppose that a rule of $\Pi_{\mathfrak{S}}^{(k+1)}$ can be applied to e. We show a contradiction for each case (according to Definition 6):

CASE 1: $(q,\delta) \to (q',\delta) \in R_{Intern}$ is applied. Then $\delta(f) \leq k$ for all $f \in I_P$. This is also a rule of $\Pi_{\mathfrak{S}}^{(\infty)}$. Contradiction!

CASE 2: $(start_q,\delta) \to (q_f,\delta').(ret_q,\delta) \in R_{Call}^{<k+1}$ is applied. This is also a rule of $\Pi_{\mathfrak{S}}^{(\infty)}$. Contradiction!

CASE 3: $(start_q,\delta) \to (q_f,\delta') \in R_{Call}^{=k+1}$ is applied. Then $\delta(f) = k+1$. This contradicts $cd(e) = k$ (which implies $\delta(f) \leq k$).

CASE 4: $(ret_f,\delta).(ret_q,\delta') \to (ret_q,\delta') \in R_{Ret}^{<k+1}$ is applied. This is also a rule of $\Pi_{\mathfrak{S}}^{(\infty)}$. Contradiction!

CASE 5: $(ret_f,\delta).(q',\delta') \to (ret_q,\delta).(ret_q,\delta') \in R_{Ret=k+1}$ is applied. Then $\delta'(f) = k+1$. This contradicts $cd(e) = k$.

CASE 6: $(ret_f,\delta) \parallel (ret_q,\delta') \to (ret_q,\delta) \parallel (ret_q,\delta') \in R_{Ret}^{=k+1}$ is applied. Then $\delta'(f) = k+1$. This contradicts $cd(e) = k$.

Remark 4. The k-context-sensitive composition would not ensure that deadlocks are maintained, as all calls from calling depth k would be modeled as in the context-insensitive composition. Hence, the same counterexample as in the context-insensitive case would be possible.

Lemma 3 (Reducing the Calling Depth of Deadlocks). *Let $\mathfrak{S}$ be a service-oriented system and I_P the set of provided interfaces. If $\Pi_{\mathfrak{S}}^{(sen)}$ has a deadlock e then it has a corresponding deadlock e' with calling depth $cd(\alpha^{-1}(e')) = 1$.*

Proof (Sketch). According to Lemma 1, there is an equivalent composition $\Pi_{\mathfrak{S}}^{(\infty)}$, where $\alpha^{-1}(e)$ is the corresponding deadlock. (The bijective function α is defined in the proof of Lemma 1(ii).) Let $f \in I_P$ be a procedure, such that $(q_f,\delta) \Rightarrow_{\Pi_{\mathfrak{S}}^{(\infty)}} d'$ where d' is a deadlock and $\delta(f) > 1$ is maximal among the atoms (q,δ) of $\alpha^{-1}(e)$. Thus, the call of f reaching the deadlock d' is non-recursive. By induction, we can entail that $(q_f, \delta|_f^1) \Rightarrow_{\Pi_{\mathfrak{S}}^{(\infty)}} d''$, where d'' is obtained by replacing each atom (q,δ') with $(q,\delta'|_f^1)$. Consequently, the derivation of the deadlock $\alpha^{-1}(e)$ has the form:

$(q_0,\delta_0) \Rightarrow_{\Pi_{\mathfrak{S}}^{(\infty)}} d_1 \parallel (q_f,\delta).e_0$
$\quad\Rightarrow_{\Pi_{\mathfrak{S}}^{(\infty)}} d_1 \parallel d_2 \parallel (q_f,\delta).e_1 \quad$ Assuming $(q_f,\delta).e_0 \Rightarrow_{\Pi_{\mathfrak{S}}^{(\infty)}} d_2 \parallel (q_f,\delta).e_1$ (1)
$\quad\Rightarrow_{\Pi_{\mathfrak{S}}^{(\infty)}} d_1 \parallel d_2 \parallel d''.e_1 \quad$ Assuming $d_2 \parallel (q_f,\delta).e_1 \Rightarrow_{\Pi_{\mathfrak{S}}^{(\infty)}} d_2 \parallel d''.e_1$ (2)
$\quad= \alpha^{-1}(e)$

where d_1, d_2 are deadlocks, $\delta_0(h) = 0$ for each $h \in I_P$, and $\delta(f) = 1$. The above assumptions (1) and (2) follow from the fact that the calling depth of f is at least two, i.e., there was a previous call of f.

By removing the information on calling depths, we can construct the following derivation within the context-sensitive composition:

$$\begin{aligned} q_0 &\Rightarrow_{\Pi_{\mathfrak{S}}^{(sen)}} \alpha^{-1}(d_1) \parallel q_f.\alpha^{-1}(e_0) \\ &\Rightarrow_{\Pi_{\mathfrak{S}}^{(sen)}} \alpha^{-1}(d_1) \parallel \alpha^{-1}(d_2) \parallel q_f.\alpha^{-1}(e_1) \\ &\Rightarrow_{\Pi_{\mathfrak{S}}^{(sen)}} \alpha^{-1}(d_1) \parallel \alpha^{-1}(d_2) \parallel \alpha^{-1}(d'').\alpha^{-1}(e_1) \end{aligned} \quad (1)$$

Since d_1 d_2, and d'' are deadlocks in $\Pi_{\mathfrak{S}}^{(\infty)}$, it follows from Lemma 1(ii) that $\alpha^{-1}(d_1)$, $\alpha^{-1}(d_2)$, and $\alpha^{-1}(d'')$ are deadlocks in $\Pi_{\mathfrak{S}}^{(sen)}$, too. Thus, $\alpha^{-1}(d_1) \parallel \alpha^{-1}(d_2) \parallel \tilde{\alpha}^{-1}(d'').\alpha^{-1}(e_0)$ is a deadlock in $\Pi_{\mathfrak{S}}^{(sen)}$. Thus, there is a derivation in $\Pi_{\mathfrak{S}}^{(\infty)}$, which corresponds to (1) yet reaches the deadlock in the first call of f:

$$(q_0, \delta_0) \Rightarrow_{\Pi_{\mathfrak{S}}^{(\infty)}} d_1 \parallel (q_f, \delta).e_0 \Rightarrow_{\Pi_{\mathfrak{S}}^{(\infty)}} d_1 \parallel d''.e_0$$

Since this derivation has at least one recursive call of f less, the calling depth of f in the deadlock $d_1 \parallel d''.e_0$ smaller than in the deadlock $\alpha^{-1}(e)$. By induction, we can show that there is a deadlock d''' in $\Pi_{\mathfrak{S}}^{(\infty)}$ reachable without any recursive call of f, i.e., for any $(q, \delta) \in atoms(d''')$ it holds that $\delta(f) = 1$. The same argument can be applied for each $g \in I_P$, whereas the deadlock d''' contains an atom (q, δ) with $\delta(g) > 1$. Hence, we can show by induction that there is a deadlock d, such that for each $(q, \delta) \in atoms(d)$ and each procedure $h \in I_P$, it holds that $\delta(h) \leq 1$. In conclusion, it follows that $e' = \alpha(d)$ is the deadlock with $cd(d) = 1$. □

Proof of Theorem 1: Let $\mathfrak{S}$ be a service-oriented system and e a deadlock in $\Pi_{\mathfrak{S}}^{(sen)}$. Lemma 3 entails that there is a deadlock e' in $\Pi_{\mathfrak{S}}^{(sen)}$ with $cd(e') = 1$. Next, it follows from Lemma 1(ii) that there is a deadlock $e'' = \alpha^{-1}(e')$ in $\Pi_{\mathfrak{S}}^{(\infty)}$ with $cd(e'') = 1$. Finally, Lemma 2 guarantees that e'' is also a deadlock in $\Pi_{\mathfrak{S}}^{(2)}$.

Remark 5. Theorem 1 entails that workflow nets can be composed, such that deadlocks of the context-sensitive composition are retained. This composition must simply unfold each workflow net twice for each asynchronous procedure in the provided interface and connect the workflow nets with the corresponding request and response nodes. The resulting Petri net is suitable for classic deadlock analyses. Granted, this composition and resulting Petri net is more complex than approaches based on [14].

5 Related Work

In this work, we have captured different kinds of context-sensitivity when composing service abstractions. There are numerous other approaches for modeling systems. Most system abstractions are described on the basis of finite state machines [11,13], process algebras [2], Petri nets [15], recursive Petri nets [6], push down systems [4,18], or process rewrite systems [3,16]. All these models either cannot model unrestricted recursive behavior or the deadlock analyses on these models is no longer decidable [5]. In [18], we have shown that this can lead to false positives when checking the protocol conformance of a service-oriented system. The notion of workflow nets was introduced by Van Der Aalst in [14,15], where their composition is explained more thoroughly. In [8,12,15], the authors did not show how to handle recursion with unrestricted service calls and whether this plays a role, for example, in the occurrence of false positives of the deadlock analysis. It is unclear, whether their composition is context-sensitive or context-insensitive. To the best of our knowledge, there is no other work discussing different approaches to context-sensitive and context-insensitive composition of service abstractions wrt. the calling depth of synchronous and asynchronous service calls and the resulting impact on deadlock analysis.

6 Conclusions

In this paper, we examined deadlock analysis of service-oriented systems by investigating different kinds of workflow net compositions, e.g., context-insensitive, context-sensitive, and k-context-sensitive, focusing on systems with unbound recursion and concurrency. We found that the context-insensitive composition completely ignores the calling context, whereas the context-sensitive considers the complete calling context. As middle ground, we introduced the k-context-sensitive composition that limits the calling context to a fixed calling depth k and ignores the calling context of deeper recursive calls. As a result, the context-insensitive composition is equivalent to the well-established workflow net compositions based on [14]. However, we have shown while deadlock analysis of a workflow net composition is conservative, if there are no recursive or concurrent asynchronous service calls. Otherwise, they can fail to identify deadlocks. To remedy this, we have shown that a 2-context-sensitive composition is sufficient to identify all deadlocks in the service abstraction. In detail, we established that if a deadlock occurs in a procedure call of a procedure f in the context-sensitive composition, then it can also occur in the first call of f. Hence, the 2-context-sensitive composition already contains the deadlock. Notably though, the result of this composition is still a Petri net, albeit a significantly larger one, when compared to the context-insensitive composition. Still, highly optimized Petri net analyzers can be employed to identify deadlocks. In conclusion, we found the limitation of current deadlock analyses of service-oriented systems and showed how to overcome it in theory.

In the future, we will focus on other undesired behaviors of service-oriented systems and their relation to the calling context. For instance, we want to investigate protocol conformance checking, whose limitations have been shown in [18]. Our intuition, however, is that protocol conformance checking cannot be limited to a certain calling depth. Although we have not proven this, we argue that the resulting language of a k-context-sensitive composition (with $k \in \mathbb{N}$) is *regular*, and thus unable to detect violations if the context-sensitive composition gives raise to a context-free language. Besides that, we will implement and compare practical approaches to identify deadlocks in a 2-context-sensitive composition, either efficiently constructing a Petri net or simulating a PRS with bound calling depth. Last but not least, we want to study the limitations of the context-sensitive composition, i.e., whether there are undesired behaviors that might be overlooked.

References

1. Aho, A.V., Lam, M.S., Sethi, R., Ullman, J.D.: Compilers: Principles, Techniques, and Tools, 2nd edn. Addison-Wesley Longman Publishing Co., Inc., Boston, MA, USA (2006)
2. Allen, R., Garlan, D.: A formal basis for architectural connection. ACM Trans. Softw. Eng. Methodol. (TOSEM) **6**(3), 213–249 (1997)
3. Both, A., Zimmermann, W.: Automatic protocol conformance checking of recursive and parallel component-based systems. In: Component-Based Software Engineering, 11th International Symposium (CBSE 2008), pp. 163–179 (October 2008)
4. Burkart, O., Steffen, B.: Pushdown processes: parallel composition and model checking. In: International Conference on Concurrency Theory, pp. 98–113. Springer (1994)
5. Giachino, E., Kobayashi, N., Laneve, C.: Deadlock analysis of unbounded process networks. In: CONCUR 2014–Concurrency Theory, LNCS, vol. 8704, p. 63 (2014)
6. Haddad, S., Poitrenaud, D.: Modelling and analyzing systems with recursive petri nets. In: Discrete Event Systems, pp. 449–458. Springer (2000)
7. Hauck, E.A., Dent, B.A.: Burroughs' b6500/b7500 stack mechanism. In: AFIPS '68 (Spring): Proceedings of the Spring Joint Computer Conference, pp. 245–251. ACM (1968)
8. Martens, A.: Analyzing web service based business processes. In: 8th International Conferences on Fundamental Approaches to Software Engineering, FASE 2005, Held as Part of the Joint European Conferences on Theory and Practice of Software, ETAPS 2005, Proceedings 8, pp. 19–33. Springer, Edinburgh, UK (2005)
9. Mayr, R.: Combining petri nets and pa-processes. In: International Symposium on Theoretical Aspects of Computer Software (TACS'97), volume 1281 of LNCS, p. 547561. Springer Verlag (1997)
10. Mayr, R.: Process rewrite systems. Inf. Comput. **156**(1–2), 264–286 (2000)
11. Nierstrasz, O.: Regular types for active objects. In: OOPSLA, vol. 93, pp. 1–15 (1993)
12. Reisig, W.: Associative composition of components with double-sided interfaces. Acta Informatica **56**(3), 229–253 (2019)
13. Tenzer, J., Stevens, P.: Modelling recursive calls with uml state diagrams. In: International Conference on Fundamental Approaches to Software Engineering, pp. 135–149. Springer (2003)
14. Van Der Aalst, W.M.P.: Application and Theory of Petri Nets 1997: 18th International Conference, ICATPN'97 Toulouse, France, 23–27 June 1997, Proceedings, chap. Verification of workflow nets, pp. 407–426. Springer, Berlin, Heidelberg (1997). http://dx.doi.org/10.1007/3-540-63139-9_48

15. Van Der Aalst, W.M.: Workflow verification: finding control-flow errors using petri-net-based techniques. In: Business Process Management, pp. 161–183. Springer (2000)
16. Weissbach, M., Zimmermann, W.: On abstraction-based deadlock-analysis in service-oriented systems with recursion. In: Service-Oriented and Cloud Computing: 6th IFIP WG 2.14 European Conference, ESOCC 2017, Proceedings 6, pp. 168–176. Springer, Oslo, Norway (2017)
17. Weißbach, M., Zimmermann, W.: On limitations of abstraction-based deadlock-analysis of service-oriented systems. In: Fazio, M., Zimmermann, W. (eds.) Advances in Service-Oriented and Cloud Computing, pp. 79–90. Springer International Publishing (2020)
18. Zimmermann, W., Schaarschmidt, M.: Automatic checking of component protocols in component-based systems. In: Löwe, W., Südholt, M. (eds.) Software Composition. LNCS, vol. 4089, pp. 1–17. Springer (2006)

Author Index

A
Alidu, Abubakari 33
Ardagna, Danilo 155

B
Becker, Steffen 219
Brogi, Antonio 65, 105

C
Calmi, Nicolas 112
Casale, Giuliano 155
Cavenaghi, Luca 112
Celesti, Antonio 57
Ciavotta, Michele 33, 112

D
Daniel, João F. L. 197
de C. Costa, Rogério Luís 146
De Paoli, Flavio 33

E
Ebrahimi, Elmira 40
Edinger, Janick 40

F
Fazio, Maria 57
Felderer, Michael 171
Filippini, Federica 112
Fischer, Mathias 3
Forti, Stefano 65, 105

G
Gao, Yicheng 155
Gonçalves, Alexandrino 146
Gottschalk, Felix 40
Gritsch, Philipp 171
Guerra, Eduardo 18, 197

H
Hästbacka, David 81, 96
Hautz, Mika 171
Hemadasa, Nisal 40
Hirmer, Pascal 219

I
Ivo, André A. S. 197

J
Junior, João José Maranhão 18

K
Kaaser, Dominik 3, 40
Klein, Kevin 219
Koll, Peter 171
Kühn, Thomas 235

L
Leite, Matheus C. 197

M
Marto, Anabela 146
Melegati, Jorge 18
Montesi, Fabrizio 181

N
Napoli, Rosario 57

P
Peressotti, Marco 181
Picotti, Valentino 181
Plebani, Pierluigi 131
Ponce, Francisco 105

R
Rabadão, Carlos 146
Ristov, Sashko 171

S
Saile, Finn 3
Sala, Roberto 155
Santos, Leonel 146
Savi, Marco 112
Schmut, Isabella 171
Schulte, Stefan 3, 40
Soldani, Jacopo 65, 105

T
Thomas, Julius 3

V
Villari, Massimo 57

W
Walz, Alexander 219
Weißbach, Mandy 235

Y
Yakubov, Diyaz 81, 96
Yang, Shudan 131

Z
Zimmermann, Olaf 181
Zimmermann, Wolf 235

The manufacturer's authorised representative in the EU is Springer
Nature Customer Service Centre GmbH, Europaplatz 3, 69115 Heidelberg,
Germany. If you have any concerns regarding our products, please
contact ProductSafety@springernature.com

Printed and bound by CPI Group (UK) Ltd, Croydon, CR0 4YY

26/03/2026

02078952-0006